FUR TRAPPERS AND TRADERS

OF THE

FAR SOUTHWEST

Beavers at Work. The beaver lured many Americans to the Southwest and was a major ingredient in the region's early economy. From Richard Lydekker, ed., *Library of Natural History* (Philadelphia: Gebbie and Company, 1901). Courtesy of Western History Collections, University of Oklahoma.

FUR TRAPPERS AND TRADERS

OF THE

FAR SOUTHWEST

Twenty Biographical Sketches

Edited by
LeRoy R. Hafen

Selected and with an Introduction by
S. Matthew Despain

UTAH STATE UNIVERSITY PRESS
LOGAN, UTAH

Utah State University Press
Logan, Utah 84322-7800

Cover illustration: A Trapper and His Pony, from a drawing by Frederic
Remington. From Henry Inman, *The Old Santa Fe Trail* (New York:
Macmillan, 1897). Courtesy of Western History Collections, University of
Oklahoma.

Cover design by Michelle Sellers

Library of Congress Cataloging-in-Publication Data

Fur trappers and traders of the far Southwest : twenty biographical sketches /
    edited by LeRoy R.Hafen : selected and with an introduction by S.
    Matthew Despain.
        p.   cm.
    Originally published: 1968.
    ISBN 0-87421-235-9
    1. Trappers—Southwest, New—Biography. 2. Fur traders—Southwest,
New—Biography. 3. Southwest, New—History—To 1848. 4. Frontier and
pioneer life—Southwest, New. 5. Southwest, New—Biography. 6. Fur trade—
Southwest, New—History—19th century. I. Hafen, Le Roy Reuben, 1893– .
II. Despain, S. Matthew, 1963– .
F800.F87 1997
979'.02'0922—dc21
[B]   97-30832
                                                                                          CIP

To
Carla J. Despain and Kalin R. Despain
and to the memory of
LeRoy R. Hafen

Contents

Illustrations

Far Southwest Fur Trade Region

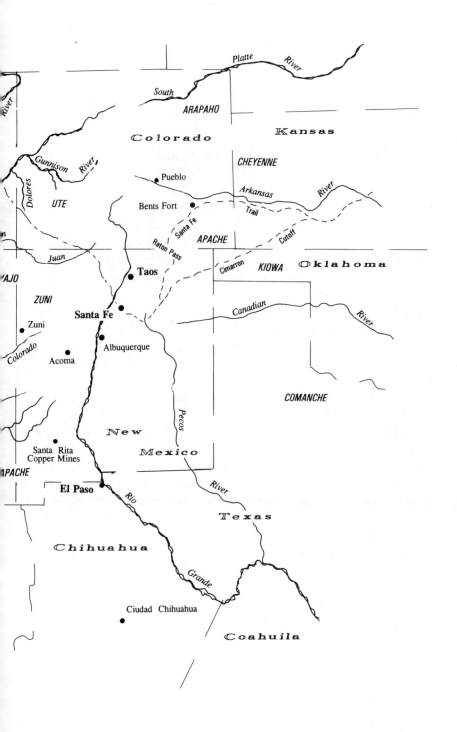

Preface

This book presents a view of the Far Southwest fur trade and the trappers and traders involved in it through twenty biographies selected from LeRoy R. Hafen's ten-volume *The Mountain Men and the Fur Trade of the Far West* (1968–1972). By focusing on the Southwest trade, the present work offers a thematic approach and, hence, a coherence that Hafen's original series lacked. Some of the biographies' subjects will be familiar to readers, and others not. The intention is not to eulogize further already popular figures but to increase the reader's understanding of and appreciation for the Southwest fur trade and its players. The sketches selected represent particular facets of the Southwest trade and are arranged to reflect, whenever possible, the trade's chronology. The book, therefore, is more than a collection of biographies and should be useful and appealing to those interested in the fur trade of the Far Southwest.

A few individuals deserve mention for their generous help. Special thanks go to Fred R. Gowans of Brigham Young University, friend and devout scholar of the fur trade, who has often urged me to explore the Southwest fur trade; to William W. Savage Jr. of the University of Oklahoma for his assistance and inimitable insight during the creation of this work; to Rodney H. Despain, an admirable cartographer and superb father; to John R. Lovett of the Western History Collections of the University of Oklahoma for his archival support; and to Carla Jenks Despain, my beautiful wife and friend, for typing the manuscript and for putting up with it and my impositions.

Introduction

by S. MATTHEW DESPAIN
Norman, Oklahoma

Taos Pueblo, which would become the hub of nineteenth-century Anglo-American trapping and trading in the Southwest, endured a long history of European contact. Spanish conquistadors under Francisco Vásquez de Coronado first happened upon the pueblo, which they called Brava, in 1540 while searching for the fabled cities of Cíbola.[1] Yet, not until the mid-1600s did Spanish colonists abide in the region. This first settlement was short-lived. Repressive Spanish treatment of the natives bred discontent that culminated in the Pueblo Revolt of 1680. Indians drove the Spanish south down the Rio Grande beyond present-day El Paso, Texas. Taos played an important role in the organization and execution of the revolt.[2]

Spanish colonizers again settled near Taos in 1720. Soon, however, hostile Comanches induced the Spanish to seek joint protection with the Indians in the pueblo. The settlement was then moved south to the Río de las Trampas for better protection and easier access to the Spanish farms. To Americans, who began arriving in the 1820s, this pueblo was known as Rancho de Taos.[3] Most Americans preferred another village in the Taos Valley known as Don Fernando de Taos. This was the hamlet they called Taos. For Santa Fe merchant Josiah Gregg, "No part of New Mexico equals this valley in . . . richness of produce and beauty of appearance."[4] Many Americans seemed to agree with Gregg's appraisal as the area subsequently was favored by the Southwest fur trappers and traders.

Taos was the Southwestern center of American fur trade activity for various reasons, one being the valley's strategic location. Its northern end formed a southern gateway into the Rocky Mountains. From Taos, trappers could follow the Rio Grande north to the San Luis Valley and from there reach the parks and major rivers of the southern and central Rockies. They could as easily venture west or south to trap rivers such as the Gila, the lower Colorado, or the Pecos. Besides being a departure point, Taos provided trappers with a fixed settlement where they could sell their pelts and procure supplies year-round. Taos also afforded the comforts and pleasantries of "civilization" and thus a place to reside during off-seasons without traveling back to Missouri. As the most northerly New Mexican settlement, Taos was remote enough (some seventy miles north of Santa Fe) to help Americans evade New Mexican officials and the payment of trading tariffs. Furs could be shipped from Taos to St. Louis and supplies smuggled in with relative ease.[5]

The community structure and cultural makeup of Taos and Santa Fe gave the Southwest fur trade a distinctive character. The trapping society in New Mexico was more stable than the transitory rendezvous system, which served mountain men in the central and northern Rockies. For instance, the percentage of Southwest fur trade men who married Hispanic American women far exceeded that of Rocky Mountain men who married Indian women.[6] Besides yielding special status and trading privileges, marriage to New Mexican women at times led to land acquisitions and increased community involvement, which contributed to the more sedentary character of the Southwest fur trade society. Marriages between Southwest fur trade men and New Mexican women generally were also more stable and longer lasting unions than mountain man marriages to Indians. One reason was the relative similarity of American and Mexican cultures in comparison to the myriad Indian societies. Then too, the more transient nature of the Rocky Mountain fur trade and its rendezvous system helped produce more precarious marriages. Conversion to Catholicism often became a prerequisite for Americans who married Spanish-American women. More often than not economics rather than fervent religious inclinations motivated such conversions. Many Americans in the fur trade also embraced Mexican citizenship because it seemingly increased economic opportunities. Of the known 360 foreigners who entered New Mexico and whose names appear in Catholic Church records between 1820 and 1850, 75 percent married Mexican women.[7] The greater percentage of trappers and traders who remained in the Southwest after the fur trade, relative to men who stayed in the northern Rockies, further demonstrates the more sedentary nature of the Taos trade.[8]

Other factors contributed to the Southwest fur trade's distinctiveness. Fur trade men found diverse entrepreneurial opportunities there that far exceeded what was available to the more isolated and nomadic mountain men. Many pursued other business ventures in addition to trapping and trading. Those who obtained land grants often turned to farming or ranching. Others took up mining, work as artisans, politics, horse trading, and distilling whiskey for trade (the local concoction commonly referred to as "Taos Lightning"). Few of these occupations were feasible concurrently with participation in the rendezvous system.

The lifeways and livelihoods of New Mexican society inevitably involved Southwest fur trade men in a well-codified legal system different from what rules governed mountain men. Without prescribed laws or a court system, mountain men conducted themselves loosely according to what may be called a kind of "legal behaviorism." Americans in the Southwest instead operated under Mexican jurisprudence. Most economic and social dealings, including business contracts, licensing, trade, criminal matters, land ownership, and even marriage, were subject to the Mexican *corpus juris*, which made laws and legal authorities a more important consideration in the Southwest fur trade.[9]

The composition of the fur trade community was also somewhat different in the Southwest. The Taos trade attracted, besides Anglo Americans, a large number of French Americans. The French had been for decades an influential presence in the southern portions of Louisiana Territory and a threat to Spain's monopoly on New Mexican commerce. French Americans were an important presence in other fur trade areas as well, but they, in combination with the prevailing Hispanic population of New Mexico, distinguished the Southwest trade from the more Anglo American- and Indian-dominated rendezvous and upper Missouri River trade.

Prior to the arrival of Americans, few New Mexicans trapped beaver. Spain, being chiefly interested in finding mineral wealth and defending its northern provinces from foreign intrusion, expressed only a modicum of interest in furs during its colonial era. What trade existed dealt primarily in coarse hides such as buffalo, bear, and deer, rarely in fine pelts like beaver and otter. This left an abundant beaver population that was enticing to Americans.[10] After the influx of Americans, some New Mexicans pursued the trade, in part because Mexican regulations enacted during the mid-1820s prohibited foreigners from trapping the region. However, since few New Mexicans did trap, New Mexican governors Bartolomé Baca (1822–1825) and his successor, Antonio Narbona (1825–1827), "thought it expedient to extend licenses to foreigners . . . upon condition of their taking a certain portion of Mexicans to learn the art of trapping."[11] Though most New Mexicans accompanying trapping expeditions appear to have been merely camp tenders, others did take up trapping.[12] Regardless of their specific roles, New Mexicans added to the Southwest trade's distinct cultural makeup.

The Southwest trappers also trapped areas that the mountain men mostly did not. Though imperious Spanish policies hindered American trapping in the Far Southwest during the early 1800s, some men, such as Caleb Greenwood, Etienne Provost, and Ezekiel Williams, did enter the region. Following Mexican independence in 1821, American traders, including William Becknell, John McKnight, and Thomas James, and trapping parties led by men such as Hugh Glenn and Jacob Fowler converged on Taos and Santa Fe. In the employ of the traders were teamsters and camp hands for the caravans. Some of them, including Ewing Young, William Wolfskill, and Isaac Slover, remained in New Mexico to trap the neighboring tributaries of the Pecos and Rio Grande rivers and even the Rio Grande's headwaters in the San Luis Valley to the north. These men became the first established American presence in the Southwest. Though mercantile transactions between St. Louis merchants and New Mexican residents initially dominated trade, the market for beaver furs soon supplanted them. Traders found that outfitting trappers in exchange for beaver pelts to sell back in St. Louis brought greater profits. Northern New Mexico thus became an important fur trading center with an increasingly influential American community at its heart.[13]

Opportunities for trapping and trading in the Southwest attracted increasing numbers of Americans, which led distraught Mexican officials to clamp down on foreign trappers. Most trappers merely circumvented these restrictions by obtaining Mexican citizenship or through special licenses, bribery, or outright evasion of officials. The remoteness of the Taos Valley only exacerbated matters by hindering official efforts at enforcement.[14]

When beaver near Taos and Santa Fe became scarce, trappers pushed further north and northwest, following established Spanish-Ute trade routes first demarcated by Fray Silvestre Vélez de Escalante and Fray Francisco Atanasio Domínguez in 1776.[15] From 1823 to 1825, trappers led by Etienne Provost, François Le Clerc, William Becknell, and Antoine Robidoux trapped the upper Colorado River and its tributaries, including the "River of the Spaniards," or the Green River.[16] In late 1824, one group under Provost's leadership reached the Great Salt Lake basin. The next spring, Provost was again trapping the Green River in east-central Utah and there met William Ashley, who would establish the famous rendezvous later that year.[17] Two accomplishments resulted from these early northerly trapping expeditions from New Mexico. First, Provost likely became the first non-Indian to behold the Great Salt Lake, preceding Jim Bridger, who is often credited with the lake's discovery.[18] Second, and more important, the Taos trappers became the first American trapping force in the central Rockies, antedating the more famous mountain men and anticipating the annual rendezvous.

In addition to Ashley's mountain men, Hudson's Bay Company brigades competed in beaver country as far southeast as northern Utah, carrying out the company's plans to create a "fur desert" that would forestall American westward expansion.[19] Consequently, most Taos trappers turned their attention south and west of Taos to the Lower Colorado and Gila Rivers. Between 1826 and 1827, many worked this region—Ewing Young, William Sherley "Old Bill" Williams, George Yount, John Rowland, Ceran St. Vrain, Sylvestre Pratte, and James O. Pattie among them. More importantly, some who trapped in that direction ventured on to California and advanced the trade between Los Angeles and Santa Fe. One group under Ewing Young, David Waldo, and David E. Jackson established a trade in California horses and mules. Other trappers such as Thomas L. "Peg-leg" Smith subsequently also recognized and sought out this valuable new commodity, and George Yount and William Wolfskill helped open a more northerly route of commerce between New Mexico and the coast, called the Old Spanish Trail. The trails these men opened would enable a later generation of Americans to reach California and aid in the United States acquisition of it.[20] Arguably, the Taos trappers' importance in opening the Far West to American expansion equals or surpasses that of the Rocky Mountain trappers.[21]

Unlike the Rocky Mountains or the upper Missouri River region, the Southwest became a haven for small-scale enterprises and independent trappers. Political barriers, harsher environment, lower quality and fewer beaver furs, and a lack of navigable waters to St. Louis markets made the region unprofitable for large investors. One major enterprise did try to enter the Southwest trade: Bernard Pratte and Company, the western department of John Jacob Astor's American Fur Company. Astor intended to gain full control of the Far West trade and believed that the furs coming out of Taos and Santa Fe threatened his attempted monopoly. But incessant failure dogged Bernard Pratte and Company and revealed the futility of large-scale trapping in such an inhospitable environment.[22]

The Southwest fur trade's "golden era" lasted from 1828 to 1833, when beaver prices and the number of American trappers reached their apex. Trappers continued working the Gila and Colorado while some ventured as far south as Chihuahua. Others turned north again to the southern Rockies, trapping regions of the Green, Gunnison, and upper Colorado Rivers. After 1828, the Taos trappers were gleaning a significant portion of the fur wealth of the Rocky Mountains. In 1831, one fur trader from St. Louis estimated that the Southwest trade accounted for one-third of the total furs shipped to St. Louis. The returns from New Mexico for the following year were equally impressive, and the only larger single shipment that year came from the rendezvous.[23] Indeed, "the Taos trappers offered the only challenge to the operations of large Missouri-based companies that dominated the Rockies."[24]

The shifting geographical orientation of the Southwest fur trade differed from that of the Rocky Mountain trade. Each group had its own region of concentration, but while Taos trappers first moved north, then south-southwest, then north again, the Rocky Mountain trappers were consistently drawn back north from the central Rockies to the Three Forks region of the upper Missouri. Moreover, the Southwest trappers were obliged to adopt different, less concentrated trapping patterns than the mountain men, owing to the region's challenging topography and climate. They nevertheless offered the only significant American opposition to the increasingly monopolized Rocky Mountain trade.

Taos's slide from economic prominence began around 1833. Beaver prices dropped as silk hats became the vogue. Trading posts like Bent's Fort on the Arkansas (only 150 miles northeast of Taos) supplanted the New Mexican settlements' strategic importance as trading depots. Indeed, Charles and William Bent took economic control of the region, placing the Far Southwest in the economic grip of American entrepreneurs. By 1840, trade of buffalo robes overtook and largely replaced that of beaver pelts.[25] Many former trappers took up the buffalo trade—some as hunters. Most, however, traded with Indians, Mexicans, and *Comancheros* for robes, using "Taos Lightning" as a primary bartering item.[26]

The influence of Taos trappers and traders in gaining American control of the Far Southwest is unquestioned. By the end of the beaver trade in 1840, the Southwest was under the economic control of Americans. American traders and former trappers owned and controlled much of Taos and constituted the largest foreign group there. It is easy to surmise, then, that their presence constituted an invasionary spearhead from America into the Southwest by means of "the more subtle and often unconscious process of economic conquest."[27] More than the Americans' economic influence, the cultural, social, and even political presence they established in northern New Mexico eventually helped determine the outcome of General Stephen W. Kearny's "bloodless conquest" of the province during the Mexican War.[28] Thus, the Taos trappers had a farther-reaching effect on the settling of the Far Southwest than the mountain men had upon more northern areas. Taos trappers formed the first settlements of United States citizens in the Far West. In contrast, the trapping grounds of the itinerant mountain men would have to be settled later by Mormons, miners, and the military.

These biographical sketches of subjects who represent the Far Southwest fur trade are reprinted unaltered from LeRoy Hafen's original series, *The Mountain Men and the Fur Trade of the Far West*. They are, to the degree possible, arranged chronologically according to the figure's place in the fur trade time line. However, many individuals portrayed here participated in different stages of the trade, while others merely represent certain traits or aspects of it. Still, this approximation of chronological order lends some coherence to the historical context and perhaps constitutes the best approach to learning history from biography. The levels of scholarship in these biographies vary, in part because the thirteen biographers range from buff to budding scholar to professional historian. Some of them should be familiar to those versed in Western history and especially to those familiar with the fur trade; others, however, are less well known. To aid readers unfamiliar with some or all of the contributing writers, biographical notes on them accompany the following brief synopses of the biographies chosen for this book.

Marcelino Baca belonged to that New Mexican-born minority of trappers who helped establish the Southwest fur trade's unique ethnic mix and character. A Taos native, Baca presumably learned trapping while accompanying American groups required to include New Mexicans in their ranks. After the Southwest trade's decline, Baca trapped in the northern Rockies. He settled with other trappers at Pueblo and Hardscrabble, Colorado, after the demise of the beaver trade.

Jules DeMun was a well-educated and articulate French aristocrat. Owing to the French Revolution and other twists of fate, he by 1812 ended up in St. Louis. There he took up trading and trapping. While on the upper Arkansas River, he realized the Southwest's fur trade potential. Many times he sought permission from Spanish officials to trap the region, but he was refused and even imprisoned. DeMun's experience shows both the early interest in Southwest fur trapping and the heavy French influence in the region. Janet Lecompte, author of the Baca and DeMun biographies, is a housewife turned historian who favors Colorado and fur trade history. Although not an academic historian, Lecompte has received praise for her work, especially for her *Pueblo, Hardscrabble, Greenhorn* (1978) about the post-fur trade life of trappers and traders. She contributed many of the best biographies to Hafen's *The Mountain Men and the Fur Trade of the Far West.*

James Kirker's multi-occupational career reflects the diverse economic character of the Southwest fur trade. Before trapping in the Southwest, Kirker ascended the Missouri as one of William Ashley's "enterprising young men." Besides the fur trade, Kirker busied himself at copper mining (at the Santa Rita mines with Sylvester and James Pattie), trading arms and ammunition to the Apache (against Mexican laws), freighting, and even scalp hunting. Author William C. McGaw, a newspaperman turned writer, actor, and stuntman for Metro-Goldwyn-Mayer, produced the Ford Motor Circus road shows of the 1950s. He later became owner, editor, publisher, and principal reporter of the *Southwesterner* of Columbus, New Mexico, a publication dedicated to Western lore.

Jacob Fowler, with partner Hugh Glenn, led one of the first Mexican-authorized American trapping ventures into the Southwest following Mexico's independence. Their modest success lured other Americans to the region. Fowler did not pursue trapping thereafter, but he had helped open the Santa Fe and Taos fur trade. Author Raymond W. Settle, an amateur historian with a fancy for the West, made his living as a Baptist minister in Missouri. Besides sermonizing, Settle wrote amply about the Far West, including a few biographies for Hafen's series. Most of his writing was on transportation in the American West, including such well-known works as *Saddles and Spurs: The Pony Express Saga* (1955) and *War Drums and Wagon Wheels: The Story of Russell, Majors, and Waddell* (1966).

Isaac Slover was among the first American trappers officially allowed into New Mexico—as part of the Glenn-Fowler expedition—and one of the first trappers to take up permanent residence at Taos. Slover worked the Colorado's tributaries with men like Ewing Young and William Wolfskill, trapped the Gila with James and Sylvester Pattie, and crossed the Southwest to California. His California venture helped open overland trading between that province and New Mexico. Author Andrew F. Rolle served in army intelligence during World War II. After the war he held the State Department's vice-consul position at Genoa, Italy. After Italy, he earned his Ph.D. from the University of California at Los Angeles and taught history at his alma mater, Occidental College, Los Angeles, as holder of the Robert Glass Cleland chair. His writings are mostly about California and Italian-Americans. His most recent work, *John Charles Frémont: Character as Destiny* (1991) is the best yet on the famous explorer.

Ewing Young arrived in Taos with William Becknell's second trade caravan in 1822 and remained to trap beaver. Between trapping ventures he also became a trader at Santa Fe and Taos and applied for Mexican citizenship to facilitate his enterprises. He gave Kit Carson his start in the fur trade and, later, trapped the Gila and Lower Colorado and worked the copper mines at Santa Rita. With Davis Waldo and David Jackson, Young pioneered trade of mules and horses from California to New Mexico. His trading career began with and continued through most of the Southwest fur-trade period and reflects many of its major phases. Historian Harvey Lewis Carter, who wrote the Ewing Young, Kit Carson, John Gantt, and Dick Wootton biographies in this collection, earned his doctorate from the University of Wisconsin in 1938. He later taught for many years at Colorado College, Colorado Springs. A good friend of LeRoy Hafen, Carter wrote thirty-nine biographies for *The Mountain Men and the Fur Trade of the Far West*, more than any other of the eighty-four contributors. Carter's best-remembered book is *"Dear Old Kit": The Historical Christopher Carson* (1968). He also spent much effort in defending Carson's reputation against detractors and in championing the stereotypical romantic image of the adventurous mountain man.

Etienne Provost typifies the many Frenchmen in the Southwest fur trade. Though Provost's activities in the region preceded Mexican independence, he is best known for his ventures afterward. He led the first major expeditions to reach the Green River and portions of central Utah from Taos and was probably the first non-Indian to see the Great Salt Lake. More importantly, his Taos trappers preceded the coming of the Rocky Mountain men in the central Rockies. Later on, Provost led American Fur Company brigades on the upper Missouri, having been, as many fur men were, recruited into John Astor's company as part of Astor's grand scheme to control the Far West trade. Author LeRoy R. Hafen, editor of *The Mountain Men and the Fur Trade of the Far West*, received his doctorate in history from the University of California at Berkeley in 1924. That same year he became director and state historian for the State Historical Society of Colorado and editor of *Colorado Magazine*, positions he held until 1954. He later taught at his alma mater, Brigham Young University, finishing his career there. Hafen wrote and edited over fifty books and more numerous articles about the American West, many about the fur trade. Few individuals have contributed as much to the history of the Far West as he.

Antoine Robidoux belonged to an influential family in the Southwest fur trade. Like his brothers, François, Michel, and Louis, Antoine first pursued trapping. He accompanied Etienne Provost's group into the central Rockies. Later, he became a trader, entered Santa Fe's political circles, and took the name Don Antonio Robidoux after gaining Mexican citizenship. Seeking Mexican citizenship was common among Americans in Mexico who became expatriated for mostly business reasons. Besides representing the Robidoux brothers, Antoine's life reflects well the social, economic, and political character of the Southwest fur trade. Author William S. Wallace taught history in northern New Mexico and Arizona public schools and at the

University of Montana during the 1940s. He then became head librarian and archivist at New Mexico Highlands University, Las Vegas, New Mexico. Wallace's best known work is *Antoine Robidoux, 1794–1860: A Biography of a Western Venturer* (1953).

William Sherley (Old Bill) Williams first was a government interpreter with the Osage, then worked for William H. Ashley, and eventually trapped in the Southwest. Like many trappers, he focused on the Gila, but he also trapped throughout much of the Southwest and the central Rockies. Williams worked for many companies in Taos and St. Louis, and his career reflects the individualistic nature of the Southwest trade, which was unencumbered by large, domineering fur companies. Author Frederic E. Voelker was an accountant in St. Louis with a deep interest in the Far West. He occasionally wrote articles for *The Missouri Historical Society Bulletin* and was chapter president of the St. Louis Westerners. Most of Voelker's writings were articles about fur trade figures; he never produced any book-length studies. He died leaving his only attempted large work, a biography of Ezekiel Williams, unfinished.

George C. Yount arrived in Santa Fe in 1826 as a trade caravan teamster, then took up trapping. Yount trapped mostly the Gila and Colorado Rivers, and his efforts index well that phase of the Southwest trade. Like many Southwest fur trade men, Yount busied himself in other economic ventures. In 1830, he accompanied William Wolfskill's group that opened the Old Spanish Trail—perhaps the most important facet of his career. A renowned paleontologist at the University of California, author Charles L. Camp periodically wrote about the American West too. In the 1940s he led an archeological dig in South Africa that discovered remains of the man-ape, genus *pleisanthropus*. He also discovered one of America's richest fossil fields in northwestern New Mexico. His writings on the American West have been influential and include books such as *James Clyman: American Frontiersman* (1928), *George C. Yount and his Chronicles of the West* (1966), and *The Plains and the Rockies: A Bibliography of Original Narratives of Travel and Adventure, 1800–1865* (1937), co-edited with Henry Wagner.

Kit Carson became the most famous trapper in American history and culture. In 1826, he fled the tedium of apprenticeship to join a Santa Fe-bound wagon train. For the next few years, Carson worked for various individuals as a teamster, cook, or interpreter. Then in 1829 he joined Ewing Young's trapping venture to California. For a number of years thereafter Carson was involved with the rendezvous system and trapped the central Rockies with Jim Bridger's brigades. After the fur trade's decline, Carson returned to the Southwest and hunted buffalo for the Bents. He gained fame as guide for John C. Frémont's various expeditions during the 1840s. He later became an Indian agent and during the Civil War directed military campaigns against the Navajo that ended in that tribe's tragic "long walk." Carson, as portrayed in numerous dime novels and popular works, became the basis of the principal stereotyped and romanticized fur trapper figure that has dominated the American popular mind to the present.

Sylvestre S. Pratte experienced a short-lived and dismal career. From Taos, he operated as the Southwest agent of Bernard Pratte and Company (part of John Jacob Astor's western empire). Unlike most Taos trappers who worked independently or for small enterprises, Pratte had large financial backing, but failure dogged his efforts. His incompetent leadership and restrictive Mexican mandates hampered Pratte's endeavors along the Gila and in the central Rockies. His life reveals the futility of large-scale trapping in the precarious circumstances and lesser abundance of the Southwest. Author David J. Weber, who wrote the Sylvestre Pratte, John Rowland, and Gervais Nolan biographies in this collection, is professor of history and current holder of the Robert and Nancy Dedman Chair at Southern Methodist University, Dallas, and specializes in the history of the American Southwest. His numerous books, articles, and awards place him among the leading Western historians today. His *The Taos Trappers: The Fur Trade of the Far Southwest, 1540–1846* (1971) remains the best work on the subject to date.

John Rowland arrived in the Southwest in 1823 in the employ of one of the Santa Fe caravans. He accompanied Etienne Provost as one of the first trappers entering the central Rockies from Taos. He later led trapping groups along the Gila River. Rowland became one of the first Americans to take a Mexican wife and obtain Mexican citizenship. Beyond trapping, Rowland operated a flour mill and a distillery. He later migrated to California and participated in the Bear Flag Revolt. Rowland's life in the Southwest embodies much that distinguishes the region's fur trade.

Gervais Nolan was a French Canadian who worked for the Montreal-based Northwest Fur Company until 1820. By 1824 he had made Taos his home. Besides trapping, Nolan pursued a number of occupations, including gunsmith, merchant, and miner. He married a Mexican woman and became a naturalized Mexican citizen. He eventually acquired massive land holdings in New Mexico totaling nearly 1.5 million acres. As much as anyone else's, Nolan's life personified the unique character of the Southwest fur trade.

Thomas L. (Peg-leg) Smith entered the Santa Fe trade as an independent trader in 1824. He first ventured northward out of Taos into the central Rockies, later turned his attentions to the Gila, then trapped the central Rockies again, working for Sylvestre Pratte. While trapping in the southern Rockies, Smith was shot in the lower left leg by Indians, shattering both bones and leaving amputation as the only remedy. The incident provided his nickname. Smith continued trapping, mostly in the region north of Taos. With the decline of the beaver trade, he turned to horse trading and stealing, mining, and other occupations. Author Alfred Glen Humpherys earned his Ph.D. from the University of New Mexico and taught at Ricks College in Rexburg, Idaho, early in his career. He also worked as a historian and interpretive ranger for the National Park Service at the C & O Canal in Washington, D.C., and at the Little Bighorn (Custer) Battlefield. Currently, he is the curator and director of the Wheeler Historic Farm, a living history museum near Salt Lake City, Utah.

William Wolfskill figured prominently in the Southwest fur trade. As one of the earliest American trappers in the region after Mexican independence, he worked the tributaries of the Rio Grande and the Pecos River. Between 1826 and 1829 he spent months trapping the Gila and trading horses. He also owned a store in Taos with a distillery and was a major distributor of Taos Lightning. But Wolfskill's most enduring legacy was opening the Old Spanish Trail between California and New Mexico. Author Iris Higbie (Wilson) Engstrand received her doctorate from the University of Southern California in 1962. She then went on to teach history at various California colleges and universities and focused her studies primarily on California's history. Her major contribution to fur trade history was her book *William Wolfskill: Frontier Trapper to California Ranchero, 1798–1866* (1965), on which her article was based.

Ceran St. Vrain's trapping and trading activities began in 1824 at Taos. His ventures were often connected directly or indirectly to Bernard Pratte and Company, and he accompanied the failing expeditions of Sylvestre Pratte. His success came after forming a partnership with the Bent brothers, William and Charles. Together, based at Bent's Fort on the Arkansas River, they gained economic dominance of the Southwest fur and Indian trade, including that in much of the central Plains and central Rockies. Harold H. Dunham, who wrote both the St. Vrain and Charles Bent articles in this collection, first taught in various New York City colleges in the 1930s. He then served as historian in the U.S. Army Transportation Corps during World War II. After the war he became professor of history at Denver University, specializing in the American Southwest. In 1959 he was a consultant for the federal government in the Indian Claims Commission proceedings in the case of *Pueblo de Taos v. United States.*

John Gantt's career represents the end of the Southwest fur trade, when beaver pelt values dropped and trading shifted from Taos to forts such as Bent's Fort and Gantt's own along the Arkansas River. Gantt was the first to pursue trading with the Cheyenne and to erect an adobe post on the Arkansas. But he eventually lost out to his better financed and more aggressive competitors, the Bents. Gantt had a rough time keeping ahead in the trading business, as did large numbers of unsuccessful and usually unknown trappers and traders who sought opportunity in the Southwest.

Charles Bent built Bent's Old Fort on the Arkansas River in 1834, supplanting Taos and Santa Fe as the region's economic and trading hub. Before building the fort, Charles and his brother William were trappers. But Charles shifted to trading and became a leading merchant in Taos. With partners Ceran St. Vrain and William, Charles spearheaded the plans for Bent's Fort and oversaw the company's affairs. He participated in land speculation (securing the large Maxwell, Las Animas, and Nolan land grants) and in politics as the United Stated Civil Governor of New Mexico. Bent's economic and political influence facilitated America's conquest of New Mexico. The National Park Service rebuilt his old fort, which is now visited by thousands of tourists yearly.

Dick Wootton arrived late to the region, near the end of the fur trade. In 1836 he hired on with one of the Bents' supply trains. He then worked for them trading with Indians but later organized his own trapping expedition to the Rockies. After the fur trade, Wootton pursued various economic ventures. He contracted to supply buffalo meat to Bent's Fort, traded with Indians, scouted for the military, raised buffalo for zoos and shows back East, and operated a saloon and hotel. Wootton died in 1893, the same year Frederick Jackson Turner proclaimed the frontier's closure.

In studies of the American fur trade, the Far Southwest and many of the trappers and traders who worked in it have been overshadowed by the more popular and romantic mountain men. Since the inception of fur trade scholarship, historians have generally ignored, neglected, or failed to deal definitively with the Southwest fur trade. In his seminal three-volume work *The American Fur Trade of the Far West* (1902), Hiram Martin Chittenden paid no regard to the Southwest or its trappers, offering little more than a disparaging paragraph about the region.[29] His disregard set the course for ensuing generations of fur trade historians. Paul Chrisler Phillips also neglected the Southwest trade in his monumental two-volume study *The Fur Trade* (1961), dealing with it scantily in a final chapter that seems more an afterthought than a concerted analysis. Likewise, David J. Wishart's more recent *The Fur Trade of the American West, 1807–1840* (1979)—an interdisciplinary examination of the complex relationships among the biological, physical, and cultural environments of the fur trade—fails to consider the Southwest trade's significant differences from the fur commerce of the Rocky Mountain and upper Missouri River regions. Similarly, the weapons and tools of the Southwest fur trade received slight notice in Carl P. Russell's *Firearms, Traps and Tools of the Mountain Men* (1967).[30]

A small number of works dealing with the Southwest trade do exist though. Robert Glass Cleland's *This Reckless Breed of Men: The Trappers and Traders of the Southwest* (1950) stresses the American fur trade as an imperial factor contributing to United States sovereignty. Cleland's chapters center on individuals, but to include heroic figures like Jedediah Smith (who had virtually nothing to do with the Southwest trade), Cleland extends the Southwest's boundaries as far north as the American-Canadian border and looks mostly at California, cheating the Southwest of its importance in American fur trade history. One appealing narrative, David Lavender's *Bent's Fort* (1954), examines the largest mercantile firm in the region.[31]

The best monograph to date on the Southwest fur business is David J. Weber's *The Taos Trappers*. Weber focuses specifically on the Taos- and Santa Fe-centered trade, granting it deserved historical recognition. His book's sweeping examination of the trade is a must for those wanting to know more about the importance of the Southwest. However, the particular experiences of notable figures are not so fully traced in it. The selection of biographies collected here adds dimension to the trade's history by bringing individual trappers to greater attention.

This collection provides an inviting and informative history of the Southwest fur trade through biographies. There are aspects of this popular approach that should be noted. Readers may find that an Anglo-centric perspective prevails throughout these biographies. That is because American historians, who have dominated the study of the Southwest, "have ethnocentrically shoved their own countrymen to the front of the stage."[32] Thus, they have made Americans, especially trappers and traders, central heroes in Southwest history while pushing Mexicans and Mexico to the periphery as nuisances to progress. Though uncontrived, the ensuing biographies are heirs to this slant.

Moreover, though biography is an entertaining and viable form of history, it has become increasingly passé among professional historians taken with the tedium of more polemical scholarship. They have left biography mostly to professional writers producing for popular audiences. The biographies here are written well and are well documented, and their historical foundations hold up even after three decades. Still, a number of contributors to the Hafen series limited themselves methodologically and accepted sources uncritically. The results often projected without analysis the ethnocentric views and prejudices of the trappers and traders toward other groups. Readers should understand that these biographies appeared as today's scholarly concerns over ethnic diversity, gender, environment, and other politically correct trepidations were in their infancy. Hence, they lack the inclinations or analytical trends of more recent historical writings; we should not judge their authors by present expectations but should instead recognize the continuing historical relevance of their writings.

Fortunately, a new generation of historians armed with an array of analytical tools is making its mark in Western history. To this group we must turn for deeper understanding of ethnicity, gender, environment, and community, hoping they will not neglect the Southwest fur trade to the degree that their forebears did. If they give it the attention it deserves, we may anticipate greater historical understanding of this unique facet of the American experience.

Notes

1. Herbert E. Bolton, *Coronado, Knight of the Pueblo and Plains*, 4th ed. (Albuquerque: University of New Mexico Press, 1991), pp. 184–86, 310–11.

2. The most authoritative work on the Pueblo Revolt of 1680 is Charles W. Hackett, *Revolt of the Pueblo Indians of New Mexico and Otermin's Attempted Reconquest, 1680–1682*, 2 vols. (Albuquerque: University of New Mexico Press, 1942). See also John Francis Bannon, *The Spanish Border Lands Frontier, 1513–1821* (New York: Holt, Rinehart, and Winston, 1970), pp. 80–86.

3. The uniting of the Spanish settlers and the Pueblo Indians (traditional enemies) for protection and survival is attributed to what anthropologist W. J. McGee defines as "the economy of solidarity." See W. J. McGee, "The Beginning of Agriculture," *American Anthropologist* 8 (1895): 366.

4. Josiah Gregg, *Commerce of the Prairies*, ed. Max L. Moorhead (Norman: University of Oklahoma Press, 1954), p. 104.

5. David J. Weber, *The Taos Trappers: The Fur Trade in the Far Southwest, 1540–1846* (Norman: University of Oklahoma Press, 1971), pp. 8–9.

6. Nearly 68 percent of American fur trade men in the Taos region married Hispanic American women, while marriages to Indian women accounted for only 39 percent of mountain man marriages. See William Swagerty, "Marriage and Settlement Patterns of Rocky Mountain Trappers and Traders," *Western Historical Quarterly* 11 (April 1980): 164.

7. Ibid., pp. 168–69.

8. Americans who remained in Taos after the trade comprised fourteen percent of all trappers and traders. Ibid., p. 171. See also Janet Lecompte, *Pueblo, Hardscrabble, Greenhorn: Society on the High Plains, 1832–1856* (Norman: University of Oklahoma Press, 1978).

9. The legal history of the American fur trade is a new and intriguing area of study. See John Phillip Reid, "The Layers of Western Legal History," *Law for the Elephant, Law for the Beaver: Essays in the Legal History of the North American West*, ed. John McLaren, Hamar Foster, and Chet Orloff (Pasadena, Calif.: Ninth Judicial Circuit Historical Society, 1992), pp. 23–73.

10. Weber, pp. 12–31.

11. Gregg, p. 160.

12. Weber, pp. 160–62.

13. Ibid., pp. 52–65.

14. Ibid., pp. 156–62, 176–90 discusses the various means by which trappers and traders circumvented Mexican restrictions.

15. LeRoy R. Hafen, *The Old Spanish Trail: Santa Fé to Los Angeles* (Glendale, Calif.: Arthur H. Clark, 1954), pp. 59–89.

16. Richard E. Oglesby, *Manuel Lisa and the Opening of the Missouri Fur Trade* (Norman: University of Oklahoma Press, 1963), pp. 66–67, 95.

17. Weber, pp. 66–81.

18. Jack B. Tykal, *Etienne Provost: Man of the Mountains* (Liberty, Utah: Eagle View Publishing, 1989), pp. 48–49; Cecil Alter, *Jim Bridger* (1925; Norman: University of Oklahoma Press, 1962), pp. 84–85.

19. Frederick Merk, *Fur Trade and Empire* (Cambridge: Harvard University Press, 1931); Gloria Griffen Cline, *Exploring the Great Basin* (Norman: University of Oklahoma Press, 1963), chapters 5, 6.

20. Weber, pp. 112–56; Hafen, pp. 131–54, 171–79.

21. Bernard De Voto, *The Year of Decision: 1846* (Boston: Little, Brown, and Company, 1943), pp. 238–46, 349–59, 368–75.

22. Weber, pp. 168–76, 195; Hiram M. Chittenden, *The American Fur Trade of the Far West* (New York: Francis P. Harper, 1902), 1:325.

23. Weber, pp. 204–7.

24. Ibid., p. 194.

25. Howard R. Lamar, *The Far Southwest, 1846–1912: A Territorial History* (1966; New York: W. W. Norton and Company, 1970), chapter 2.

26. Weber, pp. 210–29.

27. Lamar, p. 47.

28. Ibid., chapters 2, 3. The role of American trappers and traders in facilitating the conquest courses through these chapters. See also Weber, pp. 189–90.

29. Chittenden, 2:782–83.

30. See Paul Chrisler Phillips, *The Fur Trade*, 2 vols. (Norman: University of Oklahoma Press, 1961); David J. Wishart, *The Fur Trade of the American West, 1807–1840: A Geographical Synthesis* (Lincoln: University of Nebraska Press, 1978); and Carl P. Russell, *Firearms, Traps and Tools of the Mountain Men* (New York: Alfred A. Knopf, 1967). A good historiography of the Western fur trade is Gordon B. Dodd, "The Fur Trade and Exploration," in *Historians and the American West*, edited by Michael P. Malone (Lincoln: University of Nebraska Press, 1983), pp. 57–75.

31. Robert Glass Cleland, *This Reckless Breed of Men: The Trappers and Fur Traders of the Southwest* (New York: Alfred A. Knopf, 1950); David Lavender, *Bent's Fort* (Garden City, NY: Doubleday and Company, 1954).

32. David J. Weber, *The Mexican Frontier, 1821–1846: The American Southwest under Mexico* (Albuquerque: University of New Mexico Press, 1982), p. xvi.

Marcelino Baca

by JANET LECOMPTE
Colorado Springs, Colorado

As a rule, native New Mexicans did not make good trappers. Trapping was a solitary occupation and New Mexicans preferred the safety of numbers, an attitude bred into them by their forebears' precarious existence in an isolated Spanish colony surrounded for two centuries by savage tribes. During the 1830s, it is true, there were many New Mexicans employed at trading posts on the Missouri, Platte, and Arkansas rivers, and even in the roaming trapping brigades, but almost invariably as muleteers or packers. It was a rare native of New Mexico who chose to make his living as a trapper, often alone and protected only by his rifle, his wit, and his reflexes.

Marcelino Baca was one of these rare New Mexican trappers.[1] Born about 1808 at Taos, the son of Salvador and Tomasa Silva Baca, Marcelino grew up tall and strong, handsome and intelligent, and contemptuous of the race from which he had sprung. George F. Ruxton described him thus:

> Marcellin – who, though a Mexican, despised his people and abjured his blood, having been all his life in the mountains with the white hunters – looked down easily upon six feet and odd inches. In form a Hercules, he had the symmetry of an Apollo; with strikingly handsome features, and masses of long black hair hanging from his slouching beaver over the shoulders of his buckskin hunting shirt. He, as he was wont to say, was "no dam Spaniard, but 'mountainee man,' wagh!" [2]

---

[1] Joseph Meek remembered another, named Loretta, who with his Blackfoot wife became interpreter to an American Fur Company post among the Blackfoot. F. F. Victor, *The River of the West* (Hartford, 1870), 134-35.

[2] *Life in the Far West* (New York, 1849), 193. Ruxton ends his novel, of which

A Trapper and His Pony, from a drawing by Frederic Remington. From Henry Inman, *The Old Santa Fe Trail* (New York: Macmillan, 1897). Courtesy of Western History Collections, University of Oklahoma.

"Mountainee man" he surely was, and in later years he boasted of the nine years he had spent in the mountains, living on meat alone and tasting neither salt nor bread.[3]

Marcelino Baca probably learned to trap in one of the many companies of American trappers who made Taos their headquarters and outfitting point during the 1820s. He also spent some time working with his father in a gold mine (probably at the *Real de Dolores* [Old Placer], discovered in 1828 south of Santa Fe) where he learned to pan gold in wooden bowls. When in later years he showed up at Fort Laramie with a vial of gold dust he had panned on the Chugwater, it was the first gold the trappers had ever seen. But the West was more interested in fur than in gold at that time, and his discovery went unnoticed.[4]

Marcelino probably began his nine years as a trapper in 1832 or 1833. By 1835 he was a member of James Bridger's American Fur Company brigade and well on his way to acquiring his reputation of "the best trapper and hunter in the mountains and ever first in the fight."[5] His Mexican background, always mentioned by those who wrote about him, was on one occasion a decided asset to the brigade. On the Humboldt River in 1835, Marcelino spied a Digger Ute creeping towards the trappers' horses. Throwing his lasso – hardly a standard piece of trapping equipment – he caught the Indian around the neck, wheeled his horse and galloped through the greasewood, dragging the remains of the unfortunate Digger behind him.[6]

---

he says "there is no incident in it which has not actually occurred" (p. n), with an account of a party of mountaineers, "Marcellin" being the only one named, finding the frozen body of Bill Williams in "New Park" (Middle Park, Colo.). This did not actually occur, however, since Ruxton died a year before Bill Williams did.

[3] Lieut. E. G. Beckwith's report, *Report of Explorations and Surveys for a Railroad Route from the Mississippi River to the Pacific Ocean,* ii (Washington, D.C., 1855), 35.

[4] James B. Marsh, *Four Years in the Rockies, or, The Adventures of Isaac P. Rose* (New Castle, Pa., 1884; reprint, Columbus, Ohio, n.d.), 215.

[5] Ruxton, *op. cit.,* 23.   [6] Marsh, *op. cit.,* 89.

Marcelino had the well-developed flair for self-preserva-
tion that marked a successful Mountain Man. While serving in Bridger's brigade on the Yellowstone River, he went
to reconnoiter a Blackfoot fort on top of a bluff above the
trappers' camp. Near the top of the hill Marcelino was fired
on from the fort, the charge striking and breaking his ankle.
He fell to the ground, and as the Indians rushed from the
fort to finish him off, he coiled himself into a ball and rolled
down the snow-covered slope into camp.[7] Another account
of this episode on the Yellowstone dates it February 22,
1837, and refers to its hero only as "a Spaniard." [8] Still with
Bridger's brigade in the winter of 1837-8, Marcelino was
one of those sent from camp on Powder River to Fort
Laramie for supplies, returning to camp in January.[9]

Around the end of 1838, Marcelino blundered into Pawnee lands on the Platte River. The Pawnees took him captive and prepared him for a peculiarly unpleasant ritual
sacrifice: After tying the captive to a post, the Indians would
build a fire nearby and dance; as they danced, they would
approach the victim, cut off a strip of flesh, roast it in the
fire and eat it, the captive perishing miserably in the meantime. While the handsome trapper was being fattened for
such a feast, the chief's daughter fell in love with him and
begged her father to spare his life. Her wish was granted
and Marcelino was released. He took his Pawnee Poca-
hontas to wife, giving her his mother's name of Tomasa or
Tomacita.[10] If she was beautiful, the legend does not say so,
but fifteen years later she was at least possessed of "matronly
grace and dignity." [11] Their eldest son, José, was born on the

---

[7] *Ibid.,* 144.

[8] Osborne Russell, *Journal of a Trapper* (Boise, Idaho, 1921), 53.

[9] *Ibid.,* 79f. Isaac P. Rose says Bridger's camp was on Wind River. Rose, Tom
Biggs and Marcelino went to Fort Laramie for supplies, says Rose, and did not
return to Bridger's camp until spring. Marsh, *op. cit.,* 215-17.

[10] F. W. Cragin's notes of an interview with José de Jesús Valdez, Walsenburg,
Colo., Dec. 9, 1907, Cragin Collection, Pioneers' Museum, Colorado Springs, Colo.

[11] Lieut. Beckwith's report, *loc. cit.,* 35.

South Platte River near present Denver in 1839; their second son, Luis, was born at Fort Laramie in 1841; their only daughter, Elena, was born at the Hardscrabble settlement in 1846, and later married a son of Charles Autobees. After the birth of Elena, Marcelino took his wife and children to Taos where he had the children baptized and at the same time was married in the Catholic church to their mother. Tomasa outlived Marcelino, dying in 1871.[12]

When the beaver trade went to pieces, Marcelino joined other trappers who found refuge from the wreck of their occupation at Pueblo, the Arkansas River trading post and agricultural settlement at the mouth of Fountain River. In the spring of 1844 he moved with George Simpson and others to Hardscrabble Creek, thirty miles west of Pueblo, and made a new settlement. For three or four years Marcelino lived at Hardscrabble, trading with Indians and trapping occasionally, probably more for fun than profit, for by now the Indian trade had made him a wealthy man.[13]

In 1847 or 1848 the Hardscrabble settlement began to decline, and Marcelino moved to the lovely valley of the Greenhorn River, south of the Arkansas, where he kept cattle and grew corn, wheat, beans and watermelons, not only for his family's consumption, but to trade to the Indians.[14] In 1852 the Utes swooped down on Greenhorn, killing some of Marcelino's cattle, destroying his grain and

[12] F. W. Cragin's notes of an interview with Elena Baca Autobees, Pueblo, Colo., Nov. 8, 1907, Cragin Collection.

[13] Janet S. Lecompte, "The Hardscrabble Settlement, 1844-1848," *Colorado Magazine*, XXXI, no. 2 (April, 1954).

[14] Lieut. Beckwith's report, *loc. cit.,* 34-35; Cragin's notes of an interview with Elena Baca Autobees, cited. Charles Autobees testified in 1873 that Marcelino Baca, along with Archibald Metcalf, John Brown, and William New, occupied land on the Greenhorn in 1841 or 1842. If so, this early occupation was sporadic, perhaps only to grow a crop of corn, or pasture stock there for a short period. Testimony of Charles Autobees, Jan. 16, 1873, Pueblo, Colo.; "Vigil and St. Vrain Grant," Correspondence, 1868-1914, Records of the General Land Office, RG 49, National Archives, Wash., D.C.

stealing his horses. He decided to move back to the deserted Pueblo and live in the old fort while he was building a log house a mile east across Fountain River. He moved onto his new ranch and in the spring of 1853 he dug a ditch from the Fountain and planted a cornfield, but a flood washed it out.[15] Before summer he put in another crop on the Greenhorn and while he was engaged in farming it, he was hired as a guide over the Sangre de Cristo Pass to Fort Massachusetts by the party surveying a route for a railroad to the Pacific. As a guide he performed adequately; Captain Gunnison described him as an intelligent man with thirty years' experience in the mountains.[16]

In the fall of 1853, Marcelino moved back to his log house on the east side of Fountain River, where he had built ten or twelve other houses for his peons, as well as corrals for his cattle and horses (he was said to have had as many as 500 head of cattle and 50 horses). At the same time the old Pueblo was fixed up and occupied by a group of Mexicans from Taos, who in the spring and summer of 1854 put in a cornfield and did a little trading with the Utes, notably with Chief Blanco's band of Muaches.

In the early morning of December 24, 1854, Chief Blanco and his men, apparently friendly as usual, paid Marcelino's ranch a visit, asking to come inside the house. Marcelino would have let the Utes in, but an old man named Barela vehemently objected, and his wise advice prevailed. As the Indians went away, crossing the Fountain towards Pueblo, they drove off all Marcelino's cattle and horses that had not been secured in the corrals. At Pueblo the Indians were admitted, and immediately began a massacre of the seventeen men in the fort, not one of whom escaped alive.[17] Mar-

---

[15] Charles Irving Jones, "William Kroenig, New Mexico Pioneer," *New Mexico Historical Review*, XIX (Oct., 1944), 292, 296f.

[16] Beckwith's report, *loc. cit.,* 120.

[17] Janet Lecompte, "Pueblo Massacre," *Denver Westerners' Brand Book*, 1954 (Boulder, Colo., 1955), 41-48.

celino's loss of 73 head of cattle, 13 horses, and 2 mules amounted to over $4000.[18]

A month later the Utes returned to the Arkansas and killed Marcelino's brother, Benito, near Pueblo. By then Marcelino had had enough. He moved his family to New Mexico, to the little frontier village of Rio Colorado (now Red River), where he spent the remaining years of his life. When the Civil War broke out, he enlisted in the New Mexico Volunteers and was killed by a shot in the forehead during the battle with invading Texans at Valverde, N.M., on February 21, 1862.[19]

---

[18] "Claims for Indian Depredations in New Mexico," *H. exec. doc. 123,* 35 Cong., 1 sess. (ser. 959).

[19] F. W. Cragin's notes of interviews with José de Jesús Valdez and Elena Baca Autobees, cited.

Jules DeMun

by JANET LECOMPTE
Colorado Springs, Colorado

Jules DeMun was a nobleman by birth, by nature and by training. Proud and gentle, educated and articulate, of "perfect integrity and pure morals," his qualities belonged where people of high culture congregated – a palace, drawing-room or embassy. But life did not fit him to his proper niche. He was thrown by two revolutions and his love for a beautiful lady into a world where his virtues were useless. We will not find a more incongruous Mountain Man than Jules DeMun, or a more ineffectual one.

He was descended from a long line of French peers, whose seignories and castles, some dating from the twelfth century, were located in the southwest part of France, in the province of Gascony. Jules's father, Chevalier Alexandre Jacques DeMun, son of the Marquis DeMun, joined the King's Body-Guard and was sent to the Caribbean island of Santo Domingo. There he married Marie Madeleine LeMeilleur and sired four sons and two daughters – Jules Louis René, Juan Santiago María Luis (Louis), Nicolas, Augusto Ysabel Vincente (Auguste), Juliette Marie Madeleine (Cécé), and Amédée, lost at sea, unmarried. Jules was the eldest son, born April 25, 1782, at Port au Prince, where his baptismal record may yet be seen in the old church.[1]

At an early age, Jules and his brother Auguste were sent

---

[1] Marquis de Mun, "Brief Account of De Mun Family in France," *Collections,* Missouri Historical Society, v, no. 2 (Feb. 1928), 209-15; Nettie H. Beauregard, "De Mun Family in America," *Collections,* Missouri Historical Society, v, no. 3 (June 1928), 327-28. See also the account of Julius Walsh, Jules DeMun's grandson, in J. Thomas Scharf, *History of Saint Louis City and County* (Phila., 1883), II, pp. 1209-11.

to France to be educated. When the revolution broke out, the boys were disguised as peasants and hustled out of the country by a family servant, Jules hiding his Stradivarius violin under his rags. The boys escaped to England where their parents had settled after a negro revolt forced them to flee Santo Domingo. In England the boys' education was continued until the family fortunes, reduced in the two revolutions, required them to earn their livings. Jules went to Cuba in 1803, at the age of twenty-one, where he became a coffee planter and a Spanish subject. He was joined there by his brothers in 1807 and by his mother after the death of their father in 1808. By 1809, Jules was in the United States, doing business at Baltimore, Philadelphia, and finally, Ste. Genevieve, Missouri, where his mother and brother Auguste joined him. By January 1812, Jules had moved to St. Louis. There, on March 31, 1812, he married fifteen-year-old Isabelle Gratiot, beautiful and charming daughter of Charles Gratiot and Victoire Chouteau, related to all St. Louis's wealth and fashion.[2]

It was not long before Jules learned what it meant to be a poor member of a wealthy family, and especially of the great fur-trading family of Chouteau. In the summer of 1812, he went into business in St. Louis with his sister Cécé's husband, M. DePestre, but the firm was dissolved in September.[3] After that, Jules disappears briefly from the records except for a term on the St. Louis grand jury in 1813.[4] By

[2] *Ibid.*

[3] Frederick L. Billon, *Annals of St. Louis in Its Territorial Days* (St. Louis, 1888), 126; Records of the St. Louis Superintendency of Indian Affairs, Kansas Historical Society, Topeka, vol. xxx.

[4] Billon, *Annals,* 18. Jules's brother Auguste had by this time settled on Black River in southwestern Missouri where he established mills, obtained leases on salt licks and founded Lawrence County. He was killed by William McArthur during a political argument at Ste. Genevieve in September 1816. Lewis (Louis) DeMun was clerk of the Lawrence (Mo.) County Court in 1817. By 1825 he was attaché to the French Embassy in Washington. Later he went to Cuba, probably in 1819 with Jules and Isabelle, his mother, and his widowed sister Cécé (Clarence Edwin Carter, *Territorial Papers of the United States,* xv (Washington, D.C., 1951), 161-65, 280; Scharf, *St. Louis,* II, p. 1210.

the summer of 1815, Jules found himself in what he termed, a year later, the "distressing situation" of not being able to provide all the "gifts of fortune" for his wife and their baby daughter.[5] Nothing less than stringent necessity could have sent him off to the Rocky Mountains as a trapper and as partner of two of his wife's Chouteau relatives – "in the role of parasite," as Jules described himself in his journal.[6]

The fur-trading adventure of DeMun and Auguste P. Chouteau was inspired by a similar one of Joseph Philibert. Philibert had left St. Louis for the mountains on April 3, 1813, with eighteen St. Louis Frenchmen and a license to trade with the Arapaho Indians at the head of the Arkansas, Platte and Otter [North Canadian] rivers. At Boonslick in central Missouri, Philibert was joined by Ezekiel Williams and two companions, who traveled with them up the Missouri and Osage, crossing over to the Arkansas and following that river to an Arapaho village at the foot of the mountains. There Williams raised a cache of furs he had made in previous years, and started back down the Arkansas. By September, Philibert and his men had crossed the mountains into the San Luis Valley and established a hunting camp about four leagues north of Zebulon Pike's old stockade on the Conejos. On September 15, two men whom Philibert had sent to look for beaver dams were captured by forty Spaniards catching wild horses, and were taken to Santa Fe to be questioned by the commandant. Subsequently, 250 Spanish soldiers were sent to Philibert's camp to arrest him and his men, raise their caches of goods on the Arkansas and conduct them to Santa Fe. After fifty days' detention, the traders were released, but their goods were confiscated to pay the expense of their captivity. They were allowed to

---

[5] Letter of Jules DeMun to Isabelle DeMun, Riviere des Kans, July 21, 24, 25, Aug. 13, 1816, translated by Mrs. Max W. Myer, in Janet Lecompte, "Jules and Isabelle DeMun," *Bulletin,* Missouri Historical Society, xxvi, no. 2 (Oct. 1969), 30.

[6] "Journals of Jules DeMun," ed. Thomas Maitland Marshall, *Collections,* Missouri Historical Society, v, no. 3 (June 1928), 316.

remain in Taos until February 1815, when they crossed the mountains to the Arkansas Valley. On the Huerfano River, Philibert left nine of his men camped to await his return in the fall. With the others he went to St. Louis to buy goods, to enable him to barter horses from the Indians with which to bring in his furs.[7]

In July, the *Missouri Gazette* announced that Philibert had arrived at St. Louis with his "broken fortune," his year's work having been a "ruinous business." [8] But his estimate of the potential profits to be made in the mountains, expressed to Auguste P. Chouteau, Jr. and Jules DeMun, must have been encouraging. Before the summer was out, Chouteau and DeMun had succeeded in getting financial backing from merchants Pierre Chouteau and Bartholomew Berthold. Then they obtained a license "to trade on Platte & Arkansas Rivers," bought a considerable outfit, and hired a large number of engagés.[9]

On September 10, 1815, Chouteau, DeMun, Philibert and the men (some of them "traveling independently") left St. Louis, forty-six strong.[10] Day by day DeMun's diary describes their journey with controlled distaste – stifling heat, violent rainstorms, delays caused by lost horses, reports of hostile Sacs, rocky terrain and mistaken trails, batteries of

---

[7] *Missouri Gazette*, July 29, 1815, from Dale L. Morgan's collection of newspaper transcripts entitled, "The Mormons and the Far West," copy in the Beinecke Library, Yale University; letter of Ezekiel Williams, Boonslick, Aug. 7, 1816, in the *Missouri Gazette*, Sept. 14, 1816; Letter of Julius DeMun to Governor William Clark, St. Louis, Nov. 25, 1817, *American State Papers*, Foreign Relations IV, pp. 211-13 (DeMun signed himself "Julius" when he wrote in English).

[8] *Missouri Gazette*, July 29, 1815, *cited*.

[9] George S. Ulibarri, "The Chouteau-DeMun Expedition to New Mexico, 1815-1817," *New Mexico Historical Review*, XXXVI, no. 4 (Oct. 1961), 267; Carter, *Territorial Papers*, XV, p. 85; Edwin James, *Account of an Expedition from Pittsburgh to the Rocky Mountains performed in the years 1819, 1820* [1823], reprinted by R. G. Thwaites, *Early Western Travels* (Cleveland, 1905), XVI, pp. 226-27.

[10] "Statement and Proof in case of Chouteau and Demun, of their loss and treatment by the Spaniards," St. Louis, Sept. 25, 1817, *American State Papers*, Foreign Relations, IV, pp. 209-10.

mosquitoes and a diet of no bread. Around the first of October they arrived to spend a week at the Great Osage village, most of whose occupants were off hunting, having left their rush-covered lodges to filthy, verminous old squaws. Here DeMun's journal betrays the misery of its author:

> Never did time seem so long as the time I am spending here. Just imagine a person who has never been among Indians, stuck in a lodge where one must lie down in order not to be smothered by the smoke, among old carcasses whose skin is scaly from dirt and who crunch vermin with relish; having nothing to eat but corn which is often barely cooked, and not being able to set foot outside without stepping in filth, and one may judge if the situation is pleasant.[11]

Leaving the Osage village, they passed the Neosho and Verdigris rivers and crossed over into the open valley of the Arkansas, where cold and snow increased. Their horses became so weak that they dismounted and continued on foot. On November 27 they caught sight of the mountains, "like clouds on the horizon." That same day they found two beaver traps hanging from a tree, belonging to a man named Greenwood and his companion, who joined their party. They arrived at the foot of the mountains on December 8, but under what circumstances DeMun does not say, for his journal stopped abruptly the week before.[12]

Between St. Louis and the mountains, Chouteau and DeMun bought out Philibert's furs, goods, horses, and the time of his men, half of whom they had expected to find at the Huerfano camp where Philibert had left them in February. But no men awaited them on the Huerfano, for when Philibert had failed to show up by summer's end, his men had again gone over the mountains to Taos.[13] Their arrival was duly noted by Governor Alberto Maynez who wrote the

---

11 "Journals of Jules DeMun," *Collections,* Missouri Historical Society, v, no. 2 (Feb. 1928), 194-95.

12 *Ibid.,* 194-208; letter of DeMun to Gov. Clark, Nov. 25, 1817, *cited.*

13 Letter of DeMun to Gov. Clark, Nov. 25, 1817, *cited.*

Commandant at Durango for instructions.[14] In the meantime, the Frenchmen were allowed to spend their second winter in New Mexico, at the friendly village of Taos. They were treated so warmly that many of them returned in later years to make their homes there.[15]

At the beginning of January 1816, DeMun, who spoke Spanish, set out for New Mexico to fetch Philibert's men and ask permission of Governor Maynez to trap on the waters of the Rio Grande del Norte. The governor was a polite old gentleman – a man of his word, like DeMun himself – who promised to write the commandant on the subject, and gave DeMun permission to trap or trade on the east side of the mountains north of the Red River of Natchitoches (Canadian).[16]

[14] Alberto Maynez, Jan. 18, 1816, "tells of nine Frenchmen who have arrived at Taos, and that he has prevented them from marching through his country." Index of Correspondence to Commandante General at Chihuahua, Spanish Archives of New Mexico #2639, with gratitude to David Weber for his knowledge of these archives and his generosity in sharing it.

[15] See sketches in this series of Jean-Baptiste Chalifoux (vol. VII), Abraham and Antoine Ledoux (vol. III), Pierre Lesperance (vol. VI) and Joseph Livernois (vol. V), all of whom were said to have come to Taos before Mexican Independence in 1821 under circumstances that resemble the Chouteau-DeMun or Philibert expeditions. Of the eleven Chouteau-DeMun men who signed a statement on September 25, 1817, describing their captivity in New Mexico, three that I know of – Provott [Provost], Derport [Desport] and Bissonet [Bissonette] – returned to Taos in the 1820s. Signers of the statement (all with their marks) were: Jean Batiste Brizar, Baptisti Ficio, Charles Bourguinon, Joseph Cisdelle, Etenne Provott, Francois Mauant, Pierre LeGris, Francois Paket, Antoine Bizet and Joseph Bissonet. "Statement and proof in case of Chouteau and DeMun," cited. Toussaint Charboneau and Michel Carriere gave separate depositions in December 1817.

[16] Letter of DeMun to Gov. Clark, Nov. 25, 1817, cited. Maynez wrote his superior on Jan. 18, 1816, "that the Frenchman Don Julio de Mun who has just arrived at Taos, seeks a license to hunt otter [beaver] on the rivers which run into the Province of New Mexico." ("Index of Correspondence. . ." cited.) Maynez was overgenerous to DeMun. The southern and western boundaries of the Louisiana Purchase had not yet been settled and most Spanish officials would not have accepted the Red River of Natchitoches as the northern limit of their country, at least this far west (it was generally accepted as a boundary farther east). Its sources were thought to be in the Sangre de Cristo Mountains east of Taos, the Canadian River being its principal headwaters. Actually, Red River headwaters were in Oklahoma and Texas, a fact not officially determined for another thirty-five years. In 1819 the Arkansas River was accepted by both countries as the northern limit of New Mexico.

DeMun returned to the Huerfano camp where it was decided that they had too few goods and trapping outfits. Accordingly, DeMun, Philibert and the Delaware Indian guide, Cohun, left the Huerfano for St. Louis on February 27, 1816, to buy more goods and equipment. The arrangement was that Chouteau would hunt and trade until June 15, when he and his party would descend to the mouth of the Kansas to meet DeMun and a barge for transporting the furs to St. Louis.[17] Chouteau and his forty-five men apparently went north and camped with a large number of Kiowas, Arapahos and Kaskaias or Bad Hearts (Kiowa-Apache) who had assembled on Grand Camp Creek (Bear Creek, near present Denver) to trade horses for British goods with a band of Cheyennes.[18]

DeMun reached St. Louis on May 13. There he bought goods and equipment and took out a license on June 13 in partnership with "Peter Chouteau Jr." (Auguste's brother Pierre, married to Isabelle DeMun's sister Emilie) to trade with the "Arapahos, Haytons [Ietans or Comanches] etc."[19] After a precious month with his lovely wife and their two little daughters, DeMun left St. Louis on June 15 with a barge to meet Auguste Chouteau at the mouth of the Kansas. But Chouteau did not arrive at the rendezvous until August

17 "Journals of Jules DeMun," *Collections,* Missouri Historical Society, v, no. 3 (June 1928), 323; letter of DeMun to Gov. Clark, *cited.*

18 James, *Account of an Expedition, loc. cit.,* XVI, pp. 284-85. The identification of "Grand Camp Creek" with Bear Creek is made by Harlin M. Fuller and LeRoy R. Hafen in their edition of *The Journal of Captain John R. Bell* (Glendale, 1957), 148. The Chouteau-DeMun trappers may have entered North Park, headwaters of the North Platte River, as Carl I. Wheat in *Mapping the Transmississippi West* (San Francisco, 1958), II, p. 79n, and Dale L. Morgan in *The West of William H. Ashley* (Denver, 1964), pp. xliv, 263, state unequivocally that they did. Without seeing it themselves, Dr. James describes North Park and Major Long marks it on his map as "Bull Pen." Wheat and Morgan assume that the information about North Park came from Long's guide, Joseph Bissonette *dit* Bijeau [Bijou], as it well may have (it could also have come from their hunter, Abram Ledoux). But Bijeau had "repeatedly" (as James says twice) visited North Park, and not necessarily as a member of the Chouteau-DeMun party.

19 Carter, *Territorial Papers,* XV, p. 190.

10, for on his way back he had been attacked by two hundred Pawnees and had taken refuge on an island in the Arkansas (henceforth called "Chouteau's Island"), losing one man killed and three wounded. At the Kansas River they sent the furs back to St. Louis in the barge and, now numbering forty-five, started again for the mountains.[20]

At the head of the Arkansas they learned from a party of Spanish traders that Utes and Apaches, who had already killed two of Philibert's men, were hovering about. They decided to go no farther into the mountains, but again to ask the governor of New Mexico about trapping on the waters of the Rio Grande. DeMun and two others accompanied the Spanish traders south, while Chouteau and his men waited in the Sangre de Cristo Pass at the headwaters of the Huerfano River.[21]

At the new frontier village of Rio Colorado, DeMun was stopped and forbidden to go to Santa Fe. After DeMun dispatched a letter to the governor, he was led back up the San Luis Valley to await an answer to his letter. The answer came in twenty days and its meaning, if politely phrased, was unmistakable – get out of Spanish dominions and stay out! DeMun crossed the mountains again and, to show that he had nothing to hide, wrote the alcalde of Taos that his party would winter on the eastern slope. They made camp, apparently on the Huerfano again.[22]

In the middle of March, Chouteau and DeMun had intended to go to the headwaters of the Columbia in search of the Crow Indians, but Spanish traders (who brought bread, horses, flour, etc. to their camp every week or so) gave them hope of permission to trap west of the mountains in Spanish territory, for the governor had indeed written the com-

[20] Letter of DeMun to Gov. Clark, *cited;* "Journals of Jules DeMun," *Collections,* Missouri Historical Society, v, no. 3, pp. 318-26; "Statement and proof in case of Chouteau and Demun. . .", *American State Papers,* Foreign Relations IV, pp. 209-10.
[21] Letter of DeMun to Gov. Clark, *cited.* [22] *Ibid.*

mandant at Durango regarding their request. In March, DeMun went to Taos to look into the matter. There he was apprehended by two hundred soldiers who led him back to his camp to investigate a report that he and Chouteau had built a fort housing twenty thousand American troops on the Purgatory. When the Spanish soldiers found no such fort, they raised all the traders' caches of furs and goods and ordered Chouteau and DeMun to return to St. Louis. But the traders, fearful of Pawnees and of losing the profits of their spring trade, persuaded the soldiers to let them leave to the north instead of the east.[23]

The traders left, but they came back. After a fruitless attempt to cross the mountains at the sources of the Arkansas, they returned to the Greenhorn on the south side of the Arkansas, where they re-grouped. Seventeen men were immediately sent to the Platte with instructions to meet Chouteau later. Chouteau and the rest were to stay in the mountains another year. DeMun would return to St. Louis with the furs. It rained the day DeMun was to leave, so he made the unfortunate decision to lay over a day.[24]

The next day – May 24, 1817 – Spanish soldiers captured the camp and its furs and took the men to Santa Fe. There Chouteau and DeMun faced not the kindly Maynez but his ill-tempered successor, Don Pedro Maria de Allande. When they insisted that they had been captured on American soil and had a license to trap there, Governor Allande flew into a rage, exclaiming that their government had no right to issue such a license, for the boundary between the two countries was the Mississippi River! – an assertion DeMun found so heinous that he stubbornly declined to argue his own position. He and Chouteau were thrown into prison, in chains.[25]

After forty-four days' imprisonment, they were tried, sentenced to be stripped of their property and forced to

---

[23] *Ibid.*   [24] *Ibid.*   [25] *Ibid.*

kneel and kiss the document depriving them of the fruits of
their two-years' labor. With one poor horse apiece, they
were then allowed to leave New Mexico, arriving at St.
Louis on September 7, 1817. Their actual loss, according to
DeMun, was $30,380.74½. The claim and accrued interest
amounting to $81,772 was allowed in 1851 – but both Chou-
teau and DeMun were dead.[26]

We Americans have always reacted with high indigna-
tion to the fate of Chouteau and DeMun, an emotion not
entirely warranted. Their trappers on the Arkansas were
operating in a kind of no-man's land, for the boundaries of
the Louisiana Purchase were still undetermined. At this
time, Governor Allande's claim to the boundary at the Mississippi River was no more absurd than the American claim
to that at the Rio Grande del Norte, and Governor Clark's
right to issue Chouteau and DeMun a license to trap on the
headwaters of the Arkansas was at least questionable, just as
the irate Governor Allande indicated.[27] There was no justifi-
cation for Chouteau and DeMun to be camped on the
Greenhorn where they were finally captured; surely they
realized by now this was in effect Spanish Territory! Had
Chouteau and DeMun (and Philibert before them) quietly
gone about their trapping and trading, staying east of the
Rio Grande and north of the Arkansas in country claimed –
but not aggressively defended – by Spain, their expeditions
might have paid them well. But the proud DeMun, refusing
to stoop to subterfuge, insisted on obtaining Spanish permission to trap further afield. DeMun was importunate; re-

[26] Letter of DeMun to Gov. Clark, *cited; Missouri Gazette,* Sept. 13, 1817, in
Dale L. Morgan's newspaper transcripts, "The Mormons and the Far West";
Carter, *Territorial Papers,* xv, pp. 339, 343, 380. For disposition of the claim see
Ulibarri, "The Chouteau-DeMun Expedition. . .", *cited,* and "Claims on Mexico,"
27 Cong., 2 Sess., *H. Rept. 1096* (Ser. 411), p. 17.

[27] Eleanor L. Richie wrote two fine articles on this subject: "Background of the
International Boundary Line of 1819 along the Arkansas River in Colorado," *Colo-
rado Magazine,* x, no. 4 (July 1933), 145-56, and "The Disputed International
Boundary in Colorado, 1803-1819," *ibid.,* xiii, no. 5 (Sept. 1936), 171-80.

peatedly the Spaniards demanded that he get out of their country, and doggedly he kept turning up again, asking favors, until Spanish patience was exhausted.

Neither Chouteau nor DeMun ever made another trading trip to the Rocky Mountains. After his return, DeMun received letters from the King of France inviting him to settle in France and bestowing on him the Order of the Fleur de Lys as a distinguished Royalist refugee. But the honor, which he refused, did little to shore up his sagging fortunes. After a summer as the manager of John Mullanphy's store in St. Louis, DeMun and his family left for Cuba in the fall of 1819 and bought a coffee plantation which he cultivated for ten years, returning to St. Louis in January 1831. For a short time he had a trading post in southern Wisconsin. Then he was appointed secretary and translator to the U.S. Board of Commissioners adjusting titles of French and Spanish land grants in Missouri. Later he became registrar of the United States Land Office at St. Louis. In 1842 he was elected St. Louis County Recorder of Deeds, in which office he died on August 15, 1843, aged 61. He was survived by his wife Isabelle (who died 1878) and five daughters, Isabelle (Mrs. Edward Walsh), Julie (Mrs. Leon Antoine Chenie), Louise Victoire (Mrs. Robert A. Barnes), Emilie Laure (Mrs. Charles Bland Smith), and Aimee Claire (died unmarried).[28]

---

[28] Billon, *Annals,* 18; Nettie H. Beauregard, "DeMun Family in America," *cited,* 330-31; Scharf, *History of St. Louis,* II, p. 1211.

Pack Train to Santa Fe, from a drawing by Frederic Remington. From Henry Inman, *The Old Santa Fe Trail* (New York: Macmillan, 1897). Courtesy of Western History Collections, University of Oklahoma.

Arrival of the Caravan at Santa Fe. From Josiah Gregg, *Commerce of the Prairies* (New York: H.G. Langley, 1844). Courtesy of Western History Collections, University of Oklahoma.

James Kirker*

by WILLIAM COCHRAN MCGAW
Editor "The Southwesterner," El Paso

There was a general exodus of Scots from their native heath in 1681 as a result of the Test Act passed that year, making it mandatory for Presbyterians to give up their religion, swear allegiance to Charles II, and join the Church of England.

Among the thousands to flee Scotland for Ireland that year were three tall, red-haired Presbyterian brothers named Kirker. They settled in Ulster and became known as Kirker of Falls, Kirker of Armagh and Kirker of Antrim. James Kirker, destined to become perhaps the greatest Indian fighter on the American continent (if not the most famous), descended from the latter and was born on December 2, 1793, in Killead Parish – about 10 miles northwest of Belfast – the second son of Rose and Gilbert Kirker of Carnaghlis. His older brother was named Gilbert and he had two sisters, Rose and Martha.

Kirkers were traditionally either grocers or tanners and were well-to-do. Jim's father was a prosperous grocer and his Uncle James, after whom he was named, moved to Belfast as a young man and made a small fortune for that day as a tanner, operating his business for a half century on North Street.

Just a week or two before James Kirker was born, Napoleon Bonaparte had his baptism of fire before Lyons, and his subsequent rampages across Europe and North Africa

---

* This biographical sketch of James Kirker is condensed from a work in process of publication, entitled *Santiago! The Life and Times of James Kirker, King of the Scalphunters,* to which the reader is referred for citations and annotations.

sent such a tremor of fear through Great Britain that old Johnny Bull began dipping into his three traditional bins of cannon fodder – Scotland, Ireland and the public jails – to build up the army and navy to meet the Bonaparte threat. Jim's older brother, Gilbert, was conscripted, and the Kirkers decided it was time to ship their youngest boy out of danger. He was given a fat purse and put aboard a vessel bound for the United States, landing in New York City on June 10, 1810, when he was 16 years old.

On June 19, 1812, the United States Congress declared war on Great Britain and because the American navy was almost non-existent, the early fighting against England at sea was done mostly by privateers and ships sailing with *letters of marque*. Within a few days after the declaration of war, 23 privateers sailed out of New York harbor and Jim Kirker was a member of the crew on one of them, "The Black Joke," a converted Albany packet under the command of its owner Berndt J. Brunow. There were 70 in the crew and she carried seven guns, one a Long Tom, or swivel gun, midships, and two were carronades of short range for infighting.

"The Black Joke," a name taken from a bawdy popular song, had a relatively successful career as a privateer until she was captured off the coast of Brazil by the British ship "Lion." Jim was among the prisoners being taken to San Salvador on a captured American vessel, "William," in tow of the British ship, "Java," when the U.S. frigate "Constitution" hove in sight, with the small brig, "Hornet," sailing with her. Commodore William Bainbridge engaged the "Java" and after two-and-one-half hours of fighting, the "Java" was no more and the "Constitution" had earned her first great sea victory and a new sobriquet, "Old Ironsides." The "Hornet," meanwhile, captured the "William," and the latter vessel was sent back to New York in charge of Captain Davis, returning Kirker and the other prisoners. In New

York Jim's mustering out pay came to more than $1500, including his share of the many prizes taken, and with this money he entered the grocery business and matrimony, marrying a woman named "Catharine," according to Longworth's New York Directory.

They had at least one child, a son named James B. Kirker, who was to become a bookseller in New York City at 151 Fulton St., enlist in the Union Army in 1863, and to be discharged a major in the quartermaster corps. He died in 1877.

The Kirker grocery was at 41 Ferry St., a three-block-long street running near today's Brooklyn Bridge. In three short blocks there were eleven tanning and leather shops and five groceries.

Early in 1817, five relatives arrived from Belfast, Robert and David Kirker, Jim's cousins, and their sister, Jane, who was accompanied by her husband, Joseph C. Clegg, and their three-year-old son, Joseph, Jr. They visited with Jim until early spring when they planned to set out for St. Louis. Their enthusiasm for the American frontier was so infectious, Jim left with them on their journey to Pittsburgh and down the Ohio, leaving Catharine to mind the store while he was gone.

Jim's second cousin, Thomas of Tyrone, had come to America many years earlier and became the second governor of Ohio in 1807, but there is no evidence the Kirker party visited their relative on the way to St. Louis. It is probable they arrived in St. Louis on the first steamboat to dock at that Mississippi River metropolis, "The Zebulon Pike," on July 27, 1817.

The Kirker boys almost immediately threw in with the McKnight and Brady combine, a group formed by two families of brothers who controlled much of the real estate, merchandising, and nearly all of the keel-boat business of that day in St. Louis. James opened up a grocery on Cherry

Street, "under the bluffs," with David Kirker a very junior partner, or perhaps even an employee, while Robert Kirker was employed by Thomas McKnight as a sort of general manager of his riverside warehouse. Robert later accompanied Thomas to Galena, Illinois, where they were engaged in lead mining, and then to Davenport, Iowa, where Thomas died in the 1860s, shortly after the Civil War. The Cleggs lived in St. Louis initially, but later moved to Peoria, Illinois, where the Cleggs and Walkers opened a distillery known today as the Hiram Walker Distillery, and one of the present officials is Clegg Walker.

Jim's grocery apparently prospered, for despite a jarring depression that descended in 1819, Jim leased a piece of riverfront property from John McKnight and built a combination stone residence and grocery in 1821. Just about that time Cousin David left with John McKnight and Thomas James for Santa Fe, where they hoped to obtain the release of the youngest McKnight brother, Robert, who had led a party to New Mexico in 1811. Robert's $25,000 worth of trade goods was confiscated and the men were imprisoned. After nine years, James Baird, Peter Baum, Sam Chambers and some of the others were released and arrived back in St. Louis late in 1820, but for some reason Robert remained behind.

Enroute to Santa Fe, though, David Kirker disgraced himself and the Kirker name by abjectly surrendering himself and his arms to a threatening war-party of Comanches. After the McKnight and James party was saved by some Mexican soldiers, David was sent back to Missouri in disgrace, leaving with the returning Becknell caravan from Las Vegas, New Mexico, in the late fall. He was accompanied by one other member of the James-McKnight outfit, probably William Shearer, who became ill about this time and died a short while later.

When David arrived back in St. Louis early in February,

1822, it doesn't take much imagination to envision his reception, nor is it difficult to devise Jim Kirker's reaction. To say he was embarrassed at his cousin's cowardice would probably be putting it mildly. At any rate, Jim signed up with General William Ashley's first expedition for the Upper Missouri, and spent the winter on the Yellowstone with Major Andrew Henry, Ashley's early partner. Late the next spring, 1823, Jim accompanied Henry's men when they dropped down to join Colonel Leavenworth's forces to attack the Arickaree villages as a punitive action for the Ree's earlier belligerence against Ashley. Following the Arickaree assault, Jim Kirker quit the Ashley outfit in utter disgust with the inept leadership of Ashley, plus what he considered the latter's avaricious exploitation of uneducated young adventurers and rum-dumb older trappers. Kirker was no teenage adventurer, nor a rum-sodden failure fleeing the responsibilities of civilization, so he could see no percentage risking his life to gather fur pelts for Ashley on the general's terms. Jim was thirty years old with years of business experience, was well educated, and he had become well acquainted with thieves and adventurers at the tender age of sixteen while privateering. He was not at all interested in giving up to Ashley half of all the pelts he trapped, and receive in return the privilege of boating Ashley's trade goods up river, plus enough powder and lead to provide his own food and fight off Indians to protect Ashley's enterprise. Ashley wanted enough profit to further his political ambitions, save himself from bankruptcy, and a big enough fortune to enable him to marry a beautiful and socially significant young lady. The arrangement was a "sucker's game" to a man of Kirker's intelligence and experience and, after informing Ashley of his opinion, Kirker returned to Missouri with Leavenworth's forces.

But Kirker had already caught "mountain fever," and by 1824, he was itching to go again, though under much different auspices and absolutely free from Ashley's tricky gimmicks. Kirker had long been acquainted with another St. Louis grocer named Bernard Pratte and the latter's son, Silvestre, who was getting up a New Mexico expedition. This expedition eventually was to include another Sylvester, one with Pattie for a last name and a son named James Ohio, who was to write a narrative of his experiences in the wilderness. There is no hardrock evidence naming Kirker as a member of this party, but it IS known he was in Santa Fe in 1824, for he is listed in a head-count of that year. Years later Kirker's son-in-law, Sam Bean, was to write that Jim was accompanied to New Mexico by Robert McKnight, Stephen Courcier, Henry Corlew, Hugo Stephenson, Lewis Dutton, Joshua Sledd and Rufus Doane, but chronological evidence makes lumping these men in one party impossible. It is possible for Stephenson and Kirker, as well as McKnight and Courcier, to have arrived in 1824, as that is the accepted date for all of them, but Sledd, Doane, Dutton, and Corlew all arrived later. Dutton is named as a companion of Hugh Glass after the latter's grizzly bear epic, and Dutton's daughter, Simona, married Stephenson's son, Horace.

Jim Kirker made more than one trip back and forth between St. Louis and Santa Fe in the 1820s though, and it is possible these men came with him at different times. Bean knew all of these men better than he did his own father-in-law, for he lived among some of them for many years in the El Paso area. It stands to reason each of these men told him at some time or another of his coming to New Mexico with Kirker. After Jim's first trip to Santa Fe and New Mexico in 1824, he was back in St. Louis at least by February 26, 1825. On this date he is listed as a surety on a bond posted for Hamilton Carruthers in St. Louis Probate Court for the latter to act as administrator of the estate of William

Shearer, a member of the John McKnight and Thomas James expedition. James Lansdell was the other surety with Kirker.

Jim must have made an 1825 trip to Santa Fe, for in July of that year he applied for Mexican citizenship, according to information found in the papers of Donaciano Vigil by Father Stanley, the latter's biographer. Then in 1826, Kirker is credited with taking Kit Carson on his first trip to the mountains, with Kirker in charge of a train probably owned by the Turley brothers. Information on this appears in the St. Louis *Saturday Evening Post and Temperance Recorder* for July 17, 1847, in a paragraph preceding a biography of Carson, probably written by Charles Keemle, a former trapper who knew both Kirker and Carson intimately. Carson was also employed at the Santa Rita mines by McKnight and Courcier, a job Kirker probably arranged for the youngster.

Kirker came to the Santa Rita mines originally with the elder and younger Pattie, directed to do so by Silvestre Pratte. The elder Pratte operated the mines from 1824 until 1827 on a lease from the owner, a Spaniard named Francisco Lagera. The lease was terminated in 1827 when Spaniards were excluded from Mexico and their property confiscated.

Kirker joined the Patties on a trapping party with George C. Yount in 1827, but accompanied Yount back to Taos while the Patties, Nathaniel Pryor, Jess Ferguson and some others elected to go on to California. Shortly after that Kirker interested McKnight and Stephen Courcier, a Frenchman from Philadelphia, to take over the operation of the Santa Rita mines and was employed by them to guard the burro trains of ore from the mines to the mint at Chihuahua City. The mint was run by an Englishman named John Potts. It was during this period Kit Carson worked at freighting ore.

Kirker freighted for McKnight and Courcier in the summer and trapped the Gila in the winter for a number of years and in 1833 employed a young Tennessean named Benjamin David Wilson as a trapper. Wilson was later forced to leave New Mexico because of his suspected participation in the "Texian Invasion" of 1841. He went to California, intending to go on to China, but purchased the Jurupa land grant ranch and married into the family owning the Santa Ana grant, both of which comprised an area occupied today by Riverside, California. When his Mexican wife died, Wilson married the widow of Dr. Thomas Hereford and they had two daughters, Anne and Ruth. The latter was the mother of General George S. Patton, Jr., old "Blood and Guts" of World War II.

The friendship begun in 1833 between Kirker and Patton's grandfather, B. D. Wilson, lasted until Kirker's death nearly 20 years later. It was also in 1833 that Kirker's first child was born to Rita Garcia, described by Wilson as "handsome and a fine woman." Apparently Kirker had entered into a bigamous marriage with Rita, but this legal technicality was perhaps straightened out in 1831, when Catharine Kirker describes herself as "widow" in the *Longworth Directory* for that year back in New York. However, there is no evidence that her "Enoch Arden" husband was ever declared legally dead in New York courts.

In 1835 Governor Albino Perez of New Mexico granted Jim a license to trade among the Apaches and Jim took off with eighteen men to live among this tribe over the winter of 1835-36. Kirker became so intimate with the Apaches that they made him a war chief, and Mexican authorities suspected him of not only fencing stolen horses and mules for the Apaches across Texas and into Louisiana, but also of actually leading many of the Apache raiding parties. Governor Perez rescinded Kirker's Apache trading license and placed a price of $800 on his head, dead or alive, declaring Jim an outlaw. Kirker repaired to Bent's Fort on the Arkansas River in southern Colorado and laid low for a number of weeks, or until Governor Perez, himself, fell victim to a mob on August 9, 1837. He was beheaded in a revolt which many Mexicans believed to have been inspired, at least in part, by Kirker. It may be indicative of something that Manuel Armijo, an ambitious politician who aspired to succeed Perez and is charged also with having a hand in the plot, was successful in becoming governor and one of his first acts was personally and publicly to invite Kirker back to New Mexico. But their honeymoon friendship was destined to become short-lived, due to a complex set of circumstances.

On April 22, 1837, a Kentuckian named James Johnson killed Apache Chief Juan Campo (a friend of Americans to that time) and many of his tribe, in an ambush near a dry lake in the vicinity of today's Cloverdale, New Mexico. This caused the Apaches to seek vengeance on Americans everywhere, which resulted in the closing of the Santa Rita mines, operated by Kirker's friends, McKnight and Courcier. The latter had meanwhile become one of the leading citizens of Chihuahua City, while McKnight had established himself at the Corralitos Hacienda, which still exists near the ancient town of Janos, just east of the Chihuahua-Sonora border.

Courcier and McKnight sent a call to Kirker at Taos to come down, get the Apaches off their backs, and help them re-open the mines. Kirker gathered together a group of twenty-three men, mostly experienced Shawnee and Delaware Indian battlers, plus a sprinkling of Mountain Men drawn from various nationalities, and lit out for the Santa Rita Apache country. In retribution for Apache raids on the mining community, Kirker and his handful of ruffians struck at an Apache village headed by Mangas Coloradas, and succeeded in killing 55 warriors out of a total of 247, taking nine female prisoners and capturing 400 head of stock. They totally destroyed the village located on a large bluff near a mountain called today Cooke's Peak. Kirker lost one man and had eight injured in the fray, while the remaining fourteen drove the stock and carried their wounded into Soccoro, N.M. The result was that burro trains were moving once more with ore from Santa Rita to Chihuahua City and Kirker's fame as an Indian fighter became the topic of the day. And this was not just among cowed Apaches, but also among prominent Chihuahuaense, including Jose Maria de Irigoyen, who had been elected governor of Chihuahua on a platform to do something about the troublesome Apaches and had taken office the previous January 1. The governor had subsequently led several feeble campaigns against the Apaches personally, but when he heard of Kirker's exploits, he sent for him.

Irigoyan had meanwhile set up a group known as *Sociedad De Guerra Contra los Barbaros,* which was to collect a fund by taxation and voluntary contributions to the amount of 100,000 pesos, the equivalent of dollars then, to conduct the campaigns. Kirker's old friend, Estevan Curcier (or Stephen Courcier) was named president of the society, assisted by Vincente de Palacios and Juan Vivar y Balderrama. The Society for War against Barbarians (another name in Chihuahua for Apaches) called on Kirker both for advice in their future deliberations and to ask him to lead personally the campaign against the Apaches, who had frustrated the Mexicans for years by leading raids against missions, mining communities, farms and ranches. Many Mexican mining operations and hacienda ranches had become ghost towns.

Kirker's plan, set up in cooperation with the society, was to visit every key community and establish local militia units for their own defense, then to build up his force of Shawnees, Delawares, French, Scotch, Irish, Hawaiian, English and American Mountain Men to a force of about 200 for an attack on the concentrated establishments of Apaches.

After setting up several militia units in Chihuahua and New Mexico, Kirker headed back to Taos, where he hoped to recruit another 150 or so experienced Indian fighters. By late August, he had increased his force to about fifty men, according to an account written by Matt Field, an actor turning writer who had come to New Mexico and who wrote a series of articles on his adventures for the New Orleans *Picayune*.

Field was in Taos when Kirker made his first campaign under the new *Society de Guerra* plan, and describes the results in some detail in articles which eventually appeared in the *Picayune* for February 28 and March 2, 1840, some months after the attack occurred on September 5, 1839. It came about by Kirker's having purposely left some horses unguarded near the mission town of Rancho de Taos, not to be confused with San Fernando de Taos proper, some four miles to the north. The Apaches took the bait and no sooner had they stolen the horses than Kirker and his men were in pursuit. Kirker knew the Apaches better than they knew themselves and correctly surmised that they would try to escape with the horses through a defile in the mountains. Instead of chasing them into the pass, Kirker led his horsemen rapidly around the mountain by a path he knew and reached the other end of the ravine long before the Apaches arrived. There he stationed his men on the heights, setting up an ambush. The Apaches numbered about 120, according to Field, and at least twenty of that number fell at the first fire of Kirker's riflemen, while many others, clenching their teeth with pain from wounds, tried to stick on their horses as they clutched the reins and turned back the way they had come, hoping to reach the sanctuary of the mission church before Kirker's men caught them.

Kirker's Indian hunters chased the terrorized Apaches all the way back down the ravine, picking off a man here, another there, until finally the Apaches ran screaming into the walled square around the church, hoping to gain safety under the sacred roof. The Kirker men cooly loaded their rifles and began picking them off like targets on a range, then rushed them, taking many scalps. Of this affair Matt Field wrote:

> In this battle forty Indians were killed and of Kurker's [sic] party but one American and one half-breed. The stolen horses were recovered, and all the other animals in the possession of the Indians were taken as booty. Kurker himself is as brave as a lion, and a man of great enterprize, as well as skill in this kind of war fare. Having just commenced operations his force is small, but men were thronging to join him every day, and he will soon be at the head of a powerful army.

In the pay of the State of Chihuahua and with a private army, Kirker showed considerable disdain for his old friend Armijo, governor of New Mexico. In July of 1839 Kirker was one of the leading petitioners to Armijo, demanding that he bring to trial immediately two Mexicans who, early in 1838, had murdered an American trader named Andrew W. Daley, a friend of Kirker's. Even though the two confessed their guilt, they were allowed to go free. When the memorial demanding justice was presented to Armijo, the latter chose to view it as a conspiracy against him and he tried to intimidate the signers. Kirker and William Driden were credited with being the leaders of Americans, according to the Mexican historian Bustamente, and the former reminded Armijo he retained even his office through the strength of Kirker's men and arms and implied a rather unveiled threat that these men could be used many ways. Armijo ceased the punitive action against the petitioners and sent them an apology for misconstruing their motives. Armijo also promised to bring the culprits to justice as soon as they were caught. Kirker and his men caught them at once and turned them over to Armijo, who swore they would receive the due execution of the law. Josiah Gregg, another trader, who wrote *Commerce of the Prairies,* perhaps the best book on that place and period, said the two murderers were freed two years later at about the time of the Texian invasion of New Mexico in 1841.

Kirker and his men ranged over New Mexico, Chihuahua, Sonora, west Texas, and parts of what is now Arizona, dispatching Apaches and setting up local militia to cope with future depredations.

Meanwhile, Governor Irigoyan was succeeded on September 18, 1839, by his cousin with almost the same name, Jose Maria Irigoyan de la O., and the latter approved Kirker's funds and plans for future Apache campaigns as one of his first acts. However, on May 20, 1840, he was succeeded by Pedro Olivares, who on July 6, was succeeded by Francisco Garcia Conde, a military man who thought it a disgrace to have a Mexican state employ an "outsider," even though a naturalized Mexican, to protect the people from Indians. It was embarrassing to the Mexican military and Conde was a proud part of that military, so he terminated the agreement.

Kirker then retired to his hacienda at Corralitos, dispersed much of his force and waited for the Apache retribution, which he knew was inevitable. It wasn't long in coming, for soon the angered Apaches were invading even the streets of Chihuahua and slaughtering the citizens within shouting distance of the governor's palace.

Governors of Chihuahua of that period held office mostly as a result of presidential favor, and were changed frequently. Kirker was in and out as the governors changed, and finally was called back to Chihuahua by Governor Angel Trias for another major effort against the Apaches. Trias suggested that Kirker and his men be paid by the scalp, instead of a flat fee, and agreed to give them $100 for the scalp of an Apache warrior, $50 for a squaw's and $25 for a papoose's.

Kirker again brought his men together. They probably

included such hardies as Peg-leg Tom Smith, Gabe Allen, Stephen Meek, James Hobbs, John Spencer, Spiebuck (a Shawnee chief) and other lesser known mountain rough-necks, including a large Negro referred to only as Andy. Kirker stationed the crew in the Plaza de Toros, or bull-fight arena, then located on the hills surrounding the city, and began outfitting them.

Within a few days they had their first job, when a 100-burro train belonging to a Chihuahua merchant named Porras was raided by Apaches, who took the whole cargo and left only one survivor, a half-breed who came into Chihuahua to tell the horrible news. Sr. Porras called upon Kirker and said he would give half of the cargo of trade goods, as well as the horses and mules, in addition to their deal with the governor, if he would track down the Apaches and punish them for this crime. Kirker called Spiebuck, his second in command, and asked him to go ahead with the half-breed to the site of the massacre and see what he could do about picking up the Apaches' trail. When Kirker arrived with the men, Spiebuck informed him the trail was fresh and easily followed.

Kirker had ascertained previously that included in the freight items were several gallons of liquor. When he reached the site and conferred with Spiebuck, they agreed that the Apaches would proceed cautiously for a few days, then when they were sure nobody was on their trail, they would sit down and drink the whiskey. Basing their strategy on this, Kirker and Spiebuck kept the men back for a couple of days, far enough away that the Indians would not know they were being followed; then after the third day, they took to the trail and traveled rapidly. They caught the Apaches, drunk as Kirker predicted, and slaughtered the whole party of some twenty warriors.

Kirker then met with his men, telling them that one of the major Apache villages was only two or three days' travel away, just in the foothills of the Sierra Madre Mountains, and if they wanted to pick up another large bundle of $100 Apache scalps, they could do so. It was agreed to continue. They cached the Porras train merchandise and went on. They arrived at the Indian settlement shortly after dark and took up positions in the hills surrounding the camp, which was on the edge of a lake.

Kirker saw a war party of Apaches come in with fresh scalps dangling from their belts and noticed also that they had captured another multi-gallon supply of whiskey. Kirker counseled the men each to pick out an Indian in the camp below for a rifle shot, load their six-shooters and stuff them in their belts, then prepare for action at about daylight when the Indians would be too drunk and fatigued from drinking and dancing to fight.

This turned out as planned, and the Kirker men slew nearly all of the tribe, a few escaping by way of the lake, including their chief, Cochise, who recognized Kirker and swore vengeance on him as a traitor to his Indian friends.

With eighteen women captives, the scalp hunters returned to Chihuahua with more than five hundred horses and mules, all of Porras' merchandise except a lot of sugar the Indians spilled and several gallons of liquor the Kirker hunters drank. Governor Trias refused to pay the scalp money, and many Mexicans were claiming the mules and horses as their property. This vexed Spiebuck so deeply, he stripped himself of his buckskins and walked naked except for his loin cloth and a feather in his hair. He drank a bottle of brandy, stuck a knife and tomahawk in his belt, and headed for the governor's mansion. Kirker followed to make sure he and his family would not become involved as a result of Spiebuck's intended violence.

The Shawnee broke through a guard at the governor's door, grabbed Trias by the throat and threatened to kill him if he were not paid immediately for his scalps. He was paid, and returning to the bull ring, he gathered up his share of mules and horses and announced he would not stay and do business with people who would not keep their word. He then headed for Bent's Fort with more than half of Kirker's men, mules and loot, shouting back over his shoulder that if Kirker was smart he would do the same. But Jim couldn't. By this time he had a large Mexican family, with sons named James, Rafael and Roberto, and the daughter, Petra, all living in Chihuahua and under the jurisdiction of Governor Trias. He was never paid, bringing to a total of more than $30,000 the amount owed him by the Mexican government.

He was soon to gain his revenge, though, when Colonel Alexander Doniphan brought his Missouri Volunteers to northern Mexico in 1846 and about 450 of them whipped three times this number at the Battle of Brazitos, about 15 miles north of El Paso on the Rio Grande. The night after the American victory, Kirker and several of his Shawnees joined the Doniphan forces – and Chihuahua was doomed.

Kirker outlined the strategy for the campaign, explaining how the Mexican gun emplacements were in redoubts on a bluff some eighteen miles north of Chihuahua City, at a place called Hacienda Sacramento. He explained that Doniphan should approach frontally, then turn off to his right, or east, as though he were going to skirt the bluff and attack a fort some three or four miles in that direction. Then when the Mexican defenders were thoroughly confused, he was to turn back again and advance up a gently inclining slope to the rear of the Mexican battlements.

To make sure there would be no obstacles between Doniphan and his objective, Kirker took a handful of men and captured the only two places between El Paso del Norte and Chihuahua City: Carrizal and Encenillas, the latter a hacienda owned by Governor Trias and the former a military presidio that General Pershing would be unable to take sixty years later with two full companies.

The battle plan was perfect and the only hitch was the human element, which Kirker unwittingly overcame. It all started the day before the battle when Kirker and an old Missourian named James Collins "liberated" a gallon of brandy from someplace and sat down to drink it. With most of the brandy gone they got into a drunken quarrel and Collins, recalling the abject behavior of Cousin David Kirker before the Comanches more than twenty years earlier, made the mistake of calling Jim Kirker, too, a coward. Guns were drawn and Kirker was ready to commit murder on his erstwhile friend when they were stopped by General Doniphan personally, who told them a battle was planned for the next day and they could prove which was a coward and which was brave by their actions on the field.

As they lined up for battle, Kirker still angry from the insult, rode up to Collins and shouted, "The last one into that second redoubt and to grab the Mexican guideon is a damned coward," and then road off. Collins took off at the same time and they rode straight for the Mexican line, followed by Major Sam Owens, a trader who had been elected to his military office. Kirker leaped his horse completely over the first redoubt, overran the second before Collins could make it, grabbed the red banner and then, having no place else to go, ran the whole length of the Mexican riflemen with his prize in his hand, followed by Collins, who likewise came through unscathed. Not so lucky Owens, who was killed before the first redoubt.

Meanwhile, the American army had been ordered to charge, and after a short fight they won the day.

Kirker, promised a colonel's pay by Doniphan, accompanied the troops to New Orleans, then back to St. Louis and was refused his pay at both places, despite the outstanding nature of his acts.

In St. Louis he was feted, written up in the newspapers, but not paid. He returned to Santa Fe and there was waiting for Ceran St. Vrain to come by so he could seek his help in recovering the Kirker family from Chihuahua. James couldn't return there because of a $9,000 price on his head for helping Doniphan's army.

Meanwhile, his daughter, Petra, had married Sam Bean, a discharged Doniphan soldier, and they operated a hotel Kirker had bought in Santa Fe. In May of 1848 the Utes were acting up. They chased two companies of U.S. soldiers out of the hills near Raton, New Mexico, and once more the citizens turned to such Mountain Men and Indian fighters as Kirker, Old Bill Williams and others to quiet the Indians. And quiet them they did, although Williams had his elbow shattered by a Ute rifle ball; but it healed in time for him to accompany John Fremont on his fourth expedition to the Rockies and get lost in a terrible snow, mostly because Fremont wouldn't listen to him. Kirker, meanwhile, made a quick trip to Ireland and back, probably to settle an estate of his brother or one of his sisters, and was in St. Louis again in January, 1849, ready to lead a company of gold seekers to California. This he did, as far as Santa Fe, despite an attack of cholera which he overcame simply by mounting his horse and riding in agony.

Once more he waited in Santa Fe to be re-united with his family; Sam Bean was in the El Paso area trying to fix up their papers and get them on the road. Meanwhile, Jim had another offer, and guided a group to California, where he joined his old friend, John Marsh, near Mt. Diablo at a place called Oak Springs. Here he protected Marsh and his property, and at the same time Jim and the Shawnees and Delawares still with him, hunted for game which they sold to restaurants in San Francisco. They did most of their hunting in Contra Costa County, where they lived and were listed in the special 1852 census made by the state of California.

Jim died at Oak Springs, near Mt. Diablo, early in 1853. His property was taken over almost immediately by a Dr. Adams, probably in payment for doctor's bills. And since Dr. Adams used Kirker's jacal to raise skunks, it would indicate that Kirker's death was due to cancer, for Dr. Adams, a cancer specialist, thought he had found in skunk oil a cure for cancer. Or – just maybe – Kirker died from an overdose of skunk oil. Anyway, the scarred old battler was laid to rest on a high hill near Pleasanton, California, just behind a state police barracks that stands there today. A 90-year-old son of one of the early settlers has told how his father attended Kirker's funeral; that he was buried by the Shawnee and Delaware Indians and how they headed back east right after the funeral and were never more seen in California.

About the only local reminder of Jim Kirker now is a "Kirker Pass," which leads into the Mount Diablo area from the Sacramento River.*

---

* A portrait of James Kirker appears herein at page 16 .

Jacob Fowler

by Raymond W. Settle
Monte Vista, Colorado

Jacob Fowler (1764-1849), government contractor, surveyor, trapper, hunter, Indian trader, merchant, traveler,
and diarist, was born in Winchester (Westminster?), Maryland, March 1, 1764.[1] His parents, with their four sons,
Jacob, Edward, Matthew, and Robert, removed from that
place to Ligonier Valley, Pennsylvania, in 1768, and after
three more moves settled in the neighborhood of Fort Vanmeter, ten miles inland from Wheeling, Virginia, in 1778.[2]
These numerous removals westward were caused by Indian
hostility. This situation compelled the people to live in forts
during much of the year.

In 1782, when the notorious Simon Girty led a body of
Indians against Fort Henry at Wheeling, Virginia, and
neighboring posts Jacob, then only eighteen years of age,
bore a man's part in the defense of Fort Vanmeter. Many
acts of heroism were performed in those flaming days, such
as that of Elizabeth Zane, at Fort Henry in November of
that year, who dashed from the safety of the fort under
heavy fire by the Indians to bring in a keg of powder which
had been inadvertently left in the cabin belonging to her
brother Ebenezer, some rods from the gate.[3] In November,
1782, Fowler piloted 1,050 mounted men under Colonels
Benjamin Logan and one of the Bowman brothers, John or
Joseph, from Bryant's Station (Lexington) to the mouth of
the Licking River, where they joined General George

---

[1] Charles Cist, "Biography of Jacob Fowler," in Cincinnati *Western Advertiser,*
Oct. 31, Nov. 7, 1849.

[2] Cist, *op. cit.,* 4.

[3] Cist, *op. cit.,* 6; John Frost, *Pioneer Mothers of the West* (Boston, 1859), 37-46.

Rogers Clark in his successful raid upon the Indian towns along the Miami River.[4]

In the latter part of the Revolutionary War the Fowler family left the Fort Vanmeter settlement and moved to Wheeling, where Jacob formed a personal acquaintance with the famous quartet of Indian fighters – Martin, Lewis, Jacob, and John Wetzel, who lived on Wheeling Creek twelve or fourteen miles from its mouth.[5]

After the close of the war, Fowler, in partnership with Abraham Creigh and Robert McConnell, hunted on the Muskingum and its tributaries to supply the various posts and settlements in that area with meat.[6] In 1789 he, with Benjamin Hulin, loaded a flatboat with whisky, cider, and merchandise and floated down the Ohio River to the settlements of Marietta, Ohio, and Kanawha, Virginia. This was his first venture in the trading business. After the goods were all sold he went down to Cincinnati, which had been laid out a few months before, to visit his brother Matthew, with whom he took a contract to supply new Fort Washington and the town of Cincinnati with meat. Their hunting was usually ten to fifteen miles into Kentucky. That same year Fowler bought lots in the village of Cincinnati.[7]

In the spring of 1790 he went back up the Ohio River to Point Pleasant where he met his former partner Hulin, who had just had a narrow escape from Indians, and Lewis Wetzel. In the summer of 1791, Fowler returned to Cincinnati where he met General Arthur St. Clair,[8] who, upon

---

[4] Mary K. Jones, "History of Campbell County," read at Centennial Celebration, July 4, 1876, Newport, Ky., p. 3. See also Theodore Roosevelt, *Winning of the West* (New York, 1905), III, pp. 63, 70, 72, 77, 84.

[5] Charles Cist, "Obituary of Jacob Fowler," in Cincinnati *Western Advertiser,* Oct. 24, 1849.

[6] Cist, "Biography," *loc. cit.*

[7] Cist, *op. cit.,* 10-12; Benjamin Van Cleve, "Memoirs," in *Quarterly Bulletin, Historical and Philosophical Society of Ohio,* XVII, p. 18.

[8] Cist, *op. cit.,* 13, 16-17. Gen. Arthur St. Clair, governor of Northwest Territory and commander of the army.

orders from President Washington, was making preparations to lead an army of 2,400 frontiersmen against the
Indians. Fowler accepted the appointment of Assistant Surveyor under John S. Gano,[9] afterward General, marched
away with it, and served as scout and hunter. While on this
campaign he heard that his brother Matthew had been
killed near Fort Hamilton, not far from Cincinnati, by the
Indians.[10] His brother Robert escaped unhurt.

St. Clair's disastrous campaign is well known.[11] Fowler
was in the thickest of the battle until he saw the day was
hopelessly lost; then he joined his terror-stricken comrades
in their flight from the awful scene. Beyond Fort Jefferson
they met Colonel Hamtramck with 500 to 600 reinforcements and provisions for the stricken army.[12]

About 1792 Fowler sued General James Wilkinson for
scouting pay, which had been withheld on the grounds that
all he did while in service was loaf around Indian camps
with an Indian wife. The case came to trial, the jury returned a verdict in favor of Fowler, and the judge ordered
that the General be held in jail until the debt was paid.[13]

Fowler married the widow Esther Sanders, *nee* de Vie, of
Newport, Kentucky, probably not long after St. Clair's
defeat. They had at least three children – Edward, Benjamin, and Adelaide – and possibly more.[14] He built a cabin
on the site of Newport, Kentucky, and in 1793 assisted Gen-

---

[9] Roosevelt, *op. cit.*, 146, 151, 154; Cist, *op. cit.*, 17.

[10] Cist, *op. cit.*, 17, 20.

[11] Cist, *op. cit.*, 21-29; Van Cleve, *op. cit.*, 28; James McBride, *Pioneer Biography: sketches of lives of some early settlers of Butler County, Ohio* (2 vols., Cincinnati, 1869), I, pp. 148-49, 154, 156-59.

[12] Roosevelt, *op. cit.*, v, pp. 169-70. This was one of the most crushing defeats in the history of Indian warfare, exceeding in losses those of Gen. Braddock in 1755. Van Cleve, *op. cit.*, 28.

[13] Charles T. Greve, *Centennial History of Cincinnati* (2 vols., Cincinnati, 1904), I, pp. 301, 308, 371.

[14] Jacob Fowler, *Journal of* (New York, 1898), xi-xii; Mrs. James Joyce Arthur, *Annals of the Fowler Family* (Austin, Texas, 1901), 313-17; Lewis Collins, *History of Kentucky* (Louisville, 1877), 424.

eral James Taylor from Virginia, one of the main promoters
of the town, in surveying a road from that place toward
Lexington, Kentucky.[15] In 1795 he was keeping a tavern in
Newport, and the first meeting of the trustees of Newport
Academy was held in his home September 21, 1799.[16]

Like all frontiersmen of the day, Fowler was possessed
of a craving for a huge amount of land. He crossed the
Licking River to Covington, Kentucky, and bought two
thousand acres of what became the site for the city.[17]

Records concerning Fowler's activities during the ten or
twelve years following the turn of the century seem non-
existent. With the outbreak of the War of 1812 he made the
acquaintance of 26-year-old Hugh Glenn, who came to Cincinnati from Mason County, Kentucky, prior to 1811. On
October 12 of that year, Glenn and other prominent men of
Cincinnati organized the Farmers and Mechanics Bank.[18]
With the outbreak of the war Fowler became a contractor
in the Quartermaster's Department of the United States
Army with the rank of assistant quartermaster. His responsibility was to furnish the army with whiskey, beef, bread,
biscuits, bacon and other commissary supplies. General
William Henry Harrison also called upon John H. Piatt,
merchant of Cincinnati and a relative of Fowler, for rations
to sustain the volunteers and regular troops. At that time
Fowler was serving around Detroit and the Maumee
Rapids, furnishing supplies for the garrison at Fort Wayne
and British prisoners of war. In this work he frequently
came in contact with Hugh Glenn. In 1814, Fowler, Glenn,

---

[15] James A. Padgett, "Letters of James Taylor to the Presidents of the United
States," in *Register of Kentucky State Historical Society*, XXXIV (1936), 104.

[16] Jones, *op. cit.*, 7-8.

[17] Fowler, *op. cit.*, x.

[18] Cincinnati *Western Spy*, Oct. 26, 1811; Gorham Worth, *Recollections of Cincinnati, 1817-1821* (Albany, 1851), reprinted in *Quarterly Publications of Historical
and Philosophical Society of Ohio*, XI, p. 42. [For further information concerning
Hugh Glenn and his varied activities, see sketch by Harry R. Stevens in this
Mountain Men series, II, p. 161.]

and Robert Piatt, cousin of John H., formed a partnership, called Jacob Fowler & Company, to supply rations for British prisoners of war at Long Point, Ontario, and Fort Wayne. In the summer of 1816 he established a small factory in Newport and manufactured hemp bagging for dry beans and tobacco.

In 1817, Fowler signed Glenn's bond to guarantee the faithful discharge of a contract with the United States War Department. In 1818 he became Glenn's agent at Fort Crawford, in which capacity he drove cattle from Prairie du Chien in Wisconsin to St. Louis, Missouri, looking after Glenn's business as contractor to furnish supplies to various posts in the west, including Fort Osage on the Missouri River and Fort Smith at Belle Pointe on the lower Arkansas River. In November-December, 1817, Glenn accompanied Majors Stephen H. Long and William Bradford to that area.

When Glenn's contract with the government expired, he and Fowler busied themselves for the next two or three years buying large tracts of land in Illinois and elsewhere.[19]

In July or August, 1820, Glenn went to the lower Verdigris River and, with Charles Dennis as partner, opened an Osage trading post sixty miles northeast of Fort Smith on the Verdigris River, a mile above its confluence with the Arkansas. In the spring of 1821 he went back to Cincinnati for a short visit. While there, he and Jacob Fowler made plans for an expedition to the headwaters of the Arkansas River to trade with the Indians and trap beaver. Having wound up his business affairs as best he could, Glenn left Cincinnati early in June and went to St. Louis. There he employed some of the men, especially French-Canadians, for the proposed expedition. Traveling on, he reached Fort Smith on August 5 and secured a license from the Com-

---

[19] The number of acres in Glenn's name is not known but it was very great. That Fowler was also interested is certified by records in several Missouri River counties.

mandant, Major William Bradford, to trade with the Indians along the Arkansas River and its tributaries.

Fowler arrived at Fort Smith late in August, possibly with more men. On September 6 they left the fort and marched to Glenn's trading post on the Verdigris, where they remained until September 25, making final arrangements for their undertaking. Among other items Fowler carried in his personal baggage was a supply of note paper, pens, and a bottle of ink, for he meant to record such events of the journey as he thought worthy of remembrance. Every night while his companions loafed about the campfire, he sat apart writing down, in a fascinating, sometimes mystifying scrawl resembling Egyptian hieroglyphics, the events of the past day. At first glance the average reader would find it hopelessly illegible, but by close, persevering study of his sometimes weird handwriting it may be read.

One of the most charming features of the document is his unique phonetic spelling ."Where" becomes "wheare," "proceed" is written "purceed," the name of his partner Glenn becomes "glann," "bed" is spelled "beed," "here" appears as "heare," "made" is written down as "maid," "pleasant" is "pleesent," "horse," as "hors," "delighted" as "delited," and so on. His capitalization follows no pattern whatever, and to him punctuation was an unknown art. One is, however, impressed by his fidelity to his self-imposed task, for he never missed a single day's entry. When he returned home he placed the manuscript in the family archives, where it remained totally unknown for seventy-six years, until 1898, when Francis P. Harper brought out an edition of 950 copies edited by Elliot Coues. The original is now in the library of the University of Chicago.

As the cavalcade moved up the Arkansas River, it presented an interesting spectacle. There were twenty men, thirty horses, and seventeen pack mules loaded with beaver traps and Indian trade goods.[20] Day by day they trudged along the east leg of the great bend of the Arkansas, with little to break the monotony except an occasional rainstorm, the loss of a few horses to the Osage Indians, and a couple of hunters getting themselves lost in the vast prairie. Thus the first fur brigade to penetrate the Southwest got under way.

On October 26, near present Cimarron, Kansas, they camped at an old Indian fort where they discovered the tracks of shod horses – proof that white men had recently passed that way, though they had no idea who they might be. They were made by William Becknell's party [21] from Franklin, Missouri, on its way to Santa Fe. On November 14, while in camp at the mouth of the Purgatory River, the first and only casualty of the expedition occurred. Lewis Dawson was so severely mauled by a grizzly bear that he died the following day.[22]

Five days later, on November 19, they met a Kiowa chief and thirty to fifty warriors who gave evidence of a friendly disposition. The chief and two warriors remained with the expedition that night, while the others returned to the tribe to spread the news that white traders were in the country. The following day the chief traveled upstream with them. During the day the remainder of the tribe came in and set up some two hundred lodges, each containing from twelve to twenty persons.

Although Glenn and Fowler did not know it, they had

---

[20] It should be borne in mind that in planning this expedition, Glenn and Fowler intended only to trade with the Indians along the Arkansas River and trap beaver on its headwaters on American soil. On September 27, 1821, twenty-two days after they set out from Glenn's trading house, Mexico gained her independence from Spain and rescinded the restrictions on foreign traders entering the country. Our traders did not learn of this until some three months later. Fowler, *op. cit.,* 72, 74, 94, 95.

[21] Becknell's career will be narrated later in this series.

[22] Dawson made the fatal mistake of attacking single-handed and wounding a grizzly bear. No experienced hunter, white or red, would have done such a thing.

stumbled upon the spot where an Indian fair or rendezvous, as the Mountain Men called such occasions a few years later,[23] was in progress. They had finished their fall hunt and were ready to go home for the winter. They had come from as far north as the upper Missouri River and the Red River on the south. Hostilities, if any existed, were temporarily adjourned, everyone had a good time, tribes that were poor in horses bought all they could afford, and stole any they could get away with.

The following day 350 lodges of Comanches came in and also camped near the white men. Next came the Arapahoes and Cheyennes. When all had arrived, Fowler estimated they numbered from ten to eighteen thousand, of all ages and both sexes. The expedition was now in a perilous situation. The Comanches openly declared they would kill the traders and take their goods.[24] The Cheyennes were willing to help, but the Kiowas and Arapahoes, who outnumbered all the others combined, claimed the white men as their friends and property.[25] In spite of the critical, perilous situation, a party of six men led by Isaac Slover was sent into the mountains upstream on December 3 to trap beaver. On

---

[23] The first of these was held by William H. Ashley in the Green River Valley in 1825.

[24] "friday 23 nov 1821 – this morning a Councel was hild amongst the Cheefs of both the nations (Kiowas and Ietans, or Highatans or Comanches), and Conl Glann . . . was told by the Ietan Cheef that the Ware Ready to Receive the goods in his possession that His father the Presedent had sent them – But When He was told that there Was no Such goods He Became in a great Pashion and told the Conl that he was a lyer and a theef and that He Head Stolen the goods from his father and that He the Cheef Wold take the goods and Segnefyed that He Wold kill the Conl and His men too. . ." Fowler, *op. cit.*, 53-54. In 1820 Major Stephen H. Long had come through Comanche territory along the Arkansas and Canadian rivers and met this identical chief and told him that President Monroe would send him "plenty of goods and that the goods We Head Ware Sent to him and that We head no Wright to traid them." Fowler, *op. cit.*, 58.

[25] The Cheyennes joined the Comanches, but at the critical moment a large number of Arapahoes joined the Kiowas in declaring their friendship for the white man. Being outnumbered, the Comanches abandoned their warlike intentions and a battle to the death was avoided. Fowler, *op. cit.*, 54.

December 28 the remainder moved camp to a spot on the south side of the Arkansas River, opposite the site of future Pueblo, Colorado.

Two days later a party of sixty Spanish traders from Taos and Santa Fe [26] came to camp with the information that Mexico had achieved independence from Spain and that the law prohibiting foreigners, especially Americans, from trading or trapping in the country had been abolished. Consequently, Glenn decided to accompany them on their return and secure permission to enter Mexico. He set out on January 2, 1822, leaving Fowler in charge of the expedition and taking four men with him.

Glenn promised to come back or send word in fifteen days, but if he did neither they were to conclude that he had been thrown into prison. In that event they would make their way back to Missouri as best they could. The following morning five of the men mutinied because they did not expect that the Spaniards would allow Glenn, to whom they looked for payment of their wages, to return. Fowler, with the help of his brother Robert, succeeded in putting down the rebellion.

On January 20, 1822, Fowler crossed the Arkansas River to the site of future Pueblo on American soil and built a strong stockade and horse pen. On January 28 all fears concerning Glenn's safety were set at rest by the arrival of Baptiste Peno with the news that Glenn's trip to Santa Fe was successful. He had secured the desired permission, gotten a license to trap in New Mexico, and would meet Fowler and the other members of the expedition at Taos.

Fowler led the now jubilant party along the old Taos Trail [27] toward the south, following the eastern base of the

[26] Comancheros.

[27] The old Indian-Spanish route from Santa Fe through Taos and across the Sangre de Cristo mountains by way of Sangre de Cristo Pass to the Arkansas River, which Pierre and Paul Mallet followed on their historic journey from St. Louis to

Sangre de Cristo Mountains. They crossed the range through Sangre de Cristo Pass, skirted the southeast edge of the San Luis Valley, passed the site of future Fort Garland, and reached Taos on February 8, 1822, where they found Glenn awaiting them. Two days later two trapping parties were sent back up the Rio Grande to the San Luis Valley, to remain out until May 1.

On February 10, Fowler himself set out for the same area, and Glenn returned to Santa Fe. In the following weeks the three parties set their traps upstream on the Rio Grande as far as Wagon Wheel Gap, with only meager success, because the streams were all frozen over and the animals remained in their houses. The three parties returned to Taos where all had arrived by May 1. Here they remained until June 1, making preparations for their return to Missouri. On that date they went out, crossed the Taos Mountains through Taos Pass and bore east toward the Arkansas River, which they reached at the site of present Coolidge, Kansas, on June 11.

The journey eastward along that stream was without significant incident except that on June 28, in present Franklin County, Kansas, they saw the tracks of William Becknell's three wagons on their way to Santa Fe. The significance of those tracks, made by the first wagons to cross the Great Plains, seems to have been entirely lost upon Fowler.

On July 5, 1822, they rode into Fort Osage on the Missouri River. There they bought two canoes (pirogues), built a platform upon them, piled their furs and baggage upon it, and floated down to St. Louis, where they arrived about July 15. Four men were detailed to bring on their horses. After two days in the city, Fowler set out for Cincinnati by

---

Santa Fe, New Mexico, in 1739-1740. They were the first white men to enter New Mexico from the Mississippi and Missouri rivers. Folmer, "The Mallet Expedition of 1739 through Nebraska, Kansas and Colorado to Santa Fe," in *Colorado Magazine,* XVI, pp. 161-73.

water, where he arrived on July 17, 1822, having been absent over thirteen months. He crossed the Ohio River to Covington, Kentucky, and was at home with his family.

Glenn remained in St. Louis, paid off the members of the expedition, settled accounts for supplies, etc., and sold the furs they had laboriously transported on packhorses across the plains, to the American Fur Company for $4,499.64.[28] Just what Fowler's financial interest in the expedition was is rather obscure, but he undoubtedly had a stake in it. When Glenn paid his men and bills for supplies and equipment he had $2,624.85 left.

Although limited to a considerable degree, the expedition achieved certain definite results. The fact that it successfully made the round trip to New Mexico, sustained itself on the Great Plains and in the mountains for almost a year with the loss of only one man, and encountered no difficulty with the Indians or Mexicans, may be certainly regarded as notable achievements.

Furthermore, although Fowler's journal lay unnoticed for seventy-six years, and the information it contained was not available to later travelers to New Mexico, and neither Glenn nor Fowler ever made another trip, the rank and file of the members of the expedition returned to their homes on the Missouri River, St. Louis and the Illinois country. Certainly they made no secret of their great adventure. What they said encouraged others to take the long trail leading westward. In addition, some of the members, such as Isaac Slover, Nathaniel Miguel Pryor, and perhaps others returned to the southwest as hunters and trappers.

On Monday, October 15, 1849, Jacob Fowler died at his home in Covington, Kentucky, leaving a daughter, Abigail; two sons, Benjamin and Edward; one brother, Robert;

---

[28] Contract between Lieutenant Charles Ward and Jacob Fowler, June 20, 1823. National Archives, Record Group no. 94.

probably his wife; a number of grandchildren, among whom was Frances Scott; and a great-granddaughter, Mrs. Ida Symmes, who became the custodian of Fowler's journal. She was a granddaughter of Captain John Cleve Symmes, author of *The Theory of Concentric Circles* (Cincinnati, 1826), and a great granddaughter of Hon. John Cleve Symmes, member of Congress from New Jersey, who, on the north bank of the Ohio River, bought a great body of land on which the city of Cincinnati was founded.[29]

---

[29] Fowler, *op. cit.,* x.

Isaac Slover

by ANDREW F. ROLLE
Occidental College, Los Angeles

Isaac Slover, sometimes called a native of Kentucky, was perhaps born in Pennsylvania, in 1780. In 1819 he owned a farm near Saline in present-day Arkansas. Slover may also have hunted on the Grand River in Oklahoma that year.[1] He grew crops at his farm between his wanderings over the game trails in its vicinity. From 1821 to 1822 Slover was with the Glenn-Fowler trapping expedition in New Mexico in search of beaver. This party, under the leadership of Hugh Glenn and Jacob Fowler, figured importantly in opening up the Santa Fe trade and in the origins of the American fur traffic throughout Colorado, New Mexico, and California.

Several of the entries from the journal of Jacob Fowler throw light upon Slover's participation in the Glenn-Fowler venture:

> *September 26, 1821:* Heare the Rain Continued all night – Heare one of our Hunters – Slover – Lay out all night but Came in the morning.
> *December 3, 1821:* Started the trappers under the Command of Slover – with him Simpson, Maxwell, Pryer, Findlay, Taylor.
> *January 20, 1822:* Robert Fowler and Slover Caught one bever.
> *February 1, 1822:* Slover got his feet a lletle frost Bitten.

Fowler's later entries for February 21 and March 12, 1822, clearly indicate that Slover headed one of the parties of this expedition. On the north fork of the Rio Grande they killed elk as well as beaver. The party was made up mostly of

---

[1] Grant Foreman, *Pioneer Days in the Early Southwest* (Cleveland, Ohio, 1926), 39.

Kentuckians. It traversed the country west of Fort Smith, Arkansas, into the Rocky Mountains via what was later Pueblo, Colorado. The group traveled along the Arkansas River. Ascending the Rio Grande, its members went to Hot Springs Creek in the San Juan Range, returning eastward via the Kansas country.[2]

In February, 1824, Slover, with Ewing Young and William Wolfskill, began to trap the San Juan River and other tributaries of the Colorado. When they arrived back in Taos the following June, this group had amassed some $10,000 worth of beaver and other pelts.[3]

In 1828 Slover was one of the party of trapper-adventurers who made their way westward from Santa Fe with James Ohio Pattie and his father, Sylvester. The younger Pattie, in his *Personal Narrative* (1831), writes dramatically of rescuing Slover and his father, Sylvester, "from famish" along the trail. James Ohio speaks of Slover, who (judging by his age upon his death) must have been in his fifties at the time, as an old man. Pattie's own father, who was Slover's trail companion, was apparently about the same age and was to die soon thereafter. On March 12 the Pattie group was apprehended by Mexican authorities as foreign interlopers at Santa Catalina Mission in Lower California and marched northward under guard to San Diego in Upper California. There Governor José María Echeandía incarcerated them. During November of that year, however, Slover and another trapper, William Pope, received permission to return eastward via Sonora in Mexico proper, probably for purposes of repatriation.[4]

---

[2] Elliott Coues (ed.), *The Journal of Jacob Fowler* (New York, 1898), *passim*.

[3] Robert G. Cleland, *This Reckless Breed of Men* (New York, 1950), 128, 195, 198, 217; Joseph J. Hill, "Ewing Young in the Fur Trade of the Far Southwest, 1822-1834," *Ore. Hist. Soc. Quarterly*, XXIV (March, 1923), 7.

[4] H. H. Bancroft, *History of California* (San Francisco, 1884) III, p. 163, 166-167, 178; V, p. 722.

John Brown Sr., a Rocky Mountain companion of Slover's, recalled:

A party of fur trappers, of whom I was one, erected a fort on the Arkansas River in Colorado, for protection and as headquarters during the winter season. We called it "Pueblo." The city of Pueblo now stands upon that ground.

Brown further remembered that Slover came into this fort one day, trailing two mules loaded with beaver skins. He was thereupon engaged, Brown remembered, "to help me supply the camp with game, and during the winter we hunted together, killing buffalo, elk, antelope, and deer . . ." Brown found Slover to be "a reliable and experienced hunter" and further, "a quiet and peaceable man, very reserved. He would heed no warning and accept no advice as to his methods of hunting. His great ambition was to kill grizzlies – he called them 'Cabibs.' He would leave our camp and be gone for weeks at a time without anyone knowing his whereabouts . . ." Later, in California, Brown saw Slover again and talked with him about "our experiences at Fort Pueblo, and of our other companions there: James W. Waters, V. J. Herring, Alex Godey, Kit Carson, Bill Williams, Fitzpatrick, Bridger, Bill Bent, the Sublettes and others. . ."[5]

Sometime between 1837 and 1843, Slover had come back to California with a group of colonists from New Mexico. He brought along a wife, Barbara, known as Doña Barbarita. They settled near San Bernardino but Slover continued to trap the streams of California, possibly as far away as the Sierra range, for weeks at a time. In the 1850s there were still, fortunately, large quantities of trout, deer and bear to be found in the San Bernardino Valley where he lived. In

[5] John Brown, Sr., *The Mediumistic Experiences of John Brown, Medium of the Rockies* (Des Moines, Ia., 1887), quoted in John Brown, Jr. and James Boyd, *History of San Bernardino and Riverside Counties* (3 vols., Chicago, 1922), II, p. 681.

local records, incidentally, Slover himself was sometimes called Luís or Cristóbal.[6]

On October 13, 1854, near the age of eighty, Slover had a savage knife and claw fight with a grizzly bear on the north slope of Mount San Antonio in the Cajon Pass. Before his hunting companion, one Bill McMines, could kill the beast, the bear had chewed a large piece of flesh from Slover's thigh and broken his leg. Weakened by profuse bleeding, he died the following day. Although married to a Catholic, Slover was given a Mormon funeral.[7] (In 1851, when the Mormons had settled in what is now San Bernardino, he had delivered a wagon full of provisions to them; this act of welcome came out of his modest personal larder.)

Slover had settled near today's Colton, on the side of a conspicuous peak which was to be called Mount Slover. The Indians had named the place Tahualtapa ("Hill of the Ravens") while the Californians called it Cerrito Solo. Lime kiln and limestone quarrying operations began on Mount Slover in the late 1850s, and embellishments for some of the palatial marble mansions on San Francisco's Nob Hill came from there. Later, cement operations were to cut down the mountain even further.[8]

In 1873, almost twenty years after Slover died, the "Slover Mountain Colony," a realty development that bore his name, was established three miles outside San Bernardino. It consisted of a tract two thousand acres in size. A second purpose of the Slover Mountain Colony was to attract the Southern Pacific Railroad, then planning a route

---

[6] George and Helen P. Beattie, *Heritage of the Valley* (Pasadena, Calif., 1939), 60, 103-105, 117-118, 177; L. R. and A. W. Hafen, *Old Spanish Trail* (Glendale, Calif., 1954), 181, 198-199, 222, 224; *History of Napa and Lake Counties, California* (Napa, Calif., 1881), 55.

[7] Brown and Boyd, *op. cit.*, 681.

[8] Raymond M. Holt, "The Mountain They Put in Sacks," *Westways*, vol. 50 (June, 1958), 30-31.

through San Bernardino. It is appropriate that Slover's name should have become linked with the opening of one of the major lines of communication between the East and the West, for he had blazed some of the trails that later became highways.[9]

[9] William A. Conn to Judge Benjamin Hayes, April 10, 1874, and William C. Mintzer to Hayes, Sept. 8, 1874, Bancroft Library ms. CE-81.

Ewing Young

by HARVEY L. CARTER
Colorado College, Colorado Springs

Ewing Young, one of the most considerable figures of the fur trade of the Far West, was born near Jonesboro, Washington County, in eastern Tennessee, at least as early as 1794 and, more probably, as early as 1792.[1] He was the son of Charles and Mary Rebecca (Wilkins) Young, who had taken up land there in 1790. His grandfather, Robert Young, was an early Watauga Valley settler and a veteran of the battle of King's Mountain.[2] Although his father died in 1796, it is evident that his son, Ewing, received some education and it is also known that he was apprenticed to learn the carpenter's trade.

When and under what circumstances Young left his native state are unknown but, on January 18, 1822, he bought a farm, in partnership with Thomas P. Gage, at Charitan, Missouri, on the north bank of the Missouri River. On May 24, 1822, they sold the farm and, on the next day, Ewing Young joined William Becknell, who was about to set out on his second trip to Santa Fe.[3] Becknell had twenty-one

---

[1] Kenneth L. Holmes, "Ewing Young, Enterprising Trapper" (Unpublished doctoral dissertation, University of Oregon, 1963), 4-5. The researches of Dr. Holmes turned up a will of Charles Young dated May 28, 1794 (Will Book no. 1, Washington County, Tennessee, p. 176) in which mention is made of his "sons Wilken and Ewen and dater Giny." Thus, Ewing Young's birth was prior to May 28, 1794 and, if an inference may be drawn from the order of the mention of the children, Ewing was probably born during the year 1792. Prior to the investigations of Dr. Holmes, the date 1796 had been accepted for Young's birth because of his baptismal record in Taos in 1831, which gave his age as 35 years at that time.

[2] Samuel C. Williams, *Tennessee during the Revolutionary War* (Nashville, 1944), 157, reports the legend that Robert Young shot Major Ferguson at the battle of King's Mountain, with his rifle, "Sweet Lips."

[3] Holmes, *op. cit.,* 16-22. Here again Dr. Holmes has discovered material enabling a correction to be made. Young could not have been with the first Becknell expedi-

men and three wagons for this trip. This was undoubtedly the first use of wagons on the Santa Fe trail. Young had invested whatever he had from the sale of his farm in trade goods and thus made the journey as a partner in the venture. The only other members known are William Wolfskill and John Ferrell. The latter had been in the gunpowder-making business at Boone's Lick with John Day and Benjamin Cooper, and he and Young proposed to engage in this business in New Mexico.[4] The route they followed left the Missouri at present Kansas City and struck the Arkansas at the Great Bend. Joined by a party under John Heath, they continued on the Cimarron route and arrived at San Miguel twenty-two days after leaving the Arkansas.[5] The gunpowder scheme with Ferrell failed to materialize for lack of an adequate supply of nitre. Young turned instead to beaver trapping, inviting Wolfskill to join him. They trapped the Pecos River in the fall of 1822 and thus was begun his notable career as a trapper and trader.[6]

There is no record of Young's movements in the year 1823 but it is likely that he trapped on some of the more frequented streams of New Mexico and matured his plans for going farther afield, for he told Wolfskill that he wanted "to get outside of where trappers had ever been." [7] In pursuance of this aim, he organized and led a party westward to the San Juan River in February, 1824. The party was loosely organized and gradually broke up, but Young, Wolfskill, and Isaac Slover stuck together until June, 1824, when they returned to Santa Fe with over ten thousand dollars worth of furs.[8]

tion in 1821, as had previously been believed, because his involvement with land transactions precludes such a possibility.

[4] *Ibid.,* 24-5.

[5] William Becknell, "Journal of Two Expeditions from Boone's Lick to Santa Fe," in *Missouri Historical Review* (January, 1940), IV, pp. 79-80.

[6] Holmes, 42.   [7] *Ibid.,* 44.

[8] Joseph J. Hill, "Ewing Young in the Fur Trade of the Far Southwest, 1822-1834," in *Oregon Historical Society Quarterly* (March, 1923), XXIV, p. 7.

Ewing Young now had some capital with which to operate and he returned to St. Louis in the fall of 1824, possibly with Augustus Storrs, although this is conjectural. Here he purchased a supply of trade goods worth $1,206.40 in Mexican dollars. He made the return trip to Santa Fe very early in the spring of 1825 and paid $301.50 customs duty on the goods, which were itemized and valued by the Mexican authorities on April 11, 1825. The goods consisted chiefly of cotton and silk cloth, handkerchiefs, ladies' slippers, metal buttons and combs, but also included knives and hoes.[9] Young returned to Missouri with M. M. Marmaduke, leaving Santa Fe May 31, 1825, which may indicate that his goods found a ready market and that his stock needed replenishing. This time he took a number of mules, some of which were stolen by the Osage Indians. He received $216, the amount he requested, from the federal government as indemnification. The Marmaduke party arrived in Franklin, Missouri, on August 5, 1825.[10] Young must have returned to New Mexico after a very short stay in Missouri, for Major Sibley recorded in his *Journal* that he permitted one of his men, Benjamin Robinson, to go trapping with "Mr. E. Young" on November 27, 1825. Robinson died before they had gone far, and Young himself returned to Taos in ill health by January 22, 1826.[11]

While recovering his health, Young again teamed up with his old partner, William Wolfskill, who set out to trap the western rivers while Young returned once more to Missouri, this time with Major Sibley. They set out on February 26, 1826, and reached Missouri early in April. Young started back with more goods from Fayette, Missouri, on May 20,

---

[9] Young's list of trade goods is in the Ritch Collection of the Henry E. Huntington Library, doc. no. R181. See Holmes, 47-8.

[10] M. M. Marmaduke, "Journal," in *Missouri Historical Review* (October, 1911), VI, pp. 1-10.

[11] A. B. Hulbert, *Southwest on the Turquoise Trail, Overland to the Pacific Series,* II, pp. 147, 153.

1826.[12] Arriving in Taos in the late summer he found that Wolfskill's trapping venture had been unsuccessful because of trouble with hostile Indians.[13]

Young now decided to organize a trapping party strong enough to defend itself against the Indians and to recover the losses suffered at their hands. However, he was by no means the only leader of a fur brigade headed for the tributary streams of the Colorado River in the year 1826. Governor Narbona had issued licenses by August 31 of that year to Isaac Williams, Ceran St. Vrain, Michael Robidoux, and John Rowland as well as to "Joaquin Joon," as Young is styled in the Mexican documents. These separate parties amounted to over a hundred men, and probably more went than were actually licensed to go.[14]

Young originally led a party of eighteen licensed trappers in 1826, including Milton Sublette and Thomas L. (later "Peg-Leg") Smith. But he had consolidated with a group of sixteen men, of whom George Yount was one, who accepted his leadership. This large party was in the neighborhood of the junction of the Salt and Gila rivers when it encountered three survivors of a group of thirty French-American trappers, the rest of whom had been set upon and killed by Papago Indians. These three, Michael Robidoux, the leader, young James Ohio Pattie, and one other were glad to join Young's band.[15]

Stirred by the news of the massacre of the Robidoux party, Young set a successful ambush for the Papagos and

---

[12] Holmes, 53-4.   [13] *Ibid.,* 55.

[14] See Thomas Maitland Marshall, "St. Vrain's Expedition to the Gila" in *Southwestern Historical Quarterly* (January, 1916), XIX, pp. 251-60. Marshall overestimates the role of St. Vrain. The New Mexico records usually refer to Young as Joaquin Joon, Jon, or Jong; the California records used also the designation of Joaquin or Joachim Joven.

[15] Joseph J. Hill, *op. cit.,* 9-15. This reconstruction of events, first made by Mr. Hill, has been accepted universally by historians. There seems to be no doubt that Young was the "genuine American leader" referred to by Pattie. See also Robert G. Cleland, *This Reckless Breed of Men* (New York, 1952), 179-81.

exacted a heavy toll of lives for those of the dead trappers, whose mutilated bodies they gathered and buried. Having done this, Young divided his band into two equal groups to trap the Salt and Gila rivers to their headwaters. Both groups then returned to the junction of these rivers and were reunited. They then trapped down the Gila to its junction with the Colorado, which brought them among the Yuma Indians, with whom they had no trouble. As they moved up the Colorado River they enjoyed good beaver trapping. However, when they came among the Mojave Indians, Young was aware at once that they were menacingly hostile, and he built a stockade in anticipation of trouble. When a chief shot an arrow into a tree, Young put a bullet into the arrow with his rifle. The Indians, unimpressed by this display of marksmanship, attacked the trappers at daybreak but were repelled with a loss of sixteen. Young continued up river for four days, keeping men posted at night. Then, thinking the Indians had given up the chase, he relaxed his guard. Immediately the Mojaves attacked, killing two and wounding two before they were driven off. Eighteen of the trappers pursued them on horseback and killed a number, whom they hanged from trees to discourage the others. At the confluence of the Bill Williams Fork with the Colorado, Young lost three more men, who were scouting for beaver sign. The Indians were found roasting and eating their victims but managed to get away.[16]

Young now led his men along the south rim of the Grand Canyon until they reached the Navajo country south of the San Juan River. Here, for reasons not very clear, it was decided to continue northward and trap the Grand River (now the Colorado). Pattie's narrative becomes extremely vague and untrustworthy from this point. It is certain they could not have been on the Yellowstone and on Clark's Fork

---

[16] *The Personal Narrative of James Ohio Pattie,* ed. by Milo M. Quaife (Chicago, 1930), 136-50.

of the Columbia as he declares. The most probable reconstruction is that they crossed the continental divide from the
headwaters of the Grand (Colorado) in the vicinity of
Long's Peak and got upon the South Platte. Then they may
have swung in a big circle, going to the Laramie, the North
Platte, the Sweetwater, the Little Snake, the Yampa, and
finally, up the Eagle to the headwaters of the Arkansas in
the central Colorado Rockies.[17] In the process, four more
men were lost to Indians, but the remainder of the party
crossed from the Arkansas to the Rio Grande and so, back
into New Mexico, heavily laden with furs worth perhaps
$20,000.

Young must have learned that Narbona was no longer
governor and that the new governor, Armijo, was hostile to
American trappers, for he left twenty-nine packs of beaver
in the village of Peñablanca, in the care of a Mexican named
Cabeza de Baca, before proceeding to Santa Fe.[18] Governor
Armijo learned where the furs were and, in June, 1827, sent
men to confiscate them. They did so, killing Cabeza de
Baca in the process. At Santa Fe, Milton Sublette managed
to seize the two bales of beaver belonging to him and to get
away with them. Young was thereupon thrown in jail for a
time. When questioned he gave no information that would
aid in apprehending Sublette and was soon discharged.
Meanwhile, the beaver pelts had received poor care and
were sold at a low rate, but it is not thought that Young and
his men ever recovered anything despite the fact that they
had been duly licensed to trap.[19] In order to protect himself
better in the future, Young procured a passport from the
American State Department signed by Henry Clay, then
Secretary of State. He also applied for Mexican citizen-

---

17 *Ibid.*, 150-9. Pattie's dates are unreliable as well as his geography. See also
Hill, *op. cit.*, 17-18.
18 Cleland, *op. cit.*, 218-19.
19 *Ibid.*, 219-24.

ship, in company with four other Americans, on April 26, 1828.[20]

Meanwhile, he opened a store in Taos in partnership with Wolfskill, who had just brought in a fresh lot of goods from St. Louis, and outfitted a trapping party which he sent to the Gila River. This party, not having Young's redoubtable leadership, soon returned because of trouble with the Apaches.[21] He now began to make plans for an extensive trapping expedition, which he would lead in person, all the way to California. Doubtless the recent return of his good friend Richard Campbell from California had made him acquainted with the opportunities that lay in this direction. But before he set out he was to perform a signal service for other traders. The regular Santa Fe caravan had been escorted to the border by Major Bennett Riley and there turned over to the protection of Mexican troops. Although the Mexican guard was 120-strong and the traders themselves numbered sixty, word came in to Taos that the caravan was beleagured by a much larger force of Indians. Young set out, with forty men, to the rescue, but on receiving fresh news, returned and augmented his force to ninety-five men. The Indians rode off when Young and his hunters appeared; the wagon train was saved and decided to go to Taos instead of Santa Fe.[22]

In August, 1829, Young led forty trappers north from Taos into the San Luis Valley. This was to give the impression that they planned to trap in the central Rocky Mountains on American soil. Actually they never got out of Mexican territory but doubled back across western New Mexico to the Zuni pueblo. From here they went to the

---

[20] Ritch Collection, Henry E. Huntington Library, doc. R199. Young's passport was dated March 20, 1828. He applied for Mexican citizenship in order to get a Mexican provincial passport as well.

[21] Holmes, 85.

[22] William Waldo, "Recollections of a Septuagenarian" in *Missouri Historical Society Quarterly* (April, June, 1938), V, pp. 64, 77, 78.

familiar trapping waters of the Salt River. They trapped down that stream and up the Verde River with considerable success, driving off and killing some interfering Apaches along the way. Now Young divided his party and sent half of the men back to New Mexico with the furs, while he himself led the other half to California. Among the latter was young Kit Carson, who had worked as a cook for Young in Taos and who was now out on his first real trapping expedition.[23]

Leaving the headwaters of the Verde (San Francisco) River, they struck out for the Colorado just below the Grand Canyon, camping at a place long after known as Young Spring, near present Truxton, Arizona. After crossing the Colorado, finding themselves short of food, they bought from the Mojaves a mare about to foal and ate both the mare and the foal. Their route lay up the dry course of the Mojave River for several days, then down through Cajon Pass to the mission at San Gabriel, California. Here they stayed only for one night, so eager were they to get upon the beaver streams of California.[24]

They passed on to the San Fernando Valley and over the Tehachapi range to the San Joaquin River. This was the beaver paradise for which they had been heading, but as they worked down the stream they became aware that it had been trapped by another party. This turned out to be Peter Skene Ogden and his Hudson's Bay Company brigade, whom they overtook after a while. They trapped the Sacramento, as far as what is now Redding, together with Ogden's group without any argument developing. Here they parted and Young returned downstream with his party, augmented by a man who had left British employment to join him.[25]

It was now July of 1830. Young aided the San José mis-

---

[23] Kit Carson, *Autobiography*, ed. by Milo M. Quaife (Chicago, 1935), 9.

[24] *Ibid.*, 10-14. Young was the fourth American to lead an overland party to California. He was preceded by Jedediah Smith in 1826, the Patties in 1827, and by Richard Campbell in 1827.

[25] Hill, *op. cit.*, 25.

sion to recover runaway Indians, who had run off into the Sierra Nevada Mountains, sending Carson with ten men to accomplish this service for the mission. He also sold his furs to a ship captain, Don José Asero, and purchased more horses and mules. Soon after this, Indians stole sixty horses but, by swift pursuit, all but five were recovered. At this time also, three of Young's men went to Monterey to secure passports to return to Taos, but they were forced by the others to rejoin the party.[26]

In September, 1830, they started back to New Mexico, but went by way of Los Angeles where most of the men got drunk. In the course of this spree, James Higgins shot and killed James Lawrence. Young, who was not drunk, sensed bad trouble with the authorities and got the men to ride out of Los Angeles in a hurry. They went down the Colorado River to the Gulf of California, then up the river to the Gila and up that river to its source, trapping with considerable success as they went. Young now employed a stratagem by going to the Santa Rita copper mines and leaving the furs with Robert McKnight, who was working the mines. He then proceeded to Santa Fe, where he procured a license to trade with the Indians at Santa Rita. He then sent back for the furs. There was over a ton of beaver skins, and he was taking no chances of losing this catch by confiscation.[27]

It was April, 1831, when Young paid off his men in Taos. During the twenty months that had elapsed since he had set out for California, three other expeditions had made their separate ways there – those of Antonio Armijo, William Wolfskill, and Peg-Leg Smith. Young's first California expedition, besides being profitable, must be credited with the effective opening of trade with California. It is also notable that Kit Carson served his apprenticeship as a Mountain Man under so experienced a leader as Ewing Young and

---

[26] *Ibid.*, 23. The three would-be deserters were Francois Turcote, Jean Vaillant, and Anastase Carier.

[27] *Ibid.*, 27.

that Young was quick to recognize both the ability and the reliability of the younger man.

On May 11, 1831, Young was baptized by Father Martinez at Taos, but he did not apply for naturalization. He lived with Maria Josepha Tayfoya, but did not contract a legal marriage with her. Young was planning to go to California a second time and considering whether he wanted to settle there. While at San José on his first trip, he had become acquainted with John R. Cooper, with whom he had since had some correspondence in which was discussed both the possibility of developing the mule trade between California and New Mexico and the possibility of Young's settling in California.[28]

On July 4, 1831, the wagons of Smith, Jackson, and Sublette reached Santa Fe. Jedediah Smith had been killed by Indians on the Cimarron, but the other two partners brought in the goods. On July 31, 1831, William Sublette paid Ewing Young $2,484.82 owed to him by William H. Ashley. About the same time, Young formed a partnership with Dr. David Waldo and David Jackson for the purpose of beginning the mule trade Young had in mind and continuing the trade in beaver pelts.[29]

David Jackson went ahead with a letter from Young to John R. Cooper which was to facilitate his buying of mules. He set out on August 25, 1831, and arrived in San Diego early in November of that year with eleven men. Meanwhile, Young had received a passport on August 21 to travel to Chihuahua, but instead of using it he organized a party of thirty-six trappers and set out for California in October, 1831. Among them was Job F. Dye, to whom we are indebted for the following list of men who were in the party: Sidney Cooper, Moses Carson, Benjamin Day, Isaac Sparks, Joseph Gale, Joseph Dofit, John Higans, Isaac Williams,

---

[28] Holmes, 126-7.
[29] Sublette Papers, Missouri Historical Society, St. Louis, Missouri.

James Green, Cambridge Green, James Anderson, Thomas
Low, Julian Bargas, José Teforia, and John Price. They
stopped at the Zuni pueblo for supplies and then trapped
down the Salt River, catching beaver in large numbers.
There were other adventures as well. Young and Dye had a
scrape with a grizzly bear. They fought Apaches and Young
himself killed their chief. Then Cambridge Green, usually
called Turkey – a small man, but mean – killed big Jim
Anderson, who bullied him once too often. By January 1,
1832, they had moved down the Gila and were camped on
the Colorado River.[30]

Young took ten men and went to Los Angeles, arriving
February 10, 1832. He turned Green in to the authorities
for homicide. The rest of the men did not come in until
March 14, 1832. Where they spent the intervening time is
not known. Early in April, Jackson came in from the north
with six hundred mules and one hundred horses. This was
only about a fourth of what they had hoped to buy. So
instead of all driving them to New Orleans, as had been
planned originally, Jackson drove them to Santa Fe and
Young remained in California to hunt sea otter.[31] Father
Sanchez at the San Gabriel Mission had a vessel built for
this purpose which was transported now by ox-cart to San
Pedro harbor and assembled there. Young and Jonathan
Warner and several others, including two Kanakas, engaged
in the otter hunt; but Young did not like being dumped in
the surf and, after being spilled several times, left the hunt
and went to Monterey.

This was in early July and, by early October, Young had
organized fourteen men to trap the San Joaquin. There is no
record of Young's movements during this three-month
period. It has been supposed that he stayed in California.

---

[30] Job F. Dye, *Recollections of a Pioneer, 1830-1852* (Los Angeles, 1951), 18-29.

[31] Holmes, 142-52. Professor Holmes points out that Alfred Robinson, *Life in California* (New York, 1846), 140-41, almost certainly describes Young's landlubber experiences while hunting sea otter, although Young is not identified by name.

However, Maria Josepha Tafoya, back in Taos, on April 8, 1833, gave birth to a son whose paternity was attributed to Young and never denied by him. It would have been possible for Young to have returned to Taos during the summer of 1832, and if he was the true father of Joaquin Young, who later inherited his property, it is essential to assume that he did so.[32]

Regardless of Young's whereabouts during the summer it is clear that in early October, 1832, he led fourteen trappers out from Los Angeles into the San Joaquin Valley. When they reached the Fresno River they saw signs indicating that a large band of trappers had been there very recently. So they hastened on to the Sacramento, where they found a Hudson's Bay Company brigade under Michael La Framboise, who was soon joined there by another band under John Work. The combined Hudson's Bay Company party amounted to 163 persons, although only forty were trappers, the rest being women and children and Indians.[33] John Turner, one of the survivors of the massacre of Jedediah Smith's men on the Umpqua in 1827, was working for La Framboise but, after talking with Young, he openly transferred to him. Turner interested Young in going farther north than he had intended. In March, 1833, they went to the Pacific coast, about seventy-five miles above Ft. Ross, and continued north as far as the Umpqua River. Ascending

[32] The alternatives to the conclusion that Young revisited Taos in the summer of 1832 are: (a) Father Martinez, Maria Tafoya, Kit Carson, Richard Campbell, and Manuel Lefevre were all mistaken in certifying Young's paternity; or (b) Maria Tafoya experienced a pregnancy of eighteen months. The baptismal record is dated April 12, 1833, and states that the infant was four days old at that time. It is in the Chancery office, State Records Center, Santa Fe, New Mexico. However, the entry does not appear in the normal consecutive order for that date but is written on an insert, stuck in at the bottom of the page. This irregularity may provide still a third alternative, namely, that this insert was made some years later than the normal entries and that it may not be accurate as to the date of birth and baptism of Joaquin Young.

[33] Alice Bay Maloney, *Fur Brigade to the Bonaventura* (San Francisco, 1945), 22 ff.

this to its source, they crossed to the northwest shore of Klamath Lake and thence to the Klamath and the Pitt rivers, past Mt. Shasta and back to the upper waters of the Sacramento, thus completing a big circle through most difficult country. By November 13, 1833, the night of the great meteoric shower, they were camped on the shores of Tulare Lake, whence they returned to Los Angeles.[34] Young had some conversation at San Pedro with Abel Stearns about starting a sawmill, but soon they went on to trap once more on the Gila, in the winter of 1833 and 1834.[35]

When he returned to San Diego and Los Angeles, Young was discouraged by the poor results of his last trapping expedition and by his inability to get either men or tools to engage in lumbering. It was at this time, near San Diego, that he met the eccentric Oregon enthusiast, Hall J. Kelley of Massachusetts, who was temporarily stranded on his way to "the promised land." Nevertheless, after listening to Kelley expound the wonderful future of Oregon, Young declined to accompany him thither. Kelley went on to Monterey and was surprised to have Young, with seven men, turn up there during the last of June, 1834, with the declaration that he was ready to go and settle in Oregon and that, if Kelley had deceived him, "woe be unto him."[36]

They started their northward journey with over forty horses and mules belonging to Young. At San José, they stopped for five days to secure provisions, and Young went to San Francisco to get more horses, which he had contracted for before leaving Monterey. When they left San

---

[34] Holmes, 161-7. Both in the Sacramento and San Joaquin valleys, where Indian population had been plentiful, they now found many dead of a great pestilence which had ravaged those regions during their absence in Oregon.

[35] Abel Stearns Papers, Henry E. Huntington Library. A letter of Young's to Stearns dated March 14, 1834, indicates that Young had not yet given up the project for a sawmill at that time.

[36] Fred Wilbur Powell, *Hall J. Kelley on Oregon* (Princeton, 1932), 100. Kelley wrote that they first met "in Pueblo, near the port of St. Diego." This may refer to Los Angeles.

José, Young had seventy-seven horses and mules, and Kelley and the other men with Young had twenty-one, all of which Young swore were fairly bought. However, either at San José or just north of it, they were joined by nine men with fifty-six horses, of which Young said he did not know whether they were bought or stolen.[37]

This accession to the party was to be the cause of much trouble for both Kelley and Young upon their arrival in Oregon. Governor José Figueroa wrote on September 9, 1834, from Santa Clara Mission to Dr. John McLoughlin at Fort Vancouver, charging Young and the members of his party with having driven two hundred stolen horses out of California and asking McLoughlin's aid in recovering them.[38] There is no proof that Young acquired any of his stock dishonestly. On the contrary, he had always shown a disposition to cultivate good relations with the authorities in California, had helped the missions to recover stock and Indians, had given up a number of horses in his possession in 1833 upon identification of brands, and had refused to give up others.[39] This would seem to be adequate refutation of the charge that Young was a horse thief. His mistake lay in allowing the marauders to join up with him.

Young's party was overtaken in the Umpqua valley by La Framboise and his returning Hudson's Bay Company brigade. At this time, Kelley was extremely ill and Young was glad to allow him to travel with the Hudson's Bay Company captain, who was better equipped to give him medicinal care. Kelley thus arrived at Fort Vancouver a little before Young did, late in October, 1834.[40]

---

[37] *Ibid.*, 300, 351. These are the men whom Kelley called "marauders." There is not much doubt that their animals were stolen. Two of them were deserters from Joseph R. Walker's famous expedition to California in 1833. Kelley says further that these marauders tried to kill him but were prevented by Young. Their number is variously given as five, seven, and nine.

[38] A copy of this letter is in the Archives of the Hudson's Bay Company in London. The transcript of it was furnished to me by Professor Kenneth L. Holmes.

[39] Hubert Howe Bancroft, *History of California*, III, pp. 394, 410.

We do not know precisely what occurred between Ewing Young and Dr. John McLoughlin, but we know that McLoughlin had circulated Figueroa's charge of thievery against Young and that he refused to have any business dealings with him. Young felt a keen resentment over this treatment. He denied the charge and eventually received a retraction of it. But meanwhile, he had to shift for himself. It is no small tribute to his character and ability that he was able to survive in spite of the tremendous power and influence of the Hudson's Bay Company. Looking about for a likely place to settle, he pre-empted fifty square miles of land in the Chehalem valley and built a hillside cabin overlooking his domain. Here for the next two years he managed to exist, entirely independent of the hostile fur company, which refused all his overtures to trade, though willing, on occasion, to offer charity, which Young was too proud to accept. He told Lt. Slacum, in 1836, that "a cloud hung over him so long, through Dr. McLoughlin's influence, that he was almost maddened by the harsh treatment of that gentleman." [41]

But doubtless he was able to trade furs for supplies from American ships that came up the Columbia from time to time and, in 1836, he began the erection of a sawmill with Sol Smith, who had come to Oregon with Nathaniel Wyeth in the same year that Young had arrived. Also, in 1836, he announced his plans to start a whiskey distillery, with Lawrence Carmichael as partner, and bought from Wyeth's trading post, after Wyeth's departure, a large cauldron or

---

[40] Powell, 262-4. Kelley remained in Oregon until March, 1835, when he took ship for the Hawaiian Islands. He was given adequate care by Dr. McLoughlin but was segregated and not admitted to table at the fort. His account of this period is found in Powell, 181-9. It should be said that McLoughlin's treatment of Young and Kelley was an exception to his usual policy of open handed hospitality. Young's spread was located southwest of modern Portland and about twenty miles almost directly west of Oregon City.

[41] "Slacum's Report on Oregon, 1836-1837" in *Oregon Historical Society Quarterly* (June, 1912), XIII, p. 196.

copper kettle for this purpose. A temperance society was already in existence among the American settlers, having been organized February 11, 1836. Jason Lee and other missionaries asked him to abandon his plans to operate a distillery. The Hudson's Bay Company had a strict monopoly of liquor, as well as nearly everything else, up to this time. Young may have seriously intended to break into this monopoly. Or he may have foreseen the objection of the American temperance people and acted as he did for the purpose of winning their good opinion and so lessening the power of the company. At any rate, he consented to their request and stopped the erection of the distillery. He refused to take $51 which the temperance society had raised to compensate him, but later he sold the kettle to them for $50, which was a high price. It is not certain that Lt. William A. Slacum had arrived before this matter was settled, but if so he may have influenced Young's decision not to persist against the wishes of the community.[42]

Slacum, a naval lieutenant, had been ordered by President Jackson to look into affairs in Oregon. He noted the dependence of American settlers on the British company, especially in the matter of cattle. The company would lend a cow to a settler but refused to allow any to pass into private hands. In discussing the situation with Ewing Young, Slacum learned that there were many cattle in California and that some might be brought to Oregon from there. Thus was organized the Willamette Cattle Company. Young agreed to take ten men and go to California, purchase cattle, and drive them to Oregon. Slacum would transport the men to California. Settlers subscribed money for the purchase, and even Dr. McLoughlin was drawn into the scheme by the able lieutenant.[43] The *Loriot,* Slacum's brig, reached the

---

[42] Miss A. J. White, *Ten Years in Oregon* (Ithaca, 1848), 78-9. See also Courtney Walker, "Sketch of Ewing Young," in *Transactions of the Oregon Pioneer Association, 1880,* 56-7.

Russian Post, Fort Ross, February 20, 1837, and a week later sailed into San Francisco Bay, carrying Young and the cattle company treasurer, Philip Leget Edwards, and their men.[44]

In the course of his negotiations with California officials regarding the cattle deal, Young found it necessary to continue to Monterey, where he landed March 2, 1837. To secure final permission, he had to go overland to Santa Barbara. The officials wanted their palms greased and apparently Young applied the unguent by purchasing more cattle than he actually took out of California. At all events, he returned to Monterey, where he met Edwards on May 10, 1837, and took time out to visit his old friend and employee, Job F. Dye, at his still house near Monterey.[45] Then, having been authorized by General Vallejo to purchase one thousand head of cattle, he seems to have bought seven hundred at three dollars per head at San Solano and five hundred more at San José, both purchases being negotiated through the government. However, after they started north on July 27, 1837, Edwards estimated, on August 14, that they were driving 729 head. On September 9, near Mt. Shasta, they still had about 680 head. The cattle were mostly heifers and Young refused to allow any to be killed for food until August 27. They followed the Hudson's Bay Company fur brigade's old trail over the Siskiyous and reached the Rogue River, where they encountered some Indian trouble.[46] Here Edwards ceased keeping his diary but we know they reached the settlements on the Willamette early in October

---

43 "Memorial of William A. Slacum" in *Senate Document no. 24,* 25 Cong., 2 sess., pp. 12-13.

44 Philip Leget Edwards, *California in 1837* (Sacramento, 1890), 7.

45 *Ibid.,* 20. See also Doyce B. Nunis, editor, *The Diary of Faxon Dean Atherton* (1964), 55-6.

46 *Ibid.,* 20-47. The route lay over rough country where, as Edwards wrote, the mountains "appear every day to grow more difficult. Hills peep over hills, and Alp on Alp."

with about 630 head. The total cost amounted to about $8.50 per head.[47]

Of the cattle he brought through, 135 head belonged to Young himself, making him the most considerable owner of livestock in the Oregon settlements. He was now able to expand his lumbering operations on Chehalem Creek, where he cut planks from Douglas fir and oak. He built himself a larger cabin. He constructed a grist mill, too, since he farmed more than 150 acres of wheat himself and since other settlers had need of one. Of course, he continued his fur trade on a small scale. The business records that he kept were very complete and they indicate that he acted in the capacity of banker for many of the settlers.[48] There was every indication that he was the leading citizen among the American settlers and that his old troubles with the Hudson's Bay Company were over.

In 1838 he was visited by John Augustus Sutter, who was soon to settle in California on a more princely domain than Young had carved out for himself in Oregon. Father Blanchet arrived in that year and borrowed money from Young. Thomas Jefferson Farnham came overland to Oregon in 1839 and visited Young on November 12 of that year.[49] One of Farnham's men, Sidney Smith, went to work for Young and lived with him. Through the Hudson's Bay Company, Young made arrangements to import some Kanakas from Hawaii, in 1839, to augment his labor force. In 1840, he found some gigantic bones of prehistoric animals and arranged to send them by ship to Boston, where they could and did receive study from those versed in such matters.[50]

[47] Hubert Howe Bancroft, *History of Oregon*, I, pp. 139-150.

[48] F. T. Young, "Ewing Young and his Estate" in *Oregon Historical Society Quarterly* (September, 1920), XXI, pp. 197-315. Young's "Day Book" and his "Register" are given here.

[49] Thomas Jefferson Farnham, *Travels in the Great Western Prairies, the Anahuac and Rocky Mountains, and in the Oregon Territory* (New York, 1843), 95.

[50] Holmes, 249-60.

However, Young had for several years been troubled with what was called dyspepsia. The ailment seems to have persisted from the time of his first arrival in Oregon. His records show that he received medicine for it from several doctors. Early in February, 1841, he had a particularly bad attack. He lingered a short while in delirium before he died. A post mortem examination was made and it was reported "that a sack of water had formed on his brain" and "that his stomach was destroyed by acid he was accustomed to take for his indigestion."[51] It is difficult to avoid the conclusion that he had suffered for years from an ulcer of the stomach, which probably also caused his death.

Ewing Young was at least forty-seven but probably not more than forty-nine years of age when he died. His death raised a problem in the American settlement in Oregon. There was no governmental authority to take charge of the disposition of his property. His death caused the first steps toward a provisional government to be taken. His property was disposed of at public auction, with Joe Meek acting as auctioneer. Sidney Smith bought up his land claim and much of his livestock. Old Mountain Men like Doc Newell, Joe Gale, and John Turner bought tools and livestock. George Gay bought seven books for a dollar and Courtney Walker paid $3.50 for a two-volume set of Shakespeare.[52] Some have supposed that Young carried this set with him in all his wanderings, but the price indicates it was in good condition and it seems more likely that he had bought it off some New England ship during his Oregon years. His estate was probably worth a good bit more than it actually sold for.

The government used some of the money to build a jail, as it was allowed to use it until final disposition could be made. Finally, in 1854, a young man arrived in Oregon

---

[51] *Ibid.*, 266.
[52] F. T. Young, *op. cit.*, 171-97.

bearing the name Joaquin Young and armed with creden-
tials from Taos setting forth that he was the son of Ewing
Young and Maria Josepha Tafoya. In addition to these
documents, sworn to by Charles Beaubien, Christopher
Carson, and Manual Lefevre, of Taos, testimony was heard
in Oregon. Joseph Gale certified that he knew of Young's
connection with Maria Tafoya and that the young man
resembled Young very much. Robert (Doc) Newell testified
that Young had told him he had a son in New Mexico. So
Joaquin Young was awarded and paid $4,994.64 by the
Territory of Oregon.[53] Joaquin Young left Oregon for
California, where his inheritance was soon dissipated.

The only physical description that has been recorded of
Ewing Young is that of the Oregon missionary, Elijah
White, who said he was "a large finely built man six feet
and perhaps two inches in height." [54] Farnham referred to
him as "the excellent old Captain" and evidently enjoyed his
company, but told nothing of his appearance. Hall Kelley
refers to him as "bold and enterprising" and speaks of having listened to the thrilling events of his eventful life but
unfortunately he did not set down any of these events in his
writings. Kelley considered that Young had lost some of the
refinements of civilization and more than once indicates that
he stood in some fear of him. At the same time, he admired
the way Young stood up to McLoughlin and he characterized him as of undoubted patriotism.[55] In this connection,
it is to be remembered that, although Young applied for

---

[53] *Ibid.*, 199-202. During the summer of 1954, while teaching a course in Western
History at Western State College, Gunnison, Colorado, the writer had in his class
two women named Romero, the wives of a grandson and a great-grandson of
Joaquin Young. They knew of his Oregon inheritance and said that he lost most of
it in gambling. They did not know of Ewing Young except through learning of him
in my course.

[54] White was interviewed by Frances Fuller Victor in San Francisco, February
18 and 21, 1879. W. H. Gray referred to Young as "a stirring ambitious man" and
Courtney Walker characterized him as "a candid and scrupulously honest man
. . . thorough going, brave and daring."

[55] Powell, 183-4.

Mexican citizenship for business reasons, he did not complete the process.

Young's attitude towards Indians was condemned by Hall Kelley, who gave instances of the death of Indians he believed to be innocent, at the hands of men traveling with Young. Two things need to be said regarding Kelley's charges. First, Kelley, who believed the Indians innocent, was afraid to speak up in their behalf. Secondly, Young merely permitted the action of others and did not initiate it himself.[56] Young's attitude with regard to Indians was much the same as that of other Mountain Men. He did not trust them because his experience told him this was a mistake. He also believed, and acted upon his belief, that Indians should never be allowed to have the upper hand and that retaliatory action should be swift and sure. Young was not, by choice, an Indian fighter or an adventurer. He was a business man. He took only so much action in the discipline of Indians, or for that matter, the discipline of his own men, as would enable him to continue with his business in an unhampered manner.

As a business man, Young was successful in a modest way from beginning to end. Had he lived longer he might have been successful in a much bigger way. He started with very little capital and succeeded in spite of some hard financial reverses. He was extremely independent and had the habit of command. It is notable that he was the leader of every expedition that he accompanied after his arrival in New Mexico. Sometimes he sent out men whom he did not accompany but, when he was along, he was in charge. When he acted in partnership with others, he seems to have been always at least an equal partner and more often a dominating one, after his first expedition with Becknell, where he was a minor partner.

---

[56] Powell, 351-3.

Young had a good eye for business opportunity. He sensed the necessity of exploiting new and untrapped areas for the fur trade. His mule venture, though not highly successful, was soundly based. He was the pioneer Oregon cattleman, wheat man, and lumber man.[57] These were the three products for which the Pacific Northwest became most famous, and that one man should have been responsible for the beginning of all three is an indication of a high degree of business acumen on the part of that man. Young's most outstanding traits were his unerring business judgment, his marked organizational ability, and his unyielding determination in the face of adversity. For this last quality, a rare one among men, he is much to be admired.

Except for a few letters, preserved by those to whom he wrote, Ewing Young left no records to aid the historian, beyond his expense accounts in Oregon. Had he left a journal of events on even one of his many trapping expeditions, he would loom much larger in the fur trade than he does. He operated in Mexico where such records might be a liability in relations with the government and, being his own boss, he did not need to render a report to anyone.[58] But the fact that we know as much as we do about his career, and that our knowledge comes almost entirely from those who crossed or joined his path in one way or another, are indication of the magnitude of his importance in the history of the American frontier. It is also significant that what was recorded about him by others was never what he said, but what he did.

Only Jedediah Smith and Peter Skene Ogden can be said to have surpassed Ewing Young in terms of penetration of wide areas of the Far West and sheer distance covered. They

[57] F. T. Young, *op. cit.*, 171 ff. Small amounts of wheat had been grown by French-Canadians prior to Young's acreage. He was the first American to grow wheat in Oregon.

[58] Cleland, *op. cit.*, 215-16.

surpassed him in terms of priority in time, but Young surpassed them in terms of independent individual enterprise as opposed to company enterprise. Even in chronological sequence, Young was right on their heels and probably more effective in opening routes to be followed by others.[59] In the southwest, he was already experienced before such eminent characters as St. Vrain and Carson had got started. He cannot be said to have furnished so dramatic a leadership as many of the principal characters of the fur trade were able to give. Nor can it be said that he was the hero of celebrated individual exploits to the extent that even minor characters were at certain stages of their careers. But it is doubtful if anyone connected with the fur trade touched the historical development of the American Far West at more frequent or more vital points than Ewing Young.

When we think of this grandson of a pioneer on the Watauga in eastern Tennessee coming to the end of his career in the Chehalem valley of far-off Oregon, before that land had become part of the United States, and when we consider that he came to that extreme westerly spot by strenuous marches through the borderlands of what was then northern Mexico, we must realize not only the enormous geographical distance traversed but also the tremendous span of American history encompassed in the career of Ewing Young.[60]

---

[59] Holmes, 3.

[60] Archer Butler Hulbert, *Frontiers; The Genius of American Nationality.* (Boston, 1929), 56.

Etienne Provost

by LeRoy R. Hafen
Brigham Young University

Etienne Provost was so early and so persistently engaged in the fur trade of the far West that in later years he was called "The Man of the Mountains."[1] In the literature referring to him, his name is given many spellings, the most common being Provot, Proveau, and Provost. Since he did not write, we are unaware of his preference; but the early French spelling is Provost, and the pronunciation was Provo. According to his birth certificate in Notre Dame, Montreal, he was born in Chambly, Quebec, in 1785.[2] His parents[3] were Albert and Marianne (Menard) Provost.[3]

Of his early life we have no account. He first appears in the records of the fur trade as a member of the Chouteau-DeMun trading venture to the Rocky Mountains, 1815-17. This was the initial large company to exploit the fur resources of the upper Arkansas and Platte rivers. After two years of trade and two efforts to get favorable cooperation from the Spaniards of New Mexico, the Americans were captured and taken to Santa Fe. They suffered confiscation of their furs and other property. After their release and return to Missouri "Etienne Provott" and ten other men of the party made a sworn statement about their treatment in New Mexico, saying in part, "We remained in prison (some of us in irons) forty-eight days."[4]

---

[1] Joseph Nicollet's report in *House Doc. 52*, 28 Cong., 2 sess.; reprinted as "Nicollet's Account, 1839," in *South Dakota Historical Collections*, x (1920), 113.

[2] Roy M. Provost, Long Beach, California, in a letter to me of July 24, 1964, says he saw the certificate at Montreal.

[3] Stella M. Drumm, "Etienne Provost," in the *Dictionary of American Biography*, XIV, p. 250.

[4] "Statement and proof in case of Chouteau and DeMun of their loss and treat-

When Mexican independence from Spain was achieved in 1821, a number of Americans, including some previously imprisoned by the Spaniards, again turned their faces toward New Mexico. During the year 1822 four American parties of traders and trappers journeyed to Santa Fe and during the winter of 1822-23 several men pushed westward and northwestward across the continental divide to trap western waters.[5] Among these probably was Etienne Provost, who had formed a partnership with one Leclerc (Francois ?) and was in New Mexico in 1823 and perhaps earlier.[6]

By 1824 Provost was not only on Green River, but had pushed over the Wasatch Mountains into the Great Basin. There he suffered a tragedy that gave his name to the river near Utah Lake. Warren A. Ferris, a fur man in the mountains, gives some details of the affair in describing the Snake Indians and one of their chiefs:

> There is one evil genius among them, called the *"Bad Gocha,"* (mauvais gauche – bad left-handed one) who fell in with a party of trappers, led by a well-known mountaineer, Mr. E. Proveau, on a stream flowing into the Big Lake that now bears his name, several years since. He invited the whites to smoke the calumet of peace with him, but insisted that it was contrary to his medicine to have any metallic near while smoking. Proveau, knowing the superstitious whims of the Indians, did not hesitate to set aside his arms, and allow his men to follow his example; they then formed a circle by sitting indiscriminately in a ring, and commenced the ceremony; during which, at a preconcerted signal, the Indians fell upon them, and com-

---

ment by the Spaniards," in *Annals of Congress,* 15 Cong., 1 sess., II, pp. 1957-58. All of the eleven men signed with an x. Michael Carriere in a supplemental statement, said that he served the two years and was paid $200 as wages. Presumably, Provost received the same amount.

5 "Answers of Augustus Storrs to Queries Addressed to Him by the Hon. Thomas H. Benton," etc., reprinted in A. B. Hulbert, *Southwest on the Turquoise Trail* (Denver, 1932), 93.

6 See Benjamin O'Fallon's correspondence from Fort Atkinson August 1, 1823, to the Governor of New Mexico, *Bulletin of the Missouri Historical Society,* XVI (October 1959), 22-24. Provost had been out to New Mexico and had returned to the United States by August 1, 1823.

menced the work of slaughter with their knives, which they had concealed under their robes and blankets. Proveau, a very athletic man, with difficulty extricated himself from them, and with three or four others, alike fortunate, succeeded in making his escape; the remainder of the party of fifteen were all massacred.[7]

Ferris, on his map of the fur country, places Provost's name on present Jordan River, which runs from Utah Lake to Great Salt Lake. So one would assume that he means to report the misfortune as taking place on the Jordan River of today. Kit Carson told his biographer about the Provost tragedy and said that it occurred on the river named for Provost. But he does not indicate whether he meant the present Provo River that flows into Utah Lake, or the Jordan, which runs from it. In any case, the Utah Lake vicinity would be the locality of the massacre.

William Gordon, in his "Report to the Secretary of War relative to the Fur Trade," dated at St. Louis, October 3, 1831, said that in 1824 "8 men were killed at one time by the Snakes on the waters of the Colorado who were in the employ of Provost & Lubro [Le Clerc]." In the tabulation at the end of the document the party is given as "Provost & Le Clerc's Company," and the place of the tragedy as "Reta [Euta or Utah] Lake."[8]

What appears as a likely explanation of this tragedy is given by British traders. Peter Skene Ogden, in his letter of July 10, 1825, writes:

We were also informed by the Americans the cause of the Snakes

---

[7] W. A. Ferris, *Life in the Rocky Mountains*, ed. by P. C. Phillips (Denver, 1940), 308-09.

[8] Gordon's Report of October 3, 1831, in *Sen. Doc. 90*, 22 Cong., 1 sess., p. 29. The numbers given as killed vary in the different accounts. Gordon, just cited, says eight. Ogden in his letter of July 10, 1825 (*Mississippi Valley Historical Review*, XXI, p. 68) says eight; and in another place says nine (Dale L. Morgan, *West of William H. Ashley*, Denver, 1964, p. 146). Ferris, previously quoted, says four or five escaped, of a party of fifteen. Kit Carson (D. C. Peters, *The Life and Adventures of Kit Carson*, New York, 1858, p. 246) says all were killed but four, but does not give the number in the party.

not being so friendly towards us as formerly, and which I regret to state the Americans too justly attribute to us, last Summer Mr. Ross consented most probably with such villains he had to deal with, he could not prevent them to go and steal the Snakes horses in which they succeeded, 12 of Mr. Ross's party were then absent in quest of Beaver and were with a large Camp of Snakes who were treating them most kindly, but on hearing this they pillaged them of all their horses and Furs, and in the scuffle they killed a Snake chief, shortly after a party of 7 Americans and one of our deserters fall on the Snakes Camp, and the Snakes lost no time in killing them all this also has greatly irritated the Americans against us, and they would most willingly shoot us if they dared.[9]

Etienne Provost has been credited with the discovery of Great Salt Lake.[10] If the attack on his party by the Snakes occurred on the Jordan River, as Ferris indicates, then Provost must certainly have seen the lake at least in the fall of 1824, if not before. James Bridger has often been given the honor of the discovery of the lake, but there is no contemporary record of this; and it is of doubtful authenticity. It is very likely that the Hudson's Bay Company trappers under Donald McKenzie and Michel Bourdon saw the lake while trapping the upper Snake River, Bear River, and as far east as Green River in the years 1818 to 1822.[11]

After the massacre of most of his men Provost led the remnant back over the Wasatch Mountains. On Green River, near the mouth of White River is a very large grove of sweet (round-leafed) cottonwoods, the twigs and bark of which provide excellent winter horse feed.[12] While Provost and some of his men wintered here, arrangements were made for his partner Leclerc to bring out supplies from New Mexico.[13]

---

[9] From Ogden's letter, edited by Frederick Merk, in the *Mississippi Valley Historical Review,* XXI (June 1934), 67-68.

[10] See the note written by W. M. Anderson in 1834 and published in J. H. Simpson, *Report of Explorations,* etc., 17.

[11] Alexander Ross, *Fur Hunters of the Far West,* edited by Kenneth A. Spaulding (Norman, 1956), 135-39, 152-53, 207-08.   [12] We visited this grove in 1962.

The East End of San Francisco Street at the Plaza in Santa Fe. Courtesy of Western History Collections, University of Oklahoma.

Don Fernando de Taos. This small Southwest hamlet, favored by American fur hunters for its frontier amenities and remoteness from Mexican authorities, was the hub of the Southwest fur trade and ranked behind only St. Louis in importance to the Far West American fur trade. From W. W. H. Davis, *El Gringo* (New York: Harper and Brothers, 1857). Courtesy of Western History Collections, University of Oklahoma.

In the spring Provost led a trapping party northward, and on May 23rd came upon Peter Skene Ogden's company on the Weber River, some distance east of present Ogden, Utah. The Britisher records in his diary: "early in the day a party of 15 men Canadians & Spaniards headed by one Provost & Francois one of our deserters, arrived."[14] In the afternoon a party of Ashley's men, led by Johnson Gardner, also appeared, and confronted Ogden with a demand that he leave this territory, which Gardner said belonged to the United States. Being south of the 42nd degree of north latitude, they were all interlopers upon Mexican domain, except perhaps Provost, who was trading from a New Mexico base and presumably had a Mexican license.

Provost returned to the Uinta country, probably to receive expected supplies. On his way there with twelve men, he met W. H. Ashley on the Duchesne River, June 7th. Ashley, who had boated down the Green River and had cached supplies near the mouth of the Uinta, now employed Provost to return to Green River and bring back the cached goods. This accomplished, the two co-leaders pushed on, crossed the Wasatch Mountains and descended to the headwaters of Provo River.[15] Ashley crossed Kamas Prairie and descended Weber River, while Provost made a trip to the lake to trade with the Utes.[16] After rejoining Ashley on June 21st Provost appears to have continued with him to the gathering place on Henry's Fork of the Green.

Here was held the first rendezvous in the Rockies. Provost was present, and he and his men traded eighty-three beaver skins to Ashley for $207.50 and received in exchange

---

[13] Pegleg Smith said that in February, 1825, some twenty-five of Provost's men returned from the Green River to Taos. – "Sketches from the Life of Peg-leg Smith," in *Hutchings' California Magazine,* v (1860-61), 319.

[14] "Ogden's Journal," as edited by David E. Miller in *Utah Historical Quarterly,* XX, p. 181.　　　　[15] Morgan, *Ashley,* 117.

[16] Ashley records on June 22nd: "Mr. Provo who went to the lake to trade with the Euteaw Indians returned last evening." *Ibid.,* 117.

coffee, tobacco, cloth, ribbons, etc.[17] Whether or not Provost remained after the summer rendezvous of 1825 to continue trade in the mountains or returned to New Mexico is not definitely known. His partnership with Leclerc presumably was terminated at this time. Jim Beckwourth says that Provost was at the summer rendezvous of 1826, but of this we are not certain.[18] In any event, he was back in St. Louis in September 1826, and was doing business with B. Pratte and Company. The account books of this organization give details. "Etienne Provos" received cash payments, September 22 to 30, totaling $458.25; and for the same period sundries of shoes, cloth, etc., amounting to $286.38. The cash received October 2 to 14 totaled $483.55 (and the last item was entered as "paid in full").[19]

The goods received in October indicated the stocking of a trading venture, for it included 12 barrels of whiskey, 1 of brandy, and 1 of rum; 4 dozen pipes, 186 pounds of tobacco, blankets, muslin, flannel, and sundries at $1770.[20] Whether these goods were for an independent venture or one for the company is not clear.

B. Pratte & Company apparently were courting Provost. B. Berthold, a member of the company, wrote to J. P. Cabanné from Fort Lookout on the upper Missouri, December 9, 1826: "I dare not advise anything about the project with Ashley. However, it seems to me that it would be well for us to assure ourselves of Provost, who is the soul of the hunters of the Mountains." [21]

In 1827 there were charges against Provost on the books

17 *Ibid.*, 119.

18 T. D. Bonner, ed., *Life and Adventures of James P. Beckwourth* (New York, 1931), 66. Beckwourth seems to mix events of the 1826 and 1828 rendezvous.

19 B. Pratte & Company Journal M, 349, 353. I went through various Journals and Ledgers of the American Fur Company in the library of the Missouri Historical Society at St. Louis in the summer of 1967. They are each numbered by a capital letter. Hereafter they will be cited by the letter and page.

20 Journal M, 357; Ledger H, 207.

21 Morgan, *Ashley,* 307-08. The original, in French, is in the Chouteau Collection, Missouri Historical Society.

in February, July, and August. Provost may have been in the regular employ of the American Fur Company in 1828, when this company was endeavoring to break into the trade of the Rocky Mountains, where Smith, Jackson, and Sublette were dominant. Provost would be an effective agent. It is said that in the fall of 1828 he was sent by Kenneth McKenzie to contact the trappers of the mountains and try to bring them with their trade to Fort Floyd, later Fort Union, at the mouth of the Yellowstone.[22]

Apparently Provost remained in the mountains during the winter working for himself, for in early July he was at Fort Tecumseh on the Missouri and was acting very independently. McKenzie wrote to Pierre Chouteau Jr. from the post on July 7, 1829:

> Provost is just arrived from his spring hunt, he is bound for St. Louis he will not give me five minutes to write you. . . Provost goes down to St. Louis in order to get equiped & come up immediately to trade with the Crows & trap at the same time. . . I forgot to say that Provost would not give me his spring hunt, but he owes me nothing.[23]

After arriving in St. Louis in the summer of 1829 Provost formed a trading agreement with the American Fur Company. In the company's account book it is entitled "Etienne Proveau's Advanture," and the sub-title is: "For the Following Sead [said] E. Proveau's advanture by him self (E. Proveau) in half with the American Fur Company." Then follows three pages of items listed and priced, including 9 horses ($47 to $110 each), 30 beaver traps, gunpowder, lead, pack saddles, rifles, tobacco, alcohol, etc. Provost provided $1450.17. Among the goods furnished by the American Fur Company were 3 dozen scalping knives,

---

[22] H. M. Chittenden, *American Fur Trade of the Far West* (1935 edition), I, p. 330.

[23] Quoted in D. L. Morgan and E. T. Harris, *Rocky Mountain Journals of William Marshall Anderson* (San Marino, Calif., 1967), 345. Hereafter cited as *Anderson Journals*.

3 doz. Wilson butcher knives, 18 bunches of blue glass beads, and 10 three-point blankets.[24]

At the time of this business transaction Provost married on August 14, 1829, Marie Rose Salle, *dit* Lajoie.[25] The accounts show expenditures on his wedding day for a razor, shaving box, brush, and a pair of three-point green blankets; and the next day the purchase of a "lot of ground, $100," and for "making plane and plotting for house, $5.00."[26]

Etienne soon left on his trading venture, leaving a credit with the company to be drawn upon by his wife as needed.[27] He reached the mouth of Kansas River in early October[28] and was in the Crow country during the succeeding winter.[29]

The "Proveau Advanture" appears not to have turned out well. Apparently Provost was induced to give up the partnership and accept employment with the American Fur Company's Upper Missouri Outfit, being given $605.59 for his share of the joint project.[30]

In January 1831, Provost carried dispatches from Kenneth McKenzie at Fort Union to Fort Tecumseh. The next month he set out with horses and goods to support Vanderburgh on Powder River.[31] His service was highly valued, for while the usual trader was given $200 per year, Provost's salary was $1,000 for the first and second years and $1400 for the third and fourth years.[32]

In the summer of 1832 Lucien Fontenelle and Provost

---

[24] American Fur Co. Account book P, 129, 542-44, under dates of August 13-15, 1829.

[25] Stella M. Drumm in the *Dictionary of American Biography*, XIV, p. 250.

[26] Book P, 544.

[27] The books show cash paid "to his lady " as follows: August 29, 1829, $50; Dec. 12, $25; Jan. 28, 1830, $22; April 6, $50; April 10, $47; June 8, $25; July 13, $25; Aug. 9, $50; and Aug. 23, $25. *Ibid.*, 544. Periodic amounts were given to her from Sept. 13, 1830, to July 30, 1831, totaling $175. Book R, 344.   [28] Book P, 542.

[29] McKenzie's letter of May 5, 1830, Chouteau-Papin Collection, Missouri Historical Society.

[30] This item is on the books under date of Oct. 10, 1830, Book T, 381.

[31] *South Dakota Historical Collections*, IX (1918), 147-49.

[32] Upper Missouri Outfit, Book T, 381; Book W, 244.

led a "Mountain Expedition" of some 50 men and 150 horses from Fort Union to supply the company's trappers under Vanderburgh. The train got a late start (June 19) and did not reach Vanderburgh, who was waiting at Pierre's Hole, so he moved over to Green River and there met the Fontenelle and Provost pack train on August 8th.[33] After delivering the goods Provost returned with the furs in September to the Missouri River and then continued with them down to St. Louis. Here, on June 5, 1833, he was advanced $465.46 from the Upper Missouri Outfit.[34] Then he went back up the river to Cabanné's post, north of Bellevue, where he was met and described by the famous steamboat captain Joseph LaBarge, who "found that veteran mountaineer, Etienne Provost, who at that time probably knew the western country better than any other living man. He had just come in for the purpose of guiding Fontenelle and Drips, partners in the American Fur Company mountain service, and owners of the trading post at Bellevue, to the Bayou Salade (South Park, Colorado), where they intended to spend the winter trapping beaver."[35]

The party did not go to South Park, but it did go to the mountains to the rendezvous on Green River. Fontenelle remained with the trappers, and Provost brought the furs back to the Missouri River, arriving at Fort Pierre on August 29, and then continuing on to St. Louis.[36] For his year's service ending in the fall of 1833, he was paid $1400.[37]

His accounts from October 10, 1833, to February 20, 1834, amounting to $1176.34.[38] From these it appears that he was converting his home into a lodging house.[39] He is listed as a tavern keeper in Account Book X, pages 56-58, with

---

[33] Ferris, *op. cit.*, 150, 156, 158.

[34] Book V, 142. His accounts during the preceding winter are also in Account Book V, 41, 48, 50.

[35] H. M. Chittenden, *History of Early Steamboat Navigation on the Missouri River* (Minneapolis, 1962), 38-39.   [36] *Anderson Journals*, 347.

[37] Book W, 244.   [38] Book U, 280.   [39] *Anderson Journals*, 347.

charges for such items as coffee, sugar, tobacco, a barrel of rice, one of rum, and 5 barrels of whiskey ($48.88). Then in March, 1834, there is a 4-page "Invoice of Mdze sent to Lucien Fontelle in charge of Etienne Proveau to be sold in the Rocky Mountains for the account and risk of the U.M.O., 1834." Among the items are blankets, coats, beads, rifles, shot, etc., to a total of $7,256.06.[40]

Provost took the route, new to the American Fur Company, by way of the Little Blue and Platte rivers. On the same trail, and ahead of Provost, went the companies of William Sublette and Nathaniel Wyeth. W. M. Anderson, accompanying Sublette, in his diary on May 6th mentioned passing Provost, and also Cerré (with supplies for Bonneville).[41] A report that Provost was attacked on the way out by Pawnees was denied; instead, he reached the rendezvous at Ham's Fork safely, and in mid-July set out on his return.[42] From Bellevue Lucien Fontenelle sent the furs (5,309 beaver and some other skins) down river to St. Louis and wrote on September 17, 1834: "I hardly think it necessary to have them [the furs] insured, although the river is very low, but the boat will be very strong, and will have a crew formed of the very best kind of voyageurs under the eyes of Mr. Cabanné, and the superintendence of Etienne Provost."[43]

The American Fur Company Accounts show the amount due Etienne Proveau on November 26, 1834, as $611.15. A subsequent entry shows $900 due him for services in 1835.[44] In 1835 Provost went out to Fort Lucien (Laramie) and returned to St. Louis in the winter. On January 31, 1836, W. L. Sublette wrote to Robert Campbell: "Since I came to St. Louis I have been informed that the two Prevoes has got in last evening and that they left Fontenell at St.

[40] Book Y, 6-9.　　　　　　　　　　　　　　　　[41] *Anderson Journals,* 73.
[42] *Missouri Republican* (St. Louis), August 26, 1834.
[43] Printed in Chittenden, *American Fur Trade* (1935), I, p. 308.　　[44] Book X, 58.

Charles. . . Report says Fontinell Intends quiting the Company and Joining Prevo and Some Others and gouing Out that he has purchases Some goods in Liberty." [45] On February 9, 1836, Sublette wrote again: "The two Prevoes left him [Fontenelle] at Liberty, sending whiskey up to the Black Snake hills." [46]

In the spring or summer of 1836 Provost, accompanied by Toussaint Racine, made a trip to "Fort Lucien." He was paid $225 for his service; Racine received $150. [47] They may have been escorting Joshua Pilcher, who went out for the American Fur Company to Fort Laramie and to the summer rendezvous and purchased the fort from Fitzpatrick and Fontenelle. [48] On July 20, 1836, Provost's account totaled $1265.81, less $228.97 charged for land he purchased. [49] During the winter of 1836-37 Provost made a 51-day trip to Council Bluffs, for which he was paid $100 on March 21, 1837. During his absence his wife had received $80 from the company. [50]

With the caravan taking trade goods to the summer rendezvous of 1837, Provost went as assistant to Captain Thomas Fitzpatrick. Also in the company was the famous Scotsman William D. Stewart and his personal party, including the capable artist Alfred Jacob Miller. No diary of the trip has come to light, but the numerous Miller paintings and accompanying written explanations by the artist give an important record of the journey. There were about thirty wagons and carts in the train. Two of the paintings are important to us here, for they give pictures of Provost in his fifty-second year. One shows the trapper train greeting a

---

[45] Sublette's letter of Jan. 31, 1836, to Robert Campbell, Missouri Historical Society. The second Provost may have been Etienne's brother or nephew.

[46] W. L. Sublette's letter of Feb. 9, 1836, to Robert Campbell, Missouri Historical Society. Photostat in my possession. [47] Book X, 210, 383.

[48] Pilcher reports progress in letters written June 21st at Fort Lucien, Chouteau-Papin Collection, Missouri Historical Society. Also, see this *Series*, I, p. 155.

[49] Book X, 257. [50] *Ibid.*, 58.

delegation of Indians. In the front line on his white horse proudly rode Stewart, and beside him are three other men, including on his mule, plump "Monsieur Proveau, a sub-leader, with a corpus round as a porpoise." In a second painting Provost is shown, fat and round, standing beside his tent and with hands cupped to his mouth is giving the loud call to gather in the horses.[51] In his fictionalized book *Edward Warren,* Stewart described "Old Provost the burly Bacchus" as "a large heavy man, with a ruddy face, bearing more the appearance of a mate of a French merchantman than the scourer of the dusty plains."[52]

Provost came back from the rendezvous in late summer and was paid $600 for his season's work. In December he left St. Louis for the posts in the Council Bluffs region.[53] When he returned to St. Louis on February 24, 1838, he brought news of the terrible smallpox plague that had wrought such havoc among the tribes on the upper Missouri.[54] Provost appears to have gone out to the rendezvous of 1838, for which service he was paid $450; and in December of that year was advanced $40 "for traveling expenses to Arkansas."[55]

Jean N. Nicollet, with young John C. Fremont as second in command, explored and mapped the country between the upper Mississippi and Missouri rivers in 1839. In their party, that set out from St. Louis on April 4th, went Etienne Provost. He was highly esteemed by the French scientist, who wrote in his report:

I had brought up [to Fort Pierre, present South Dakota] with me from St. Louis only five men who for my purposes were certainly worth ten. Four of them had proved themselves by numerous journeys

---

[51] M. C. Ross, *West of Alfred Jacob Miller* (Norman, 1951), plates 76 and 197, with accompanying written descriptions. Also see the frontispiece of this volume of the *Mountain Men* series for a reproduction of the latter painting referred to above.

[52] Quoted in *Anderson Journals,* 348.   [53] *Ibid.,* 348.

[54] J. A. Hamilton's letter of Feb. 25, 1838, in the Chouteau papers, Missouri Historical Society.   [55] *Anderson Journals,* 349.

across the prairies, as well as voyages over the Rocky Mountains. One
of they was Etienne Provost, known as "L'homme des montagnes," –
man of the mountains. I may remark here that these western voyageurs
are distinguished from the same set of men who do service in the
northern lakes by their never singing; and although apparently sullen
and discontented, are most faithful, cautious and courageous in the
midst of all dangers.[56]

Fremont's appraisal was almost identical.[57] Provost was
paid $750 for his service.

The business accounts show that Provost was in St. Louis,
at least in February, August, and November, 1840. This
year he formed a partnership with Clement Lambert.
"Proveau and Lambert, Tavern Keepers" did business during the winter of 1840-41.[58] During 1841 and 1842 his name
appears in many of the fur company business accounts, and
from April to September of 1842 he worked for the Upper
Missouri Outfit at $50 per month.[59]

Provost gave important assistance to James J. Audubon
when the great naturalist ascended the Missouri River and
gathered specimens for his collections and his famous draw-
ings. Provost was paid $50 per month from June 13 to
October 19, 1843.[60] Edward Harris, who accompanied
Audubon and kept a good journal of the expedition, mentions Provost frequently. On June 24 he writes:

Bell went out with Provost before breakfast to try and shoot a Doe in
the point of the woods above the Fort by imitating the cry of a Fawn
on an instrument made by Provost yesterday, he did not succeed.
After breakfast . . . I took Provost's call with me and tried it
in a small island of timber . . . at the first call a Doe came
within 30 feet of me.

June 29. Went out with Provost and killed two does by using his
call to bring the animals close. . .

July 8th   Squire killed a deer, using Provost's call.[61]

---

[56] Nicollet's Account in *South Dakota Historical Collections,* x (1920), 112-13,
reprinted from *House Document 52,* 28 Cong., 2 sess.   [57] *Ibid.,* 77.
[58] *Anderson Journals,* 349.   [59] *Ibid.*
[60] P. Chouteau Jr. & Co., Ledger GG, 348, Mo. Hist. Soc.

The party left Fort Union August 16th and returned down the river. At St. Charles, on the bend of the river a little above St. Louis, Provost became "extremely drunk," left the party, and went by land to St. Louis.[62]

Provost went up the Missouri River again in 1844 and was at Fort Union in October of that year. A year later his arrival at Fort Pierre on November 2, 1845, was noted.[63] His last voyage up river appears to have occurred in 1848, on a steamboat commanded by Joseph LaBarge.[64] Even though sixty-three years of age, old Provost still commanded respect and exercised authority among both whites and Indians. Captain LaBarge tells that the Yankton Sioux were preventing the men on the bank from loading wood on the steamboat.

> [Provost] then went out himself onto the bank where the Indians were, and said, "Now, men, come out here and get this wood." They came and loaded up. "Now go on board," he said, and they went entirely unmolested. Provost went last, and before descending the bank, turned toward the Indians and asked them: "Why don't you stop them? Are you afraid of *me*?" The truth is they were afraid of him, . . . and understood that he would stand no foolishness.[65]

Chittenden tells of Provost's skill in managing recruits being taken up the Missouri for service with the fur company.

> It was a favorite pastime with that veteran mountaineer, Etienne Provost, who was often sent up in charge of recruits, to compel an early settlement which would determine all blustering and quarreling. He would form a ring on the forecastle and compel every braggart to make good his claims before the assembled passengers and crew. One after another would succumb, until one man would emerge from the

---

[61] J. F. McDermott, *Up the Missouri with Audubon: Journal of Edward Harris* (Norman, 1951), 113-14, 119-20. For other incidents see pages 27, 98, 103, 124, 137, 140, 165, 169, 172-73, 176.   [62] *Ibid.,* 189.

[63] *South Dakota Historical Collections,* IX, p. 211.

[64] Morgan, in *Anderson Journals,* 350.

[65] Chittenden, *Steamboat Navigation,* 180.

contest victorious over all the others. He would then be awarded the championship, and receive a red belt in token thereof.[66]

Provost died in St. Louis on July 3, 1850.[67] His funeral service was held in the St. Louis Cathedral, still standing west of the new, impressive, 630-foot Gateway Arch in the Jefferson Memorial to Westward Expansion.

His wife and a grown daughter survived him. His estate papers are preserved in the Probate Court Records at St. Louis, where I examined them in July, 1967. A purported will of April 1, 1839, was denied by the widow and was not accepted by the Probate Judge, Peter Ferguson. "Mary Provot," the widow and her daughter Mary were the only heirs. An inventory of the estate and the final expenses are itemized. The real estate and personal property included the home at Second and Lombard Streets, St. Louis; some pieces of land in Lee County, Iowa; and lots in Keokuk, Iowa, and Nashville, Tennessee. Cash on hand was $102.70 and household furniture was appraised at $78.95.[68]

Etienne Provost was a legendary character in his own lifetime. When the Mormons founded a town beside Provo River in 1849 and named it Provo, they were unaware that the fabled character they honored was still alive in St. Louis.

---

[66] *Ibid.,* 128-29.

[67] The notice in the *Missouri Republican* of July 4th said: "Died. Yesterday afternoon, about 4 o'clock Mr. Etienne Provot, an old resident of this city.

"The friends and acquaintances of the family are invited to attend his funeral, This afternoon, at 4 o'clock, from his late residence on the corner of Lombard and Second streets, to the Cathedral burial ground."

[68] Among the furniture and household items listed were: 12 chairs, $12; 1 rocking chair, $2; 1 bureau, $8; 1 spitton, 10 cents; 1 setee, $1; 1 clock, $8; 1 glass globe, 50 cents; 1 picture of President of the U.S., 10 cents. The funeral expenses included: Extra fine finished velvet coffin with handles and overcase delivered, $25; for Hears [hearse] and 5 carriages, $17.50; 6 pairs gloves and 2 pieces of crepe, $7; 16 W Spurm Candles at 45 cents, $7.20; burial service St. Louis Cathedral, $6; attendant clergyman to cemetery, $3.

"Final Medicine" from the druggist: mustard, 10 cents; Flaxseed, 5 cents; Black tea, 5 cents; rice, 5 cents; pins, 5 cents; ginger, 10 cents; oil, 5 cents; Laudanum, 10 cents; whiskey, 10 cents; ginger, 10 cents; vinegar, 5 cents; Brandy, 10 cents; mustard, 10 cents; total $1.00.

Antoine Robidoux

by WILLIAM S. WALLACE
New Mexico Highlands University, Las Vegas

Joseph Robidoux II, the father of Antoine, was born in Canada in 1750, and moved to St. Louis in 1770. He was engaged in a successful fur trading enterprise and eventually acquired land holdings in Florissant, a suburb of St. Louis. In 1782 he married Catharine Rollet, from Cahokia, Illinois. Antoine Robidoux was the seventh of ten children from this union and was born in the newly acquired Robidoux home in Florissant, September 24, 1794.[1]

Upon the death of Joseph II in 1809, Antoine's oldest brother, Joseph III, took over the operation of the family business. Little is known concerning Antoine's early years. The earliest record shows that he enlisted in an artillery company in St. Louis on April 23, 1813, and was honorably discharged from the unit one month later.

Antoine Robidoux appears to have been in his late twenties when he first went to Santa Fe; the exact date is unknown. A petition of Antonio and Luis Robidoux for naturalization is dated at Santa Fe July 16, 1823.[2] Passports of February 29, 1824, and June 29, 1825, signed by William Clark, give Antoine permission to travel through the Indian Territory to Mexico.[3]

Records of Robidoux trips to New Mexico are found in the James Kennerly diary, kept at Fort Atkinson near Council Bluffs on the Missouri River. On September 30,

---

[1] This brief biographical article is based on the present author's book, *Antoine Robidoux, 1794-1860: a Biography of a Western Venturer* (Los Angeles, 1953). See that volume for the principal citations of sources. A portrait of Robidoux appears herein at page 15.

[2] Ritch Papers, no. 111, Henry E. Huntington Library.

[3] Found in the Huntington Library.

1824, Kennerly records: "Robidoux party started for St. Afee to day." The return trip is thus reported on August 30, 1825: "Tiltons Boat arived. & Robideaus party from Tous [Taos, New Mexico]." In a fortnight the party is again heading for New Mexico: "September 14. . . Robidous party started to day to Tous."[4]

The year 1825 may be established as the time of Antoine's permanent association with Santa Fe, Taos, and the intermontane corridor, northwest of New Mexico. From this year on, documentary sources link him regularly with these places rather than St. Louis. For the next two or three years he was evidently busy with trapping the numerous river valleys of the corridor area and getting the feel of the land.

Antoine became infatuated with the daughter of a Spanish captain of Santa Fe, Carmel Benevides, whom he married in 1828. Following his marriage he petitioned for and received naturalization as a Mexican citizen, taking the name of Don Antonio Robidoux. Becoming an expatriated American in Mexico at this time was linked more with the exigencies of business than any unpatriotic motive. Many American trappers and merchants in the Mexican-dominated areas of the West became citizens at this time in order to circumvent the Mexican law which limited the granting of trapping and trading licenses to Mexican nationals. David Waldo, a fellow American and friend of Antoine who participated in the Santa Fe trade for many years, also became a Mexican citizen. Waldo was later one of those who helped Antoine in his negotiations with the United States government to obtain a pension. A more immediate reason for Antoine's becoming a Mexican citizen was the loss of a stock of goods in Santa Fe by brother

---

[4] Edgar B. Wesley, ed., "Diary of James Kennerly, 1823-1826," in *Missouri Historical Society Collections,* VI (Oct. 1928), 75, 78, 80. We cannot be certain as to which of the Robidoux brothers led these parties, but Antoine was most likely the leader.

Francois because they were not Mexican citizens. Once a citizen, Antoine lost no time in improving his position. In 1830 he entered Santa Fe's political circles and within a few months had managed to capture the presidency of the *junta del ayuntamiento,* or town council, of Santa Fe.

Antoine Robidoux's activities in the intermontane corridor were to bring him the distinction of being one of the first penetrators of the entire corridor. Also, he was the first to remain long enough in a large section of the corridor to establish himself as one of the first permanent fixtures in the long and colorful history of Western America. This distinction came about through his establishment of a small fort on the banks of the Gunnison River, a short distance below the mouth of the Uncompahgre River, in what is now western Colorado.

The remains of the Gunnison fort site were finally obliterated in the 1880s by the incoming ranchers. The fort appears to have been located on a slope facing northwest and about forty chains southwest of the junction of the Uncompahgre and Gunnison rivers. The area in the vicinity of the fort was formerly well supplied with trees, but subsequent land clearing activities of ranchers and farmers have left the site a clear field. The Indians of western Colorado, Utah, southern Idaho, southwestern Wyoming, and of much of the remainder of the central portion of the corridor received their first regular taste of northern Indo-European civilization by the establishment of the fort on the Gunnison. Later Antoine's operations extended to a second fort which he constructed near the forks of the Uinta River and White Rocks Creek, in northeastern Utah.

The fort on the Gunnison seems to have been ready in time to take advantage of Senator Thomas Hart Benton's legislation which resulted in an appropriation for improvement of the route from Fort Osage on the eastern frontier to Taos on the west, and completed by 1825, thus opening the flourishing Santa Fe trade on a large scale. The Gunnison fort was located in the north and south travelway used by the trappers traveling from the New Mexico settlements to the beaver-rich valley of the Green River and on to Brown's Hole and, later, to Fort Bridger. The Gunnison fort was probably erected in the mid-1820s and the other, Fort Uintah, in the early 1830s. Judging from the disagreements in literature touching on the Robidoux forts it is doubtful whether exact dating will ever be possible unless some new documentary material is discovered.

For information on the activities of Antoine's forts by contemporary witnesses only two sources exist. The first of these is the recorded impressions of a Methodist clergyman from Ripley County, Indiana, who passed through the Gunnison Country in 1842 on the return trip of a journey he made to the Oregon Country. His comments on Antoine and his establishments are highly colored, but for lack of a variety of sources on the subject, they are useful.

Of Fort Uintah, the fort on the Gunnison, and his journey through the Gunnison Country to Taos he commented:[5]

> We had to wait there [at Fort Uintah] for Mr. Rubedeau about 18 days, till he and his company and horsedrivers were ready to start with us to the United States. This delay was very disagreeable to me, on account of the wickedness of the people, and the debauchery of the men among the Indian women. They would buy and sell them to one another. One morning I heard a terrible fuss, because two of their women had run away the night before. I tried several times to preach to them; but with little, if any, effect.
>
> Here I heard the mountain men tell of the miserable state of the Indian root-diggers. Numbers of them would be found dead from pure starvation; having no guns to kill game with, and poor shelters to live in, and no clothing except a few skins. These creatures have been known, when pressed with hunger, to kill their children and eat them! and to gather up crickets and ants; and dry them in the sun, and

[5] Joseph Williams, *A Narrative of a Tour from the State of Indiana to the Oregon Territory in the years 1841-42* (Cincinnati, 1843, reprinted 1921), 80-84.

pound them into dust, and make bread of it to eat! These creatures, when traveling in a hurry, will leave their lame and blind to perish in the wilderness. Here we have a striking example of the depravity of the heathen in their natural state. I was told here, of a Frenchman, who lived with an Indian woman, and when one of his children became burdensome, he dug a grave and buried it alive! At another time he took one of his children and tied it to a tree, and called it a "target," and shot at it, and, killed it!

Mr. Rubedeau had collected several of the Indian squaws and young Indians, to take to New Mexico, and kept some of them for his own use! The Spaniards would buy them for wives. This place is equal to any I ever saw for wickedness and idleness. The French and Spaniards are all Roman Catholics; but are as wicked men, I think, as ever lived. No one who has not, like me, witnessed it, can have any idea of their wickedness. Some of these people at the Fort are fat and dirty, and idle and greasy.

July 27th. We started from Rubedeau's Fort, over the Wintey River, and next crossed Green and White Rivers. Next night we lay on Sugar Creek, the waters of which was so bitter we could scarcely drink it. Here two of Rubedeau's squaws ran away, and we had to wait two days till he could send back to the Fort for another squaw, for company for him.

August 1st. We camped under a large rock, by a small stream, where we could get but very little grass for our animals. Next night we lay under the Pictured Rock, and being sheltered from the rain, slept very comfortable. Next day we traveled over rough roads and rocks, and crossed the Grand River, a branch of the Colorado, which runs into the Gulf of California, at the head thereof. Next day we crossed another fork of Grand River, and came to Fort Compogera, below the mouth of the Compogera River.

The last fork of the Grand River to be crossed by the party was what is now known as the Gunnison River. During the era of the Mountain Men it had been known as the Blue River. The Spanish appear to have called it the Rio San Xavier. A major tributary of the Gunnison, the Tomichi, was the name applied by the Indians to the entire course of the Gunnison River. The "Compogera River" was one of several forms used for spelling the name of the river which the Indians have called since time immemorial the "Uncompahgre."

August 14th (Sunday). I preached to a company of French, Spaniards, Indians, half breeds, and Americans, from Proverbs xiv, 32: "The wicked is driven away in his wickedness: but the righteous hath hope in his death." I felt the power of the word, and I believe some of the people felt it also. I spoke plainly and pointedly to them, and felt as though I would be clear of their blood in the day of eternity.

Next day we started to go through New Mexico, which is a long distance out of our route, to shun the range of the Apahoc Indians; and at night we camped on a small creek. Tuesday morning, we started, and crossed Union River; and next day, crossed Lake River, and lay that night on a small creek. Here are good, clear streams of water; but rough, hilly roads – rocky, sandy, and gravelly; good grazing for our animals all the way.

August 19th. We could see snow on the mountains. We had a very cold rain. Next day we came to Rubedeau's wagon, which he had left there a year before. He hitched his oxen to it, and took it along. This morning my moccasins were frozen so hard I had to thaw them by the fire before I could put them on. Here we had reports of Indian hostilities having commenced near Santa Fe, in New Mexico. Rubedeau sent an express to see whether it was so, and found it to be false.

Sunday, 20th. The frost was like a little snow. My blanket, which I used for a tent-cloth, being rained on the night before, was now frozen quite stiff and hard. We left this beautiful plain, which lies between two mountains, with a fine stream of water running through it. How different my feelings were on this Sabbath day, with my gun on my shoulder, and my butcher-knife and tomahawk by my side, in this heathen land, than they would have been in the pulpit with my Bible and Hymn-Book in my hand. On Sabbath evening I tried to preach to them; but being wet and cold after traveling through mountains and plains, we had but little satisfaction. Next morning my blankets and mocassins were frozen hard again. Some snow and rain fell during the night. I pray God to give me more faith, more patience, and more courage to preach the Gospel.

We are now on the waters of the Del Norte River, which falls into the Gulf of Mexico, and are passing the North Mountain. We are now traveling down Tous Valley, which leads down to Tous (a Span-

ish village) and Santa Fe. This is a beautiful valley, about eighty or a
hundred miles long. We remained sometime in this valley, encamped
by some beautiful streams of water, waiting for the express to return.
We then traveled for several days about a south course, and encamped
in the neighborhood of Tous. Here I tried in vain to persuade our
company to leave Rubedeau; for he would detain us too late, as winter
was coming on. It will be recollected that there were only four of us
in company, bound for the United States; and Rubedeau had hired
three of them to stay with him.

Having crossed a "Lake River" and passed down the
"Del Norte River," there is little doubting that the party
followed the route from the fort on the Gunnison which led
along the south side of the Gunnison River, its main course
being impassable because of the Black Canyon of the Gunnison which extends from a short distance up the river from
the fort to the upper valley of the Gunnison at present-day
Sapinero, Colorado. The trail then left the Gunnison at its
junction with the Tomichi up which it followed to the
Cochetopa Creek and thence over Cochetopa Pass and south
to the valley of the Rio Grande. Antoine's having picked
up one of his wagons along the trail is adequate testimony
to its use by the time of the early 1840s.

By Joseph Williams' repetition of the term "wickedness"
it may be surmised that there were a number of individuals
living in the forts. The eighteen days wait before setting out
for Taos suggests preparations for a movement of no small
proportions, and his care in itemizing the residents at the
Gunnison fort would suggest a body of individuals large
enough to make an impression upon him which, psycho-
logically, is indicative of more than just a few. Particularly,
since he felt there were enough present to preach to them.

Returning to Fort Uintah on October 7, 1842 (immediately following his arrival in the south with Williams),
Antoine was accompanied by a New Englander, Rufus B.

Sage, who has left the other account of a visit to a Robidoux fort. Sage tells us:[6]

A small party from a trading establishment on the waters of Green river, who had visited Taos for the procurement of a fresh supply of goods, were about to return, and I availed myself of the occasion to make one of their number.

On the 7th of October we were under way. Our party consisted of three Frenchmen and five Spaniards, under the direction of a man named Roubideau, formerly from St. Louis, Mo. Some eight pack mules, laden at the rate of two hundred and fifty pounds each, conveyed a quantity of goods; — these headed by a guide followed in Indian file, and the remainder of the company, mounted on horseback, brought up the rear.

Crossing the Del Norte, we soon after struck into a large trail bearing a westerly course; following which, on the 13th inst. we crossed the main ridge of the Rocky Mountains by a feasible pass at the southern extremity of the Sierra de Anahuac range, [an old name for the La Plata Mountains], and found ourselves upon the waters of the Pacific.

Six days subsequent, we reached Roubideau's Fort, at the forks of the Uintah, having passed several large streams in our course, as well as the two principal branches which unite to form the Colorado.

Sage makes no mention of the fort on the Gunnison. While at Fort Uintah, where he remained for ten days, Sage managed to make notes on matters concerning Fort Uintah as well as some of the fanciful tales of mountain men concerning civilized white tribes living in the wilds and a lost city. It might logically be assumed that he, being a New Englander, would have been as aware of "wickedness" as an Indianan, especially since the Indiana of Williams' day was itself still in the opening stages of experiencing the first shudders of civilization. However, Sage had nothing to say on the morals of Antoine and his companions. Of Fort Uintah and its activities in general Sage noted:

---

[6] Rufus B. Sage, *Scenes in the Rocky Mountains* (Philadelphia, 1846), 178, 182; or reprint ed. by L. R. and A. W. Hafen (Glendale, Calif., 1956), *in Far West and Rockies Series,* v, pp. 89-90, 97-98.

The trade of this post is conducted principally with the trapping parties frequenting the Big Bear, Green, Grand, and the Colorado Rivers, with their numerous tributaries, in search of fur-bearing game.

A small business is also carried on with the Snake and Utah Indians, living in the neighborhood of this establishment. The common articles of dealing are horses, with beaver, otter, deer, sheep, and elk skins, in barter for ammunition, firearms, knives, tobacco, beads, awls, etc.

The Utahs and Snakes afford some of the largest and best finished sheep and deer skins I ever beheld, – a single skin sometimes being amply sufficient for common sized pantaloons. These skins are dressed so neatly as frequently to attain a snowy whiteness, and possess the softness of velvet.

They may be purchased for the trifling consideration of eight or ten charges of ammunition each, or two or three awls. . . Skins are very abundant in these parts, as the natives, owing to the scarcity of buffalo, subsist entirely upon small game, which is found in immense quantities. The trade is quite profitable. The articles procured so cheaply, when taken to Santa Fe and the neighboring towns, find a ready cash market at prices ranging from one to two dollars each.

According to Sage, on this trip a total of about one ton of "goods" was hauled. This fact, plus his neglect to mention the Gunnison fort, may indicate that Antoine had developed a second trail for servicing Fort Uintah, either to save time or avoid the rougher, growth-shrouded Uncompahgre Plateau sector where supply trains were more vulnerable to attack. One ton of supplies would indicate only one fort was being serviced at that moment; each probably being serviced individually. A second trail may have left the old trail in southwestern Colorado and proceeded down the Dolores River to the Colorado, and then up the Colorado and across to Fort Uintah.

About the time Antoine was preparing to return to Fort Uintah with Sage, Dr. Marcus Whitman was starting out from his mission of Waiilatpu at the opposite end of the intermontane corridor, near present-day Walla Walla, Washington. Whitman's objective was Boston, where urgent affairs of the American Board of Commissioners for Foreign

Missions required his presence. With Asa L. Lovejoy as a companion he started out on October 3, 1842, on the first leg of his journey. Fourteen days and 528 miles later, they arrived at Fort Hall; a fort constructed at the confluence of the Portneuf and Snake rivers by Nathaniel Wyeth in 1834. After a two-day rest a new guide was retained and they pushed on to Fort Uintah, having decided to go south to Santa Fe along the east side of the corridor to avoid Indian hostility and escape the harsh winter that had set in early that year.

Sometime about November 1, they arrived at Fort Uintah where they met Antoine and possibly Sage. Also at the fort was Miles Goodyear, often termed "Utah's first citizen," a trader and trapper in the central portion of the corridor at that time. A fresh guide took Whitman and Lovejoy from here on to the fort on the Gunnison. On this leg of their journey they were forced to ford the Colorado River at present-day Grand Junction, Colorado. Lovejoy has left a description of that crossing.[7]

> This stream was some one hundred and fifty, or two hundred yards wide, and looked upon by our guide as very dangerous to cross in the present condition. But the Doctor, nothing daunted, was the first to take the water. He mounted his horse, and the guide and myself pushed them off into the boiling, foaming stream.
>
> Away they went completely under water – horse and all; but directly came up, and after buffeting the waves and foaming current, he made to the ice on the opposite side. The guide and myself forced in the pack animals; followed the doctor's example, and were soon drying our frozen clothes by a comfortable fire.

At the Gunnison fort the weather was getting colder. A guide obtained at the fort lost his way a few days after leaving the fort and forced a delay until another one could be sent from the fort. Food gave out and the pack animals and a dog were butchered. Probably despairing of ever getting

---

7 W. H. Gray, *History of Oregon* (Portland, 1870), 325.

back to Boston, and on the point of giving up, they stumbled into a group traveling from Taos who were able to give them enough food to last until they reached Taos, in the middle of December.

Because the severity of the weather encountered by Whitman is unlike that to be found south of the fort on the Gunnison it may be that he took the Gunnison-Cochetopa Pass trail. On modern highways this trail may be followed in a general way by taking U.S. Highway 285 from Santa Fe to Alamosa, Colorado; Colorado State Highway 17 from Alamosa to Moffat. From Moffat a back road to Saguache connects with Colorado State Highway 114, which then proceeds to Cochetopa Pass and down the Gunnison Valley. The San Luis Valley, through which this trail passed, may be entered from the east by what is now called Mosca Pass. At the time Captain Gunnison's expedition crossed this pass it was noted in the expedition's journal that they had crossed "Roubideau's Pass." In 1848 Frémont, on his fourth expedition, had also used Robidoux Pass. Being a gateway from the east as well as the south, and having been formerly named after Antoine, it is possible that Antoine left the trail just described occasionally to go directly to the Missouri Country from his forts without first going south to Taos or Santa Fe.

Indian hostility was increasing throughout the 1830s and 1840s because of one of the West's first manufactured products, a strong whiskey known as "Taos lightning," which increased the wrath of the Indian, who was already plagued with having his fellows kidnapped and sold into slavery in the villages of New Mexico and being promiscuously slaughtered by the whites. The illegal use of "fire water" was quite enough to bring the Indian hostility to a head. Therefore, it is little wonder that only two years after Sage's trip to Fort Uintah, the Utes attacked the fort, killed the men, carried off the women, and touched off a period of warfare that was to continue in the intermontane corridor's various regions for another forty years. The following letter, exchanged between the Sublette brothers, records how the news of the massacre at Fort Uintah was received at Taos:

TAOS, OCTOBER 20, 1844

DEAR BROTHER I come to this place a fieu days since mearly to pass the time and get provisions for the winter as there is nothing to be done. Brother Solomon is here with me and is doing nothing as my self.

The Youteau Indians are at ware with the Spaniards and whites a Spaniard come in a fieu days Since who was trapping with one other his companion was killed he escaped went to the Fort of Rubadoux where he found them all killed five or six Spaniards and one American from there he came to this place without shoes coat or no provisions which took him 14 days the Spaniards have a new gavenor in office he has raised the duty on the traiders – it was at Five hundred dollars pr wagon he has got it to six. . .   A. W. SUBLETTE

To: W. L. Sublette, St. Louis.

Late in 1844 (or early in 1845) Antoine abandoned his fort on the Gunnison and moved to St. Joseph, Missouri.

In 1846 he joined General Stephen Watts Kearny as an interpreter in Kearny's campaign to the West in the War with Mexico. After the occupation of New Mexico he remained with Kearny in the advance on California. On December 6, 1846, Antoine received a lance wound in the back during the battle of San Pasqual. The St. Joseph *Gazette's* obituary of Antoine presumed that he had lived in California for several years. His brother Louis by this time had become a major landowner in Southern California having acquired control of large portions of what are now San Bernardino, Orange, and Riverside counties.

Antoine's residence in California remains speculative. In any event, residence in California was not taken up immediately, because Antoine later asked for reimbursement of expenses incurred in taking a boat from California to New

Orleans. The pain of the wounds received at San Pasqual was responsible for his returning to Missouri by boat, according to the report of the Congressional Committee on Military Affairs (*House Reports no. 226,* 34 Cong., 1 sess., III), "via Peru, Jamaica, and other places." The last five years of his life were spent in St. Joseph where he died on August 29, 1860.

There is no record of Antoine and his wife Carmel ever having any children of their own, but they did adopt a young girl while living in Santa Fe named Carmelette. When the family moved to St. Joseph just before the Mexican War, Carmelette was by then a young woman. Shortly after arriving in St. Joseph she married Isador Barada, a friend of the Robidoux clan. Shortly after the birth of their first child, a girl named Amanda, Carmelette died quite suddenly and Carmel, no longer having any ties in St. Joseph since the death of Antoine, returned to Santa Fe with Amanda. Later Amanda married an Indian agent and Carmel lived with them until her death in 1888 at Durango, Colorado.

William Sherley (Old Bill) Williams

by FREDERIC E. VOELKER
St. Louis Westerners

William Sherley Williams, fourth of the nine children of Joseph and Sarah (Musick) Williams, was born June 3, 1787, in a cabin on Horse Creek, old Rutherford County, North Carolina. Both parents, of predominantly Welsh ancestry, were natives of Virginia. During the Revolution, Joseph served against both the British and their Cherokee allies until incapacitated by a bad leg wound.[1]

In the remote area of the Williams farm, under the east front of the Blue Ridge, where "educational facilities were . . . meagre and insufficient," the Williams children were taught the fundamentals, some Latin, and the Baptist precepts by a knowledgeable mother. One of the boys, Lewis, became a famous Missouri preacher.[2]

About 1793, encouraged by "a kind of proclamation issued by the Governor of the Spanish posts at the Illinois" (Upper Louisiana Territory) inviting settlers, many members of the Musick-Williams clan of North Carolina decided to move west. In July 1794, Joseph Williams disposed of his 650 acres in Rutherford County, packed up his family and goods and joined the exodus.[3]

---

[1] William Terrell Lewis, *Genealogy of the Lewis Family in America* (Louisville, 1893), 57, 187, 191-92; William R. Vaughan's copy of Sarah Williams' family *Bible* record (ms.); Record of Deeds, Book E-1 (ms.), 413-14, Rutherford Co. Reg. of Deeds, Rutherfordton, N.C.; writer's notes of an interview with C. E. Vaughan, Owensville, Mo., grandson of the subject's sister Arabella, May 28-29, 1936. The Williams farm lay in that part of old Rutherford Co. now within Polk Co.

[2] Clarence W. Griffin, *History of Old Tryon and Rutherford Counties, North Carolina* (Asheville, 1937), 122; R. S. Duncan, *A History of the Baptists in Missouri* (St. Louis, 1882), 79; writer's field notes, Aug., 1937; C. E. Vaughan interview, *loc. cit.*

[3] *Debates and Proceedings in the Congress of the U.S.* (Washington, 1834), 624; Record of Deeds, *loc. cit.*, Book M-Q, 237-38.

The only regularly traveled route northwest, a rough horse-trail, crossed the Great Smoky Mountains near Warm Springs, on the French Broad River, some fifty-five miles from the Williams farm, went northwest across Tennessee and into Kentucky at Cumberland Gap, thence by the Wilderness Trail to Crab Orchard, and farther northwest to the Falls of the Ohio (Louisville). The clan crossed the Ohio there or at some point downstream, and ultimately reached Whiteside Station, Northwest Territory, fifteen miles south of St. Louis.[4]

In the summer of 1795 Joseph Williams and his family crossed the Mississippi into Spanish Louisiana Territory and halted at a fortified settlement called Owen's Station, or Village à Robert, sixteen miles northwest of St. Louis and five miles from the Missouri River. On August 26, 1796, the Spanish government granted Joseph eight hundred arpens of land (about 680 acres) on the south bank of the Missouri, four miles west of Owen's Station.[5]

From the new farm the Williams boys ranged widely, hunting, trapping, perfecting woodland skills. Will, as his family called him, gradually expanded his trapping radius, and one day, after a long hunt, arrived at a village of the Osage Indians, on the waters of the Osage River, two hundred miles from home. There he decided to stay. He was about sixteen when one day he suddenly appeared at home and announced that thenceforward he would live as an Osage.[6]

---

[4] Thomas Perkins Abernathy, *From Frontier to Plantation in Tennessee* (Chapel Hill, 1932), 154-55, 157 (map); William Allen Pusey, *The Wilderness Road to Kentucky* (N.Y., n.d.), 1, 15, 50 (map), 55, 62, 65-66, 113-29; Col. David R. Musick, autobiographical note (typescript copy), Etta Musick Nason papers (private), St. Louis. Warm Springs is now Hot Springs, Madison Co., N.C.; and Whiteside Station is now Columbia, Monroe Co., Ill.

[5] Hunt's Minutes, vol. 1 (typescript copy), 208, Mo. Hist. Soc., St. Louis; *American State Papers, Public Lands* (Washington, 1861), VIII, pp. 852-53; Field Notes, U.S. Surveys, St. Louis County, Mo. (ms.), II, p. 169, Surveyor's Office, Clayton, Mo. Owen's Station is now Bridgeton, St. Louis Co., Mo. The Williams farm was confirmed as U.S. Survey 282.

[6] Duncan, *op. cit.*, 79-80; Draper's Notes, vol. 22, Trip 1868, 1 s (ms.), 167-68;

Will settled with the Big Hill band of the Great Osages who liked and respected him. He learned their language, hunted with them, counseled them in their dealings with the whites, acquired considerable influence among them, undoubtedly was adopted by the Big Hills, married, in native manner, one of their girls by whom he had two daughters, Sarah and Mary, and remained with them nearly a quarter of a century.[7]

While pursuing the indispensable, westward-ranging buffalo, Will learned much about the immense area between the Osage country (along the waters of the lower Missouri and the middle Arkansas) and the Rocky Mountains, and there are indications he may have reached some northwestern beaver streams and the settlements of the Spanish Southwest long before the organized brigades of beaver hunters.[8]

Vaughan interview, *loc. cit.;* writer's notes of an interview with Perry and Josie Williams, Brinktown, Mo., grandchildren of the subject's brother John W., June 2, 1936.

[7] John Joseph Mathews, *The Osages* (Norman, 1961), ix, x; *American Missionary Register* (cited below as *A.M.R.*), vol. II, no. 10 (Apr. 1822), 402; writer's notes of a conference with members of the William S. Mathews family, Pawhuska, Okla., Aug. 30, 1933. John Joseph Mathews is the grandson of Sarah (Williams) Mathews, daughter of the subject.

[8] George Champlin Sibley, in *The Road to Santa Fe,* ed. Kate L. Gregg (Albuquerque, 1952), 253; John D. Hunter, *Memoirs of a Captivity Among the Indians of North America* (London, 1824), 455; George Frederick Ruxton, *Life in the Far West* (N.Y., 1849), 123; *Denver Republican,* Oct. 5, 1897, interview with Philander Simmons; [M. C. Field], "The Old Man of the Mountains," New Orleans *Daily Picayune,* Jan. 4, 1844; statement of Anson Rudd, Aug. 2, 1901 (typescript), Pioneer Envelope, F. W. Cragin Papers, Pioneers' Museum, Colorado Springs, Colo.

Operating independently, frequently alone, and keeping no written record, so far as known, the precise date of Williams advent in the Rocky Mountains is problematical. He appears to have known his way around the mountains before his first recorded trip. There is a living tradition among the Osages that some of their people had reached not only the Ute country, but the land of living "Cliff Dwellers" still farther southwest, at least seventy-five years before Williams first met the Osages. Mathews, *op. cit.,* 149-53. That Williams made excursions with the Osages far to the west, *ca.* 1803-1825, can hardly be doubted.

Ruxton indicated Williams first went to the mountains about 1807; Simmons said Williams went to what is now Colorado in 1808; Field indicated Williams had been in the mountains since 1815; and Rudd indicated Williams went to the mountains in 1807. All these men were personally acquainted with Williams.

When, in the spring of 1812, war broke out on the Missouri frontier, and Britain's Indian allies north of the Missouri River began their murderous raids, Will volunteered for service with Captain James Callaway's Company C, Mounted Rangers, assigned as scouts and spies in the area "northeast of St. Charles," in the Missouri Point-Piasa country along the Mississippi. He appears on the company roster as "fourth sergeant." His length of service is problematical, but he was back at the Osage village by December 1813. On September 15, 1814, his daughter Mary was born.[9]

Williams is recorded as official interpreter for George C. Sibley, United States Indian Agent and factor at Fort Osage on the Missouri River, from May 13, 1817, to June 30, 1818, and probably served in that capacity for a longer period; and he also pressed and packed furs at the fort. His daughter was baptised in the Catholic faith in July 1819; and on April 28, 1820, he sold to a kinsman the forty acres of the home farm willed him by his father, who had died the preceding January.[10]

In July 1821, a sub-station of the United States factory was established on the Marias des Cygnes River, about five miles from its mouth, near the Osage villages, with Paul Baillio as sub-factor and Williams as official interpreter. Next month a band of New England missionaries, sent by the United Foreign Missionary Society with the blessing of the government, arrived in the Osage country.[11]

9 John R. Callaway papers (mss.), Joseph Maher Coll., Mo. Hist. Soc., St. Louis; Edgar B. Wesley, "James Callaway in the War of 1812," *Missouri Historical Society Collections,* vol. v, no. 1 (Oct. 1927), 77; Register Baptismalis Nationis Osagaiae (ms.), [7], Monastery of St. Francis de Hieronymus, St. Paul, Kan.

10 Receipts from Wm. S. Williams to G. C. Sibley, June 30, 1817 (mss.), Fort Osage papers, Ret. Files, Ind. Trade, Off. of Ind. Affrs., Washington; Geo. C. Sibley Memo. Book, 1812-1818 (ms.), Sibley papers, Lindenwood Coll., St. Charles, Mo.; Register Baptismalis, *loc. cit.;* General Records, Book I-J (ms.), 283, Off. Recorder of Deeds, City Hall, St. Louis, Mo. A military post, Indian agency and factory, Fort Osage was established in 1808, on the south bank of the Missouri, some fifty river miles east of present Kansas City, Mo.

11 *A.M.R., loc. cit.,* vol. I, no. 12 (June 1821), 485; vol. II, no. 7 (Jan. 1822), 275; vol. II, no. 9 (Mar. 1822), 351; vol. II, no. 10 (Apr. 1822), 405.

This was an important event in Williams' life because it revealed his intellectual capacity, and his impatience with the white man's civilization and Christianity as he saw them practiced; it led to many a widely spread humorous tale about "Parson Williams"; and, it appears, contributed to his domestic infelicity and his leaving the Osages, who were being crowded by whites and "removed" Indians.

To the missionaries Williams immediately became a benefactor by furnishing practical information about the Osages, and volunteering his services as interpreter and translator. By the end of 1821 he had produced a two-thousand-word Osage-English dictionary, had a grammar well under way, and was constructing sentences.[12] Subsequently completed, the material was made into a book.[13]

In the late summer of 1822 Williams served as guide and interpreter in the Osage country for generals Henry Atkinson and Edmund P. Gaines and other army officers on tours of military inspection and of conciliation between the Osages and their enemies, the Cherokees and their allies.[14]

By this time relations between Williams and the missionaries had cooled, due to Williams' reluctance to interpret sermons orally, and the missionaries' uncertainty about the "accuracy" of his translations; and because of his great influence with the Osages, they dared not preach without his approval. By this time, too, Williams had acquired, in the

---

12 *Ibid.,* vol. ii, no. 8 (Feb. 1822), 329; vol. ii, no. 10 (Apr. 1822), 402, 406; vol. ii, no. 12 (June 1822), 489.

13 *Washashe Wageressa Pahugreh Tse: The Osage First Book* (Boston, 1834). The volume nowhere names the compiler. The title literally translates: Osage First Lines of Writing. James Constantine Pilling, *Bibliography of the Siouan Language* in Bulletin [5], Bureau of Ethnology (Washington, 1887) names as compilers: William B. Montgomery and W. C. Requa, two of the missionaries instructed by Williams. It is a small book of 126 pages with "familiar sentences in Osage and English interlinear," and selections from the Old and New Testaments, and spelling lessons in the Osage. Only five hundred copies were issued and the work is now very scarce.

14 Journal of Union Mission, Aug. 29 and Sept. 2, 1822 (ms.), Okla. Hist. Soc.; *A.M.R., loc. cit.,* vol. iii, no. 5 (Nov. 1822), 186; vol. iv, no. 2 (Feb. 1823), 41, 43; vol. iv, no. 3 (Mar. 1823), 75.

accepted Osage manner, two more wives. His thoughts and his manner of life distressed the missionaries and they fervently prayed for his redemption, while Williams continued to interpret for them.[15]

When the act of Congress abolishing the Indian factory system became effective among the Osages in the late summer of 1822, the sub-factory on the Marias des Cygnes was closed and Williams lost his job as its interpreter. He became an independent trader among the Indians of the middle Arkansas River area, and appears to have prospered. About this time he moved with his enlarged family to a new Osage village not far from his trading post on the Neosho (Grand) River. On May 30, 1824, he was granted a one-year license to trade with the Osages and immigrant Kickapoos at the "Fork of Grand River."[16]

During the summer and early fall of 1824 Williams devoted considerable time, as interpreter, to the case of Bad Tempered Buffalo, Little Eagle, and three other Arkansas Osages charged with the murder of Major Curtis Welborn; all parties being poachers on Choctaw land in Arkansas Territory. This included trips to Cantonment Gibson and the Arkansas Osage village to arrange the surrender of the Indians, and to Little Rock for the trial. Only Bad Tempered Buffalo and Little Eagle were convicted, and five months later pardoned by President John Quincy Adams.[17]

---

[15] *A.M.R.*, loc. cit., vol. III, no. 3 (Sept. 1822), 92; vol. III, no. 5 (Nov. 1822), 185-86; vol. III, no. 6 (Dec. 1822), 212; vol. V, no. 9 (Sept. 1824), 272-73, 275; vol. VI, no. 7 (July 1825), 217.

[16] *Ibid.*, vol. III, no. 5 (Nov. 1822), 188; vol. IV, no. 2 (Feb. 1823), 44-45; vol. IV, no. 3 (Mar. 1823), 75; vol. VI, no. 7 (July 1825), 217; Boat Account, Fort Osage, 1823-24, and Blotter, 1823 (mss.), Sibley papers, *loc. cit.;* License no. 16, 1824, Indian Trade (ms.), Mss. Div., Wisc. Hist. Soc. The "Fork of Grand River" was the area on the Neosho (Grand) River where several feeder streams reached the river, in the extreme southeast corner of present Kansas. Deliberate vagueness was characteristic of many early Indian trading licenses.

[17] *A.M.R.*, loc. cit., vol. V, no. 5 (May 1824), 138-40; vol. V, no. 6 (June 1824), 178-79; vol. V, no. 10 (Oct. 1824), 301-04; vol. VI, no. 1 (Jan. 1825), 22; Journal of Union Mission, *loc. cit.*, Dec. 4, 1823, June 10 and Aug. 27, 1824; President Adams pardon (ms. copy), Osages, Ret. Files, Off. Ind. Affrs., Washington.

Later that fall, perhaps by pre-arrangement, Williams headed for the Rocky Mountains. He probably had little time for trapping on his long trans-mountain trip to a camp near Flathead (Salish) House, a Hudson's Bay Company post on Clark's Fork of the Columbia River. There, as a free trapper during the early winter of 1824-1825 he worked closely with a brigade of William H. Ashley's trappers under Jedediah S. Smith; and they encountered plenty of Indian hostility.

According to Thomas Eddie, one of Smith's men, Williams, hunting afoot up the fork for meat, ran into a hostile party of Blackfeet, wandering far from their home grounds east of the mountains, killed four of them and escaped by slithering into a side canyon, where he hid for two days while the Indians hunted for him. On the third day he sneaked to the top of a crag in time to watch his frustrated enemies leave the vicinity. Fearing the presence of more Blackfeet on the banks of the fork, Williams fashioned a rude raft and quietly floated down Clark's Fork to the trappers' camp.[18]

It appears that about this time, Williams, at thirty-seven, prematurely acquired the cognomen "Old Bill" by which he was known the rest of his life.

By the end of May 1825, Bill had arrived back at the Osage village. When the land cession treaty between United States Commissioner William Clark and the Osages was signed on June 2, 1825, in St. Louis, one section of land was reserved for each of Williams' daughters; and Williams, at the request of the Osages, was awarded $250 for "credits given" them. During the next two months Bill put his business affairs in order and prepared for a long absence.[19]

---

[18] Boat Account, Fort Osage, 1823-1824 (ms.), Sibley papers, *loc. cit.;* Frank Triplett, *Conquering the Wilderness* (St. Louis, 1883), 431-32, 454-55. See also the writer's "Thomas Eddie," in this *Series,* I, p. 276, and the sources there cited.

[19] Journal B, 1825-1826, Bernard Pratte & Co. (ms.), 170, Mo. Hist. Soc., St. Louis; Power of attorney, June 13, 1825, Williams to his brother James, Gray Twp., Gasconade Co., Mo. (ms.), Cons. Files, U.S. Gen. Acctg. Off., Washington.

By August 1 he had joined the government expedition under George C. Sibley, Thomas Mather and Benjamin H. Reeves, commissioners, to survey and mark the trade road from Fort Osage to Santa Fe, New Mexico, and negotiate its rights-of-way through the Indian country. Bill was engaged as "Interpreter, Runner, Hunter, etc." Because of his wide acquaintance and high reputation among the Osages his initial duty was to call their leaders to a treaty council on the Neosho River at the place Sibley named "Council Grove." The signature of William S. Williams, interpreter, was among those affixed to the pact on August 10.[20]

From Council Grove, Bill rode to summon the headmen of the Kansa village, some forty-five miles northwest. The treaty with the Kansas was signed August 16 at Sora Kansa Creek, and again Bill was signatory.[21] Sibley consistently minimized Bill's services as diplomat and interpreter.[22]

The expedition headed west, crossed the Little Arkansas and struck the Arkansas about 270 miles west of Fort Osage. They followed the north bank of the river about 190 miles, crossed to the south bank and traveled south forty miles across the "Cimarron Desert" to the Cimarron River, which they followed to Upper Cimarron Spring, rode south and crossed the North Canadian River, passed Rabbit Ears Mountain, and continued west to a point about seventy miles directly east of Taos, New Mexico. From there they were guided a hundred devious miles through the Sangre de Cristo mountain mass by "Francisco Largo (a civilized Comanche Indian)" to Taos, where they arrived October 30, 1825.[23]

---

20 Voucher 8, Settlement 452, Mexican Road Commrs., 1836 (ms.), G.A.O.; Sibley, op. cit., 7, 34, 57, 59, 253; Indian Treaties, comp. S. S. Hamilton (Washington, 1826), 419. Council Grove is now a municipality in present central Morris Co., Kan.

21 Sibley, op. cit., 59, 61-63, 252-53; Indian Treaties, op. cit., 421. Sora Kansa Creek is a small branch of Turkey Creek, flowing near present Elyria, McPherson Co., Kan.

22 The late Dr. Kate L. Gregg, editor of the Sibley journals (sup.), expressed to the writer a concurring opinion.

On November 14 Bill was granted a leave of absence to go trapping, and started "down the Rio del Norte" (Rio Grande). The record is silent as to his destination, but the lower Rio Grande waters as well as the Gila headwaters toward the southwest were acknowledged beaver waters. Bill returned to Taos on February 24, 1826, reported "good success," and began gambling. On March 9 he was still gambling and had "not yet joined the Service"; and that ended his tenure with the road commissioners.[24]

Soon after that Bill started back to the Northwest and, losing no time, joined his companions of the 1824-1825 season at or near Great Salt Lake. They set out for the Yellowstone by way of Bear River, turned east, and between Bear River Divide and Commissary Ridge picked up the Sublette Cut-off, followed it and crossed Green River in the vicinity of Names Hill. As they approached the Wind River Mountains they had daily skirmishes with the pugnacious Blackfeet. When they arrived at a point about twenty miles east of Sublette's Spring, Bill and three others started north into the mountains on a short hunt, with the intention of crossing the mountains and rejoining the main party east of the mountains.[25]

In the southern end of the Wind River Mountains Bill's trappers were thrice attacked by Blackfeet, but came off with Williams, Bill Gordon and Joe Lajeunesse only superficially wounded. They fled along the route laid out, probably over Sioux Pass, onto the Little Popo Agie and the

23 Sibley, *op. cit.*, 63-66, 68, 70-80, 82, 84-111, 254-60. The point 270 miles from Fort Osage would be the vicinity of present Sterling, Rice Co., Kan.; and 190 miles farther west would be at about present Deerfield, Kearny Co., Kan.

It appears that from present Mt. Dora, just west of Rabbit Ears Mountain, both in present Union Co., N.M., they followed a fairly easy road to the neighborhood of present Springer, Colfax Co., N.M. Some earlier road maps (*e.g.* Conoco) show a dirt road following this identical route.   24 Sibley, *op. cit.*, 132, 152, 155.

25 Triplett, *op. cit.*, 415, 432-33. Triplett had the details from Thomas Eddie, one of the main party. Names Hill is in present northeast Lincoln Co., Wyo. Sublette's Spring is in present south central Sublette Co., Wyo.

Popo Agie, which they followed to its junction with Wind River, which presently becomes the Bighorn. There they joined the main party and continued down the Bighorn. They eluded a Blackfeet ambush, but not without serious wounds, and arrived at their semi-permanent camp on the Yellowstone near the mouth of the Bighorn.[26]

Late in the summer of 1826 Bill returned to New Mexico where, on August 29, at Santa Fe, he and Ceran St. Vrain and their thirty-five "servants" were given a "passport" by Governor Antonio Norbona "to pass to the State of Sonora [Arizona] for private trade." Although Norbona suspected that the trappers' real purpose was to hunt beaver his official records protested that the "passport" did not include the privilege of "lingering" to trap beavers on the rivers of Sonora. Undeterred, that fall the trappers penetrated deep into the Apache country north of the Gila, working it and its upper affluents.[27]

One day, as Bill worked alone, he was surprised by the Apaches, captured, "stripped of everything, clothes, arms, traps and mule and turned loose in the desert." Stark naked, afoot, and without a weapon, he headed northeast toward Taos. After a 160-mile travail through the White Mountains, the arid valley of the Little Colorado, and the desert country of the Zunis, Bill was picked up among the mesas by the Zunis, taken to their pueblo, ceremoniously welcomed, provided with a blanket and moccasins, and "treated with great veneration and almost worship." After he left the Zunis he appears to have spent some time during the sum-

---

[26] Triplett, *op. cit.,* 416-18, 433-39. Sioux Pass is in present southwest Fremont Co., Wyo. Their semi-permanent camp was near present Bighorn, southwest Treasure Co., Mont.

[27] Thomas Maitland Marshall, "St. Vrain's Expedition to the Gila in 1826," in *Southwest Historical Quarterly,* vol. XIX, no. 3 (Jan. 1916), 253, 255, 257-58. There is much more to the story, involving politics, Mexican-Indian relations, bribery, personalities, etc. The entire subject of Mexican-trapper relations invites scholarly exploration. See Thomas J. Farnham, *Travels in the Californias* (N.Y., 1846), 84-86.

mer of 1827 among the Navahos. Ultimately he made it back to Taos, some two hundred miles.[28]

Bill left Taos early in the fall of 1827 with a trapping party led by Sylvestre S. Pratte, with Ceran St. Vrain as clerk, bound for Green River. On their way north they camped in Park Kyack, a lush basin full of game, girt on the west and south by the snowy Park Range (Continental Divide), on the east by the Medicine Bow Mountains. The North Platte River rises in the park and emerges northward between spurs of the Sierra Madre and Medicine Bows. There, on October 1, Pratte sickened and died, and was succeeded by St. Vrain. They went on to Green River waters, where they wintered. In April 1828, the party broke up, and most of the men, probably including Bill Williams, reached Taos about May 23.[29]

From the spring of 1828 to the spring of 1830 Bill apparently became better acquainted with the Utes, their country, and other recesses of the Rocky Mountains theretofore known only to the natives; and acquired wide repute for an accurate knowledge of his range. At Taos, in the spring of 1830, he met young Jesús Archuleta, who began a tenure as Bill's loyal retainer by accompanying him on a trip to South Park and the valley of the South Platte.

They went north over Raton Pass and, keeping east of the mountains, arrived at a point near Manitou Springs where they swung around Pike's Peak and crossed the mountains into a splendid hunting ground, South Park, headwaters

---

[28] James J. Webb's signed statement (ms.), Webb papers (private), St. Louis, Mo.; William Ingraham Kip, "The Last of the Leatherstockings," in *The Overland Monthly*, vol. II, no. 5 (May, 1869), 409; *St. Louis Globe-Democrat*, Dec. 24, 1911; W. T. Hamilton, *My Sixty Years on the Plains* (N.Y., 1905), 102.

[29] Ceran St. Vrain to B. Pratte & Co., enclosing undated memo. of acct., cert. of services, etc., dated Sept. 1, 1829 (mss.), Bent-St. Vrain Papers, P. Chouteau Maffitt Coll., Mo. Hist. Soc., St. Louis. The letter, probably sent from Taos, is undated and was received in St. Louis Sept. 28, 1828. Park Kyack, also known to the mountain men as The Bull Pen, The Buffalo Pasture, New Park, and North Park (its present name), occupies most of Jackson Co., Colo.

country of the South Platte. Though their route north out of the park is uncertain, it seems likely they went as far northwest as Williams Fork of the upper Colorado River, then circled southward to the South Platte, followed it to about its junction with Cherry Creek, and went south by an unknown route to the Arkansas, which they followed to Bent's Fort.[30]

On September 4, 1832, at the bid of John Harris, a motley crew of some seventy-five trappers and adventurers from the New Mexico settlements, including Bill Williams and another seasoned trapper, Aaron B. Lewis, and Albert Pike, a young Easterner of literary proclivity, rendezvoused in the valley of the Rio Pueblo de Picuris, on the western slope of the Sangre de Cristo Mountains, about twenty-seven miles south of Taos. The announced intention was to trap "the Cumanche country, upon the heads of the Red river and Fausse Washita." They left on the sixth, and the entire course trended southeast.[31]

They crossed the mountains near Tres Ritos into Mora Valley, continued to the junction of the Mora River and Sapello Creek, where they struck the Santa Fe Trail and followed it to a point six miles beyond the Gallinas River crossing. There they left it and crossed to the Pecos River at Anton Chico. Eleven days and nearly ninety miles of following the Pecos brought them to Bosque Redondo, where they left the river and headed toward the western escarpment of the Llano Estacado (Staked Plain), up which they wound to a Comanche trail.[32]

The trail led them down the Double Mountain Fork of the Brazos River, a succession of depressions holding more

[30] *St. Louis Globe-Democrat,* Dec. 24, 1911. See note 37.

[31] Albert Pike, "Narrative of a Journey in the Prairie," in *Publications of the Arkansas Historical Association* (Conway, Ark., 1917), IV, pp. 94-96; Writers' Program, W.P.A., *New Mexico* (N.Y., 1940), 377. Originally included in Pike's *Prose Sketches and Poems* (Boston, 1834), his "Narrative" was reprinted in 1835 with emended text in Pike's newspaper, *The Arkansas Advocate.* The 1917 printing copies the 1835 text.

[32] Pike, *op. cit.,* 95-96, 98-101; Writers' Program, *New Mexico,* 355, 370, 377.

or less water. For eighteen days and well over two hundred miles they followed the fork across the arid *llano,* met nominally friendly Comanches, lost and recovered the trail, lost men by desertion, and hunted with little success. Near the junction of the Double Mountain Fork and its South Branch the outfit got lost in the sand hills and broke up.[33]

Ill-conceived, misdirected, with overtones of deceit and fraud, and with constantly impending Mexican and Comanche treachery, the expedition never reached the waters of either the Red or the Washita; and beavers, like the buffalo, were always "just ahead" and not one beaver was taken. Bill Williams returned to Taos in time to outfit for the 1832-1833 trapping season.[34]

In middle November 1833, Bill, as guide, left a trappers' camp on Ham's Fork, a tributary of Black's Fork of Green River, with a Rocky Mountain Fur Company outfit under Henry Fraeb. They headed for Green River and, as the signs indicated a good season, expected to remain out until about March 1, 1834, and appear to have done so. Bill was back in Taos before April 1.[35]

Some time before this Bill had taken up residence in a Taos adobe with a Mexican widow with three children. It is known that her maiden name was Antonia Baca, and she came of a good family. One son, Jose, was born about 1834 to Antonia and Bill, who probably lived together for some years after that.[36]

Bill now sought wider knowledge of the Far West. According to the narrative of Jesús Ruperto Valdez (Pepe) Archuleta, his camp keeper, Bill arranged a two-man "ex-

[33] Pike, *op. cit.,* 102-15; William Curry Holden, "Comanche Trail," in *The Handbook of Texas,* ed. Walter Prescott Webb (Austin, 1952), I, p. 386; *Id.,* Anon., "Double Mountain Fork of the Brazos River," 515.   [34] Pike, *op. cit.,* 94-115.

[35] Thomas Fitzpatrick to William Sublette, Nov. 13, 1833 (ms.), Sublette Papers, Mo. Hist. Soc., St. Louis; Hiram Martin Chittenden, *The American Fur Trade of the Far West* (Stanford, 1954), I, pp. 260, 476.

[36] Statements at Taos of Juan Santistevan, Apr. 24 and 27, 1908, and Teresina (Bent) Scheurich, Apr. 29, 1908, Early Far West Notebook XII (ms.), 47-49, 53-55, 58-59, F. W. Cragin Papers, *loc. cit.;* Lewis, *op. cit.,* 192.

ploring expedition" into the vast Mexican land between the middle Rio Grande settlements and the Pacific, finding "his own trail" from near Zuni Pueblo "clear through to the missions" in California, to test stories he had heard from "Indians and priests . . . of some very wonderful things" farther west. It was to be a leisurely reconnaissance, spiced with hunts and visits with strange people.[37]

Bill gathered Pepe and "two fine saddle horses," three pack mules, ammunition, only four traps, and left Taos on April 1, 1834, for Santa Fe, where he bought food staples and medicines, and followed the old Chihuahua Trail to Albuquerque. There, says Archuleta, they visited the "mission" (San Felipe Neri Church), where Bill assisted "the padres in translating some Bible lessons into Navajo lingo."[38]

They continued down the old trail to Isleta Pueblo, left it to cross westward to Laguna Pueblo, turned southwest into "a maze of canyons and *cul de sacs*," skirted the Malpais (lava beds), headed south into the San Augustine Plains, and watered at Horse Springs. They worked west and north around the Datil Range into very rough country, and discovered that a volcanic hill they climbed to spot a better trail contained within its crater the fabled Zuni Salt Lake.[39]

---

[37] Archuleta's narrative was first published in the *St. Louis Globe-Democrat*, Dec. 24, 1911, partially subtitled: "The Story of Bill Williams, . . . told here for the first time," and with the narrator's portrait. Its authenticity has been questioned; however, the results of certain tests and investigations (too numerous and lengthy to recount here), applied to the story, are sufficient to convince us that, despite occasional anachronisms and other lapses, the narrative is essentially true in all matters of which the narrator could have had personal knowledge; and that part has been accepted as substantially correct. One important change has been made — in order to harmonize with an established chronology, and in the absence of reliable conflicting testimony, the events have been shifted from the years 1832-1835 to 1834-1837.   [38] Hamilton, *op. cit.,* 102.

[39] Isleta is fifteen miles south of Albuquerque, Laguna fifty miles west of Isleta. The Malpais, in present Valencia Co., N.M., is twenty-five miles southwest of Laguna. Horse Springs, in the west central part of the San Augustine Plains, in present Catron Co., N.M., is about fifty miles directly south of The Malpais. The Datil Range is in present western Catron Co., N.M., and the Salt Lake in the northwest corner of the county.

By a devious trail they arrived at the "extreme border house where a civilized man lived," the Cienega Amarilla rancho of Pedro Sanchez, whom Bill had met at Zuni Pueblo in 1827. Continuing west, they crossed the Little Colorado River, and one day met a hunting party of Hopis who directed them to the Petrified Forest. Fascinated, they rode through it to a Hopi village where they learned enough about the Grand Canyon to urge them toward its rim, and after a zig-zag trip they camped above Marble Canyon, where they sat in enchanted stupor.[40]

Next morning they started south, ran into the formidable canyon of the Little Colorado, retreated eastward to a river crossing, and rode south and west to the neighborhood of what became known as Bill Williams Mountain, where they spent the winter of 1834-1835 in a Walapai village. In the spring they rode west to the Colorado River where, at another Walapai village they met Padre Gonzales, a wandering Franciscan who, since they were seeking enjoyment, not hardship, dissuaded them from crossing the inhospitable Mohave Desert.[41]

They crossed the Colorado, Bill and Pepe in a canoe, the animals swimming, headed upriver and generally followed the north bank to a low mountain, probably in the Muddy Range, from which they descried the cottonwood fringe along the Virgin River. From that point their northward course is undefined; but thirty-five days later they were at Great Salt Lake, and finally, after many summer days and

[40] Cienega Amarilla (Yellow Meadow) lies in present western McKinley Co., N.M., and eastern Apache Co., Ariz., centering near St. Michaels, Ariz. Marble Canyon is the northern arm of the Grand Canyon, above the mouth of the Little Colorado.

[41] Bill Williams Mountain, in present southwestern Coconino Co., Ariz., is believed to have been named by Bill's friend Antoine Leroux. In both instances Archuleta called the Indians "Maricopas," but it is believed that he referred to the Mata'va-kapai (north people), a subdivision of the Walapai. See John R. Swanton, *The Indian Tribes of North America* in Bulletin 145, Bur. of Am. Ethnol. (Washington, 1952), 366. The *padre* could well have been Rubio Gonzales, "the Zacatecan," exiled from a California mission during secularization, just prior to this time.

hundreds of mountain miles, they found a Hudson's Bay Company camp on Lake Coeur d'Alene, where Bill out-fitted for the trapping season and Pepe went to cook for a camp at Lake Pend d'Oreille.[42]

Bill called for Pepe in the spring of 1836 and they rode southeast up Clark's Fork, Hell Gate and Bitterroot rivers, and east across the main Rockies to Bozeman Pass, where they descended to the Yellowstone. The next season, 1836-1837, with a fifty-trap line, they worked the Yellowstone waters, took six hundred skins and headed for the summer rendezvous on Green River near the mouth of Horse Creek, where they sold out and headed for Bent's Fort, where Bill took charge of a Bent-St. Vrain wagon train going to Santa Fe.[43]

Later in 1837 Bill again went out to the Colorado River. He appears to have traveled from the Bill Williams Moun-tain neighborhood through the Santa Maria country and down that stream to Bill Williams Fork of the Colorado which he followed to its mouth. There he met Antoine Leroux who reported Bill had "found water all along in holes & some beaver." The next summer, 1838, Bill was at the rendezvous on the Popo Agie, near its junction with Wind River.[44]

Bill's trapping now became sporadic. The steady decline of the fur trade, as the Mountain Men knew it, was making trapping unprofitable, and many trappers sought other fields: they hunted meat for the trading posts, guided trad-ing, missionary, and immigrant parties, loafed around the Indian villages, lived off the country on long pleasure hunts, served as interpreters, and "collected" California horses. It

---

[42] The Muddy Range is in present central Clark Co., Nev. The shores of lakes Coeur d'Alene and Pend d'Oreille, respectively in present Kootenai and Bonner cos., Idaho, were well-known fur trade camp grounds.

[43] Here ends Archuleta's story of the "exploring expedition."

[44] Richard H. Kern diary, Oct. 23, 1851 (ms.), Huntington Library, San Marino, Cal.; James B. Marsh, *Four Years in the Rockies* (New Castle, 1884; reprinted Columbus, n.d.), 225-26; Edwin L. Sabin, *Kit Carson Days* (N.Y., 1935), I, p. 277.

probably was during the years 1838-1841 that Bill pursued his comfortable relationship with the Utes, and he was reliably reported to have had a succession of Ute consorts.[45]

In the spring of 1840, after careful planning and local "arrangements" by scouts, a band of "Chaguanosos" descended upon Southern California in a sweeping raid on its horse herds. In this well-organized enterprise, which included American trappers, New Mexicans, French-Canadians and Indians, including mission apostates, Bill Williams had a directing hand. Its main objectives were the horses, once mission property but, since secularization of the missions in 1834, largely abandoned, with ownership in controversy.[46]

Late in April the Chaguanosos ran off about twelve hundred horses from the San Luis Obispo Mission herd and, by mid-May had collected about 1800 more, mostly from San Gabriel Mission and the *ranchos* between it and the abandoned San Bernardino *assistencia* (mission station), on the road to their main rendezvous in Summit Valley, just south of the climb to Cajon Pass. The three thousand animals were grazed in the lush valley, and driven up the pass onto the Mohave Desert, on the way to the Bent's Fort horse market on the Arkansas River, a hard journey of about a thousand miles.[47]

The scarcity of grass and water, and the relentless pace to elude pursuing Californios and predatory Indians, cost

[45] Micajah McGehee, "Narrative," in *Fremont's Fourth Expedition,* ed. LeRoy R. and Ann W. Hafen (Glendale, 1960), 144; Thomas E. Breckenridge, autobiographical notes dictated to C. W. Watson about 1894 (typescript), 44, 46, Harriet (Breckenridge) Knott papers (private), Hannibal, Mo.

[46] George William and Helen Pruitt Beattie, *Heritage of the Valley* (Pasadena, 1939), 37-38, 140; George D. Brewerton, "A Ride with Kit Carson," in *Harper's New Monthly Magazine,* VII (Aug. 1853), 316; Eleanor Frances Lawrence, "The Old Spanish Trail from Santa Fe to California," 1930 (typescript), 68, Bancroft Library, Berkeley, Cal.

[47] [California] Departmental State Papers: Prefectures & Juzgados, Angeles (ms.), IV, pp. 72, 88, 100, 105-06, Bancroft Lib.; Beattie, *op. cit.,* 140-43, where the affair is well summarized; G. W. Beattie to the writer, April 23, 1940.

the Chaguanosos some 1500 animals before they had cleared the desert. They probably lost many more along the Old Spanish Trail before reaching Bent's Fort; and there is a story that Bill turned his surviving share into Bent's corral and settled for a barrel of whiskey.[48]

About this time Bill took a notion to visit the folks back in Missouri. Late in 1840 he started from Taos for his old home and apparently was beyond Bent's Fort when he changed his mind, turned back and spent some time at the fort. However, in the summer of 1841 he went all the way, probably visited the Osage villages, went to see his little granddaughter, Mary's child Susan, who was living with an uncle in Neosho, Missouri, and remained to spend the winter of 1841-1842 with his aged mother and his brothers and sisters in Gasconade and Franklin counties; and many are the tales in the Ozark foothills of Bill's memorable return to Missouri.[49]

Early in 1842 Bill went to St. Louis to outfit a trading expedition. His partner was George Perkins, an experienced free trapper, and they recruited six others, including a young greenhorn, William T. Hamilton. Well armed, equipped and mounted, with wagons and pack horses loaded with merchandise and supplies, they left St. Louis early in March and followed the Missouri River to Independence, where they sold the wagons, and with an augmented pack train headed west. They probably followed the Kansas, Smoky Hill and Saline rivers. They crossed to the South Platte near the mouth of Cherry Creek where they traded with a Cheyenne village.[50]

---

[48] Dept. State Papers, *loc. cit.*, 105-06; Micajah McGehee, "Rough Notes of Rough Times in Rough Places" (typescript), 53-54, Private Papers of James Stewart McGehee, St. Louis, Mo. (transcript in writer's collection).

[49] Simeon Turley to Jesse B. Turley, Apr. 18 and Aug. 3, 1841, Turley Papers, Mo. Hist. Soc., St. Louis; interviews with C. E. Vaughan, Perry and Josie Williams, and conference with the William S. Mathews family, *loc. cit.*; writer's notes of an interview with Walter Williams, Brinktown, Mo., June 2, 1936.

[50] Hamilton, *op. cit.*, 18-25.

They rode north to trade for furs and buffalo robes at the Sioux villages east of Fort Laramie, and sold their purchases to another trader for cash, thus setting a pattern for the trip – buying and selling promptly for an immediate cash profit. They moved west along the North Platte and the Sweetwater to the Oregon Trail Crossing and northwest to nominally Shoshoni country east of the Wind River Mountains where, on Little Wind River, they had a battle with a band of Blackfeet, all of whom, according to Hamilton, were killed.[51]

On Wind River they met Bill's "old friend" Washakie and his Eastern Shoshonis, and learned that Blackfeet war parties hovered nearby. The recent deaths of two strange trappers and the theft of Shoshoni horses called for war. Bill Williams led in planning a three-pronged campaign by combined Mountain Man-Shoshoni forces, which resulted in a series of skirmishes and battles in the area east of the mountains, between the Owl Creek Mountains and the Bull Lake Creek-Wind River timber belt, in which the enemy lost twenty-one men, many horses and much property, and the allies one Shoshoni warrior. Both the victory and the celebration which followed were still being recalled by the Shoshonis nearly a century later.[52]

Bill's party traded with the Shoshonis, induced Washakie to take the accumulated skins to Jim Bridger's camp on Black's Fork of Green River, trapped Bull Lake, crossed Wind River Mountains to the head of the Green, worked down river, and crossed to Bridger's where they found Washakie and his Shoshonis with the skins, which they sold on the spot. They moved southeast to Brown's Hole near the junction of the Green and the Yampa, from which they made excursions into the Uinta Mountains. About September 1, after promising to return to Brown's Hole the fol-

---

[51] *Ibid.,* 35, 42, 44-49, 51-58.
[52] *Ibid.,* 60-80; A. F. C. Greene to the writer, July 10, 1937.

lowing spring to lead a trapping and trading expedition toward the farther West, Bill left for Taos.[53]

Next March 1843, Bill got some traps at Bent's, and went to Brown's Hole from which he and Perkins led about forty Mountain Men, with a pack train of trade goods, northwest on a trip of several thousand miles and two years' duration. They preferred to associate and trade with peaceful Indians, but if they encountered some with opposite inclinations they were prepared to take care of them in Mountain Man style. They did both and lost few men.[54]

They crossed the Uinta Mountains, went north to the Snake River and down it to work the Blackfoot, then returned to follow the Snake west to Fort Boise, a Hudson's Bay Company post near the mouth of the Boise; and crossed the Blue Mountains to the Umatilla River, and continued west to the John Day and the Deschutes, pausing to visit a Hudson's Bay camp on the Columbia near the mouth of the Deschutes (perhaps near The Dalles). They went south beyond the head of the Deschutes to Upper Klamath Lake, near which they went into winter quarters. It was from this camp apparently that Bill Williams, accomplished long-distance traveler, returned to Taos.[55]

In the spring of 1844 Bill left Taos, stopped to visit The Pueblo on the Arkansas, set out "for to'ther side of the 'big hills,'" and in due time arrived at the Klamath Lake camp. Soon after this the trappers broke camp and went to explore Lost River to its head. On the way back down river, to Tule Lake, the sink of Lost River, they were attacked by Modoc Indians and in the ensuing battle, according to Hamilton, the trappers lost three men, the Modocs about thirty.[56]

[53] Ibid., 81, 83-84, 86, 88, 92-93, 97, 99, 101.

[54] Charles W. Bowman, "History of Bent County," in History of the Arkansas Valley, Colorado (Chicago, 1881), 829; Hamilton, op. cit., 123-24.

[55] Ibid., 124, 126, 133, 138-46.

[56] George S. Simpson to George C. Sibley, Apr. 10, 1844, Sibley Mss., vol. II, [1-3], Mo. Hist. Soc., St. Louis; Hamilton, op. cit., 146-47, 153.

The trappers rode east to Clear Lake, and on to a branch of Pit River, thence almost directly south to Honey Lake where they set up a temporary camp. Three months later they rode east to skirt Pyramid Lake, on to the Truckee River, and across to Carson River, where they turned north to Humboldt Lake and went up the Humboldt River northeast to Thousand Springs Creek and the waters of Goose Creek. Then, in big jumps, they crossed to Raft River, to the Bear, to the Green, and probably used South Pass to get on to Wind River and follow it north to the Hot Springs where they rested. They resumed the journey by crossing the country southeast to the North Platte and following it east to Fort Laramie. There, in the summer of 1845 the party disbanded, and Bill returned briefly to Taos.[57]

Bill went up to visit the Mountain Men living at The Pueblo, and was there in August 1845, when Captain John C. Frémont, of the United States Topographical Engineers, induced him and Kit Carson to serve as guides on a journey officially indicated to be an examination of "unexplored" western regions, preparatory to the publication of a reliable map of the West. The party, nearly sixty strong, went up the Arkansas, detouring the Royal Gorge, past Williams Fishery (Twin Lakes), crossed the Sawatch Range over Tennessee Pass onto the head of Eagle River, followed the Eagle to the Colorado, and crossed over to White River which they followed to its junction with the Green, where they were joined by Joseph R. Walker, then crossed the Wasatch Mountains to Utah Lake, and went down the Jordan to Great Salt Lake. At a camp somewhere between the Cedar Mountains and the lake there was a serious disagreement between Frémont and the guides about the route across the Salt Desert, as the result of which, on October 27,

---

[57] *Ibid.*, 158-59, 161, 165, 167, 172, 174-77.

the day before the party started across the desert, Bill left the party.[58]

Bill is recorded at Bridger's Fort in July 1846; and about mid-June 1847, during the war with Mexico, he was one of the Mountain Men engaged to guide and guard the wagon train being taken from Fort Leavenworth across the plains to Santa Fe with Colonel Alton R. Easton's volunteer infantry battalion of St. Louisans. There was trouble with the Comanches, but the troops arrived practically intact at Santa Fe late in August. Some time between the fall of 1847 and the spring of 1848 Bill drifted up to the American Fur Company's Fort Union on the Yellowstone, and later in 1848 returned south.[59]

Bill arranged a sort of loose partnership with Josiah J. Webb of Webb & Doan in the spring of 1848 to trade with travelers along the Santa Fe Trail, and apparently was engaged in that enterprise when he was called to serve, with other Mountain Men, as scout and guide for Major W. W. Reynolds in a military campaign, starting from Taos, against a large band of Ute and Apache raiders who had been harassing the northern New Mexico settlements. The Indians were followed to Cumbres Pass in the southern extremity of the San Juan Mountains, where a fierce battle resulted in the rout of the Indians, after thirty-six of them and two soldiers were killed and many on both sides wounded, including Bill Williams, "who behaved himself

[58] Frederick S. Dellenbaugh, *Fremont and '49* (N.Y., 1914), 289-93; U.S. 28 Cong., 2 sess., *Sen. Ex. Doc.* no. 1, pp. 221-22; John Charles Frémont, *Narratives of Exploration and Adventure* (N.Y., 1957), 440-42; W. J. Ghent, *The Early Far West* (N.Y., 1936), 344; Thomas S. Martin, "Narrative of John C. Fremont's Expedn. to California in 1845-6," dictated to E. F. Murray, Sept. 5, 1878 (ms.), 9-10, Bancroft Library; Breckenridge notes, *loc. cit.*, 42-43; Abstract of expenses and supporting vouchers, Fremont's third expedition, Settlement 7634, Mar. 9, 1849, Cons. Files, Gen. Acctg. Off., Washington.

[59] Edwin Bryant, *What I Saw in California* (N.Y., 1848), 145. Bryant, who recorded the Bridger's Fort visit, disguises Bill Williams under the name "Bill Smith." *Daily Missouri Republican*, July 10, Aug. 12, Sept. 6, Oct. 23, 1847; *St. Louis Daily New Era*, Aug. 27, 1847; John Palliser, *The Solitary Hunter* (London, 1860), 87-88.

gallantly" and "was shot in the arm, shattering it most horrible." [60]

Bill was at The Pueblo on the Arkansas River on November 21, 1848, when Captain Frémont arrived with his fourth exploring expedition seeking a guide. Despite his conviction, based on unfailing signs of extremely severe weather ahead, that it was far too late in the season for the successful mountain crossing Frémont anticipated in his search for a practicable railroad route to California, Bill yielded to Frémont's pleas and agreed to guide the expedition. They left The Pueblo next day.

They went up the Arkansas and crossed over to the Mountain Men's Hardscrabble settlement, near the east foot of the Wet Mountains, where they packed the 120 mules with an additional supply of corn and, thirty-three strong, went southwest across the Wet Mountains and the Wet Mountain Valley to Robidoux (Mosca) Pass across the Sangre de Cristos. At the west end of the pass they veered north to round the sand hills in San Luis Valley and head northwest toward Saguache Creek on the west side of the valley; and there the trouble began.

According to Thomas Fitzpatrick's understanding (not to be discounted), after a discussion of the route with Frémont, it was the latter's intention, after crossing San Luis Valley, to "steer directly for California, leaving the two hitherto traveled routes, one north [the old trail up Saguache Creek to Cochetopa Pass] and the other south [the old Spanish Trail through Abiquiu] of him and passing midway between the two" [up the Rio Grande to its head]. Fitzpatrick was by no means sure that Frémont could "find a practicable route."

---

[60] Account books, 1848-1850: Ledger, 27, Day Book, 10-12, Cash Book, 1, Webb papers, *loc. cit.*; W. W. Reynolds to Sterling Price, Aug. 6, 1848, Old Files Sec., Exec. Div., Adj. Gen. Off., War Dept., Washington; Betty Woods, *101 Trips in the Land of Enchantment* (Santa Fe, 1956), 46. Cumbres Pass lies about athwart the Colo.-New Mex. line, some forty miles southeast of Pagosa Springs, Colo.

Bill Williams well knew the extreme difficulty, if not the impossibility of crossing the main middle ranges of the Rocky Mountains in winter; and as the winter settled into dangerous severity, with snow storms, deepening drifts, fierce winds and killing drops in temperature, he tried to lead the expedition from the sand hills toward what he considered the least formidable crossing – the Saguache Creek route, a course Frémont, according to Fitzpatrick, had already rejected. Consequently, even before they had left the sand hills, Williams was halted and the expedition turned southwest toward the Rio Grande. From then on Williams ceased to function as "the" guide; others, such as Henry King and Alexis Godey, veterans of former Frémont expeditions, but unacquainted with the Rio Grande country, occasionally essayed to find a trail; and while Frémont continued to seek information from Williams and argue with him about the route, generally he disregarded Bill's few words of counsel, and Bill's responses were mainly to questions from other members of the party.

Accordingly, Frémont's course was followed up the Rio Grande to the mouth of Alder Creek, where he decided to leave the river and head north into the mountains. Whether or not Williams advised this move is unclear. All accounts indicate that no trail up Alder Creek was thought to exist, yet, incredibly, according to Richard H. Kern, one of the party, King "reported to the Colonel [Frémont] that he had found a wagon road," and thereupon "undertook the pilotage," and soon after that they "found a tolerable level road," which later seems to have disappeared in the deep drifts.

They followed the canyon of Alder Creek north to the junction of its East and West forks, then struggled up the West Fork. Bucking strangling icy winds, watching frozen mules drop dead in their tracks, beating out a path for the surviving animals, almost inch by inch they pushed and twisted up the snow-choked canyons and slippery mountain sides, a little west of north, to a point near the mouth of Long Gulch, then wound irregularly northeast to a camp near the sources of Embargo Creek, just below the summit ridge of La Garita Mountains.

Storms beat back their first attempt to surmount the ridge; at the second try they scaled it and camped just beyond on a head stream of Wanamaker Creek, where the fury of the storms isolated them for five days. Men became snow-blind and badly frostbitten, food for men and animals had about vanished, and one by one the mules died. Bill Williams sagged down upon his mule in a frozen stupor, but soon revived. In this desperate situation a lull in the storm permitted them to move from their exposed position back to the Embargo Creek camp, from which, on December 26, Frémont dispatched Henry King, as leader, Bill Williams, Tom Breckenridge and Frederick Creutzfeldt to the New Mexico settlements for help, allowing them sixteen days for the round trip of about 350 miles, or nearly twenty-two miles a day through snow covered country on foot.

Because they had to break through the drifts, and because of dwindled supplies, they carried, besides their rifles and knives, a minimum of food and equipment. It took them three days in bitter weather to descend Embargo Creek twenty miles to the Rio Grande, arriving with their food exhausted, and desperately weary. On the ensuing eight-day struggle down river to the point where it turns southeast, they subsisted on a hawk, an otter, parched boots (replaced by strips of blanket), belts and knife scabbards.

Near the bend they discerned, farther toward the east, the smoke of a Ute camp, which gave hope to all but Bill Williams. He explained why he could not approach the Indian camp. He confessed that some years before he had absconded with a consignment of tribal furs, and besides, had "led the soldiers against" the Utes (a reference to the 1848 campaign), and could not blame them for seeking his scalp.

He suggested the party leave the Rio Grande, cut across country and avoid a big river bend.

Bill's plan was adopted and, weak and starving, desperate, and chewing charred leather, they crept along until within a quarter mile of the river, where King lay down to rest, and soon died. They crawled to the river, where Breckenridge happily managed to kill a deer. Revived, they were preparing to travel when they saw four horsemen. Williams shouted and waved his rifle, and soon Frémont, Godey and two others rode into the desolate camp on horses somehow acquired from the Utes.

Accounts differ as to how Williams and his two companions reached the Red River settlement (Questa). According to Tom Breckenridge, Frémont's party rode on, leaving them to make the fifty mile trip as best they could; but, according to Frémont, taken to Questa by his party. Meantime, in the mountains, men froze and starved to death.

Thus ended Frémont's disastrous fourth expedition, its toll ten men and 120 mules dead, twenty-three men crippled and ill (some never completely recovered), nearly all the equipment and personal possessions lost, and an acrimonious, continuing controversy over responsibility for the disaster that has never been resolved to the satisfaction of reasonable men. For persisting in an apparently impossible "central" course during a deadly combination of winter elements; for his failure to designate Williams as the permanent, responsible guide, and permitting or even encouraging "amateur" pilots to try to find the trails, Frémont is to blame. For consenting to guide the outfit in the face of overwhelming indications of failure for a leader with whom, three years before, he had had a serious disagreement; and for his failure to get the "rescue" party (of which he was not the leader) to the settlements after the death of King, and deliver relief to the main party within the allotted time (all of which must be considered in the light of the very difficult

circumstances under which the party attempted to operate),
Bill Williams is responsible. And if it was he who actually
led the party up Alder Creek, whether by accident or design,
he must be held accountable for that.[61]

By the middle of February 1849, Williams and his companions were in Taos, where they rapidly recuperated; and
about the middle of March, Williams and Dr. Benjamin J.
Kern, the expedition's physician, left Taos with a few Mexican attendants for the scene of the debacle to recover the
doctor's medical equipment and supplies, his brothers' (both
Edward M. and Richard H. Kern, members of the expedition, were trained artists) art materials and personal papers,
and whatever expedition property and personal effects could
be salvaged. Almost as soon as they were out of sight, rumors
began to circulate that they had been murdered.

Bill and the doctor reached the disaster area, gathered
what they could and headed for Taos. On March 21, 1849,

---

[61] No attempt has been made to document specific points in the account of Frémont's fourth expedition. About two hundred published and unpublished sources on
it exist and have been consulted, from brief contemporary newspaper items to good-
sized volumes, the most useful and impartial of which is *Frémont's Fourth Expedition, op. cit.,* a compilation and digest of the most important documents on the subject. Other sources: Richard H. Kern to J. H. Simpson, Aug. 27, 1850, *Daily Missouri Republican,* Aug. 14, 1856; E. S. Erickson to the writer, June 23, 1942, with a
sketch map of the camp sites, which Erickson first visited in 1928, and Dec. 13, 1942,
with an annotated Forest Service map of the Alder Dist., Rio Grande N.F., Rio
Grande and Saguache cos., Colo., within which the main disaster scene is located;
Dellenbaugh, *op. cit.,* 390-403; Allan Nevins, *Frémont, Pathmarker of the West*
(N.Y., 1939), 348-69; J. Loughborough, *The Pacific Telegraph and Railway* (St.
Louis, 1849), iv-xi, 77, 79, which tackles the problem of where to lay the rails, and
criticizes in detail Frémont's choice of route; Francis Grierson [Benjamin H. J. F.
Shepard], *The Valley of Shadows* (Boston, 1948), 234-61, gives a most interesting
retrospective account, touched with mysticism, of the expedition from the Missouri
to Taos; William Brandon, *The Men and the Mountain* (N.Y., 1955), a dramatic
account of the expedition which uses a number of the sources but is far from
exhaustive.

Despite the rumors, which originated with Frémont and his family, there is no
reliable evidence that the three survivors of the "rescue" party subsisted for a time
on the body of King. For an important contribution to the question see Will C. Ferril,
"The Sole Survivor," in *Rocky Mountain News,* Aug. 30, 1891, with Tom Breckenridge's fully detailed account of the movements of the "rescue" party, and his forth-
right written reply to Ferril's direct question concerning the alleged cannibalism.

probably not far east of the Rio Grande, and southwest of Mount Blanca, they were shot and killed. The preponderance of evidence seems to indicate that they were murdered by Utes, with the connivance of their own Mexican retainers. Despite rumors that their bodies were recovered, no reliable record has been found to support them.[62]

Bill Williams, lean and sinewy, stood six feet one in his moccasins, and possessed unusual strength. His facial features were small, his eyes steely blue, his face darkly weather-bronzed; his head was covered with a tangle of red hair, and he was usually well bearded.

He so excelled in the skills demanded by the trapping business that he became a legend in his own time. He was an excellent horseman, a tireless walker, an expert trailer, indefatigable in the pursuit of the beaver, and a tricky, unorthodox, effective fighter. His ability to snake himself, his animals, and his fur packs through dangerous Indian country commanded the admiration of his fellow Mountain Men. His way with Indians was uncanny. Despite the "double wabble" with which he handled his battered old Hawken rifle, he shot "plumb center." Under the prod of necessity his mental-physical co-ordination was extraordinary.

Bill Williams tagged his furs: "William S. Williams, M.T." (Master Trapper), and no one in the mountains could better claim the "degree." His traps and a sound business sense (he was a notoriously sharp trader when dealing with "company men") brought him handsome profits which he spent gambling, drinking, buying "fofarraw" for his wives and fair companions, and helping others.

Despite his high-pitched, cracked voice Williams was an impressive speaker, an able *raconteur,* and could be a superb

[62] B. L. Beal to I. H. Dickerson, Mar. 26 and May 1, 1849, Old Files Sec., Org. Div., Adj. Gen. Off., War Dept., Washington; *Daily Missouri Republican,* July 7, 1849; *Frémont's Fourth Expedition, op. cit.,* 171, 229-30; Louis B. Sporleder, Sr., The County of Huerfano (typescript), 306, Hist. Colls., Univ. of Colo., Boulder, Colo.

actor, sometimes playing the "typical" Mountain Man. Of a superior intelligence, with intellectual attainments, he did not fit the public image of a trapper. "An educated man with a critical knowledge of Greek and Latin," and an appreciation of good literature, an understanding of history, politics and comparative religion (he was, in fact, an experimenter with religions), he transcended the image. Also, he had a sound sense of humor, and was something of a practical joker.

The impression Williams allowed or even led others to gain of his apparent profound belief in Indian religious precepts and mythology, including atavism involving the bear and metempsychosis involving the elk, caused them to regard him as a congenital eccentric. How much of his "belief" was conviction and how much mere mental pose remains undetermined; however, the common idea that he was a superstitious ignoramus has been exploded.

Williams prepared a series of sketch maps of the mountain country he knew best, one of which was used as the basis for a section of an excellent official map. Besides his Osage primer and his rendering of scriptural English into the Navaho, he prepared an account of his experiences among the Apaches, Zunis, and Navahos. He sometimes kept a notebook; and he tried his hand at watercolor sketching. (All but the primer are lost.) Williams spoke frontier North Carolina-Missouri English, the Mountain Man's mixed idiom (which he helped construct), French, Spanish, and many Indian languages and dialects besides those mentioned.

Despite his tough, uncouth exterior, Williams' fondness for children, interest in young apprentice trappers, charity toward the less fortunate and, except when doubted, helpfulness to those seeking geographical information about the West, reveal his redeeming traits. Generally he was considered an honest man and a brave one, and rated a good man to have around in a tight spot. He was not a vicious man, as some later writers, without apparent reason, have averred, but an implacable, formidable foe when confronted by overt enmity.

Two portraits of Williams, an oil and a watercolor, were made by Edward M. Kern, neither of which has been found.[63]

---

[63] Documentation for the above statements is scattered through many fur trade sources, and a complete listing would extend far beyond our space. See particularly *Frémont's Fourth Expedition, op. cit.,* 143-46; Field, *loc. cit.; St. Louis Globe-Democrat, loc. cit.;* Ruxton, *op. cit.,* viii, 123-27.

George C. Yount

by CHARLES L. CAMP
University of California, Berkeley

In the years after the close of the Revolution, emigrant backwoods families, as well as wandering hunters and adventurers poured across the Alleghanies seeking to expand their energies and fortunes in new lands. Most of them had just enough taste of frontier life to want more. So the great westward movement developed. The large Jacob Yount family was one unit in this throng of trans-Alleghany pioneers. They kept on moving west in 1804 until they became among the earliest of the trans-Mississippi settlers.

Jacob Yount's farm on Dowden Creek, Burke County, North Carolina, had been the home for himself, his wife, Amarilla, and their eleven children. Among these was George, a sturdy, blond boy of ten, born on the Carolina farm on May 4, 1794. Jacob's grandparents, Hans George and Anna Marie Jundt had come to Pennsylvania from Alsace in 1731 "to escape despotism and opression." Jacob's father, John, had changed the spelling of the family name to Yount and the descendants to this day maintain the original German pronunciation, though but few others do.

After crossing the Mississippi into Missouri, the migrant Yount family stayed for a time in the vicinity of Cape Girardeau. A few months later they packed up again and moved into unsettled country farther west, near White River in a dangerous frontier where it was necessary to post guards at the corners of the fields and set up constant vigilance against Indian raids. George grew up among these rugged surroundings, became expert with his rifle and the techniques of running a frontier farm. There was but little chance for schooling for anybody and none at all for George. He never learned to read and write, but he did train and improve a splendid memory which enabled him to repeat conversations he had heard years before. He did finally learn painfully to scratch out his signature, and to use it sometimes when he wished he hadn't. Unfortunately his lack of schooling accompanied an over-generous nature, too trusting of those who would try to fleece him.

George with an elder brother, Jacob, took an active part in the War of 1812 in the hinterland. He was twice called up, once to Cap-au-Gris, where a future trapping companion, Lt. Sylvester Pattie was also serving. After these stirring times he started a farm of his own, drove stock and found time to court and marry Eliza Wilds, a young girl from Kentucky. They prospered for several years until George foolishly placed his life savings into the hands of a neighbor for "safekeeping." These funds mysteriously disappeared. George's father-in-law became concerned over the competence of Eliza's husband. Ill feeling developed and George went off to engage himself as a teamster on the long road to Santa Fe. He arrived there in the autumn of 1826 evidently in the same caravan as the runaway boy, Kit Carson.

At Santa Fe the trading had slacked off. The Mexicans seem to have spent most of their savings on the goods brought in the previous season by the first cargo trains. The commerce of the prairies had hit an economic low, but beaver trapping had extended into the Gila and Colorado country (southwestern Arizona) the previous year. George joined a party of these trappers, fitted out by Ewing Young, a man of some experience in the region. The country they entered, along the headwaters of Gila and Salt rivers, was infested by Coyotero Apaches who had harassed, robbed and driven out a trapping party the previous season. In this early party were some men, the Patties, S. Stone, Alexander K.

Branch, Milton Sublette and Thomas L. Smith (later known as Peg-leg), most of whom joined Young and Yount at the copper mines of Santa Rita in this fall of 1826.

Still in the field was a party of French trappers under Michel (Miguel) Robidoux who had moved in with the Papago-Pima Indians at their village on the Gila. Unaccountably and foolishly, Robidoux had permitted liberties with these normally peaceful people. In consequence his party was exterminated in a horrible night massacre and Robidoux himself barely escaped. The Young-Yount party came on this scene a few days later, buried the remains of the poor Frenchmen, found their traps still in the river and set about giving the Pimas a royal thrashing. They have been pretty good Indians ever since.

From here, in the vicinity of present Avondale, Arizona, the trappers scattered in various directions, up the tributaries of the Gila and Salt rivers. Young and Yount worked their way down the Gila to the Colorado where they made dugout canoes of cottonwood logs and trapped up to the Mohave villages. They even visited the ancient salt mines along the lower Virgin River, needing the salt to preserve their beaver skins.

At the Mohave villages, the Pattie men and Tom Smith separated from Young-Yount, Milt Sublette and the rest. They didn't get along too well, and Tom Smith had an especial dislike for Ewing Young. At all events the Patties tried going out southeast, went down into Spencer Creek Canyon evidently and lost three men who had separated to trap there. The Indians killed them, cut the bodies to pieces and roasted them. Yount later said that the leader of this murdered party was one "Burr." Was this the "E. Bure" (Du Breuil?) of the Narbona documents?

Pattie and his associates tried to go on westward after this encounter but they didn't get far on account of the vertical cliffs of the lower Grand Canyon. Becoming disgusted with "those horrible mountains" they evidently turned back, crossed over the Colorado and went up the Virgin River Valley and as far as the Sevier, leaving the tracks observed by Jed Smith that summer (1827).

Young's party with Yount meanwhile had packed up their bundles of beaver fur and gone across a barren country to Zuñi Pueblo. They landed at Taos only to have their entire fur catch confiscated by the Mexican authorities. Yount found himself destitute again but this reinforced his determination eventually to succeed. Realizing what a wealth of beaver lay along the lower Colorado, he organized a party of twenty-four men for the fall (1827) hunt. His party again included the eight Pattie men although this doesn't seem to have been very sensible. William Workman is sometimes mentioned as the leader and (Hiram?) Allen, "of Mohave notoriety." This was the same Allen who had been with Ashley on the Missouri in 1823. He is also mentioned by Pattie along the Gila in 1826. And he is one of those who confirmed the Hugh Glass story when Glass told it to George Yount. Glass, Allen and Yount may have been together there in Arizona either in the spring or fall of 1827.

Pattie's men and dates have been questioned. There actually seems to be a fair record of both. His men were Nathaniel Pryor, Richard Laughlin, Jesse Ferguson, Isaac Slover, William Pope and Edmund Russell. All these evidently separated from Young, Workman and Allen on the Gila, went down to the Colorado and across Baja California to San Diego, California, where Sylvester Pattie died in a Mexican jail. Pattie mentions a "Dutchman" at this period, who could scarcely be anyone but George Yount, as there were no Germans in his detachment. Yet this Dutchman appears at a time in his story when George Yount was not present.

As to the accuracy of Pattie's dates, an article in the *St. Louis Times,* July 7, 1829, which gives the names of his

California party also says that they left Santa Fe on August 18, 1827, bound for the Gila, which agrees with the date given by Pattie except that his date is given erroneously as 1826. It seems that Pattie's editor must have had a memorandum of dates which may be accepted for the time he was with Yount where the dates are a year too early on nearly every count.

After the separation on the Gila, the Yount detachment went on down to the Colorado delta, thence up river again to Mohave land and further difficulty with that nation who had recently massacred Jed Smith's second party at its crossing of the Colorado. Something had turned these Indians against the whites. The Young party found themselves in overwhelming danger. The slick Mohaves were entreating them to come to their village and enjoy the charms of a "beautiful squaw" they had captured from Jed Smith's party. This was a little too obvious for Allen to swallow. He turned the men homeward as fast as possible out of the Circean clutches and temptations. On the way they followed the "trail" or tracks of the Patties the previous spring. This evidently led them into Spencer Canyon, scene of the Burr massacre. One man who had "been with Burr" was with them again this year. He wanted to raise some packs of fur he had cached in the canyon. But the steep cliffs along this route were just as difficult for the Younts as for the Patties. They tried all sorts of ways of boosting their animals along with ropes, and after nearly starving they finally went south to the uplands near San Francisco Peak, crossed the Little Colorado at Grand Falls, visited Hopi Land and eventually found their way back to Zuñi again in an exhausted state.

During a brief stay at Workman's (?) Taos distillery in the summer of 1828, George Yount managed by trickery or some sort of smuggling operation to keep his fur catch from confiscation. He made at least enough on it to pay his debts at Taos and organize another trapping venture for the vast

regions to the north, the middle branches of the great Colorado. In his dictated narrative he is not clear about the year
of this trip. It surely took place in the fall and winter of
1828. They met the Ceran St. Vrain ("Savery") party while
camped on the Green and they encountered one of the worst
winters on record (1828-29) in the region of the Great Salt
Lake. They holed up in Bear Valley when they found their
way blocked by ten-foot snow drifts. Yount froze his feet
and had many noteworthy adventures.

Perhaps they stayed over and spent the next winter also in
the same vicinity since it must have been here that Yount
met Jed Smith's man, Arthur Black, who had returned from
Oregon in the spring of 1830. From Yount's story, Black
was retailing stories of Jed Smith's discovery of gold in
California with other tales of the land which seem to have
set up an eternal fire in the adventurous soul of George
Yount. The gold stories were probably whole-cloth fakes
but the fact seems to be that Yount saw Black that spring
or summer (1830) and there is no evidence that Black ever
came down to Taos.

Yount's visit to California may have been encouraged too
by the divorce proceedings that were being advertised in the
Missouri papers in the winter of 1829-30. Communication
with his family was never vigorous, had now broken down
entirely and messages were being intercepted at the distaff
end of the line, or so thought George.

Making preparations for a long journey he returned to
Taos, or at least as far as Abiquiu, where he and members
of his party joined William Wolfskill's trappers westbound
along the Old Spanish Trail in the fall of 1830. This great
expedition to California, by a route largely untraveled, was
the most difficult, extended and important one of Yount's
ubiquitous career, a regular odyssey.

The route came to be known as the summer (or northern)
variant of the Old Spanish Trail. The southern (or winter)

variant of that trail had been traveled part-way by Escalante, and was completely traversed by the Mexican trader,
Antonio Armijo who made a journey over it from Santa Fe
to Los Angeles in 1829-30. Jedediah Smith was the first to
travel along the westward extension of the trail through
central Utah into California in 1826 and again in 1827.

Smith must have left a barely traceable track followed
by Wolfskill and Yount until they reached Clear Creek
branch of the Sevier River. Here they failed to turn to the
right and instead went on up the main river toward where
Panguitch, Utah now lies. Here they found themselves on
one of the high plateaux, marooned in a violent mid-winter
storm and bitter cold at an elevation of some 10,000 feet.
They came down from these heights toward present Cedar
City and Little Salt Lake in a fairyland of plentiful game.
Reaching the Mohave villages they intimidated the Indians
by a clever show of force: a little brass cannon mounted on
a pack-saddle. Later expeditions avoided the river route
entirely and cut off through the desert where Las Vegas is
now.

They paid their respects to Father Sanchez at San Gabriel
Mission. He welcomed them cordially despite their rough,
battered appearance, just as he had welcomed Jedediah
Smith in years before. Yount was impressed with the size
and organization of the great missionary establishment, and
the missionaries were equally astonished at Yount's expert
marksmanship. This skill was put to good account some
weeks later when he took up sea-otter hunting at Santa
Barbara. The trick was to shoot the otters when they popped
their heads out of water to breathe; all this from a small
boat in rough water. Kanakas went along to dive over and
retrieve the otters before they sank.

Yount adapted the idea of the trappers' bull boat to this
work, using the hides of sea elephants. He coasted Santa
Cruz Island in one of these and used larger boats for trips

to the more southern islands, even far down off the coast of Baja California. Continuing the pursuit of otter and beaver in San Francisco Bay and the Sacramento delta, Yount and George Nidever rescued a tiny starving Indian child, abandoned during an epidemic of cholera. George Yount raised the little girl and she eventually married another Indian.

George Yount visited Sonoma, made himself useful to the missionaries and especially so to General Vallejo. He split out shakes ("shingles") and roofed one of Vallejo's new houses and he took charge of Sonoma Mission for a short time, thus ingratiating himself. Through the good offices of his new friends he secured a large grant of land near the head of Napa Valley. To obtain title legally he was required to become a Mexican citizen and to be baptized a Catholic. He then received the baptismal name of George de la Concepcion Yount, and he rarely, if ever, used this middle name. Incidentally, it was the only middle name he ever had although the name "Calvert" has been ascribed by error.

When he received his grant it was expected that he was to assist in defending the northern frontier against raids by wild Indians. Accordingly, he responded to early calls from Vallejo to join punitive expeditions to Russian River and into Lake County. While chasing the wild Hoter ("Jota") band in Pope Valley, Yount had two horses shot out from under him, his cap shot off and he barely escaped with his life.

At his famous Napa ranch, Yount had built a Kentucky style block house, a big log-adobe house the next year, a saw mill and a flour mill, the first of their kind to be found in the region. He raised stock, introduced grain and other crops, became famous as a vineyardist and pioneer fruit and berry farmer. He was the first white man to establish himself so far from civilization in California and the first white settler in Napa Valley.

In 1855, five years after the death of his divorced wife, he married Mrs. Eliza Gashwiler, the widow of a minister from New York State. She took over the management of affairs that rapidly grew too complicated for him to handle properly. Open-handed and liberal in offering help to strange travelers, he was often imposed upon. Miscreant squatters ("campers") took over and refused to be ousted. Thieves stole stock and fruit. The primitive courts were slow in giving relief. He had as many as seventeen court cases against the squatters pending at one time.

The first overland emigrant families came with the Bidwell-Bartleson party in 1841. Among those were old friends and neighbors from Missouri, including Joseph B. Chiles who planned to go back the next year. Yount asked him to bring the Yount family out to California. Eliza would not leave her new husband but the two daughters came, leaving Robert, the son, behind. After Robert's early death, his widow and her daughter came out and lived on the Yount farm.

Yount took no part in the Bear Flag revolt, respecting the rights of his hosts the Mexican authorities. At the same time he held the respect of the American settlers, having gone their bonds and done other favors. His home became a famous center for trail-worn hunters, emigrants and settlers in the days before the Gold Rush. He was blessed for his hospitality and kindness to such waifs as the destitute child survivors of the Donner Party who had special reason to love and honor him.

Many were led to believe that Yount's dreams were influential in the rescue of the Donners. He no doubt had heard of the plight of that party and his dreams may have stimulated him to speed assistance. His credence of dreams and omens dated from his childhood associates in Missouri who were superstitious about such things as comets and earthquakes. He also had some imaginary gold mines. His religious feelings were strong, influenced by the local Protestant ministers. He became a prominent Mason, Bible bearer for the Yountville chapter. He donated the plot for the Yountville cemetery, in which he is buried, and he contributed to various churches. He died at his ranch on October 5, 1865, at the age of 71. His monument is carved to represent phases of his life as a hunter, trapper, farmer and pioneer. There were many famous pioneers at Napa and Sonoma and Yount was regarded as the most famous of them all. Yount's portrait appears in this volume at page 24.

George Yount was known under various names. Peg-leg Smith called him "Dutch George," James Pattie evidently referred to him as the "Dutchman" and quotes some alleged humorous remarks. In some of the Southwestern reminiscences he is identified as "Captain Youtz" and "Captain Buckskin." His uncompleted "Memoirs" cover the first thirty years of his life. A more complete story is the "narrative" dictated to the Rev. Orange Clark in 1855. This was edited by me under the title "The Chronicles of George C. Yount" from manuscripts now largely in the Huntington Library and published at Denver by Old West Publishing Co., 1966. References to other material on the life and times of this renowned pioneer may be found in my book.

Kit Carson

by HARVEY L. CARTER
Colorado College, Colorado Springs

Of all the hardy and adventurous trappers who roamed the western mountains, only Kit Carson became so widely known that he achieved the status of a national hero. As this is written, nearly a century after his death, his name and fame are still familiar to the general public. As Daniel Boone typified the early frontier, so Kit Carson typified the frontier of the Far West. It is a curious fact that Carson was born within a few miles of Boonesborough, Kentucky, and grew up in the Boone's Lick Country in Missouri, near which the last years of the older pioneer were spent.

Christopher Houston Carson, called Kit from a very early age, was born on his father's farm two miles northwest of Richmond, Madison County, Kentucky, on December 24, 1809, being the sixth of ten children of Lindsey Carson and his second wife, Rebecca Robinson Carson.[1] In October 1811, Lindsey Carson sold his farm, and then moved to Howard County, Missouri, probably in the summer of 1812. Lindsey Carson was killed by a falling tree in 1818 and his

---

[1] Lindsey Carson (1745-1818) was the eldest son of William Carson, born c. 1720 in Ireland, who emigrated to America in the 1740s and settled first in Pennsylvania and later in North Carolina, where he married Eleanor McDuff. Lindsey saw irregular service in the American Revolutionary War. By his first wife, Lucy Bradley (d. 1794) his children were William, Sarah, Andrew, Moses, and Sophia. The family moved to Kentucky about 1792. After the death of his first wife, Lindsey married Rebecca Robinson. Their children were Elizabeth, Nancy, Robert, Matilda, Hamilton, Christopher, Hampton, Mary, Sarshall, and Lindsey. A tradition in the family was that Christopher was born while his parents were in North Carolina on a visit. Such a visit seems most unlikely in the circumstances of pioneer life and Kit Carson himself gave no credit to the story. See Quantrille D. McClung, *Carson-Bent-Boggs Genealogy* (Denver, 1962), 10-16.

widow, in 1821, married Joseph Martin by whom she had other children.[2]

At the age of fourteen, Kit was apprenticed to David Workman of Franklin, Missouri, to learn the saddle making trade. Acquiring an increasing dislike for the work, he ran away in August 1826 to Independence, where he joined a wagon train bound for Santa Fe. The advertisement of the saddler for the return of the runaway apprentice described him as a light-haired boy, who was small for his age, but thick-set. A reward of one cent was offered for his return![3]

Upon the arrival of the wagon train in Santa Fe, in November 1826, young Carson went almost immediately to Taos. There he spent the winter with Mathew Kinkead, who was fifteen years older than Kit and already a Mountain Man of two seasons' experience.[4]

In the spring of 1827, Kit started back to Missouri with a wagon train but, meeting a west bound train on the Arkansas River, he transferred to it as a teamster and went as far as El Paso. Returning to Taos for the winter, he worked as a cook for Ewing Young, in return for his board. In the spring, he repeated his experience of the previous year by changing from an east-bound to a west-bound train. This time he went all the way to Chihuahua, as interpreter for a merchant, Colonel Trammell. He then worked as a teamster for Robert McKnight at the Santa Rita copper mine.[5] Tir-

[2] *Ibid.* The names of the Martin half-brothers and a Martin half-sister of Kit Carson have not been found. Several Carson men married Boone women.

[3] M. Marion Estergren, *Kit Carson: A Portrait in Courage* (Norman, 1962), 24-25, reprints the advertisement, which originally appeared in the *Missouri Intelligencer*. It is not known who headed the wagon train. Certainly it was not Charles Bent, as many biographers have stated. Bent first went to Santa Fe in 1829.

[4] Mathew Kinkead was also born in Madison County, Kentucky, and had come to Santa Fe from Boone's Lick, Missouri. This may account for his hospitality to the sixteen year old Carson. The fine sketch of Kinkead by Mrs. Janet S. Lecompte in volume II of this Series, 189-99, rescues this Mountain Man from an undeserved obscurity.

[5] Kit Carson's *Autobiography,* edited by Milo M. Quaife (Lincoln, 1965; original edition Chicago, 1935), 6-9. Trammel was probably Richard Campbell.

ing of this, he returned to Taos in August 1828. Just a year later, he left Taos as a member of Ewing Young's first great trapping expedition to California. It was under Young, an old and capable hand at the game, that Kit learned the secrets of successful beaver trapping and the arduous art of survival under difficult conditions. Young found in Carson an apt pupil, who became a trusted lieutenant before they arrived back in Taos in April 1831. They had trapped the Arizona streams, both going out and coming back, and had penetrated as far as the Sacramento River in California.[6]

Like his fellow trappers, Carson now lived high for a few months on what he had earned during the last two years. By fall, the several hundred dollars he had earned by trapping were gone and he was glad to sign up with Thomas Fitzpatrick for a beaver hunt in the Rocky Mountains.[7] After trapping the Platte, the Sweetwater, and the Green, they wintered on the headwaters of Salmon River. In April 1832, trapping on Bear River and on Green River once more, they met the Sinclair party from Arkansas and learned that Captain John Gantt was trapping in New Park. Carson and three others left Fitzpatrick to work for Gantt, remaining in his employ about a year.

During January 1833, while they were camped on the Arkansas River, a band of fifty Crows stole nine of their horses. Carson was among a dozen men who went in pursuit, recovered the horses by stealth and then attacked the Crow camp for the pure excitement of doing it. During their spring hunt on the Laramie, two deserters made off with 400 pounds of beaver. Gantt sent Carson and another man after them but they were unsuccessful in catching the thieves.

[6] *Ibid.,* 9-21. Carson's *Autobiography* is the most reliable source available and is cited in preference to other sources, as a rule. For details of Young's expedition, which are not given here, see my sketch of Ewing Young in volume II of this Series, 385-87.

[7] Fitzpatrick was in Santa Fe because he had accompanied Smith, Jackson, and Sublette on the trading expedition in which Jedediah Smith lost his life.

However, they spent some time in one of Gantt's cabins on the Arkansas River.[8] From this base, Carson, Mitchell, Meek, and three Delawares, Tom Hill, Manhead, and Jonas, made an excursion into the Comanche country where they had quite an adventure. Attacked by a band of 200 Comanches, they cut the throats of their mules and forted up behind the bodies of the animals. With three firing, while the other three reloaded, they held off a dozen attacks, killing 42 Comanches. The horses of the attackers shied at the scent of fresh blood from the dead mules and would not approach very near. When night came, the six defenders headed back for the Arkansas on foot, abandoning their beaver.[9]

Upon their arrival, some of Gantt's men found them and told them that the rest were trapping in the Bayou Salade, or South Park. There they had trouble with horse-stealing Indians but Carson and three others recovered the animals. Flushed with success, Carson proposed to charge four Indians that were sighted at some distance, only to find that they belonged to a band of sixty. The charge turned into a headlong retreat until they reached the safety of their own camp. Soon after this, Carson and two others left Gantt and trapped the high mountain streams on their own. They had good luck and disposed of their beaver in Taos, in October 1833.[10]

[8] Carson's *Autobiography*, 22-29.

[9] Carson did not mention this incident in his *Autobiography*. Joe Meek described it fully but gave the date as May, 1834. This is obviously an impossible date insofar as Carson is concerned. It has caused some to reject the incident as one of Meek's more imaginary flights. However, it fits in perfectly, if dated a year earlier, when Carson was on the Arkansas River. Both Meek and Carson agree in saying that they afterward trapped in the Bayou Salade and Meek recounts the death of Guthrie by a stroke of lightning, while standing in Fraeb's tent. Thomas Fitzpatrick reports the death of Guthrie in his letter of Nov. 13, 1833, Sublette Papers, Mo. Hist. Soc. See Frances Fuller Victor, *River of the West* (Hartford, 1870), 154-58. Contrary to some opinion, I see nothing improbable about the story when the matter of the date is satisfactorily settled.

[10] Carson's *Autobiography*, 29-33.

Before the month ended, Kit joined Richard Bland Lee, who had a stock of trade goods to barter with the trappers in the mountain. They took the Old Spanish Trail and found Antoine Robidoux, with twenty men, on the Uinta River. While Lee traded with Robidoux, Kit pursued an Indian horse thief for 130 miles, killed him, and recovered the horses. Word was brought in that Bridger and Fitzpatrick were on the Little Snake River so, in March 1834, Lee and Carson went there. Lee sold the rest of his goods to Fitzpatrick but, after a month, he and three others left to become free trappers on the Laramie.[11]

After their hunt, on the way to join Jim Bridger's party and attend the summer rendezvous on Green River, Kit had what he described as his "worst difficult" experience. He had just fired at an elk, when he was rushed by two large grizzly bears. He managed to climb a tree, but lost his gun in the process, and had to remain there several hours until the bears finally decided they could not shake him out of the tree.[12]

At the rendezvous, Carson sold his beaver and bought supplies at high prices. When the rendezvous broke up in September, Carson joined a party of fifty under Bridger, which was headed for the Three Forks of the Missouri. The Blackfeet were so troublesome that they returned to the Snake River and camped there till February 1835. About thirty Blackfeet ran off eighteen of their horses and Carson was one of a dozen men who pursued them. In the ensuing fight, Kit saved the life of Mark Head but was painfully

---

[11] *Ibid.,* 33-37. I believe Carson to have been mistaken in referring to Lee as a partner of Bent Brothers and St. Vrain, although there may have been some temporary business association. The *Missouri Republican,* October 14, 1834, reported the return of "Capt. R. B. Lee, U.S. Army," from Santa Fe with eleven Bent and St. Vrain wagons. Carson stated that his employer was "Capt. Lee, U.S.A.," so it was not Stephen Louis Lee, as often has been assumed, for he was never an army officer.

[12] It was Carson's niece, Teresina Bent Scheurich, who supplied the "worst difficult" phrase. It is doubtless a fair sample of Carson's language.

wounded in the shoulder himself. He recovered in time to participate in the spring hunt, after which Bridger's party attended the rendezvous on Green River in the summer of 1835.[13]

It was at this rendezvous that Kit had his celebrated duel with a big Frenchman, whom he called "Shunar," who was attached to the party of Captain Drips. This man was a braggart and bully, who had beaten up several French trappers, which emboldened him to challenge the Americans. There is also some reason to believe that he and Kit Carson were both interested in the Arapaho girl that Carson married some time afterward. At any rate, Carson told him to shut up "or he would rip his guts." Both men went for a gun, mounted horses, and defied each other. Shunar's rifle bullet grazed Carson's head and neck, singeing his hair. Kit, at the same time, shot his antagonist in the forearm with a pistol. Carson started to get another pistol but Shunar begged for his life. Carson displayed marked resentment toward Shunar when he recounted the story in later years.[14]

Carson remained with Bridger's brigade for the fall hunt. On September 7, 1835, with Joe Meek and a dozen others, he encountered the remnant of Joseph Gale's party on the Madison River and the following day they combined to

---

[13] *Ibid.*, 39-42.

[14] *Ibid.*, 42-44. "Shunar's" name was probably Chouinard, Chinard, or something of the sort, since he was French. The earliest account is found in Samuel Parker, *Journal of an Exploring Tour beyond the Rocky Mountains* (Ithaca, 1838), 79-80. The Reverend Mr. Parker, a missionary, was present at the rendezvous, although he does not specifically say that he was an eyewitness. Neither he, nor Carson in his *Autobiography*, says that Shunar was killed. Dr. De Witt C. Peters, *Story of Kit Carson's Life and Adventures* (Hartford, 1874; original edition, 1858) relates the incident, 110-16. Dr. Peters contends that Kit did not intend to kill Shunar (whom he calls "Captain Shunan") but his argument is unconvincing. Stanley Vestal (pseud.), *Kit Carson: Happy Warrior of the Old West* (Boston, 1928), 117-27, relates upon flimsy authority, that Carson got another pistol and killed Shunar; this would have been plain murder. Vestal characterized Dr. Peters as "an ass," which may be so; but the braying of Peters is somewhat preferable to that of Vestal, both with reference to this incident and to the comparative value of their books.

stand off an attack by eighty Blackfeet. When winter set in, they retired to the vicinity of Fort Hall. In the spring of 1836, Carson, with Alexis Godey and four others, went over to Thomas McKay and his Hudson's Bay Company outfit. They trapped the entire length of the Humboldt (then called Mary's River) but did poorly. McKay then went to Fort Walla Walla and the Americans made a nearly starving return to Fort Hall. When McKay returned with plenty of horses, Carson accompanied him to the rendezvous of 1836, at the confluence of Horse Creek and Green River.[15]

Carson now cut loose from McKay and rejoined Bridger, who trapped the tributaries of the Yellowstone with a large number of men. In February 1837, while encamped on the Yellowstone opposite the mouth of Clark's Fork, a skirmish with some Blackfeet occurred. Bridger predicted they would be back in greater force and his men built a strong fort of cottonwood and brush. On February 22, the Blackfeet returned, eleven hundred strong. They built small conical forts suitable to cover ten men each and some skirmishing took place. However, the big fight which everyone anticipated failed to develop because the Blackfeet withdrew, alarmed by an appearance of aurora borealis. The spring hunt was made in the Crow country. At the rendezvous in July 1837, held on Horse Creek for the third consecutive year, Carson met Sir William Drummond Stewart.[16]

---

[15] For the period 1835-1839, Carson's recollection of events, as set forth in his *Autobiography,* 45-62, is somewhat confused and his chronology is demonstrably in error at several points. His dating of his service with McKay (whom he calls McCoy) is correct. His dating of the meeting with Joseph Gale's men as 1839 is four years off. See Osborne Russell, *Journal of A Trapper,* edited by Aubrey L. Haines (Portland, 1955), 30-31; also Victor, *op. cit.,* 167-69.

[16] The year 1836-1837 Carson characterized as uneventful due to smallpox among the Blackfeet. This is obviously wrong. He also placed the fort building episode in 1839, which is two years off. Russell, *op. cit.,* 53-4, gave the date correctly and Meek in Victor, *op. cit.,* 196-7, gave it within a month of the actual time. A comparison of the three accounts is interesting. All mention the small conical forts by means of which the number of Indians was estimated at 1100.

Mexican Girls. Many American trappers and traders were enchanted with New Mexican women. Marriage to them often yielded social, political, economic, and other advantageous perks. From George Wilkins Kendall, *Narrative of the Texan Santa Fe Expedition* (New York: Harper and Brothers, 1847). Courtesy of Western History Collections, University of Oklahoma.

For the fall hunt, Lucien Fontenelle took charge of more than a hundred trappers, of whom Carson was one. Bridger acted as guide or pilot for the party. They moved farther east this year and winter quarters were established on Powder River. Carson said it was the coldest winter of his recollection and they did not move out of camp till April 1, 1838. They passed quickly to the Yellowstone and thence to the Gallatin and finally to the Madison. Because of the great smallpox epidemic of 1837, there was no trouble with Blackfeet. However, on June 3, while scouting ahead up the Madison, Kit and a half dozen others came upon a large camp of Blackfeet. After reporting this, Kit went with forty men to attack the village. The trappers maintained the offensive for three hours, when their ammunition ran low, which enabled the Indians to counter attack. During the ensuing retreat to camp, Kit saved the life of Cotton Mansfield and, in his turn, was helped out of danger by David White. With ammunition replenished and with reinforcements from their camp, the trappers routed the enemy at last. This battle Kit described as "the prettiest fight I ever saw."[17]

After attending the rendezvous in the summer of 1838 on the Popo Agie and renewing his acquaintance with Stewart, Carson and seven others decided to go to Brown's Hole. There he joined two of the proprietors of Fort Davy Crockett, Philip Thompson and Prewitt Sinclair, who made a trading expedition that fall to the Navajo country.

---

[17] Russell, *op. cit.,* 81, 86-88; Victor, *op. cit.,* 230-32. *Robert Newell's Memoranda* edited by Dorothy Johansen (Portland, 1959), 35-36. Carson's recollection was that he spent the fall and winter of 1837-1838 at Fort Davy Crockett but this is one year too early. He definitely described the camp on Powder River and said he was there. Russell, Meek, and Newell all agree in saying that the Powder River camp was during the winter of 1837-1838. Russell said they broke camp March 25; Meek said March 1, Newell said March 29, and Carson said April 1. It is possible that small parties moved out for the spring hunt at slightly different times. Russell's description of the fight with the Blackfeet on June 3, 1838 does not agree too well with Carson's recollection, but both Russell and Meek mention Cotton Mansfield. Carson is two years off in his date for Powder River camp.

On his return, he spent the winter of 1838-1839 as a hunter for the fort. In the spring of 1839, he rejoined Bridger's party but soon teamed up with Dick Owens and three Canadians for a hunt of three months duration in the Black Hills. They had a good catch of beaver and returned to the rendezvous on Horse Creek in July, 1839.[18]

When it broke up, he and Owens went for a short time to Fort Hall, but soon returned to Brown's Hole, falling in with Doc Newell's small party on Black's Fork on August 23. They all arrived at Fort Davy Crockett on September 1, 1839. Later that month Carson participated in a fight against a band of Sioux that passed that way. In the horse stealing episodes that occurred later that fall, Owens was among the horse thieves and Carson was among those who disapproved of the thievery and tried to recover the horses for the purpose of returning them to the Shoshones from whom they had been stolen.[19]

In the spring of 1840, Carson went with Jack Robertson to Fort Uintah and sold such peltry as he had to Antoine Robidoux. That fall he trapped with six others on Grand River and spent the winter at Fort Davy Crockett in Brown's Hole. In the spring of 1841, he made a hunt in Utah and in New Park and sold his catch at Fort Uintah, remaining there till September 1841[20]

---

[18] My reconstruction of Carson's chronology puts him in Brown's Hole during two consecutive years, 1838-1839 and 1839-40, broken only by his hunt with Owens during the spring of 1839, which Carson placed one year too early. The Black Hills where they hunted are the Laramie Mountains, always so called by the trappers. There is no indication that the Black Hills of South Dakota were meant. Suppositions to this effect are based on the erroneous assumption that this hunt used the Powder River camp as its point of origin. Bearing these corrections in mind, see Carson's *Autobiography,* 54-56.

[19] *Newell's Memoranda, op. cit.,* 38-39; Victor, *op. cit.,* 259-260; see also LeRoy R. and Ann W. Hafen, *To the Rockies and Oregon* (Glendale, 1955), in *Far West and the Rockies Series,* vol. III, pp. 174-177, where E. W. Smith's Diary confirms Carson's presence at Fort Davy Crockett. It is probable that Carson's Indian wife died about this time. My thanks are due to the editor, Dr. Hafen, for advice and encouragement in making the revision of Carson's chronology that has been presented here.

[20] Carson's *Autobiography,* 62.

Beaver had been getting very scarce for the past few years and the price had also declined. Mountain Men were being forced to leave the mountains or face starvation. Carson was no exception. His wife had died and he had two children to support. In company with Old Bill Williams, Bill New, Colorado Mitchell, and a trapper named Frederick, they started for Bent's Old Fort on the Arkansas, where Carson took a job as hunter at a dollar a day. About this time, if not before, he took another squaw as wife.[21] In April 1842, he decided to return to Missouri with one of Bent's wagon trains. He visited friends and relatives, put his daughter Adaline in school, and went on to St. Louis. Feeling out of place after so long an absence, he boarded a steamer ascending the Missouri. On the boat he met John C. Frémont, of the Topographical Engineers of the U.S. Army, who was hoping to employ Captain Andrew Drips as guide for a government expedition to the Rocky Mountains. Carson told him he could do the job. Frémont liked him and, after checking on his reliability, offered him $100 a month.[22]

It should be noted that Carson was employed as a hunter at Bent's Fort only from September 1841 to April 1842. He could not have been, in that time, the leader of an independent band of trappers and Indian fighters as so many writers have depicted him. All such statements are traceable to the

---

[21] Carson does not mention his Indian wife, Waanibe, or his daughter by her in his *Autobiography*. It is not possible to say when they were married (by Indian custom) but Adaline, the first child, was probably born in 1837. Several sources mention a second daughter, who died at about the age of three by falling into a kettle of boiling soap in Taos. F. W. Cragin Papers, The Pioneer's Museum, Colorado Springs, Colorado, Notebook XII, p. 21. Cragin's informant was Carson's eldest daughter by his last marriage, Teresina (Mrs. DeWitt Fulton Allen), in an interview of March 18, 1908, at her home in Raton, New Mexico. On the question of his second squaw, see note 26 below. It must also be noted, at this point, that Carson's residence at Bent's Old Fort, in September 1841, was his first connection with that famous place. He could not have helped to build it, as many writers have stated, because it was not built until 1834 and Carson was last on the Arkansas, prior to 1841, in May 1833, at which time he was employed by John Gantt not by William Bent. In addition, he was a hunter and trapper not a bricklayer.

[22] Carson's *Autobiography*, 65-66.

stories of Oliver P. Wiggins and it is highly doubtful if any credence can be placed in any of the statements made by Wiggins insofar as Kit Carson is concerned. It may be well to state here that Kit Carson was a free trapper for a good many different employers, as has been shown; that he was a hunter for Fort Davy Crockett and Bent's Fort, but that he never commanded any body of men engaged in the fur trade, or in buffalo hunting, nor was he in command during any of the Indian fights in which he took part over the years.[23]

Carson's meeting with Frémont occurred when he was thirty-two years old and Frémont was twenty-eight. Frémont was just launching his career of western exploration. For Carson, this was the turning point of his life. He now had the chance to continue his life in the west on a different basis. His knowledge of the country and how to survive as he traveled over it must now be employed in directing and serving a new sort of enterprise. Carson took his duties seriously and measured up well.

Frémont's first expedition surveyed South Pass and climbed Fremont Peak in the Wind River Range, which he erroneously believed to be the highest elevation in the Rocky Mountains. Carson climbed with the rest; if the

---

[23] The life story of Oliver P. Wiggins was dictated by Wiggins to Dr. F. W. Cragin and occupies considerable space in his notebooks. Cragin himself had doubts of the veracity of Wiggins. I have gone over the material carefully and it is my belief that nothing said by Wiggins regarding Carson can be accepted. See Lorene and Kenny Englert, "Oliver Perry Wiggins: Fantastic Bombastic Frontiersman" in *The Denver Westerners Monthly Roundup* (February, 1964) XX, pp. 3-14, which reaches the same conclusion. Another writer on Carson, William F. Drannan, *Thirty-One Years on the Plains and in the Mountains* (1900) has been exposed as a fraud in W. N. Bate, *Frontier Legend* (1954). Wiggins has been accepted by Charles Coutant, E. L. Sabin, Stanley Vestal, David Lavender, Bernice Black-welder, and M. Morgan Estergren, among writers on Kit Carson. Sabin and Vestal have been widely quoted by other writers. All have been deceived by Oliver P. Wiggins, who may have seen Carson but was certainly never acquainted with him in the intimate way he claimed and probably not at all. LeRoy Hafen has informed me that he knew another similar fraudulent character, Col. Dick Rutledge, who paraded in long hair and buckskin suit in Denver in the 1920s.

government wanted to pay him for climbing mountains, he would do it. He educated Frémont with respect to Indians; occasionally he and Frémont squabbled but it was soon forgotten and neither ever said a harsh word about the other that would be made public. Charles Preuss, Frémont's German-born cartographer, felt that Carson insisted on warning them about Indians in order to make himself more important. Preuss enjoyed good eating, however, and he appreciated the fact that Carson would take the trouble to get the fattest buffalo cow even though it meant more work.[24] Carson was with the first expedition from June 10, 1842, to August 31, 1842, leaving it when Fort Laramie was reached.[25] Where he spent the next four months is not recorded. He says that he went to Bent's Fort in January 1843, and from there to Taos where he was married to Marie Josefa Jaramillo, younger sister of the wife of Charles Bent, on February 6, 1843.[26] Carson was thirty-three and

---

[24] Charles Preuss, *Exploring With Fremont,* translated and edited by Erwin G. Gudde and Elizabeth K. Gudde (Norman, 1958), 47, 70. Preuss referred to Carson as "Kid Karsten." This was not in levity, as his translators believe, but in ignorance, for he writes of the young of the beaver as "kids" not as kits.

[25] John C. Frémont, *Narrative of the Exploring Expedition to the Rocky Mountains in the Year 1842 and to Oregon and California in the Years 1843 and 1844.* (New York, 1846), 5-51.

[26] Quantrille D. McClung, *Carson-Bent-Boggs Geneology* (Denver, 1962), 72-73, reproduces the Baptismal Certificate of Carson as well as the Marriage Certificate. Carson had become a Catholic and had been baptized on January 28, 1842, in Taos. This was while he was hunter at Bent's Fort and it may be surmised that he was contemplating marriage to Josefa at this time. Concerning the question of whether Carson had a second Indian wife, a Cheyenne squaw, called Making Out Road, I am inclined to think that he did for a short time, until she left him. This has been denied, on the authority of Teresina Bent Scheurich, by recent Carson biographers such as M. Morgan Estergren and Bernice Blackwelder. However, Jesse Nelson, husband of Susan Carson, Kit's niece, told F. W. Cragin in an interview dated July 9, 1908, that this was true and also that he lived for a time with Antonina Luna who later married Bill Tharp. My belief is that Carson habitually concealed these connections from the women of his family, in accordance with the standards of the time, but did not attempt to conceal them from the men. Adaline was tangible proof of his first marriage, so that could not be concealed, but he did not mention her in his *Autobiography.* For Jesse Nelson's statement, see F. W. Cragin Papers, Notebook VIII, p. 83.

his bride was fifteen. L. H. Garrard, who saw her four years later, credited her with a rather haughty kind of beauty.[27]

In April 1843, Kit left Taos to accompany an east-bound wagon train of Bent Brothers and St. Vrain as a hunter. They encountered Captain Philip St. George Cooke endeavoring to protect some Mexican traders from attack by Jacob Snively and other Texans. Cooke could only police the Santa Fe Trail within American territory. Carson was offered $300 to carry word to Governor Armijo of New Mexico, so that he could provide protection for the American traders. Dick Owens accompanied Carson as far as Bent's Fort, and Carson went on to Taos where he asked the alcalde to forward the information to the governor. He then carried messages for Armijo to the traders with a Mexican companion. They were beset by Indians. The Mexican offered to be captured and let Carson escape. Carson, admiring his bravery, stayed with him and they bluffed the Indians out of their hostile intentions. When Carson reached Bent's Fort, he learned that Cooke had disarmed the Texans and that Frémont had just passed by on his second expedition and wanted Carson to accompany him.[28]

Carson caught up with Frémont, who sent him back to get mules at Bent's Fort. He rejoined Frémont at Fort St. Vrain a few days later. Frémont reached Fort St. Vrain on July 4, 1843, and it was a full year later, on July 2, 1844, that the expedition returned to Bent's Fort. During that time they had explored the Great Salt Lake, traversed the Oregon Trail to Fort Vancouver, explored southeastern Oregon and northwestern Nevada, crossed the Sierras in winter to Sutter's Fort, visited the California towns, re-

---

[27] Lewis Hector Garrard, *Wah-to-Yah and the Taos Trail* (Norman, 1955; original edition, 1850), 181.

[28] Carson's *Autobiography*, 69-73. Cooke's journal covering this affair may be found in *Mississippi Valley Historical Review* (1925-6), XII, pp. 72-98, 227-55.

crossed by Oak Creek Pass to the Mojave River, and followed a difficult desert route back to the Rocky Mountains of Colorado, which they crossed by an unusual path.[29] The crossing of the Sierras in winter was rather foolhardy and the party was lucky to come through as well as it did. Thomas Fitzpatrick, as well as Carson, guided this expedition but Frémont never became friendly with him as he did with Kit. Alexis Godey received a share of the admiration Frémont expressed for Carson, particularly in the well-known incident in which the two pursued some Indian thieves on behalf of a Mexican and came back with two scalps.[30] Joseph R. Walker, a famous Mountain Man, joined them in the desert on the way back and his knowledge was useful to the expedition. But no one displaced Carson as Frémont's ideal frontiersman and so he gained his hold on the public imagination when Frémont's reports were published.

Carson now spent several months at his home in Taos. In March 1845, he and Dick Owens decided to try farming on the Little Cimarron, about 50 miles east of Taos and Josefa joined him there after he had a cabin built. But in August word came that Frémont was at Bent's Fort on his way to California and wanted his services again. Carson and Owens sold out quickly and joined Frémont, while Josefa went back to Taos.[31] They crossed the Nevada desert south of the Humboldt, split into two groups, one headed by Frémont, the other by Theodore Talbot and Joseph R. Walker. Carson remained with Frémont, crossing to Sutter's Fort. Through some misunderstanding, Walker was not on the Tulare Lake Fork where they had expected to meet him.

---

[29] Frémont, *op. cit., passim.*

[30] Preuss, *op. cit.,* 127, expressed disgust at the Carson-Godey exploit, so highly praised by Frémont. He also stated that Carson was disgruntled because Godey was entitled to both scalps. However, after Tabeau's death at the hands of Indians, Preuss modified his attitude to some extent; *ibid.,* 130.

[31] Carson's *Autobiography,* 87-88.

Carson and Owens were sent to look for him and found him on the San Joaquin.[32]

After Frémont had second thoughts about defying General Castro at Gavilan Peak, he led his party northward into the Klamath Indian country. Here Lieutenant Gillespie reached him with news that war with Mexico had been declared. The Klamaths were hostile, however, and it was Carson's vigilance that enabled a night attack to be repelled. Carson, on this occasion, referred to Godey as a fool for exposing himself in the firelight to the arrows of the Indians. Two good men, Basil Lajeunesse and a Delaware named Crane, were killed. Punitive measures were taken and the Delawares felt better. But Carson felt that the Klamaths were even tougher warriors than the Blackfeet.[33]

When they got back to Sutter's Fort, events began to move swiftly. The Bear Flag party was organized and, with help from Frémont's men, fought the Californians in Petaluma Valley and drove them back to San Rafael. Frémont stopped to rest here and sent Carson, with Granville P. Swift and Jack Neil, ahead to scout. They captured Francisco and Ramon de Haro and their uncle, Jose de los Berreyesa, who had landed from a boat at the Embarcadero. Carson rode back and reported this to Frémont and asked what should be done with the prisoners. Frémont said, "Mr. Carson, I have no use for prisoners – do your duty." Carson returned, conferred with Swift and Neil, and they had the prisoners shot. They were influenced by the killing of two young Americans, Cowey and Fowler, by Californians, and by the rumor that this had been done in a barbarous manner. Thus, it was considered to be retaliation.[34]

---

[32] *Ibid.*, 89-93; John C. Frémont, *Memoirs of My Life* (Chicago and New York, 1887), 432-55.

[33] Frémont, *Memoirs*, 487-96. Carson's life was saved by Sagundai, one of the Delaware chiefs, a few days after the night attack.

[34] The account of this controversial episode is taken from William M. Boggs, "Manuscript about Bents' Fort, Kit Carson, the Far West and Life Among the

When the California Battalion of mounted riflemen was formed, Carson became a private in one of the companies and served until he was detached on September 5, 1846, by Frémont to carry dispatches to Washington, D.C., with an escort of 15 men. One month later, he met General Stephen Watts Kearny at Socorro, New Mexico, and was ordered by him to exchange places with Thomas Fitzpatrick. It now became Fitzpatrick's task to deliver the messages to Washington and Carson's task to guide Kearny's small force to California. Carson accepted his fate most reluctantly but brought Kearny safely to Warner's Ranch by December 2, 1846. However, a force of Californians had gathered at the Indian village of San Pasqual in a belated effort to oppose American occupation. This force Kearny attacked on December 5, at the same time sending Alexis Godey and two companions to get help from Commodore Stockton at San Diego, thirty miles away. When Godey and his men returned, they were captured by the Californians, who now had Kearny surrounded. Burgess, one of Godey's men, was exchanged but was unable to say what measures were being taken by Stockton. It was in this situation, that Kit Carson and the naval lieutenant, Edward Fitzgerald Beale, volunteered to go through the enemy lines for reinforcements. A young Delaware Indian, a servant of Beale, also went and was actually the first to get through. Beale and Carson also made it, so much exhausted that it took Carson several days and Beale much longer to recover.[35] Stockton had already sent the required aid, so the heroic journey had been unnecessary. Carson participated in the battle of San Gabriel and when Frémont arrived in mid-January, rejoined him.

On February 25, 1847, Frémont again sent Carson with

Indians," edited by LeRoy R. Hafen in *Colorado Magazine* (March, 1930), VII, pp. 62-63. Boggs had it directly from Carson, whom he questioned about it. More blame attaches to Frémont than to Carson for the shooting. Frémont, in his *Memoirs,* 525, placed the blame on his Delaware Indians!

[35] Carson's *Autobiography,* 108-117.

dispatches to the war department in Washington. Beale accompanied him and they reached Washington in June 1847. Carson returned to California, bearing dispatches from President Polk, arriving in Los Angeles in October 1847.[36] During the winter he was assigned to scouting duty and, on May 4, 1848, he left once more as a courier to Washington. This transcontinental trip is the one made famous by the detailed description written by Lieutenant George D. Brewerton and published in *Harper's Magazine*.[37]

Carson and Brewerton parted company in Taos. Carson picked up ten men in Taos and went first to Fort Leavenworth. From there, he went on to Washington alone and was back in Taos by October 1848, having stopped to visit briefly in St. Louis.[38] During the winter, Kit acted as a guide for two expeditions under Major Benjamin Beall, policing the Indians north and east of Taos.[39] He was at home when Frémont came to Taos, in January 1849, from his disastrous attempt to make a winter crossing of the San Juan Mountains. Frémont stayed at Carson's house for several days.

In April 1849, Carson and Maxwell started farming and ranching operations at Rayado, on land to which Maxwell had a claim which was eventually made good. But Carson

---

[36] *Ibid.*, 117-122. Carson called on President Polk, on June 7 and again on June 14, 1847, presenting Frémont's side of his controversy with General Kearny. Carson was in California when the court martial decided, January 31, 1848, in Washington, to uphold Kearny's charges.

[37] George D. Brewerton, "A Ride with Kit Carson" in *Harper's Magazine*, (August, 1853) VII, pp. 306-334. The article added substantially to Carson's fame. It seems probable, although it is not certain, that Carson carried the letter which first acquainted the rest of the country with the discovery of gold in California.

[38] F. W. Cragin Papers, Notebook VIII, pp. 51, 75, 77. Jesse Nelson (1827-1923) was Cragin's informant. He mentioned Jim Dawzle, George Simpson, Louis Simmons, Auguste Archambeau, and another Frenchman, Lawrence, as among the ten, in addition to himself, who went to Fort Leavenworth. He said that Carson resigned as lieutenant in the regular army at Fort Leavenworth. However, Carson's commission had never been approved by the Senate.

[39] Carson's *Autobiography*, 127-29.

was in demand as a guide for military units and was often absent from the ranch.[40]

In November 1849, when Major Grier endeavored to rescue Mrs. White and her child from the Jicarilla Apaches, Carson was added as a guide, although Antoine Leroux and Robert Fisher were already so employed. The failure of Major Grier to order an immediate attack, when the Apache camp was found, gave the Indians time to kill Mrs. White before making off. In the Apache camp was found a yellow back novel, possibly the property of Mrs. White, which represented Carson as a great Indian fighter, and it saddened him to think he had failed to save her life. Returning, they encountered the worst snow storm Carson was ever in, and did not reach Barclay's Fort until November 25, although Fisher and a few others came in on November 23.[41]

In March 1850, Kit led a pursuit of nine Indians, who had stolen horses from his ranch, and killed five of them. Two months later, he and Tim Goodale drove about fifty horses and mules to Fort Laramie to trade with the emigrants. Goodale went to California and Carson, on his way home, learned at the Greenhorn settlement of an Apache ambush. Charles Kinney, a Mountain Man living at Greenhorn, was the only one he could get to accompany him. They evaded the Indians and got through to Taos. That fall, Kit

[40] *Ibid.*, 130-131; also F. W. Cragin Papers, Notebook VIII, pp. 49, 83. Jesse Nelson, husband of Carson's niece, Susan, settled at Rayado in 1851. He said that Carson bought the old Army hospital at Rayado, when the soldiers moved to Fort Union in 1851, and the Nelsons lived in it with the Carsons. When Kit was away, Josefa would leave Rayado for a visit with her relatives in Taos.

[41] Carson's *Autobiography*, 131-36. Alexander Barclay's Diary gives details of the storm under the dates mentioned. Carson said he had heard that Leroux advised a delay and a parley with the Indians. Dick Wootton, who was present, and who had no great love for Leroux, blamed Grier for the decision. See also Forbes Parkhill, *Blazed Trail of Antoine Leroux* (Los Angeles, 1965), 134-42. The dime novel found was probably Charles Averill, *Kit Carson, Prince of the Gold Hunters,* which was published in 1849, and is thought to have been the first of many thrillers exploiting the real and imaginary adventures of Carson. Carson did not participate in the California gold rush.

arrested a man named Fox, who was charged with planning to murder Samuel Weatherhead and Elias Brevoort, in order to rob a wagon train of theirs. The arrest was made at the request of Lieutenant Oliver Taylor of the Dragoons, to whom the plot had been divulged but nothing could afterward be proved in court.[42]

In March 1851, Kit took a dozen wagons and went to St. Louis to get goods for Lucien Maxwell. On the way back he decided to follow the Arkansas to Bent's Fort and fell afoul of a Cheyenne band that was seeking revenge for the flogging of one of their chiefs by order of an officer of Colonel Edwin V. Sumner's command. Kit had only fifteen men, of whom thirteen were Mexicans. He talked the Indians out of the notion of immediate revenge and sent off a rider to Rayado for help. The rider first met Colonel Sumner, who refused help, but Major Grier at Rayado sent aid. As Jesse Nelson described the incident, twenty Cheyennes, with a whole village nearby, made the threat. A big Indian had a hatchet over Kit's head, Nelson had a gun on this Indian and another Indian had a bow, with the arrow pulled back to the head, on Nelson. Ah-mah-nah-ko, the son of Old Bark, a Cheyenne Chief, recognized Kit and averted the crisis. He also warned Kit that the Cheyennes would try to ambush him and Nelson felt that this friendly act saved their lives.[43]

In March 1852, Maxwell and Carson got together eighteen men to go trapping, with Carson in charge. They trapped South Park, followed the South Platte to the plains, then on to the Laramie River, then into New Park and Old Park in turn, finally crossing to the headwaters of the

[42] Carson's *Autobiography*, 138-41. The Elias Brevoort Manuscript, in the Bancroft Library, Berkeley, California, substantiates Carson's account.

[43] Carson's *Autobiography*, 141-46. Nelson's account is in F. W. Cragin Papers, Notebook VIII, pp. 61, 65, 69. There is a drawing of Ah-mah-nah-ko and his wife in Lieutenant J. W. Abert's Report, *House Exec. Doc. no. 41, 30 Cong., 1 sess.* (Serial 517.).

Arkansas and trapping it till it emerged from the mountains. This was more of a pleasure trip, organized as a final farewell to the old life that Carson loved so well, though they were quite successful in catching beaver.[44]

The next year, 1853, Carson and Maxwell made their famous sheep drive to California. Carson left in February and arrived over the California Trail in August. Maxwell arrived a little later; John Hatcher had been the first to set out and the first to reach California. The sheep cost not more than fifty cents each and were sold at $5.50 per head. Carson and Maxwell returned from Los Angeles across Arizona, arriving back in Taos on Christmas day, 1853.[45]

Carson now learned that he had been appointed Indian agent and entered upon the duties connected with that difficult assignment, which were to occupy his time and provide his living until 1861. During this time he made his residence at Taos, whither the Indian delegations came to transact their business. During the earlier years, the Indians were very restless and often hostile. Carson accompanied a number of military expeditions against them under various army officers.[46] He was also a very good agent, doing his best to carry out the orders of the government but retaining always a sympathetic understanding of the Indians and

---

[44] Carson's *Autobiography*, 146. It would be interesting to know the names of the men who made this hunt. It seems probable that it included a number of the old Mountain Men who took the sheep to California in 1853. The expedition resembled Sir William Drummond Stewart's farewell trip of 1843 in its conception and purpose. No other reference of any value has come to my attention on this matter.

[45] *Ibid.*, 146-48. Carson's achievement in respect to the sheep drive has been overrated. Dick Wooton had made such a drive a year earlier. Also, while Carson mentions only Maxwell and himself and two other men as participating, there were 33 men in all, and the sheep were in several herds. Louis Simmons, and his wife, Carson's daughter Adaline, went on this drive and remained in California as did John L. Hatcher. See F. W. Cragin Papers, Notebook I, p. 24. Cragin's informant was Jake Beard, interviewed at Trinidad, Colorado, October 31, 1904. Beard was one of those who made the trip.

[46] Carson's *Autobiography*, 149-70, contains details of these various expeditions which will not be given here.

their problems. He did what he could to improve their situation and the Indians had much respect for him. He was handicapped by his illiteracy and by his inability to keep his accounts in a satisfactory way. He was forced to pay some one to help him in these matters, for the government would make him no allowance for such expenses.[47]

In the fall of 1856 occurred an altercation between David Meriwether, Territorial Governor of New Mexico and Superintendent of Indian affairs, and Carson, as Indian Agent, which led to Meriwether's suspension of Carson and to his lodging charges of disobedience, insubordination, and cowardice against him. Carson acknowledged his misconduct and was re-instated. An examination of Meriwether's account of the incident, dictated in his old age, leads to the conclusion that Carson merited censure on the first two charges. He was not guilty of cowardice, although a faulty judgment of Indian demonstrations led him to be over cautious on this occasion. It speaks well for him that he acknowledged his error.[48]

It was in 1856 that Kit Carson, prompted by the desire to capitalize in a financial way upon the tremendous and far-flung reputation he had achieved, dictated his autobiography and turned it over to Jesse B. Turley, to be used as Turley thought proper for their joint benefit. The actual writer of Carson's memoirs was neither Turley nor Dr. Peters nor Mrs. Peters. It was John Mostin, Carson's secretary. However, Turley undoubtedly transferred the manuscript to Peters, who used it in writing a biography of Carson

---

[47] A fair evaluation is that of Marshall D. Moody, "Kit Carson, Agent to the Indians of New Mexico, 1853-1861," in *New Mexico Historical Review* (January, 1953), XXVIII, pp. 1-20. Concerning Carson's illiteracy, it should be said that there is ample evidence to indicate that he could neither read nor write, except for the ability to sign his name, C. Carson. Two recent biographers, M. Marion Estergren and Bernice Blackwelder, contend that he was literate but the evidence presented is unconvincing.

[48] David Meriwether, *My Life in the Mountains and on the Plains,* edited by Robert A. Griffin (Norman, Okla., 1965), 226-33.

which he published in 1858. Peters was able to supply quite a few details from having heard some of Carson's stories during his two years as an army surgeon stationed in New Mexico, 1854-1856. In addition, there was much padding of a rather unrealistic nature, which caused Carson to remark on having it read to him that he thought Dr. Peters "had laid it on a leetle too thick"[49]

In 1860, while hunting in the San Juan Mountains, Kit had an accident. He was leading his horse, when the animal fell and rolled down a steep slope, dragging Carson after him entangled in the reins. He never fully recovered from the injury to his chest that he incurred at this time.

In 1861 he resigned as Indian Agent and entered the United States Army as colonel of the First New Mexico Volunteer Infantry. He participated in the battle of Valverde, under General Canby, and was brevetted brigadier general for his services in that battle. There followed, in 1863-1864, a long and arduous campaign against the Navajos, planned and directed by General Carleton and ably executed by Carson, who destroyed their crops and penetrated their stronghold in the Cañon de Chelly. Although Carson had carried out a "scorched earth" policy, he was as generous as possible in all his recommendations for government policy toward the conquered Indians.[50]

In November 1864, he was ordered by General Carleton to invade the Kiowa and Comanche country, having under

---

[49] For a discussion of the recovery of this manuscript and of Turley's connection with it, see Milo M. Quaife's introduction in his edition of the *Autobiography*, so frequently cited heretofore. Information regarding Jesse B. Turley is to be found in Jesse Nelson's statement in F. W. Cragin Papers, Notebook VII, p. 59. The identity of Carson's scribe has been established by comparing the handwriting of the manuscript in the Newberry Library, Chicago, with that of a holograph letter of John Mostin, Taos, New Mexico, September 22, 1856, a copy of which was kindly furnished to me by Mr. Dale L. Morgan.

[50] See Estergren, *op. cit.,* 231-33; 238-50. Also Raymond E. Lundgren, ed., "A Diary of Kit Carson's Navajo Campaign, 1863-1864," in *New Mexico Historical Review* (July, 1946), XXI, pp. 226-46.

his command 335 men and 75 scouts. With this force he penetrated to the old Bent trading post of Adobe Walls, on the Canadian River, and gave battle to about 3,000 Indians, chiefly Kiowas but with some Comanches, Apaches, and a few Arapahoes as well. Fortunately, Carson had two small howitzers, which Lieutenant Pettis employed to good effect. Carson lost two men, estimated the Indian loss at 60 (others placed it higher), and withdrew in good order. It was his opinion that, but for the howitzers, the Indians would have wiped them out. He prudently resisted sentiment on the part of some to engage the Indians again, judging correctly that they had been taught a good lesson.[51]

This battle occurred almost simulanteously with Colonel Chivington's massacre of the Cheyennes on their Sand Creek reservation. When Carson heard of what had happened there, he was extremely indignant, especially at the killing of Indian women and children.[52]

After this, Carson commanded briefly at Camp Nichols and then made a trip east, stopping at Fort Leavenworth, St. Louis, Washington, and New York. In July 1866, he was assigned to the command of Fort Garland, north of Taos in Colorado territory, where General W. T. Sherman visited him in September of that year.[53] Carson was mustered out of the army on November 22, 1867. He had already decided to settle at Boggsville, Colorado (near present Las Animas) where William Bent had made some land available to him and Tom Boggs. His family was already established there.

In February 1868, however, he made another trip to Washington on behalf of the Ute Indians, always his favorite tribe. He also went to New York and Boston to see if medical men could help his chest and neck pains. He arrived back in mid-April, much exhausted by constant

---

[51] Estergren, *op. cit.*, 253-61.

[52] James F. Rusling, *Across America* (New York, 1874), 138.

[53] *Ibid.*, 139-40.

coughing, caused by an aneurysm which had developed and caused spasms in the bronchial tubes. On April 13, 1868, two days after his return, Josefa gave birth to a girl, her seventh living child, and died ten days later.[54] Kit died exactly one month later, May 23, 1868, at Fort Lyon, where he had been taken about a week earlier at the suggestion of Dr. Tilton, the army surgeon at the fort. Kit knew that his end was near and asked Aloys Scheurich to prepare him a buffalo steak and some coffee. After eating, he smoked his clay pipe until the final hemorrhage that produced his death. His will, dated May 15, 1868, named Tom Boggs as guardian of his children, a duty which Boggs carried out as best he could. The remains of Carson and his wife were removed to Taos in January 1869, where their graves are still to be seen.[55]

Kit Carson was not very impressive to look at. The Carson men were usually large. Kit was the runt of the family. Numerous people have described their surprise and disappointment on first seeing him. William Tecumseh Sherman described him as "a small stoop-shouldered man, with reddish hair, freckled face, soft blue eyes, and nothing to indicate extraordinary courage or daring."[56] He was long in the body and short in the legs, which helps to account for Frémont's great admiration for Kit as "one of the finest horsemen I have ever seen."[57]

Carson was catapulted into fame by Frémont's *Reports*.

---

[54] The children of Christopher and Josepha Jaramillo Carson were as follows: Charles, b. 1849, d. 1851; William (Julian), b. October 1, 1852; Teresina, b. June 23, 1855; Christopher, b. June 13, 1858; Charles, b. August 2, 1861; Rebecca, b. April 13, 1864; Estafanita, b. December 23, 1866; Josefita, b. April 13, 1868. There are numerous descendants of several of these children. See Quantrille D. McClung, *Carson-Bent-Boggs Genealogy* (Denver, 1962), 74-75 ff.

[55] Albert W. Thompson "Thomas O. Boggs, Early Scout," in *Colorado Magazine* (July, 1930), VII, p. 159.

[56] William T. Sherman, *Memoirs* (New York, 1875), I, pp. 46-47.
A portrait of Carson appears herein at page 14.

[57] Frémont, *Narrative*, 9.

It is doubtful if government documents ever achieved such popularity before or ever will again. The question arises as to how Carson came to be the sole beneficiary of Frémont's hero worship. Basil Lajeunesse was his favorite. He spoke of Dick Owens and Alexis Godey with the same praise that he lavished on Carson, declaring that under Napoleon, all three would have become marshals.[58] Both Godey and Lajeunesse were French, as were most of Frémont's men, and the American public was not looking for a French hero. Jesse Benton Frémont described Carson as "perfectly Saxon . . . clear and fair." Carson was the type that the American public could take to its heart. Owens was with Frémont only on the third expedition; Fitzpatrick and Walker were older men, whose reputations were already established within their limited world. Carson alone seemed to fill the popular conception of the all-American boy-hero.

By a similar process, an earlier generation had made an idol of Daniel Boone. Despite the ease with which it has been demonstrated that many others had the same qualifications or even better ones for being frontier heroes, both Boone and Carson have retained their place in the public affection with remarkable success. The answer lies in their simplicity. They were not self-seeking; fame came to them, and they accepted it with becoming modesty. The very lack of those qualities of leadership, which others had in greater degree, was what enabled Boone and Carson to survive untarnished in public estimation.

Of the two, Carson had more ability than Boone, as a glance at Carson's army career will show. Carson loved the free and easy life of the trapper as well as Boone. But he also had a devotion to duty that made him a sucessful army officer. There was nothing of the self-advertising showman in Carson. His autobiography is a straightforward, un-

---

[58] Frémont, *Memoirs*, 427.

adorned account, which has the ring of truth for any reader.
In 1866, when shown the cover of a magazine on which he
was depicted with one arm around a woman he had just
saved from a number of Indians shown biting the dust,
Carson gazed intently at the picture for a short time. Then
he said, "Gentlemen, that thar may be true, but I haint got
no recollection of it." [59]

It has been pointed out that there were two ways in which
Carson suffered at the hands of literary people. First, there
was Dr. Peters and a long line of later biographers, who
made him into a genteel, manly type, acceptable to mid-
nineteenth century standards of proper behavior. There
was also an avid crew of hack writers of dime novels, who
made him into a blood and thunder hero who turned up to
rescue emigrant parties most providentially and always in a
manner that bore slight resemblance to reality. Strangely
enough, these two widely different literary types were frequently combined. [60]

Yet there is less difference between the real Carson and
his legend than is usually the case with frontier heroes. This
is because Carson was really a man of many admirable
qualities and few reprehensible traits and because he really
did lead a strenuous and adventuresome life.

Bill Bent, Montana pioneer and squaw man, said, "In the
light of my own experiences I can come to but one conclusion and that is my uncle Kit was an over-rated man.
These same hair-breadth escapes, these same trials caused
by hunger and cold have been gone through by many a man
who has helped make this country and not one word has

---

[59] Henry Inman, *Old Santa Fe Trail* (New York, 1898), 381.

[60] The analysis presented here is that of Kent Ladd Steckmesser, *Western Hero
in History and Legend* (Norman, 1965), 13-53. This is a perceptive study, marred
only by the author's perpetuation of the myth that Carson was the leader of his own
band of trappers, known as the "Carson Men."

been written into the story of their deeds." [61] Bent was both right and wrong. It was not that Kit was overrated (although he was, to some extent), so much as that others, who were just as deserving, were underrated or not rated at all. Yet, if history must single out one individual to receive all the credit that should be shared with others of his kind, it is difficult to find a more deserving candidate for the honor than Kit Carson.[62] He was a diamond in the rough.[63]

[61] A. J. Noyes, *In the Land of the Chinook* (Helena, 1917), 88-89. The Montana pioneer claimed to have been born in St. Louis in 1846, and to have been the son of William Bent, of Bent's Fort, and Sarah Sullivan. I have been unable to verify this or to fit him into the Bent family. However, his observation on Carson is of interest, regardless of his parentage.

[62] Allan Nevins, "Kit Carson, Bayard of the Plains," in *American Scholar,* (Summer, 1939), VIII, pp. 333-49, concludes that Carson was not greater than others of his kind but more typical. The comparison with Bayard was originally made by Frémont; perhaps Crillon would have been a more accurate choice from French history. Dixon Wecter, *Hero in America* (New York, 1941), makes no mention of Kit Carson, as unaccountable omission in such a book.

[63] My former colleague of many years, Dr. Elizabeth B. White, a scholar of rigorous historical standards, on learning that I was engaged in preparing a sketch of Carson admonished me, "Don't be too hard on Kit; we need a few legends." For a much fuller treatment of Carson, see my new edition of his memoirs, published under the title *"Dear Old Kit": The Historical Christopher Carson* (Norman, 1968).

Sylvestre S. Pratte

by DAVID J. WEBER
San Diego State College

Sylvestre S. Pratte's career as a Mountain Man comprised a scant two years, during which he operated out of Taos on the edge of Mexico's far northern frontier. Yet, from the moment of his arrival there, he was one of the most powerful trader-trappers in the area. Although Pratte's name appears often in the annals of fur trade history, his activities have never been examined and their significance assessed. Perhaps his premature death robbed him of some of the notoriety that his contemporaries came to achieve.

The eldest son of prominent merchant General Bernard Pratte and Emilie Sauveur Labbadie, Sylvestre Pratte was born in St. Louis on September 22, 1799.[1] Nothing is known of his education or upbringing, but his family connections make it seem unlikely that he fit the prototype of the uneducated and unwashed Mountain Man. Pratte's marriage, for example, on June 5, 1822, was to Odille Delassus, a daughter of Major Camille Delassus, brother of the last Spanish Governor of Louisiana.[2] As young Pratte grew to manhood his father became increasingly involved in the Missouri River fur trade. By 1818 General Pratte, along with such notables as Manuel Lisa, had become one of the partners in Cabanné and Company. This organization folded within a year, but Pratte, Bartholomew Berthold, Pierre Chouteau and Jean Pierre Cabanné reorganized into

---

[1] Frederick Billon, *Annals of St. Louis in Its Territorial Days from 1804 to 1820* (St. Louis, 1888), 181.

[2] *Ibid.*, and (St. Louis) *Missouri Republican,* June 12, 1822.

what would popularly be known as "the French Company." By 1823 their official name would be Bernard Pratte and Company.[3]

Although we know very little of Sylvestre Pratte's initial involvement in the fur trade, it seems likely that he received his first taste of the business while in the employ of one of his father's companies. By 1820 young Pratte seems to have had some experience, for spring of that year found him and Anthony Vasques of St. Louis operating as licensed traders on the Missouri River. Their stay was shortened when, before dawn on May 21st, Sac Indians raided their camp and killed one of the hired men. Pratte, Vasques, and three others, fled to their boat and escaped downstream to the army encampment at Council Bluffs. Returning six days later with troops, they found most of their trade goods and furs destroyed or stolen. The partners claimed a loss of $1,098, for which they waited six years for the federal government to reimburse them $464.[4] This would not be the last of Sylvestre Pratte's misfortunes as a fur trader.

Following his altercation with the Sacs we lose sight of Pratte's career for a few years. In 1823 he was working for his father's company, and autumn of 1824 found him leading a group of "French Company" traders to winter on the James River in present-day South Dakota.[5]

While Bernard Pratte and his eldest son were pursuing

[3] Richard Oglesby, *Manuel Lisa and the Opening of the Missouri Fur Trade* (Norman, 1963), 168-71; Stella M. Drumm, "Bernard Pratte," *Dictionary of American Biography*, xv, pp. 180-81.

[4] "Relief to Citizens U.S. for Indian Depredations," 22 Cong., 1 sess., *House Doc. 38* (Serial 217), pp. 29-31, reference courtesy of Janet Lecompte; (Franklin) *Missouri Intelligencer*, April 28, 1826. "Vasques" also appears in these sources as "B. Vasques."

[5] Bartholomew Berthold to B. Pratte and Co., St. Louis, November 14, 1823, and Jean Pierre Cabanné to Pierre Chouteau, Jr., October 11, 1824. The original letters are in the Chouteau Collections, Missouri Historical Society, St. Louis, Missouri, hereinafter cited as CC. Portions of each are translated in Dale L. Morgan (ed.), *West of William H. Ashley, 1822-1838* (Denver, 1964), 61-62, 155.

the traditional trade along the Missouri and its affluents, more venturesome traders and trappers had begun to discover the fur wealth of the Rocky Mountains. By 1824, beaver trapped in the southern Rockies, and brought East over the Santa Fe Trail from New Mexico, had begun to excite traders along the Missouri. One of these was Jean Pierre Cabanné, a partner in Bernard Pratte and Company.[6] Cabanné's interest in New Mexico had been stimulated in part by the success of one of the company's occasional employees, Joseph Robidoux. In the fall of 1824 Cabanné was eager to outfit an expedition of his own into northern Mexico. When he reached his post at Council Bluffs, however, too few company hunters remained to staff a party. Cabanné blamed this shortage on Sylvestre Pratte, who had stopped at the Bluff on his way north toward the James River that fall. Pratte, Cabanné discovered, "had asserted that the [Rocky] mountains remained exclusively to Robidoux, & that the Company did not want to 'send' any more, . . . accordingly he had even believed to do well in dismissing a part of the engagés." Thus, instead of competing with Joseph Robidoux, Cabanné was forced to buy a one third interest in Robidoux's Mexican adventure.[7] This humiliation certainly contributed to Cabanné's disenchantment with Sylvestre Pratte.

During the winter of 1824-25, while Sylvestre Pratte traded for buffalo robes and assorted peltries on the James River, Cabanné laid plans for a large expedition to travel to Santa Fe in the spring. Although Pratte and Company had purchased a one-third interest in a small trading party that former employee Ceran St. Vrain steered to Taos that

---

[6] Cabanné to Pierre Chouteau, Jr., Establishment at the Bluffs, November 8, 1824, cc; Morgan, *West of Ashley*, 99. The beginnings of the fur trade from New Mexico, as well as other aspects of the Mexican trade in which Pratte was engaged, are discussed in greater detail in my doctoral dissertation, "The Taos Trappers: The Fur Trade From New Mexico, 1540-1846," University of New Mexico, 1967.

[7] Cabanné to Chouteau, October 11, 1824, in Morgan, *West of Ashley*, 155.

winter,[8] Cabanné entertained loftier ambitions. Apparently because of his father's position, twenty-six-year old Sylvestre Pratte was selected to lead the company forces into New Mexico. Cabanné's post near Council Bluffs was to be the jumping-off point for the group. When Pratte returned from the James River that spring, however, he continued downstream to St. Louis. By June 5th Cabanné wanted him back. He urged Pierre Chouteau: "If Pratte or Papin have not already left, hasten their departure; I have several engagés here; not only do they cause me a great deal of trouble and increase expenses, but they may very well become impatient waiting."[9] Despite a rumor that Pratte was on his way to the Bluffs in mid-June, not until July 26th did he reach Cabanné's post.[10] Bitter that the expedition had not left a month and a half earlier, Cabanné vowed that he would "not think of the Mountains again." Sylvestre Pratte became the chief object of his vitriol. "How," Cabanné asked Pierre Chouteau,

> can a young man who seems to be guided by a sense of good have so little success in what he undertakes? I write you these few lines separately to avoid giving pain to a good father and one who has so many rights to our esteem.[11]

Two months later Cabanné repeated these sentiments, predicting that, with Sylvestre Pratte as its leader, "the expedition to the Mountains will undoubtedly be unsuccessful." Bernard Pratte, he thought, was "much to be pitied, for having children who, by their incapability, show themselves

---

[8] St. Vrain's account in Books D and M of Pratte and Company, CC, a copy of which was graciously furnished to me by Janet Lecompte.

[9] Cabanné to Chouteau, Near the Bluffs, June 5, 1825, quotation from the translation in CC.

[10] Cabanné to Chouteau, Near the Bluffs, June 12, 1825, CC; Edgar B. Wesley (ed.), "Diary of James Kennerly, 1823-1826," *Missouri Historical Society Collections,* VI (October 1928), 76.

[11] Cabanné to Chouteau, Near the Bluffs, July 27, 1825, quotation from the translation in CC. Portions of this document also appear in Morgan, *West of Ashley,* 156.

so little worthy of him." [12] Crusty Cabanné's gloomy pre-
dictions of young Pratte's failure would prove to be true.

On July 30th the New Mexico expedition finally got
under way. The delay in leaving had one unexpected advantage that would not be appreciated for several generations. It enabled a young Kentuckian named James Ohio
Pattie to join the party and chronicle some of its adventures
in his famous and controversial *The Personal Narrative of
James O. Pattie*.[13] If Pattie is to be believed, the group
numbered one hundred and sixteen men – a large responsibility for young Pratte. Pausing on the way to trade buffalo
robes with some Pawnee on the Platte, and deerskins with
Utes on the Arkansas, Pratte's contingent finally reached
Taos on October 26th. Pratte displayed some knowledge of
local traditions by *caching* a part of his trade goods before
entering the village, thereby avoiding payment of customs
fees.[14]

Unlike the independent trappers who had been working
out of New Mexico since its opening to American commerce in late 1821, Pratte enjoyed the financial backing of
a large Missouri River fur trading firm. Thus, it is not
surprising that he came to dominate the local trade almost
from the moment of his arrival. Foreigners were prohibited
to trap in New Mexico, but Pratte managed to obtain a
license from Governor Antonio Narbona, through the good
offices of the customs collector, Juan Bautista Vigil y
Alarid. Late that fall, or perhaps early the next spring,
Pratte dispatched at least two different trapping parties.
A dozen or so men were sent to the headwaters of the Rio
Grande while Ceran St. Vrain led eighteen or twenty men

---

12 Cabanné to Chouteau, September 16, 1825, CC.

13 (Philadelphia, 1962). Pattie records leaving on July 30, 1824. Dale L. Morgan
(*West of Ashley*, 206, n. 337), has conclusively shown that 1825 was the correct
year.

14 Pattie, *Personal Narrative*, 11-38; Kate L. Gregg (ed.), *The Road to Santa Fe,
Journal and Diaries of George Champlin Sibley* (Albuquerque, 1952), 114.

to the Utah Lake area.[15] Pratte also seems to have had a stake in other trapping ventures during the 1825-26 season. For example, a group of seven trappers, which James Ohio Pattie accompanied to the Gila River, included three of Pratte's men. Pratte himself probably spent the winter in the Mexican settlements. In February he was at Taos.[16]

The season had not yet ended before Pratte's plans were interrupted by the first of several imbroglios with Mexican officials. Acting under orders from Santa Fe, the alcalde of Taos confiscated about six hundred and thirty pounds of beaver fur belonging to Pratte and Francois Robidoux. Traveling to Santa Fe to protest, the two owners learned that opposition to American trappers had hardened and that the territorial legislature had revoked their licenses. Pratte and Robidoux somehow succeeded in convincing Governor Narbona of the injustice of this *ex post facto* legislation. He released their furs and extended the protection of their licenses to cover the trappers who were still in the field. Later that season Pratte's groups from Utah Lake and the headwaters of the Rio Grande got their furs to market without interference from Mexican officials.[17] Pratte's next legal difficulty had less happy results.

In November of 1826, when another group of Pratte's trappers showed up at Taos, Governor Narbona ordered their furs to be confiscated. The alcalde of Taos, however, was unable to carry out the governor's order. The trappers who were guarding the furs, the alcalde courageously explained, did not have a key to the building. In the meantime, Pratte, who apparently had the key, hurried to Santa

15 Papers relating to the embargo of S. S. Pratte's furs, November 12, 1826, Mexican Archives of New Mexico, State Records Center, Santa Fe, New Mexico. Hereinafter cited as MANM.

16 Pattie, *Personal Narrative,* 46; Gregg (ed.), *Road to Santa Fe,* 150.

17 Agustín Durán to the Alcalde of Santa Fe, May 12, 1826; rough draft of a letter from Durán to an unknown person, March 1, 1827; Narbona to Durán, May 12, 1826, from a copy made on November 29, 1826, all in MANM.

Fe to protest the order on the grounds that the men had left in February before his license had been rescinded. This time Narbona remained unmoved. Pratte, he claimed, had told him that only three men were still trapping when, clearly, there had been more. Pratte denied saying this and at least one prominent Mexican official, treasurer Augustín Durán, sided with Pratte. Extant documents do not reveal the outcome of the case.[18]

While Pratte waged a legal battle for possession of his furs, another of his trapping brigades engaged a more dangerous enemy. By autumn of 1826 American trappers had discovered the beaver-rich waters of the Gila and its tributaries, and were converging there in force. Fickle Governor Narbona had at first issued licenses to four different American parties before changing his mind and rescinding them. One of these groups, Narbona reported, was led by Michel Robidoux and Sylvestre Pratte. Pratte probably only financed the party, however, for we have seen that he spent that autumn in Taos and Santa Fe. It was fortunate. Only three of the twenty-man party survived an Indian attack.[19] Yet, Pratte may also have held a stake in two other parties that were hunting on the Gila. Peg-leg Smith, who seems to have been traveling with the party led by Ewing Young, referred to it as "a company of fifteen men fitted out by Mr. Pratt." Returning from the hunt the following spring, Smith recalled finding "his warm-hearted patron, Mr. Pratt, one of nature's gentlemen," at Taos.[20] Ceran St. Vrain led still another of the bands which worked the Gila that autumn; it seems likely that he was either backed by Pratte or directly in his employ. St. Vrain had

---

[18] Papers pertaining to the seizure of S. S. Pratte's furs, November 12, 1826, MANM.

[19] Pattie, *Personal Narrative*, 75-80. For a summary of the 1826 hunt on the Gila see the introduction to this *Series*, pages 67-70.

[20] "Sketches from the Life of Peg-leg Smith," *Hutchings' Illustrated California Magazine,* v (Jan. & Feb. 1861), 320, 336.

worked for Pratte during the previous season and would be second-in-command to Pratte on an expedition in the fall of 1827.

Despite Pratte's manifold interests, business was not going well. The explanation is not entirely clear. Certainly the troubles with Mexican officials and the massacre of the Robidoux party had been costly. By December of 1826, however, probably before news of the Robidoux disaster had reached St. Louis, Bernard Pratte and Company had lost faith in Sylvestre Pratte. Pierre Chouteau, Jr., a partner in the firm, wrote to the elder Pratte:

> . . . as for the unfortunate business at Taos I do not dare to think of it. If it were not for these inexhaustible fur-drafts I would be of a mind to await with resignation the sad end of this expedition, but these drafts! Who can know where they will lead us? . . . where in our wretched St. Louis is a trustworthy man to be found who is able to terminate this business with the least loss possible.
>
> I am sorry, my dear General, that force of circumstances obliges me to return to a subject that is as painful to me . . . as for you to hear.[21]

Within a year, signs of Pratte and Company's displeasure at young Pratte's conduct were even more manifest. In the summer of 1827 Santa Fe trader David Workman, in the words of his attorney, "sold merchandise and loaned money to S. S. Pratte, for which he took two bills drawn by young Pratte on B. Pratte and company of St. Louis. The bills were duly presented, dishonored and protested." Workman was perplexed, for he knew that in 1826 Bernard Pratte's company had honored young Pratte's drafts.[22] Clearly, General Pratte's attitude toward his son's conduct had changed.

Paradoxically, Sylvestre Pratte's position in New Mexico had become even more important. By 1827 he was no longer

---

[21] Pierre Chouteau, Jr., to B. Pratte & Co., New York, December 17, 1826, quotation from the translation in cc.

[22] Abiel Leonard, Franklin, Missouri, to H. R. Gamble, St. Louis, October 1, 1828, in Hamilton R. Gamble Papers, Missouri Historical Society, St. Louis, Missouri.

simply Bernard Pratte and Company's agent in northern Mexico. Pratte and Company, while retaining its name, personnel, and considerable independence, had reached an agreement with John Jacob Astor's giant American Fur Company whereby it became its Western Department. The merger had had informal beginnings in March of 1825 when Astor's chief lieutenant, Ramsay Crooks, had married Sylvestre Pratte's sister, Emilie.[23] Probably unaware of this merger, and that he had lost the confidence of his employers, Sylvestre Pratte continued to trap and trade out of Taos.

In January of 1827, only a few months after the massacre of Michel Robidoux's group, Pratte outfitted another party of trappers whose destination the alcalde of Taos vaguely described as "outside of the boundaries of the Mexican Federation." Of the twenty-two participants, all but two were of French ancestry, including Ceran St. Vrain, Charles Beaubien and other lesser lights.[24] Unfortunately, nothing more is known of the activities of this group.

In the fall of 1827, perhaps in an attempt to recoup his losses, Pratte himself led thirty-six men to trap the southern Rockies and the Green River country. This latter area William Ashley considered sacrosanct. Ashley had unsuccessfully tried to reach an agreement with Bernard Pratte and Company not to allow "any person trading for them at Taus [Taos] or any other place or places, directly or indirectly to interfere" with his operations in the Green River area.[25] Pratte, however, would not agree to this. So, with Ceran St. Vrain as clerk, and Peg-leg Smith, Alexander Branch, Old Bill Williams, Milton Sublette and Joseph Bissonette form-

---

[23] David Lavender, *The Fist in the Wilderness* (New York, 1964), 377, 356-57.

[24] David J. Weber (ed. and tr.) *The Extranjeros: Selected Documents from the Mexican Side of the Santa Fe Trail, 1825-1828* (Santa Fe, 1967), 37.

[25] Ashley to Pierre Chouteau, Jr., Lancaster, Pennsylvania, February 2, 1827, in Morgan, *West of Ashley,* 159-60; Lavender, *Fist in the Wilderness,* 378.

ing part of the company, Sylvestre Pratte led a formidable contingent into the mountains. In addition to this large group of thirty-six, Pratte had outfitted a smaller party led by Antoine Leroux, and perhaps other groups as well.[26] Auspicious appearances notwithstanding, Pratte's venture would be marred by tragedy. Trapping their way north, the men reached North Park on the headwaters of the North Platte toward late September. There, Pratte sickened and died on October 1st.[27]

Although James Ohio Pattie had found him "ill in bed" in May of 1825, there is no evidence that Pratte suffered from any chronic condition. Ceran St. Vrain, who was with him at the end, reported to General Pratte that his son's "sickness had been of short duration," while Peg-leg Smith later reminisced that Pratte had died "in a paroxysm of hydrophobia, having been bitten upon the hand some several months previous, by a lap-dog, to which no attention was paid, as there was no indication of the dog's being rabid." [28] Almost a year passed before news of Pratte's death reached his family. In mid-September of 1828 rumor reached the Missouri that Pratte had been attacked by Indians. Not until September 30th did the St. Louis *Missouri Republican* carry a small notice that the eldest son of General Pratte had died on the headwaters of the Platte. Sylvestre's brother, Bernard, Jr., soon to be famous in his own right, was appointed administrator of his estate. Sylvestre Pratte died childless and his wife subsequently remarried.[29]

---

[26] Testimony of Joaquin Leru in hearings before Juan Estevan Pino, Santa Fe, June 6, 1828, MANM.

[27] Declaration of Pratte's trappers, September 1, 1829, CC.

[28] Pattie, *Personal Narrative*, 66; St. Vrain to Pratte, Taos, September 28, 1828, CC; "Sketches from the Life of Peg-leg Smith," 420.

[29] Cabanné to Pierre Chouteau, Near the Bluff, September 22, 1828, CC, portions translated in Morgan, *West of Ashley*, 176; (St. Louis) *Missouri Republican*, November 25, 1828; Billon, *Annals of St. Louis*, 181.

Even Pratte's final trapping expedition would prove to be unsuccessful. When Ceran St. Vrain piloted the party back to New Mexico in the spring of 1828 he found that "Expenses made for going for Biver" came to $6,915.41½. They had snared only $5,780.50 worth of furs. To make up the difference St. Vrain sold some of Pratte's personal belongings – his horses, mules, rifle, pistol, traps, gloves and some trade goods. Yet, a deficit of over $500 still remained which St. Vrain paid out of his own pocket.[30] Included in the inventory of Pratte's estate were notes from sixteen different persons, totaling $1,867½, all owed to Sylvestre Pratte. The list of notes was forwarded to his bereaved father, but many of these may never have been collected. In January of 1831, Ceran St. Vrain, at Taos, informed Pratte and Company: "it is possible that I will be able to Collect, Some of the debts due to the estate of S. S. Pratte, as yet I have not Collected the first cent."[31]

The money that was owed to Pratte's estate, it would appear, was insignificant in comparison to the debts that young Pratte had incurred on his father's account. The general eventually paid all of his deceased son's bills, but as one contemporary told it, "it is purely from parental feeling that Genl Pratte pays one cent on those drafts."[32]

Sylvestre Pratte's career, which seemed so promising before ending in failure, raises a number of questions. Was Pratte simply the victim of bad luck, or had Cabanné correctly discerned some weakness in Pratte's character that led to his misfortunes? Or, had Mexican officials been able to exert sufficient pressure to make it unprofitable for large American companies, such as Pratte represented, to operate

---

[30] St. Vrain to Bernard Pratte, September 28, 1828; inventory of Sylvestre Pratte's estate, 1828, both in cc.

[31] St. Vrain to Pratte & Co., January 6, 1831, cc.

[32] Moss[?] Prewitt to H. R. Gamble, Fayette, June 5, 1829, quoting a man named Glasgow, Hamilton R. Gamble Papers.

in New Mexico? Did Pratte's lack of success deter other
companies from entering the area?[33] Whatever the reasons
for Pratte's failure, his premature death gave him no opportunity to defend himself from contemporary detractors or
future historians. Thus, the questions may remain un-
answered.

[33] One authority has noted that "the Southwest never had an Astor. Limited opportunities for small operators continued almost to the end." J. W. Smurr in Paul
Chrisler Phillips, *The Fur Trade* (2 vols., Norman, 1961), II, pp. 469-70.

John Rowland

by DAVID J. WEBER
University of New Mexico

Although he is best known as a successful California rancher and co-leader of the Workman-Rowland immigrant party of 1841, John Rowland also had an earlier career as a Mountain Man in New Mexico.

The ninth child of William and Sarah Latham Rowland, two English immigrants, John Albert Rowland was born on April 15, 1791, near Port Deposit, Maryland.[1] His formative years were apparently spent in Pennsylvania,[2] but little else is known about him until the early 1820s.[3] At that time John Rowland was among those American trappers and traders who wandered into Mexico's northern frontier during her first years of independence from Spain. He seems to have come to New Mexico in 1823,[4] probably

---

[1] Leonore Rowland, *The Romance of La Puente Rancho* (Covina, California, 1958), 1. Sources vary on the year of Rowland's birth but 1791 seems correct. This date also appears on Rowland's tombstone (Rowland, 41). A portrait of Rowland appears in the present volume at page 16.

[2] Rowland considered himself to be from Pennsylvania, as did his contemporaries. W. H. Chamberlin, visiting Rowland in 1849, reported that "Mr. Rohland was formerly from Harmony, in the neighborhood of Pittsburg. He is of German descent and would be known amongst a thousand as one of the Pennsylvania Dutch." Lansing B. Bloom, "From Lewisburg (Pa.) to California in 1849; Diary of William H. Chamberlin," in *New Mexico Historical Review*, XX (Jan.-Oct. 1945), 258.

[3] Leonore Rowland, citing a WPA Writer's Project, "La Puente Valley, Past and Present," by Janet and Dan N. Powell as her source, says: "As a young man, he went to Boston to study surveying. After completing the course, he became a United States surveyor and trapper. In Boston he joined a company of trappers and with them he set out to seek his fortune in the vast, adventurous, very little known country to the west. For a time he lived in Ohio. Later he went to St. Louis, Missouri. . ." (p. 1).

[4] Rowland's obituary, *Los Angeles Herald*, Oct. 15, 1873. Rowland's marriage record (Baptismal Book, Taos-38, Box 70, p. 195, Archives of the Archdiocese of Santa Fe, Santa Fe, New Mexico) indicates that he had been baptized in the parish

traveling over the Santa Fe Trail from St. Louis with other seekers of Mexican silver and furs. In the fall of 1824 he joined the many trappers who, inspired by the earlier success of Ewing Young and William Wolfskill, set out for the Green River from their New Mexico base.[5] Unfortunately there is no evidence linking Rowland to any specific trapping party in that year. We only know that his group was attacked by Indians.[6] Peg-leg Smith, who spent that winter in Taos, later recalled that in February of 1825 "Hopper, with his little band from Green river arrived, accompanied by Antonio Rubedoux, John Roland and some twenty-five men of Provost's company."[7]

Nothing is known of Rowland's activities during the next winter except that, on October 27, 1825, he married María Encarnación Martínez of Taos.[8] He was probably the first American trapper to marry a New Mexican in the Mexican period.

The fall of 1826 saw a large-scale movement of American trappers from New Mexico to the Gila River basin. Four of their groups have been identified; one of them, composed of some eighteen men, was led by John Rowland. Regrettably, no details of his route or personnel have been preserved.[9] Trapping within Mexican territory was appar-

---

of Taos. No record of this exists, so it seems likely that the baptism occurred between August 3, 1823, and August 29, 1824, a period in which Taos baptismal records are missing.

[5] See the introduction to this *Series*, p. 65.

[6] *Los Angeles Herald*, Oct. 15, 1873.

[7] "Sketches from the Life of Peg-leg Smith," in *Hutchings' Illustrated California Magazine*, v (1861), 319.

[8] Baptismal Book, Taos-38, Box 70, p. 195, Archives of the Archdiocese of Santa Fe.

[9] Thomas Maitland Marshall, "St. Vrain's Expedition to the Gila in 1826," in *Southwestern Historical Quarterly*, xix (Jan. 1916), 251-60. See also the introduction to this *Series*, p. 67. The documents on which Marshall relied shed no additional light on Rowland (the original documents in Hermosillo have apparently been lost in a fire, while those in the AGN in Mexico City cannot be located at the present time. Fortunately, transcripts of them are preserved in the Bancroft Library).

ently prohibited to foreigners at that time and Mexican officials attempted to apprehend the Gila expeditions.[10] Ewing Young, one of Rowland's Taos neighbors,[11] had his furs confiscated,[12] but Rowland's party apparently escaped and smuggled its furs to safety. Nevertheless, Rowland was among the first foreigners who immunized themselves from this annoying prohibition when, on July 8, 1829, he became a Mexican citizen.[13]

In 1830, his trapping activities now legal, Rowland requested and received a license to trap.[14] New Mexico officials, perhaps remembering his illegal foray to the Gila in 1826, remained suspicious. The following year Governor José Antonio Chávez told Rowland:

> The license which you request is granted with the warning that the interested party ought to care, very scrupulously, that no fraud is committed against the National Treasury, for in that case it will be necessary to bring to bear all of the weight of the law concerning this matter.[15]

On August 23, 1832, Rowland again requested a license, this time to lead fourteen or more men on a trapping expedition. Governor Santiago Abreú granted permission on the same day, but stipulated that "at least two thirds of the group be composed of Mexicans and naturalized citizens and the other [third] of foreigners which you say are necessary to direct and care for your hunt."[16]

---

10 Marshall, "St. Vrain's Expedition to the Gila," 255.

11 John Rowland, deposition in the case of Joaquin Young vs. the Territory of Oregon, Nov. 1, 1855. – MS in the Bancroft Library.

12 Robert Glass Cleland, *This Reckless Breed of Men* (New York, 1950), 218.

13 List of those naturalized in New Mexico in 1829, 1830 and 1831, Ritch Collection, no. 113, Huntington Library, San Marino, California.

14 Rough draft of a letter to John Rowland from an unknown official, Santa Fe, September 5, 1830, Mexican Archives in New Mexico, State Records Center, Santa Fe, New Mexico. Hereinafter cited as MANM.

15 Rough draft of a letter to John Rowland, Santa Fe, August 20, 1831, in the governor's letter book, Oct. 22, 1830-Aug. 23, 1831, MANM.

16 Official certification by the alcalde of Taos, José María Martínez, that John Rowland is allowed to trap beaver, Aug. 29, 1832, MANM.

No record has yet been found of where Rowland trapped or who his companions were in these later years. That his base was Taos is certain, and he was probably an independent trapper. A later generation remembered that

> he was of a most fearless disposition. . . While engaged in trapping he was in several Indian fights in which he was severely wounded, his body bearing many a scar resulting from the wounds received in the conflicts through which he had passed.[17]

Sometime in the mid-1830s, perhaps as early as 1833, Rowland left the beaver streams of the Southwest to younger men and devoted his talent and attention to his growing Taos enterprises.

Even while trapping, John Rowland had entered into other business ventures. George Nidever, who visited Rowland and his family in Taos in 1831, remembered that he had a flour mill.[18] Another contemporary, Antonio Barreiro, wrote in 1832 that Ranchos de Taos "is famous for its brandy still, owned by Don Juan Rolliens, a foreigner from North America."[19] Doubtless other Mountain Men were among the greatest consumers of his "Taos lightning," as the locally-made product came to be called. In addition to operating his distillery and flour mill, Rowland occupied himself with community affairs[20] and with his growing family. Between May 28, 1826, and August 3, 1841, eight

---

[17] *Los Angeles Herald*, Oct. 15, 1873.

[18] William Henry Ellison (ed), *The Life and Adventures of George Nidever, 1802-1883* (Berkeley, 1937), 21.

[19] Lansing B. Bloom (ed.), "Barreiro's Ojeada sobre Nuevo Mexico," in *New Mexico Historical Review,* III (July 1928), 86. Bloom adds that "According to local tradition, supplied by Mr. L. Pascual Martinez of Taos, a 'John Rawlins' lived at Taos in the early '30s. He and a brother were engaged in the fur trade and later established a distillery, or *vinatero*, about three miles up the little Rio Grande cañon, in charge of one Pedro Antonio Gallegos."

[20] He participated in local politics. See, for example, Feb. 3, 1837, and April 16, 1837, MANM. In 1836 he was scheduled to join other Taos citizens, including Carlos Beaubien, Alexander Branch, David Waldo and Luis Lee on a march against the Navajo. Rowland contributed four mules to this expedition, September 1836, MANM.

known children were born to John and María Rowland.[21]

John Rowland appears to have had only marginal interest in the Santa Fe-Missouri trade. The name of his brother, Thomas, appears frequently in custom house records beginning in 1835, however, and John may have been a silent partner in "Thomas Rowland y companía." In 1837 John Rowland's connection with the Santa Fe trade was not as silent as he might have wished. Several persons testified at his arraignment that his mules, laden with flour, had met the caravan from the United States on the "Rio Colorado," [22] disposed of their burden and returned to Taos with merchandise from the wagons. Rowland had thus avoided paying both import and export duties. He was ordered to remain in Santa Fe pending further evidence, but the outcome of the case is not known.[23] The first record of Rowland's open participation in the commerce of the prairies is in 1839 and 1840.[24] It seems not unlikely that furs represented a portion of Rowland's legal and extra-legal trade with St. Louis, but this must remain speculative.

In 1841 John Rowland and his Taos partner in the distillery business, William Workman,[25] were suspected of collaborating with the controversial Texas-Santa Fe Expedition. The previous year both had been named temporary commissioners for the Republic of Texas by its president,

---

[21] Fray Angelico Chávez, "New Names in New Mexico, 1820-1850," in *El Palacio*, 64 (1957), 372-73. Chávez incorrectly dates the birth of Rowland's first child as May 28, 1825, instead of May 28, 1826 (Baptismal Book, Taos-38, Box 70, Archives of the Archdiocese of Santa Fe).

[22] Probably the present day Red River in north central New Mexico in the area of Questa.

[23] Case before Santiago Abreú, Santa Fe, July 18 and 19, 1837, MANM.

[24] Libro Manual de Cargo y Data, New Mexico, Jan. 1, 1839 through Dec. 31, 1840 (entry of Aug. 30, 1839), MANM. *Manifiesto* of goods (cotton linen) presented by John Rowland at the custom house at Santa Fe, Nov. 7, 1840, MANM.

[25] Letter of Simeon Turley, quoted in LeRoy R. and Ann W. Hafen, *Old Spanish Trail* (Glendale, 1954), 204.

Mirabeau Lamar.[26] Probably, as George Wilkins Kendall suggested, this was done "without their knowledge or consent,"[27] but the true nature of their involvement with and sympathy toward the Texans has never been assessed.[28] In early September of 1841, Rowland and Workman, who had been preparing to leave New Mexico at least as early as April, led an emigrant party of some twenty-five men to California. By the following spring the two had succeeded in obtaining over forty-eight thousand acres of Mexican land near San Gabriel Mission, the Rancho de la Puente. Rowland returned to Taos, gathered up his large family and was back at La Puente by December 12, 1842.[29]

John Rowland's California career is well known.[30] He was among those who, between 1843 and 1845, opposed Governor Manuel Micheltorena and, in the Mexican War, he sided with his former countrymen, the Americans. In the fall of 1846, when some Mexicans in southern California rebelled against American rule, Rowland was captured in a skirmish at El Chino ranch.[31] In his later years he was known as a retiring individual and a family man. This seems to have some foundation, for at El Chino, his fellow prisoner, the former New Mexican Luis Robidoux, remem-

---

[26] William C. Binkley, "New Mexico and the Texan Santa Fe Expedition," in *Southwestern Historical Quarterly,* XXVII (Oct. 1923), 95.

[27] George Wilkins Kendall, *Narrative of the Texan Santa Fe Expedition* (London, 1844), I, p. 272.

[28] Hafen and Hafen, *Old Spanish Trail,* 204.

[29] Details concerning their preparation and journey appear in Hafen and Hafen, 199-215.

[30] For a general account see Mary Elizabeth Harris, "John Rowland and William Workman, Pioneers in Southern California" (unpub. MA thesis, University of California, Berkeley, 1932). See illustration of Rowland's home, herein page 18.

[31] "Benjamin David Wilson's Observations on Early Days in California and New Mexico," foreword and explanatory notes by Arthur Woodward, in Historical Society of Southern California *Annual Publication,* XVI (1934), 98, 103, 105-110. Rowland to Manuel Alvarez, La Puente, Feb. 23, 1843, Read Collection, no. 263, State Records Center, Santa Fe, New Mexico.

bered Rowland pleading with his captors to "cut off a leg, and leave me undisturbed with my family."[32]

After the excitement of the Mexican War, Rowland's activities centered around his ranch. His portion of La Puente contained cattle, horses, vineyards and, as in Taos, a distillery and a flour mill.[33] He was among California's first and most important wine manufacturers, selling the product commercially throughout the 1850s and 1860s.[34] The location of La Puente, near the route of immigrants and the Butterfield Overland Stage, probably afforded Rowland many opportunities to reminisce with former Mountain Men. We know, for instance, that Kit Carson visited him in 1848.[35] In 1852, following the death of his first wife, Rowland married a widow, Charlotte Grey.[36] In 1857 a Catholic Church was built at the ranch and when Rowland died there, on October 14, 1873, he was buried in its cemetery, the "Acre of God."[37]

---

[32] Luis Robidoux to Manuel Alvarez, California, May 1, 1848, Read Collection, no. 260.

[33] Hubert Howe Bancroft, *History of California,* VII (San Francisco, 1886), 759. Major Horace Bell, *On the Old West Coast,* ed. by Lanier Bartlett (New York, 1930), 20. Bloom, "From Lewisburg to California," 258.

[34] Iris Wilson, "Early Southern California Viniculture, 1830-1865," in *Historical Society of Southern California Quarterly,* XXXIX (Sept. 1957), 244-45.

[35] Roy M. Fryer, "The Butterfield Stage Route," in *Historical Society of Southern California Quarterly,* XVII (March 1935), 18, 20. Rowland to Manuel Alvarez, La Puente, May 1, 1848, Read Collection, no. 266.

[36] His first wife died in the fall of 1851 and Rowland remarried on September 16, 1852. L. Rowland, *La Puente,* 32, 33, 66.

[37] Marco Newmark, "The Workman Family in Los Angeles," in *Historical Society of Southern California Quarterly,* XXXII (Dec. 1950), 317. L. Rowland, *La Puente,* 41.

Gervais Nolan

by DAVID J. WEBER
University of New Mexico

An illiterate trapper, Gervais Nolan appears to have left no record of his activities. His association with the fur trade of the Rocky Mountains rests on the scantiest of evidence and one looks, nearly in vain, for his name in the sources of the period. The little that we do know of Nolan, however, suggests an interesting career as a trapper, gunsmith, merchant, miner and land-owner; and one's interest is heightened by the infrequent appearance of Nolan's name in the historical record.

Gervais Nolan was a native of St. Charles, Canada, and the son of "Francisco Nolán and María Angela Coplatrur [?]."[1] The date of his birth is, thus far, unknown. In 1816 Nolan joined the North West Company in Montreal, working for them for the next four trading seasons, although it is not clear in what capacity. He traveled west, at least as far as the company depot at Fort William on Lake Superior, and may have spent the 1818-1819 season in Athabasca.[2] In 1820, after receiving his pay from the North West Company, Nolan left Canada with a group of merchants. Four years later, in 1824, he arrived in New Mexico where, known as Gervasio Nolan, he was to make his home.[3] Although one source has it that Nolan wandered into New

---

[1] Marriage Book, Taos-39, Box 36. Archives of the Archdiocese of Santa Fe, Santa Fe, New Mexico.

[2] North West Company Ledger in the Archives of the Hudson's Bay Company, F.4/32, p. 752. Letter to this writer from the Secretary of the Hudson's Bay Company, London, October 7, 1965.

[3] Nolan's petition for naturalization to the Ayuntamiento of Taos, February 22, 1829, Ritch Collection, no. 109, Huntington Library, San Marino, California. "Gervasio" was also spelled "Gervacio."

Mexico as a result of a broken compass,[4] it seems more likely that his trip was premeditated.

Gervasio Nolan settled in Taos, the village which many trappers and traders found attractive at this time, and here practiced the trade of gunsmith.[5] On August 5, 1828, he married María Dolores "Lalanda," the twelve-year-old daughter of Jean Baptiste Lalande,[6] the first American to establish commercial contact with Santa Fe.[7] Five children are known to have been born to Gervasio and María Nolan between 1830 and 1841.[8] In the few years following his marriage Nolan purchased several tracts of land in Taos, two of them from sons-in-law of the deceased Jean Baptiste Lalande.[9]

Nolan's fur trading activities in New Mexico must be largely hypothesized. During his first years in the area trapping was illegal for foreigners and he may have been one of those who was never caught and thus never heard of. When Mexican naturalization requirements were eased,[10] Gervasio

---

[4] Joseph Tassé, *Les Canadiens de L'Ouest* (Montreal, 1878), 186. Tassé claims that Nolan, Pierre and Antoine Leroux, Charles Beaubien and others, all employees of the Hudson's Bay Company, set out to trade with Indians when they lost their compass. Taken prisoner to New Mexico, their lives were spared only by the intervention of Manuel Alvarez. They were then sent to Mexico City and released! Tassé gives no source for this story and its obvious fictional quality impugns the veracity of the compass incident.

[5] Nolan considered himself a gunsmith when he was applying for naturalization in 1829. The *alcalde* of Taos referred to Nolan as a gunsmith in 1827. Statement of Manuel Martínez, Taos, November 12, 1827, Ritch Collection, no. 97.

[6] Marriage Book, Taos-39, Box 36. Fray Angelico Chávez, "Addenda to New Mexico Families," in *El Palacio*, v. 63 (1956), p. 242.

[7] LeRoy R. Hafen and Carl Coke Rister, *Western America* (Englewood Cliffs, N.J., 1950), 246.

[8] Fray Angelico Chávez, "New Names in New Mexico, 1820-1850," in *El Palacio*, v. 64 (1957), pp. 368-69.

[9] Year of 1847, First Book (Book "A"), Record of Land Established by Law, Federal Bureau of Land Management, Santa Fe, New Mexico. These transactions occurred between 1829 and 1831.

[10] A new naturalization law was decreed by the Mexican Congress on April 14, 1828, see Manuel Dublan and Jose María Lozano, *Legislación Mexicana* (Mexico, 1876), I, pp. 66-68.

Nolan and Charles Beaubien were the first Mountain Men to take advantage of the new legislation. Both requested naturalization on February 22, 1829; it was granted to them on June 25 of the same year.[11] Although Nolan was now able to trap legally within Mexican territory, we have documentary evidence of his doing so on only one occasion. In the winter of 1830-31, he went on a trapping expedition with other Mexican citizens. The group obtained some fifty pounds of beaver pelts. Nolan purchased his partners' shares and sold the total to "a foreigner of North America." The *alcalde* of Taos, Rafael Antonio de Luna, officially witnessed this transaction in order to enable the foreigner to export the furs legally.[12]

In the main, however, Nolan's reputation as a Mountain Man must be based on "guilt by association." In 1827, for example, he traveled from Taos to Missouri and back again in the company of Manuel Alvarez, Thomas H. Boggs, Paul Baillio, Luis Robidoux, Vincent Guion and Francois Guerin – all known fur traders.[13] At that time the export of specie was taxed by the Mexican government but furs were not. Nolan may have been among those Americans who would "try to take back on their return trip, instead of money, beaver skins."[14]

Nolan's interests apparently shifted to mining in the 1830s. Reputedly he acquired a large fortune in "commercial speculations," and then wasted "enormous sums in

[11] Nolan's request for naturalization is in the Ritch Collection, no. 109. Beaubien's request is in the Mexican Archives in New Mexico, State Records Center, Santa Fe, New Mexico. Hereinafter cited as MANM. Record of their receiving naturalization appears in "List of those naturalized in New Mexico in 1829, 1830 and 1831," Ritch Collection, no. 113.

[12] Statement of Rafael Antonio de Luna, Taos, July 21, 1831, MANM.

[13] Statement of Manuel Martínez, Taos, April 7, 1827, MANM. Permit to pass through Indian country, William Clark, Superintendent of Indian Affairs, July 23, 1827, Ritch Collection, no. 95. List of persons arriving in Taos on November 12, 1827, Manuel Martínez, Ritch Collection, no. 97.

[14] Antonio Barreiro, "Ojeada Sobre Nuevo-Mexico" in H. B. Carroll and J. Villasana Haggard (eds.), *Three New Mexico Chronicles* (Albuquerque, 1942), 108.

order to discover famous treasures which, according to legend, were to be found under the ruins of Gran Quivira."[15] In 1835 he operated a store and a forge in the mining town of Real del Oro.[16] For the next decade we find him associated with both Taos and the mining region southeast of Santa Fe. Dr. Frederick A. Wislizenus recorded meeting "Mr. Nolan, a French resident of New Placer [San Francisco del Tuerto]," in 1846.[17] In 1849 or 1850 Nolan and his son, Fernando, went to California in search of gold. There, while he was mining near Marysville, his papers and effects were burned in a fire.[18]

Nolan is best known to historians as a holder of Mexican real estate. In 1843, when he was a resident of the valley of Taos, he was awarded some eight hundred thousand acres of the San Carlos River valley in southern Colorado. Ceran St. Vrain, Carlos Beaubien and Luis Lee were purportedly on hand as witnesses when Nolan took possession of the land. Kit Carson and St. Vrain later testified that persons in Nolan's employ had cultivated and occupied the area.[19] In 1845 Nolan came into possession of nearly six hundred thousand more acres, in the little canyon of the Red River, south of the famous Beaubien-Miranda grant. He was then a resident of Real del Oro, San Francisco del Tuerto. His brother-in-law, Tomás Benito Lalanda, executed the necessary documents.[20]

15 Tassé, *Les Canadiens de L'Ouest,* 187.

16 Teniente de Policía del Rio del Oro, Juan Venavides, to Alcalde Manuel Doroteo Pino, Real del Oro, February 26, 1835, MANM.

17 A. Wislizenus, *Memoir of a Tour to Northern Mexico* (Washington, 1848), 31.

18 Rafael Romero to F. W. Cragin, Mora, New Mexico, March 7, 1908, Cragin Collection, Pioneers' Museum, Colorado Springs, Colorado. This story is verified in a petition of the heirs of Gervasio Nolan, Santa Fe, February 27, 1860, in New Mexico Land Grant Papers, microfilm in the University of New Mexico Library, reel 16, report 39, file 9.

19 United States 37 Cong., 2 sess., *House Exec. Doc. 112,* serial 1137. These papers are summarized in LeRoy R. Hafen, "Mexican Land Grants in Colorado," in *Colorado Magazine,* IV (1927), 86-87.

Gervasio Nolan returned to New Mexico after his California adventure and died there on January 27, 1857.[21] The varied career of this Mountain Man suggests that he deserves to be remembered as one of the more substantial of the foreign-born citizens who made Taos their home in Mexican New Mexico.

---

[20] Tomás Benito Lalanda, born on January 1, 1814, was an older brother of Nolan's wife, see Chávez, "Addenda to New Mexico Families," 242. Papers concerning this land grant are found in New Mexico Land Grant Papers, microfilm in the University of New Mexico Library. Also, many of these papers are reproduced in U.S. 36 Cong., 2 sess., *House Exec. Doc. no. 28,* serial 1097.

[21] Hafen, "Mexican Land Grants in Colorado," 86.

Thomas L. (Peg-leg) Smith

by ALFRED GLEN HUMPHERYS
Ricks College, Rexburg, Idaho

Thomas L. Smith started life on the edge of civilization in Garrard County, Kentucky, on October 10, 1801. He was one of four boys and nine girls born to an Irish immigrant, Christopher Smith.[1] Before running away from home at age fifteen, Tom received enough schooling to enable him to read and write, which aided him as a trader and trapper. His life among the Indians began shortly after leaving Kentucky. Running away to Nashville, Tom obtained a position from a former neighbor, Mr. Scott, as a cook on a trading expedition of three flatboats headed for New Orleans. However, Tom left the river at Natchez and spent the summer of 1817 traveling and trading among the Choctaw and Chickasaw Indians on his way back to Nashville.[2]

Smith turned west after meeting Antoine Robidoux at a council on the Wabash River in the fall and winter of 1817.[3] While at this council of the Miami, Pottawotamie, and Wabash tribes, Smith caught the chills and fever, which delayed his journey until spring. Still suffering from the ague, Smith went to his sister's home in Boone's Lick (Boonesville), Missouri, where he started to farm. However, in 1820, he and Antoine Robidoux made a two-year expedition into Kansas and Nebraska Territory where they trapped, as well as traded with the Sioux and Osage Indians.[4] During the time Smith was trapping and trading,

---

[1] "Sketches From The Life of Peg-leg Smith," *Hutchings' California Magazine,* v (Oct. 1860), 150.

[2] "The Story of an Old Trapper," in *San Francisco Bulletin,* Oct. 26, 1866, p. 1.

[3] *Ibid.*   [4] *Hutchings' California Magazine,* Oct., 1860, p. 203.

Iturbide succeeded in obtaining Mexican independence from Spain. This opened the Santa Fe area to United States trade over the Santa Fe Trail. In 1824 Agustus LeGrande organized a large party of wagons and pack animals to trade in Santa Fe. Thomas Smith was part of the caravan of 1824, but says he was an independent trader with his own mules and goods.[5] Smith and a few others left the main body and proceeded to Taos.

There Smith traded during the summer. In late August a party of some eighty trappers journeyed northward into the Utah and Snake Indian country of present Utah and Colorado. Smith accompanied this group, but was a free trapper working on his own. The party started along the Rio Grande in early September 1824, trapping for beaver as they progressed. As they neared the headwaters of the river, Smith saw that the party was much too large for successful trapping. He persuaded other free trappers to go with him to the Grand River. These included Hopper, Marlow, LeDuke and three Mexicans. This party of seven, with horses and mules, crossed the Sierra Madre to the Grand River, and trapped this stream as they descended, living on their supplies of flour and beaver tails.[6]

Upon approaching the confluence of the Green and Grand rivers, the party divided. Five trapped up the Green, while LeDuke and Smith moved south to the San Juan River.

Enroute they had an encounter with the Ute Indians, and lost five of their horses. The two white men chased the Indians right into their camp, says Smith, and demanded the return of their horses. Their boldness so impressed the Utes that they returned the horses. Crossing to the San Juan River and proceeding southward, the two trappers suffered from lack of water and food until they stumbled into a Navajo village. Here they conducted a profitable trade.[7]

[5] *Alta California,* March 8, 1858, p. 1.

[6] *Hutchings' California Magazine,* Oct. 1860, p. 204.

[7] *San Francisco Bulletin, op. cit.*

From the barter, they loaded six pack mules with skins and finely-woven serapes before continuing southward to the Moquis (Hopis). The trappers were impressed by the clean, dome-shaped huts they found in the Moqui village, and as trading progressed, they were told that the industriousness was due to the influence of a recently-departed Spanish priest.[8]

Arriving back in Taos in December 1824, Smith used profits from this venture to erect a still in partnership with James Baird, a former member of the McKnight party.[9] But in the Spring, Smith joined a party of ten men being organized and outfitted by Ceran St. Vrain. Their purpose was trapping the San Juan, Dolores, St. Miguel, and other tributaries of the Grand River. The party set out about the close of February.[10]

Upon reaching the headwaters of the Dolores, they divided and the main group descended the Dolores, while Smith and Hopper went on to the Rio del Norte. Here they trapped the upper portion of the river, finding several herds of horses roaming wild in this area. Smith and Hopper were successful in catching and breaking several of these wild horses, and also obtained a few beaver pelts. During their trapping Smith and Hopper had several contacts with hostile Arapaho Indians, and decided to return to Taos with their pelts and horses, so the venture yielded some returns.[11]

Smith spent the fall and winter in Taos. In the early spring of 1826, in company with several other Americans and Mexicans, he set out into present southeastern Colorado to trap. While on this expedition, the party was chasing a buffalo when a large party of Comanches approached suddenly at full speed, yelling and whooping. The trappers were confused and panic-stricken. Smith brought some order by rallying a few around him to make a stand. The

8 *Hutchings' California Magazine*, Oct. 1860, p. 205.

9 Paul C. Phillips, *The Fur Trade* (Norman, Okla., 1961), II, p. 517.

10 *Hutchings' California Magazine*, Jan. 1861, p. 319.   11 *Ibid.*

Comanches were on faster horses and armed with spears; therefore, retreat would have been disasterous. Convinced that they could succeed because they were about equal in number and had the advantage of firearms, they faced the Indians. This sudden change of tactics caused the Comanches to stop and make signs of peace. They called for a conference and sent a man to talk to Smith midway between the two groups. After a conference the Comanches departed, but Smith learned a lesson from this experience, for he later intimated he would not again be found in such a crowd.[12]

Upon return from this expedition Thomas Smith met Ewing Young, who had returned that spring to Santa Fe from St. Louis. Young became ill, but hired a party of twelve trappers, one of whom was Smith, to penetrate the Gila area on an expedition[13] in September of 1826. This party traveled to the head of the Salt River where they enjoyed a good catch, but the Apache Indians disrupted their trapping and forced the trappers to return to the rancho of Señor Chaves on the Rio Grande, where they waited about two weeks for Ewing Young to arrive with aid.[14]

Ewing Young recruited an additional party of sixteen men and proceeded to meet Smith and the others at Señor Chaves' rancho. About two weeks after Wolfskill and Smith first arrived at the rancho, Ewing Young arrived. Negotiations were started in an attempt to make amends with the trappers who had suffered such a defeat only weeks before. Some discussion was pointed towards the recovery of the lost traps as well as revenge on the Indians. Smith definitely wanted revenge, and unless this concession was obtained he threatened to depart on a separate expedition down the Rio Grande. Most of the party agreed to return to the Salt and

---

[12] *Ibid.*

[13] George C. Yount, "Chronicle of George C. Yount," in *California Historical Society Quarterly*, II (April 1923), 10.

[14] *Hutchings' California Magazine,* Jan. 1861, p. 320.

Gila Rivers upon the promise that no treaty be made with the Indians that had pursued them.[15] Smith and Milton Sublette were among those who agreed to continue with Ewing Young, but William Wolfskill didn't make this second journey to the Gila.[16]

The combined parties headed west under the direction of Ewing Young as captain. They recrossed the same trail to the headwaters of the Salt River in an effort to recover their traps. To their dismay they found, upon arrival, that all the traps were gone. Making the best of the situation, the party set new traps where they could get to the Salt River. The party also kept a watchful eye for Indians because they suspected that they were being observed. After a few days the Coyoteros found that they were unmolested by the trappers, and becoming brave by reason of their own numbers, began to show themselves openly within a few hundred yards of the trappers. The hot blood of Smith wanted an all-out attack upon the "red devils," but Ewing Young persuaded Smith to engage in a more subtle plan. The group retired to a grove of cedar trees and proceeded to chop down enough trees to build a substantial log pen for their stock to prevent the Indians from stealing or stampeding the horses and mules. These logs could also serve as a protection in case of attack by the Indians.[17]

It was only twenty-five days since the Indians had moved against the small party of trappers, and now a larger, reinforced group awaited the Apaches. According to a prearranged plan among the trappers, Young extended an invitation to the Indians to come into the camp on friendly terms. Six Indians came forward to the camp, a chief and five others. The chief was dressed to fit his station, for he wore a broad-brim palmetto hat, a white cotton shirt with

---

[15] *Ibid.*, 321.

[16] Joseph J. Hill, "Ewing Young in the Fur Trade of the Far South West," in *Oregon Historical Quarterly,* XXIV, p. 9.

[17] *Hutchings' California Magazine,* Jan. 1861, p. 321.

scarlet sleeves, and scarlet leggings. As the Indians entered the camp the chief demanded flour and held out a blanket as a container. Ewing Young began to scoop large double handfuls of flour into the blanket when, according to plan, Smith poked his gun under the blanket and fired. The chief was engulfed in a cloud of flour as he fell. The white cloud had not yet settled on the scarlet leggings when five rifles sounded and the other Indians were shot. At the conclusion of the encounter several Indians had been killed and a horse that had been stolen from James Ohio Pattie the year before was recovered.[18]

Having thus gained victory over the Apaches, Ewing Young's party could now commence trapping in earnest. After about a month they were surprised to meet James Ohio Pattie, the trapper Robidoux, and one other man, the only survivors of a massacre by the Papagos.[19] Rallying to the cause of the ill-fated Robidoux party, Smith and the rest of the party of Ewing Young raided the Papago village by way of an old stream bed. The raid was a complete defeat for the Indians, and Smith distinguished himself by killing and scalping the first Indian in the battle.[20]

After soundly defeating the Papagos the party continued under the direction of Ewing Young, trapping the Salt River and its tributaries before continuing down the Gila to the confluence with the Colorado. At this junction the party was greeted peaceably by the Yuma Indians, which was in definite contrast to the subsequent relations had with the Mojaves farther up the river. Even though Jedediah Smith had been well-received by the Mojaves in the fall of 1826, just a few months before the Young party arrived, Young and his men were not to fare so well.[21]

---

[18] *Ibid.*

[19] For details of the meeting of these two groups see: *Personal Narrative of James Ohio Pattie* (ed. Timothy Flint), 123-135, and Robert Glass Cleland, *This Reckless Breed of Men,* 179.

[20] Yount, *California Historical Society Quarterly,* II, p. 9.   [21] Cleland, 183.

The party stopped three miles above the first of the Mojave villages in a grove of cottonwood trees. Because of their apprehension of uneasy feeling among the Indians, the trappers cut down several cottonwood trees and erected a breastwork of cottonwood logs and packs of beaver skin. With this protection they waited for the Mojaves to act. As the day wore on more hostile signs were shown, and finally a Mojave chief speared one of the trapper's horses. Four of Young's men opened fire and killed the Indian. The trappers prepared for an attack. More logs and packs were piled upon the breastwork, and lookouts were sent up the cotton-wood trees to warn when the attack was to come. The Mojaves waited until just before dawn when they hoped to catch the trappers asleep. However, the trappers were warned and ready. The attack was strong, with the Mojaves using bows, arrows and war clubs, but the riflemen behind these breastworks easily turned back the attacks, leaving sixteen Indians dead.[22]

Though this was not a crushing blow to the Indian forces, the trappers were able to move out unmolested. They continued up the Colorado, assuming that the danger had passed. On the evening of the fourth day the trappers posted a small guard but almost all fell asleep. Unknown to the Young party, the Mojaves had followed the trappers, waiting for just such a moment. Creeping close to the camp under the cover of darkness, they stationed themselves within easy bow shot. On a signal the camp was flooded by a shower of arrows that fell upon the sleeping men. Two trappers were killed and two others were wounded in this surprise attack. Pattie's bedfellow was killed beside him and sixteen arrows hit his blanket and pinned it fast to the ground with two of the arrows piercing his hunting shirt.[23]

The trappers then divided into two groups, one to trap and the other to stand guard as a precaution against further

---

[22] *Ibid.*   [23] *Ibid.*

violence while they traveled up the Colorado River. Two miles beyond the mouth of the Virgin River as the trappers came to camp after placing their traps for the night, "Dutch George" Yount produced a handful of nuggets that he had picked up in a dry creek bed.[24] Not knowing whether it was gold or copper, Smith took the nuggets. Using two stones he rounded one of the nuggets to the right size to fit his gun. That night, using the bullet, he went hunting and killed a goat for the company, shooting it with what later proved to be a gold bullet.[25]

At this same camp a decision was made by Smith to leave the main group and trap the Virgin River. He had approached several in the party beforehand, but now only Stone, Branch, "Dutch George," and two Mexicans cast their lot with Smith. This small party built rafts and crossed the Colorado. The Young party continued along the Colorado; but since Smith did not like the canyon that was along the main stream, his group proceeded up the Virgin River.[26]

The Virgin River, even in early 1827, yielded only indifferent success in trapping, and the party began to run short of food. Along the Virgin, through present Nevada, Arizona, and Utah, they came across several groups of Piute Indians. These were poor, shy, and they hid from the small trapper party. Finally in an effort to talk and trade with these Indians, Smith had his party hide while he approached a rather large band alone. They were fearful and shy but he spoke several words to them in their own language and offered them some goods. They had him stand some distance from the group so he threw them some beads and buttons. With this they opened talks, but said they didn't have food but that the beaver had been heard striking the water with their tails in the big river to the east. Then

---

[24] *Hutchings' California Magazine,* Feb. 1861, p. 334.

[25] John M. Bludsworth, "Golden Bullets," in *San Diego Union,* May 15, 1892.

[26] *Hutchings' California Magazine,* Feb. 1861, p. 334.

the Indians ordered him to leave as they pointed in the direction of the big river.[27]

Smith and his party traveled eastward until they came to the river spoken of by the Piutes, which may have been the Sevier. The catch was very disappointing, with only one beaver being taken. In order to satisfy hunger, they dug roots and boiled their rawhide ropes, as well as the rawhide covering of their beaver packs. They continued to travel northward, and on the third day on this river they were forced to kill a mule and divide it among the six. As they traveled they found the going very difficult. The country was not only barren and mountainous, but also criss-crossed by deep canyons and gullies. They were forced to make many detours around these chasms, and some detours lasted for several days' journey. They made their way eastward toward the Colorado, spending forty or fifty days traversing this rough country.[28] While Smith was wandering, the main body of the Ewing Young expedition crossed the Rocky Mountains and returned to Santa Fe.[29]

Smith had made an earlier expedition along the Colorado and San Juan in 1824, and now he and Stone thought they saw a peak in the distance that they recognized. Being without food, Smith consented to let his dog, Blank Calio, be killed to provide the sustenance which enabled the party to reach the mountains, where Smith killed several deer.[30]

Smith now took a more southerly route in the general direction of New Mexico. They were anxious to return, for they had been away nine months and the spring trapping season had passed. Upon reaching the rancho of Trujillo, twelve miles above Albuquerque, they learned that Young had arrived before them in Santa Fe and that his entire catch of furs had been taken by the government.[31]

---

[27] *Ibid.*   [28] *Ibid.*   [29] Cleland, *op. cit.*, 185.

[30] *Hutchings' California Magazine*, Feb. 1861, p. 335.

[31] Paul C. Phillips, in his *The Fur Trade*, II, p. 517, states that in 1824 the central

The situation really came to a head when James Baird, with whom Thomas Smith had previously erected a still, made a formal complaint to the Mexican government. Baird had become a Mexican citizen since his return to Santa Fe after being released from prison with the rest of the McKnight party. He had hopes of dominating the local fur trade and had exercised control over the Gila, but Ewing Young and Thomas Smith had invaded this area and Baird wanted to regain control.[32] Governor Don Manuel Armijo was favorable to Baird and took measures against Ewing Young.

Smith learned at the Trujillo ranch that Young had returned with about twenty thousand dollars worth of beaver skins.[33] Smith was told that Young had hid the skins in the house of Don Luis Cabeza de Vaca, which was located in Rio Abajo outside of Santa Fe. They also told Smith that the alcalde and the soldiers broke into the house, killing de Vaca and removing twenty-nine packs of beaver skin. The furs were taken to the Guardia in Santa Fe where they were spread out in the sun to dry and prevent spoilage. Smith's friend, Milton Sublette, seeing two packs of furs that were his, grabbed them and carried them away before the eyes of the whole garrison.[34] Unless Smith took great care, his furs would now suffer the same fate. He thus chose to detour around Santa Fe and get his catch to Mr. Pratte in Taos, some eighty miles to the north. The party now had to miss all the settlements or travel by night, so it was in early eve-

---

government had passed an act stating that only citizens could trap in the Mexican territory and that the furs of foreigners would be confiscated. This law was left to the local governors to enforce, and there were ways of side-stepping the ordinance by working with the governors. Both Governor Baca and his successor, Narbona, believed Mexico needed their own trappers, and therefore granted licenses to groups if they would take some Mexicans along on the trip. Hill, in *Oregon Historical Quarterly*, XXIV, p. 12, states that when Ewing Young left on his expedition, Narbona had granted him such a license, but while he was on his expedition, Armijo succeeded Narbona as governor in May, 1827.

[32] Phillips, *op. cit.*, II, p. 517.   [33] Cleland, *op. cit.*, 187.

[34] Hill, in *Oregon Historical Quarterly*, XXIV, p. 12.

ning that they left the Trujillo ranch. They traveled until they felt they were past all the houses, and then made camp about two o'clock in the morning. Then they proceeded to make an early start northward with the purpose of traveling without official detection.[35]

To the surprise of the group they found a cabin straight ahead about a mile from their camp. The lay of the ground was such that they had to pass right by the house. As they drew near, the door of the cabin opened and out stepped the alcalde. Smith, in looking at the mules, saw that one of the packs had come uncovered and beaver skins were showing. The truth was out. The alcalde produced a paper from the governor ordering him to seize all beaver skins as contraband. Smith had made up his mind not to surrender the furs, and therefore he told the alcalde that the law was not in existence when he had left and that he had worked hard to obtain the beaver in order that he might discharge a debt to Mr. Pratte for his outfit. He then offered the alcalde thirty dollars as a gift (or bribe). At this point the wife of the alcalde came out of the house and Smith recognized her as one to whom he had given a silk shawl some eighteen months before. This woman argued Smith's case very well, and finally a bargain of some gun powder, lead, and a few butcher knives were added to the thirty dollars, and the party continued with the skins.[36]

Journeying onward the party came to Riitos, and hiding their packs in the trees, they stopped for breakfast. Soon they were surrounded by men, women, and children who fed them tortillas and eggs. However, it was not long before the children discovered the packs, but Smith told them that they were in the trees to keep them out of the sun, and nothing more was said. They left and pushed on to the Rio Grande and hid the furs in a cave that Smith had discovered earlier. From here they rode into Taos the following day.[37]

[35] *Hutchings' California Magazine*, Feb. 1861, p. 336.
[36] *Ibid.*   [37] *Ibid.*

A few days later the beaver were smuggled into Taos and sold to Mr. Pratte. This return called for a celebration and dance that aroused all the people of the village. A long-haired scalp that had been taken by Smith was carried on a pole which led the procession of the entire population of Taos.[38]

Spending the summer of 1827 in Taos after the expedition along the Colorado, Smith refreshed himself. After selling his furs and paying his debts, he investigated the possibilities of another trapping expedition, and finding one being organized by Sylvester S. Pratte to trap in the mountain area north of New Mexico, Smith joined. While Pratte led this expedition personally as the agent for B. Pratte and Company in Missouri, Ceran St. Vrain acted as clerk.[39]

The Pratte expedition was not large, which Smith found to his liking. Several others had joined the group, including a number of Frenchmen and an American, Alexander Branch. They outfitted themselves with horses, mules, traps, rifles, lead, powder, and trade items such as scarlet cloth, and then traveled north from Taos for the fall trapping season. The prospects were good for obtaining beaver in the high mountain streams of present Colorado. Smith had been on a few of these streams before, and Ewing Young had taken a good catch there on his return from the Colorado. With pressure prohibiting American trappers from operating along the Gila according to the decree of 1824, the brightest hope in the fall of 1827 was the mountain area to the north.[40]

The party traveled northward along the mountains until they came to the headwaters of the North Platte River, and here the group divided. The main body stayed on the Platte in the North Park area while Smith started for the Big

---

[38] *Ibid.*

[39] Affidavit of the Taos trapping party, Sept. 1, 1829, Missouri Historical Society, St. Louis (in the P. Chouteau-Maffitt Collection).   [40] See footnote 31.

Sandy alone. They were having moderate success, but they felt that by separating they could increase their catch. Smith caught several beaver on the Big Sandy, and was increasing the catch when a wandering band of Arapahoes came across his traps. The Indians discovered that Smith was alone and started to stalk him. In view of the hostility of the Arapahoes, Smith decided to ride back to the meeting point on the Platte. Leaving most of his gear behind, Smith rode hard for several days, stopping only briefly to rest and eat some jerked meat he was carrying in his shot pouch.[41]

After Smith waited several days for the main body to return to the meeting place in North Park, the group finally arrived. Then news was told of unfortunate luck on the North Platte. Sylvester Pratte had died, and they were in hostile territory.[42]

The trappers united and requested Ceran St. Vrain, who had been clerk in the company, to take the leadership. They also requested that their wages be paid from the estate of Pratte, and this Ceran agreed to do. With this agreement the men cheerfully entered under St. Vrain's command. They planned to continue trapping, for they had taken only three hundred beaver skins.

Organizing and making plans consumed ten days while they were camped in North Park on the headwaters of the Platte.[43] Smith felt that he should go out again, but St. Vrain tried to persuade him not to expose himself so openly to the Indians and to danger.[44] Just then a shot rang out and a puff of smoke came from a nearby clump of bushes.[45] Smith gave a cry of pain as the rifle bullet struck him in the

---

[41] *San Francisco Bulletin.*

[42] *Ibid.* This source says Pratte was killed by Indians; but he died of other causes. See St. Vrain's letter in the Bent and St. Vrain Papers, Missouri Historical Society, St. Louis.

[43] Affidavit of the Taos trapping party, Missouri Historical Society, St. Louis.

[44] *Hutchings' California Magazine,* Mar. 1861, p. 420.

[45] *San Francisco Bulletin.*

left leg just above the ankle,[46] shattering both bones. His gun was leaning against a tree, and as he stepped for his rifle, both bones stuck in the ground. Grabbing his gun, he fired at the clump of bushes from whence the shot had come.[47]

Open war was on, and the trappers held off the Indians[48] as they battled for more than an hour. Smith had taken a buckskin thong and ligated his wound to control the bleeding.[49] The battle ended with the trappers counting nine Indians killed and several wounded. A dead Indian was found in the clump of bushes where the first shot originated. Beside the Indian was Pratte's rifle, which had been used to injure Smith.[50] Smith called upon his companions to cut off his foot, but they refused, not knowing how nor wishing to cause Smith any pain. Smith then called to Joseph Bejux,[51] who was the cook, to bring his knife. Using this knife, Smith cut the torn muscles at the point of the fracture. Since the achilles tendon was all that was left to hold on the battered foot, Milton Sublette took the knife and severed it. Sublette suggested using a hot iron to stop the bleeding, but Smith refused.[52] Smith again used his buckskin thongs to bind up the arteries and control the bleeding.[53] Employing an old dirty shirt, they bound up the wound and waited.[54]

Supposing that Smith would bleed to death, the trappers reassured him that they would not leave him until his death. The party members, even though months from any civilization, determined to help Smith all they could. Within

---

[46] Nolie Mumey, *James Pierson Beckworth* (1957), 45.

[47] *Hutchings' California Magazine,* Mar. 1861, p. 420.

[48] James Hobbs, *Wild Life in the Far West* (1875), 57; and *Hutchings' California Magazine,* 420, name Crow Indians as the offenders.

[49] "The Scapel Under Three Flags," in *California Historical Quarterly,* IV (1925), 157.

[50] *San Francisco Bulletin.*   [51] Affidavit of the Taos trapping party.

[52] *Hutchings' California Magazine,* Mar. 1861, p. 420.

[53] *Alta California* (San Francisco), March 8, 1858.

[54] *Hutchings' California Magazine,* Mar. 1861, p. 420.

twenty-four hours the bleeding had stopped, which surprised most of these seasoned trappers. The party remained encamped here in North Park for another day while Smith regained enough strength to travel.[55] Because it was October, and winter was approaching, the group decided to move out. The two men who were appointed to look after Smith, carried him for two days by hand in a litter as the party traveled.[56]

The route was northward down the Platte to Sage Creek and then up Sage Creek across the divide to Savery Creek, which flows into Little Snake River, or as it was then named, St. Vrain's Fork. After two days on the trail, the party devised a litter that could be carried between two mules in tandem fashion. The Little Snake River was difficult to follow, for the bottom lands were in very narrow strips. Rocky canyons slowed the party, but even worse, the principal tree that grew there was the bitter cottonwood which was not liked by the beaver. As a result the catch was small as they moved southward down the Little Snake River. Leaving the Little Snake about fifty miles above the

---

[55] If all the accounts referring to this famous deed of Thomas L. Smith are to be accepted, Smith would be a surgeon of considerable experience in amputation. His foot would be wandering for years from the Mojave Desert of California to the Bear Lake Valley of Idaho and out onto the plains into the Crow country rather than staying put in Colorado. His problem grows with the sources, for in combining them he had frostbite, gangrene, and an arrow wound, not to mention the rifle ball that was the real source of trouble. Next comes the mystery of who shot him. Spanish, accuse some, Crow Indians say others, but the real identity of the Indian tribe is lost. However, Crow Indians were in the area stealing a few of the party's horses. *(Hutchings' California Magazine)*. Most accounts cut the leg off below the knee while in reality it was cut closer to the ankle. Who cut it off? Smith, himself, did the major part with Milton Sublette assisting, but certain accounts give him a complete hospital staff of companions and Indian doctors. Many instruments were reportedly used; hunting knives, butcher knives, Indian saws, keyhole saws, pocket saws, as well as a personally handmade saw filed from a knife. For this deed and for his life, Smith has been called a hero, courageous, fearless; as well as a drunkard, rowdy, roustabout, immoral, gold-seeker, and horse thief. Isn't legend wonderful?

[56] *Hutchings' California Magazine,* Mar. 1861, p. 420.

mouth, they crossed westward to the Green River where they prepared to spend the winter.[57]

The party reached the Green River the last part of November 1827, about a month after Smith had been shot. About the same time Smith noticed that one of the bones protruding from his stump was loose and could be wiggled. He used a pair of bullet molds for forceps and with the help of Milton Sublette, he pulled out the bone.[58] A few days later about forty lodges of Ute Indians joined the trappers to spend the winter.[59] These were the same Utes that had been impressed with Smith's courage in demanding return of his stolen mules several years earlier. Wakara, not yet an independent chief, was said to be in the group.[60]

The Utes were sorrowed to learn that Smith had lost his leg for they called him, "Tevvy-oats-at-an-tuggy-bone" (the big friend). A ritual was started in an effort to heal the wound. Chanting, along with crying and wailing, started the ceremony, and proper incantations were called upon. Then the women and children, chewing roots, gathered around Smith and spit upon the wound. They kept this up for several days, chewing and spitting in an effort to effect a cure. Because of, or in spite of, the unusual remedy, Smith continued to improve, and the Utes felt their treatment had been successful. Not long after this the remaining bone fragment that protruded was loose enough that again the bullet-mold forceps could be used to extract it. From this point on it was a matter of gaining strength.[61]

During his recovery the trappers had fashioned a wooden leg of either oak or hickory for him. About the first of March 1828, he was well enough to walk around some on this peg, and as a result his trapper friends gave him the

---

[57] *Ibid.*   [58] *San Francisco Bulletin.*
[59] *Hutchings' California Magazine*, Mar. 1861, p. 421.
[60] Paul Bailey, *Walkara, Hawk of the Mountains* (1954), 24.
[61] *Hutchings' California Magazine*, Mar. 1861, p. 421.

sobriquet, Peg-leg Smith.[62] The Utes also changed their name for him to Wa-ke-to-co, the man with one foot.[63]

After passing what St. Vrain described as "the most rigorous winter I have yet experienced,"[64] the trappers planned to return the property of Sylvester Pratte to St. Louis that spring. In April 1828, the party set out under the direction of St. Vrain. Peg-leg was now able to travel by riding on a horse with his peg stuck in the stirrup. After five days of travel in a general eastward direction, they came across a large trace left by Indians. This could be signs of friendly tribes, but because of their recent experiences with hostile Indians the party made a complete check of the powder and lead supply. In the event that the Indians proved hostile and fighting was necessary, the St. Vrain party found their ammunition insufficient to carry on a battle. Not wanting to take the risk of attack and defeat, they agreed to return to Taos. The travel was not difficult for they reached Taos about May 23, 1828.[65]

The party returned with about a thousand beaver pelts. Three hundred had been taken before Pratte was killed, and seven hundred were caught on the way to the winter camp and in the spring trapping. In addition to these furs the estate of S. S. Pratte contained seven mules, eight horses, seventeen traps, sixteen yards of scarlet cloth, three yards of blue cloth, one pair of gloves, one-third of a piece of webbing, one rifle gun, a pair of pistols, and one rifle barrel.[66] These items were sold by St. Vrain to pay the men their wages.[67]

---

[62] *Alta California.* Accompanying the article in *Hutchings' California Magazine* is a woodcut portrait of Smith, which is reproduced herein at page 17.

[63] *San Francisco Bulletin.*

[64] Letter from Ceran St. Vrain to Messers B. Pratte & Co., September 28, 1828, St. Louis (in the P. Chouteau-Maffitt Collection).

[65] Affidavit of the Taos trapping party.   [66] *Ibid.*

[67] On the 28th of September, 1828, St. Vrain wrote to Messers B. Pratte and Company in St. Louis, and gave an account of the happenings and the death of Pratte.

The next expedition made by Smith was to the rendezvous at Bear Lake Valley in the summer of 1828. From
this trading festival Peg-leg joined a group that trapped the
Santa Clara and Virgin Rivers. Taking a good supply of
pelts from these rivers, the party chose Smith and one other
man to travel to Los Angeles during the first part of 1829 to
sell the furs, which found a ready market. However, Smith
got drunk and the alcalde ran him out of Los Angeles, so
Smith rounded up a band of from three to four hundred
horses and drove them to Taos.[68]

For the next few years Smith trapped in the mountains of
Colorado, and on one of these expeditions he led Albert
Pike and Aaron B. Lewis to the head of the Green River
and then on to the headwaters of the Arkansas in the spring
of 1832.[69] However, as the fur trade declined Smith turned
more to trading, especially in horses, and he formed a firm
friendship with the Ute chief, Wakara, and James P. Beckwourth. Together they conducted a horse-trading venture
to Los Angeles in 1836 and purchased a few animals, but
ran off a greater number. They drove these animals to Bent's
Fort where good horses were in demand.

In the summer of 1839 Beckwourth and Peg-leg Smith
engaged the services of Wakara and one hundred fifty of
his band to go on a full scale raid of the horse herds in all
of Southern California. Following the Old Spanish Trail
they sent Beckwourth ahead to spot the herds while making
a pretense of hunting sea otter. Meeting in Cajon Pass in
the spring of 1840, the party divided into small groups and
raided all the horse herds on the ranchos and missions.
About five thousand head were stolen, but the Californians
organized and gave chase, recovering two thousand, while

---

[68] Eleanor Lawrence, "Peg-leg Smith, His Story," in *Touring Topics* (Oct. 1932),
21.

[69] Albert Pike, *Prose Sketches and Poems* (1834), 33.

Smith and Wakara succeeded in retaining three thousand head.[70]

While at Bent's Fort, Smith trapped on the Purgatory River with Kit Carson and James Hobbs until the spring of 1841. With horses to trade or sell, Smith established a trading post on the Oregon Trail in Bear Lake Valley.[71] This remained his headquarters until 1850. Selling horses to the Oregon pioneers and to the Mormons,[72] Smith was a well-known person to the pioneers that traveled west. During the rush for California gold in 1849 and 1850, many travelers left accounts of their trading with Smith for horses and food.[73]

Gold in California finally lured Smith away from the mountains and he left for the goldfields in the fall of 1850, making his headquarters at the ranch of an old trapping friend, William C. Moon, near Sacramento. The many friends of Peg-leg who had received aid from this trader on their overland trek, petitioned the California Senate to come to the aid of Smith.[74] On May 3, 1852, with the endorsement of both Governor John Bigler and Johnson Price, Secretary of State of California, the Senate unanimously passed a resolution petitioning the senators and representatives from California to secure reimbursement from the national government for Thomas L. Smith.[75]

In 1854 Smith organized and led an expedition from Los Angeles to the mouth of the Virgin River in search of the gold that Smith had once found there.[76] The party was

---

[70] LeRoy R. and Ann W. Hafen, *The Old Spanish Trail* (1954), 237.

[71] Hobbs, p. 51.

[72] "Journal History" (L.D.S. Church Historian's Office, Salt Lake City), Nov. 15, 1848.

[73] Reuben Cole Shaw, *Across the Plains in Forty-Nine,* ed. by M. M. Quaife (1948), 103; and many other narratives.

[74] Sardis Templeton, *The Lame Captain* (Los Angeles, 1965), 216.

[75] California State Senate *Journal* for 1852. Petition for relief of Thomas L. Smith, May 3, 1852.   [76] *Alta California.*

disappointed in their gold search, and returned to California later in the summer of 1854 with part of the Fremont expedition.[77]

The final days of Peg-leg Smith were spent in and around San Francisco, where he frequented the corner of Montgomery and Clay Streets and depended upon friends for charitable support.[78] A friend, Major Hensley, secured admittance for Peg-leg to the city and county hospital at San Francisco. Mr. Hensley was the president of a steamship line with offices in San Francisco, and he lived with his family in San Jose. It seems that Peg-leg had rendered assistance to Major Hensley while Smith had his trading post on Bear River. Now the major kept him supplied with whiskey and tobacco while in the hospital. W. C. McDougall visited him at the hospital and reports that Peg-leg was passing the time in the old accustomed border-life style: smoking, chewing, and drinking to the last.[79] The days were gone when Peg-leg would stand on the edge of the sidewalk of Montgomery Street and astonish everyone by giving war whoops from several Indian tribes. He remained in the hospital for several years, until his death on the fifteenth of October 1866, at the age of sixty-five.[80]

[77] S. N. Carvalho, *Incidents of Travel and Adventure in the Far West* (1857), 234.   [78] *Alta California.*

[79] Bludsworth, *San Diego Union.*   [80] *San Francisco Bulletin.*

William Wolfskill

by IRIS HIGBIE WILSON
Long Beach, California

Of that notable group of Mountain Men who afterwards became permanent and influential settlers in the Mexican province of California during the pre-gold rush era, William Wolfskill stands as an important member.* Born in Madison County, Kentucky, on March 20, 1798, of American parents descending from German and Irish ancestry, Wolfskill was a typical example of his generation's pioneer tradition.[1] In the fall of 1809, when Boonesborough, Kentucky, seemed to be overcrowded with newcomers, the Wolfskill family, numbering fourteen, set out for Missouri. With the encouragement of Daniel Boone, several Kentucky families cleared and fenced a small tract of land in Howard County, then beyond the fringe of any settled area. During the War of 1812, the Indians of the Missouri River region were particularly menacing and at the age of fourteen William Wolfskill could handle a Kentucky rifle with considerable skill.[2]

When the war ended in 1815, Wolfskill returned to Kentucky to attend school. Two years of "formal education" were adequate for the young frontiersman and he returned to the family homestead at Boone's Lick. In May of 1822, Wolfskill and several of his Howard County neighbors joined Captain William Becknell's second expedition to

---

* A full book-length biography of William Wolfskill, by the contributor of this sketch, is to be issued in 1965 by the publisher of the present series.

[1] James M. Guinn, *A History of California and an Extended History of Los Angeles and Environs* (Los Angeles, 1915), II, p. 24.

[2] *History of Howard and Cooper Counties, Missouri* (St. Louis, 1883), 92-6; Will C. Ferril, "Missouri Military in the War of 1812," *Missouri Historical Review*, IV (October, 1909), 38-41.

Santa Fe. When the party broke up in New Mexico, Wolf-skill remained in the area and trapped beaver during the summer and fall of 1822.[3]

In January of 1823, Wolfskill and a New Mexican with whom he had trapped on the Pecos River the preceding fall, set out on a trapping venture down the Rio Grande to El Paso del Norte. During the course of the journey, the two men found it necessary to build a small brush hut for protection against the snow and bitter cold. A few nights later, while sleeping in the hut, Wolfskill became the victim of what he imagined was an Indian attack. He realized that he had been shot in the chest with a rifle, but the force of the ball had fortunately been slowed by passing through a blanket and his right arm and left hand. Wolfskill left the hut and made his way on foot to the nearest Mexican settlement, Valverde, which lay at a distance of twenty-five miles. Much to his amazement, his companion turned up a few hours later with the story that he had been attacked by Indians and his partner, Mr. Wolfskill, had been killed. The New Mexican was arrested after the falsity of his report was verified and Wolfskill, almost unable to believe that a person would go to such trouble to steal a few beaver traps and an old rifle, returned to Santa Fe as soon as his strength permitted.[4]

By August of 1823, Wolfskill was back in the New Mexican capital. After some local trapping with a few trusted companions, he journeyed to Taos, arriving in the valley at Christmas time. During the month of February, 1824, Wolfskill fitted out for a trapping expedition to the head-waters of the San Juan River and other tributaries of the Colorado. The party was numerous at first, but as it con-

---

[3] Henry D. Barrows, "Story of an Old Pioneer [William Wolfskill]," Los Angeles *World*, Sept. 24, 1887.

[4] Henry D. Barrows, "William Wolfskill, the Pioneer," *Annual Publications of the Historical Society of Southern California*, v (1902), 290.

tinued around the west side of the Sierra Madre, various
members worked down different streams until Wolfskill
remained with just two companions, Isaac Slover and
Ewing Young. They remained out until beaver season was
over and returned to Taos in June with furs worth almost
ten thousand dollars.[5]

In November of 1824, Wolfskill left Taos to go south
with a party led by a Captain Owens for the purpose of
buying horses and mules to take to Louisiana. They bought
the animals in the northwestern part of Chihuahua and
drove them as far as the Presidio del Norte. Near this point
the party was attacked by Indians and several of the men,
including Captain Owens, were killed. Several of the animals which had not been captured by the Indians were
recovered by Wolfskill and another member of the party.
With money left by Captain Owens, Wolfskill purchased
some additional mules and the two men started home to
Missouri.[6]

Because of the danger of Indian attacks, Wolfskill and
his companion thought it best to return home by way of the
Mexican settlements along the Gulf. They started down by
way of the Rio Grande and hoped to eventually gain passage
on a schooner bound for New Orleans. Failing to make
connections, Wolfskill continued on alone by land to Natchitoches, Louisiana, and then caught a steamer which took
him to St. Louis. Weary from his long journey and in poor
health because of his chest wound, the young adventurer
arrived at his father's home in Boone's Lick in June of 1825.
Several months later, Wolfskill traveled to San Felipe de
Austin to rejoin his companion who was waiting with the
mules. They drove the Mexican animals, which later became known as "Missouri Mules," across Louisiana and

[5] Joseph J. Hill, "Ewing Young in the Fur Trade of the Far Southwest, 1822-
1824," *Oregon Historical Quarterly*, XXIV (March, 1923), 7.

[6] Barrows, Los Angeles *World*, Oct. 1, 1887.

Mississippi to Greenborough, Alabama, where they sold them at a good profit. Wolfskill remained in Alabama for the winter, but in March of 1826 returned to Missouri by way of Mobile and New Orleans. Once again in Boone's Lick, Wolfskill gave the proceeds of the sale to Captain Owens' family.[7]

After remaining in the Missouri area until the summer of 1826, Wolfskill joined Ewing Young on another venture to New Mexico for the purpose of trapping the Rio Gila. Upon their arrival in Santa Fe, Young took sick and the leadership of the expedition fell to Wolfskill. Among the original eleven members of the party were Milton Sublette and George Yount, both of whom had arrived with the Santa Fe caravan of that summer. The group was later joined by five trappers led by Thomas L. "Peg-Leg" Smith and Maurice Le Duc.[8] After two or three weeks on the Gila River, the expedition ran into difficulty with Indians and was unfortunately forced to return to Santa Fe empty-handed. Wolfskill then drove a band of horses from Sonora, Mexico, to Independence, Missouri, and spent the next year in the United States.

In 1828 Wolfskill left Missouri for the last time, making his third trip westward over the Santa Fe trail. Once in New Mexico he sold the majority of his trade goods to Ewing Young, and these two men entered into a partnership with Solomon Houck for the purpose of fitting out a party to trap the waters of "the California valley."[9] Young, however, made another trip to the Rio Gila while Wolfskill went to El Paso in the spring of 1829 to purchase a supply

---

[7] *Ibid.*

[8] Joseph J. Hill, "New Light on Pattie and the Southwestern Fur Trade," *Southwestern Historical Quarterly*, XXVI (April, 1923), 253; "The Story of an Old Trapper. Life and Adventures of the Late Peg-Leg Smith," San Frarncisco *Daily Evening Bulletin,* Oct. 26, 1866.

[9] J. J. Warner, "Reminiscences of Early California from 1831 to 1846," *Annual Publications of the Historical Society of Southern California,* VII (1907-08), 190.

of wines, brandy and other goods which could be sold in Taos. Wolfskill remained in Taos the balance of the year awaiting the return of Young, who with eighteen men including Kit Carson, had continued on to California.[10]

In March of 1830, Wolfskill made legal application for Mexican citizenship [11] and in July of that year prepared for an expedition to California to hunt beaver. He also expected to find Young somewhere on the Pacific Coast. Wolfskill's party consisted of about twenty men whose names can be found in the ledger of financial transactions which were made during the trip.[12] Among those who definitely accompanied Wolfskill to California were John Lewis, Zachariah Ham, Ziba Branch, Alexander Branch, Francisco Le Fourri, Baptiste St. Germain, Samuel Shields, José Archuleta, George Yount, Love Hardesty, Martin Cooper and Lewis Burton. Eleven members of the company were employees of Wolfskill and the others were free trappers under the leadership of Yount.

The route which Wolfskill's party followed after its departure from Taos was not recorded at the time, but it can be generally traced through descriptions made in later accounts by several of the participants. Wolfskill's own statement, which his son-in-law Henry Barrows faithfully recorded, is the most succinct, although it may have been edited by Mr. Barrows:

> Last of Sept., 1830, the party, with Mr. Wolfskill at its head, left Taos for this then far off Territory of California. They came by a route farther north than that usually adopted by the Spaniards in

---

10 Edwin L. Sabin, *Kit Carson Days, 1809-1868* (New York, 1935), 39ff; Christopher Carson, "Kit Carson's Story as Told by Himself," MS., n.d., Bancroft Library.

11 José Guillermo Wolfskill to the Governor of New Mexico, Petition for Citizenship, San Gerónimo de Taos, March 25, 1830; Mexican Archives of New Mexico, no. 2496b; Recommendation for Approval of Citizenship, March 25, 1830, Mexican Archives of New Mexico, no. 2497; Santa Fe, New Mexico.

12 William Wolfskill, "Ledger of Accounts, 1830-1832," MS., photostat, Huntington Library, San Marino, Calif. For a complete discussion of this expedition see LeRoy R. and Ann W. Hafen, *The Old Spanish Trail* (Glendale, Calif., 1954).

traveling between California and New Mexico – their object being to find beaver. They struck the Colorado just below the mouth of the Dolores, at the head of the "Great Cañon," where they crossed; entering the Great American Basin, striking the Sevier; thence southward to the Rio Virgin, which they followed down to the Colorado; thence descending the Colorado to the Mojave; where they hoped to obtain some provisions of which they were in want, and also to find beaver. From there they took across to the sink of the Mojave River, through the Cajon Pass to San Bernardino, and finally to Los Angeles, where they arrived in February, 1831.[13]

In contrast to the somewhat vague and circuitous routes of previous expeditions, Wolfskill's group charted a track which traversed the entire distance across the Great Basin and led directly into southern California. Explorers and fur traders such as Father Garcés and Fathers Domínguez and Escalante in 1776, Jedediah Smith in 1826-27, Ewing Young in 1829, and Antonio Armíjo in 1829-30 had followed parts of the same trail, but to Wolfskill belonged the honor of having marked the first route feasible for pack trains which covered the entire distance from Taos to the Pacific.[14] Wolfskill's path was called the "Old Spanish Trail" because it was considered to be a continuation of a trail used by the Spaniards since 1765, but in reality it was a new route discovered during the Mexican period.

Several of the members of Wolfskill's party, after reaching California, advantageously disposed of their woolen blankets, called *serapes* or *fresadas,* to the rancheros in exchange for mules. These blankets were typical of the region of New Mexico and frequently used by trappers and other travelers out of Santa Fe. They were very thick, almost impervious to water, and their high quality impressed the Californians. At the same time, the mules of California were much larger and of finer form than those used in the Mis-

---

[13] Wilmington *Journal,* Oct. 20, 1866. See also Charles L. Camp (ed.), "The Chronicles of George C. Yount," *California Historical Society Quarterly,* II (April, 1923), 38ff.

[14] Gloria Griffen Cline, *Exploring the Great Basin* (Norman, 1963), 165.

souri and Santa Fe trade. Their appearance in New Mexico caused quite a sensation, especially when it was learned that they had been received in trade for blankets. Juan José Warner later wrote that out of the bargain made by Wolfskill's men "there sprang up a trade, carried on by means of caravans or pack animals between the two sections of the same country, which flourished for some ten or twelve years." [15] On the other hand, a more recent source states that these trappers should not be thought of as having begun the caravan trade over the Old Spanish Trail because two months after Wolfskill's arrival in California "30 men from New Mexico, merchants in wool, bringing passports" appeared in Los Angeles. Since these businessmen apparently had no other purpose in going to California except to trade merchandise for mules, their transactions were those which actually began the new commerce.[16]

The Wolfskill party reached the ranch of Don Antonio María Lugo on the outskirts of Los Angeles on February 5, 1831. Here the accounts of the various trappers were settled. Financially, the expedition was not successful as a trapping venture, and Wolfskill was left in debt. Rather than continue hunting the elusive beaver, he and George Yount associated themselves with Samuel Prentice, Nathaniel M. Pryor and Richard Laughlin to build a vessel in which to hunt sea otter. This enterprise was made possible through a confusion of Spanish terms. Wolfskill had been granted a license to hunt *nutria* by the Governor of New Mexico. *Nutria* in California correctly meant "otter," whereas it was a provincialism of New Mexico to use the same word to mean "beaver." [17]

---

[15] J. J. Warner, *An Historical Sketch of Los Angeles County* (Los Angeles, 1876), 33.

[16] Eleanor F. Lawrence, "Mexican Trade between Santa Fe and Los Angeles, 1830-1848," *California Historical Society Quarterly,* x (March, 1931), 27-9.

[17] Warner, "Reminiscences of Early California," 192; George W. Beattie and Helen P. Beattie, *Heritage of the Valley* (Pasadena, Calif., 1939), 27.

View of the Copper Mine. The Santa Rita del Cobre (copper mines) provided men in the Southwest fur trade one of many entrepreneurial alternatives to trapping and trading. From Lieutenant Colonel W.H. Emory, *Notes of a Military Reconnaissance* (Washington D. C.: Wendell and Van Benthuysen, 1848). Courtesy of Western History Collections, University of Oklahoma.

Junction of the Gila and Colorado Rivers. From John R. Bartlett, *Personal Narrative of Explorations and Incidents* (New York: D. Appleton and Company, 1854). Courtesy of Western History Collections, University of Oklahoma.

With the aid of Father José Sánchez of Mission San Gabriel, who supplied both material and Indian laborers, Wolfskill and his associates built a schooner under the direction of Joseph Chapman, an apprenticed ship-builder originally from Boston, with timber cut and hauled from the San Bernardino Mountains. The schooner, perhaps the first built in California, sailed from San Pedro harbor in January of 1832.[18] Wolfskill and his partners worked the vessel from as far south as Cedros Island to north of Point Conception, but the former Mountain Men failed as sea otter hunters. They sold the schooner to Captain William S. Hinckley, who sailed her to the Hawaiian Islands.

William Wolfskill decided at this time to settle down in the pueblo of Los Angeles and direct his energies toward the cultivation of the soil. After successfully petitioning for a tract of land, Wolfskill worked part-time as a carpenter while his newly planted crops took root. Within a few years, he became one of the leading vineyardists of the country, having affirmed his belief that a vine, "if well cared for, would flourish one hundred years."[19] William and his brother John, who had reached Los Angeles from Santa Fe in 1838, acquired a vineyard in March of that year which contained four thousand vines and the two planted thirty-two thousand additional vines during the next few years. Through the acquisition of adjacent lands, William – called "Don Guillermo" by his Hispanic neighbors – increased his holdings to 145 acres in the central part of Los Angeles and eventually planted eighty-five thousand vines.[20]

In the year 1841 Wolfskill planted a two-acre orange orchard, the first commercial enterprise of that kind in Cal-

---

[18] Barrows, "William Wolfskill" (1902), 293, says the vessel was named *Refugio,* but Alfred Robinson, *Life in California* (San Francisco, 1891), 132, gives the name as *Guadalupe.* Bancroft in his Marine List (*History of California,* III, p. 382) cites the *Guadalupe* as weighing 60 tons, built by Joseph Chapman and launched at San Pedro in 1831. The schooner probably had two names.

[19] Harris Newmark, *Sixty Years in Southern California* (New York, 1930), 199.

[20] John H. Hittell, *The Resources of California* (San Francisco, 1863), 200.

ifornia, on land which was later occupied by a passenger depot of the Southern Pacific Railroad. Obtaining the young trees from the Mission San Gabriel, Wolfskill experimented in the cultivation of lemons, limes and other citrus fruits in addition to some deciduous varieties. During the early 1850s he acquired a tract of land along the San Gabriel River and by 1857, when there were not more than one hundred orange trees bearing fruit in the whole county, Wolfskill planted several thousand and thus established the largest orange orchard in the United States. Many of the seeds for these trees came from the Hawaiian Islands.[21]

Also in 1841 William Wolfskill journeyed to northern California to look for a ranch on the then-vacant public domain. At the suggestion of his friend Juan José Warner, Wolfskill selected lands lying on both sides of Putah Creek, the course of which ran along the western border of the Sacramento Valley in present-day Yolo and Solano Counties. In 1842 he petitioned Governor Juan Bautista Alvarado for a grant of land containing four square leagues, or about eighteen thousand acres.[22] His brother John drove a herd of livestock northward to put on the ranch and when the grant was finally confirmed, John purchased one-half of the land. During the gold rush, John Wolfskill made large profits in the cattle business and at one time sold one thousand head of cattle for $40,000 cash. In 1856 William Wolfskill sold his half of the ranch to his brother Mathus and two other purchasers for $71,000.[23]

---

[21] J. Albert Wilson, *History of Los Angeles County* (Oakland, Calif., 1880), 183; John L. Von Blon, "Here Oranges like Ruddy Lanterns Shine," *Touring Topics,* xxv (November, 1933), 13.

[22] *The United States vs. William Wolfskill,* Case no. 232, U.S. District Court Records, Northern District of California, San Francisco.

[23] A sketch of the active part taken in the historical development of California by John R. Wolfskill, Sarchel Wolfskill and William Wolfskill, typescript with notes in the handwriting of David R. Sessions (Bancroft Library, Univ. of Calif.), Deed of Wm. Wolfskill to A. and G. B. Stevenson, Mathus Wolfskill and Edward McGary, July 5, 1856.

By the early 1840s Wolfskill had constructed a large rambling adobe ranch house on his Los Angeles property and was active in the local affairs of the pueblo. In January of 1841 the ex-trapper married Doña Magdalena Lugo, daughter of Don José Ignacio Lugo and Doña Rafaela Romero de Lugo of Santa Barbara, and the couple became the parents of six children. Two of Wolfskill's sons, Joseph and Luis, were especially interested in agriculture, and the boys assisted in the cultivation of such new plants as the eucalyptus tree from Australia, the soft-shelled almond, the chestnut and the persimmon tree, all of which were unknown in California.[24] In addition, Wolfskill was successfully engaged in the wine-making industry, which had proven to be a profitable venture. In 1859 when the total vintage for California was reported to be 340,000 gallons of wine, William Wolfskill produced 50,000 gallons, or a little over fifteen percent of the total.[25] The value of Wolfskill's vineyards and orchards was placed at $80,000 by the Los Angeles County Assesor's office in 1858.[26]

Wolfskill always maintained a firm interest in education and established a private school in his home during the 1850s for members of his family and the children of his neighbors. The curriculum of the school included a thorough course in English and Spanish as well as basic mathematics and a study of music. Among the students in his school were the sons of other former Mountain Men such as John Rowland and Lemuel Carpenter, who had settled on nearby ranches. Wolfskill also subsidized the first public school in Los Angeles which threatened to close after the completion of its first term in 1854.[27]

---

[24] Newmark, *op. cit.*, 125, 562.

[25] Henry D. Barrows, "Letter from Los Angeles," San Francisco *Daily Evening Bulletin*, Oct. 24, 1859.

[26] *The Southern Vineyard*, Sept. 18, 1858. Property was assessed then as now at a figure much lower than its actual value.

In 1860 Wolfskill bought Rancho Lomas de Santiago, eleven square leagues of pasture land in present-day Orange County, for $7,000. He maintained the rancho to graze his large herd of cattle and horses. When the drought of 1863-64 hit the majority of southern California livestock, Wolfskill drove his herds through Cajon Pass to grassy Mojave River bottom lands and managed to save all but about twenty-five percent of his animals. In spite of this successful move, Wolfskill sold the rancho, plus an interest which he held in the neighboring Rancho Santiago de Santa Ana, to Flint, Bixby, and Company and James Irvine in 1866. He received the same price for the property that he had paid six years before.[28]

Wolfskill also bought Rancho Santa Anita, which consisted of between nine and ten thousand acres in Los Angeles County, for $20,000 in 1865. Wolfskill used the land for agricultural purposes and eventually left it to his son Luis, who sold it for $85,000 in 1872. Another piece of property which came into the hands of William Wolfskill was Rancho San Francisco, the site of present-day Newhall, which was sold to the Philadelphia Oil Company during the first California oil boom for seventy-five cents an acre.[29]

On October 3, 1866, William Wolfskill died at his Los Angeles residence. His sixty-eight years had spanned not only the important epoch of the far western fur trade, but had witnessed the founding of an Anglo-Californian society. The former Mountain Man contributed his share to the economic and cultural development of the Far West. Perhaps as the result of his many activities, Wolfskill spent little time writing. All that exist today from his own hand

[27] Roy M. Cloud, *Education in California* (Stanford, Calif., 1952), 32; Joseph E. Pleasants, "Los Angeles in 1856," *Touring Topics,* XXII (January, 1930), 37.

[28] Robert Glass Cleland, *The Irvine Ranch of Orange County* (San Marino, Calif., 1962), 53.

[29] Ruth Waldo Newhall, *The Newhall Ranch* (San Marino, Calif., 1958), 44-7.

are a few business letters and his account books. If he kept a diary, it has not been discovered, and he passed away before Hubert Howe Bancroft began compiling information for his "Pioneer Register and Index." It has been possible, however, to gain an insight into the character of William Wolfskill through the writings of his contemporaries, who agreed without exception that he was a man of intelligence, sincerity and resourcefulness. Major Horace Bell, one of the early California rangers, summed up the prevailing opinions when he commented that "Mr. Wolfskill was a very remarkable man; in fact, he was a hero – not the kind of a hero poets like to sing about, but still a hero. A man of indomnitable will, industry and self-denial; an American pioneer hero; one who succeeds in all he undertakes, and is always to be trusted, of the kind of men who enrich the country in which they live." [30]

[30] Major Horace Bell, *Reminiscences of a Ranger* (Santa Barbara, Calif., 1927), 58. A portrait of Wolfskill appears at page 20 of the present volume.

Ceran St. Vrain

by HAROLD H. DUNHAM
University of Denver

Ceran St. Vrain (May 5, 1802-October 28, 1870) was
recognized by his contemporaries as one of the outstanding
Mountain Men of the American Southwest. From fur trapping and trading, he progressed to a position of business,
military and political prominence that made him one of
New Mexico's leading citizens. His personal qualities,
which included kindliness, courage, reliability and reserve,
indicate that he was a true gentleman. The fact that only a
few of his personal and business papers seem to have survived helps explain why he has not yet been portrayed in a
full-scale biography.[1]

Ceran's father, Jacques Marcellin Ceran de Hault de
Lassus de St. Vrain, was born in French Flanders in 1770,
and migrated to St. Louis, Missouri, in 1795, five years after
his own father had fled the early stages of the French Revolution.[2] By 1796 Jacques had married Marie Felicite Du-
breuil and settled down in a home near Spanish Lake, St.
Louis County. There, in this predominantly French community, on May 5, 1802, Ceran St. Vrain, the second of ten
children, was born to the couple. Unfortunately, very little
is known of Ceran's early life. To be sure, his father was
well acquainted with some of the leading French families
of the town. He held minor political office and owned a
generous land grant in southeastern Missouri, along with

---

[1] The life of C. St. Vrain is sketched in D. Lavender, *Bent's Fort* (1954), *passim;*
N. Mumey, "Black Beard," in *Denver Westerners Monthly Roundup*, XIV, no. 1
(Jan. 1958), 4-16; and *Dictionary of American Biography* (1928-36), XVI, pp. 305-
06.

[2] P. A. St. Vrain, *Genealogy of the Family of De Lassus and St. Vrain* (1943), 15.

smaller grants near St. Louis, so the family must have lived
in fairly comfortable circumstances.

Ceran may well have received some formal education in
a town school.[3] While the grammar and spelling of his
known letters, beginning with the mid-1820s, reveal numerous deficiencies, Ceran's writing was in English, rather
than French, and it displayed at times rather elegant pen-
manship. Possibly the death of his father in 1818, when
Ceran was in his mid-teens, prevented the latter from receiving a more complete schooling, such as that provided for
Bernard Pratte, Jr., and Charles Bent, two of Ceran's
friends.

The father's death probably meant that the large family
became a burden to Madame St. Vrain, so Ceran went to
live with the Bernard Pratte, Sr., family. It was during this
period that Bernard, Jr., transferred to a school in Kentucky
to complete his education. Pratte, Sr., served as a partner in
two fur trading companies before forming Bernard Pratte
and Co., in 1823.[4] It was perhaps inevitable that as a youth
living with the Prattes, Ceran should have become a clerk
in the company's St. Louis store, progressed to managing
fur shipments, and then entered into the trade of the company's Missouri River posts.[5] From such experiences, he
progressed into the Santa Fe trade in his early twenties, yet
just how this shift occurred is not clear.[6]

In any case, by 1824 St. Vrain had formed a partnership

---

[3] The reference to St. Vrain's formal schooling is based on inference from several
sources, rather than any direct source. At least one of his younger brothers went on
to college.

[4] *D.A.B.*, xv, pp. 180-81; and J. T. Scharf, *History of St. Louis City and County*
(1883) I, pp. 196 fn., and 674.

[5] James Conklin recalled in 1877 that St. Vrain was a clerk in St. Louis for B.
Pratte, Berthold and Co., merchants. R.I. 1723. Ritch Collection, Huntington Library,
San Marino, Calif.

[6] The family genealogy states that St. Vrain entered the Santa Fe trade when he
was about twenty-one. St. Vrain, *Genealogy*, 20. Conklin, cited in the previous footnote, asserts that St. Vrain left for New Mexico in 1823.

with Francois Guerin, secured from Pratte a supply of
goods for the New Mexican and the Indian trade, and about
November 1824 left St. Louis for New Mexico.[7] His trip
proved to be a long and troublesome one lasting five months,
for he did not reach Taos until March 20, 1825.

Five weeks later, St. Vrain reported to Pratte, Sr., that
since he had reached Taos he had sold few goods; furthermore, merchandise was selling at reduced prices. He therefore considered two possible alternatives. First, he hoped to
be able to sell out all his wares, primarily to Provost and
Le Clerc when they came in from their spring hunt, and
secondarily, to other trappers. He expected that he could
make "verry profitable buisness" deals in that manner. On
the other hand, should there be no such transactions, he
planned to buy up articles that would suit the market in
Sonora, and go there to purchase mules.

In some undisclosed manner (St. Vrain declared that the
"reasons were two teajus to mention") the partnership of
St. Vrain and Guerin was dissolved by April 1825. St. Vrain
paid Guerin $100 in cash, gave him two mules, and pledged
himself for the full amount owed Pratte and Co. At the
same time, St. Vrain sent east with Guerin a small shipment
of beaver skins, the receipts from which were to be placed
partly to his own account. Shortly thereafter St. Vrain took
on a new partner, for by the summer of 1825 the firm of St.
Vrain and Baillio had been formed.[8]

The new partners outfitted a party of hunters and trap-

---

[7] Letter from C. St. Vrain to B. Pratte, dated on its face at Taos, Apr. 7, 1824,
but on the outside, in St. Vrain's handwriting, "29, 1825." A further notation on the
outside shows that it was received June 10, 1825. Chouteau Collection, Missouri
Historical Society, St. Louis.

[8] Two letters from Lt. Col. A. R. Wooley to "St. Vrain and Ballio, Merchants,"
dated Ft. Atkinson, Sept. 14, 1825. Records of the War Dep't, U.S. Army Com-
mands, 6th Infantry Letterbooks, Record Group 98. National Records and Archives,
Wash., D.C. Re Baillio at Ft. Osage, see A. H. Favour, *Old Bill Williams, Mountain
Man* (1936), 51-2.

pers, with expectations of a large profit.[9] This party may
have been one to which Thomas L. (later called Peg-leg)
Smith belonged, although there is some conflict of dates
here in the record.[10] By July 1825 St. Vrain wrote his
mother from Taos that he had sold out the greater part of
his merchandise very profitably. This success ruled out the
necessity for the Sonoran venture, although he still retained
a small stock of goods on hand. This latter he hoped to
dispose of to fur trappers who had not yet returned to Taos
from their spring hunt.

St. Vrain complained that he might have to spend the
coming winter, 1825-26, in "this miserable place," as he
called Fernandez de Taos. Actually, he may have intended
to convey the impression of regret over the delay in not
visiting his Missouri home because a combination of business and personal affairs detained him. Among the latter
may have been an intention to establish a home in Taos, for
at least by the following year he had acquired his first
wife.[11] St. Vrain did report that already he had become able
to speak Spanish well enough to dispense with an interpreter
in his business dealings.

By early April 1826, St. Vrain had returned to the States
and was preparing a new expedition for New Mexico.[12]
This effort may have been reported in the *Missouri Intelligencer* for April 14, 1826, when it noted that a company
of about 100 men, including those who had lately returned
to Missouri, would be ready to start within a few weeks for

---

[9] Letter from C. St. Vrain to Madam F. St. Vrain, dated July 1825. Mo. Hist.
Society, St. Louis.

[10] "Sketches from the Life of Pegleg Smith," *Hutching's Illustrated California
Magazine* (July 1860-June 1861), v (1861), 319; and D. L. Morgan, *The West of
Wm. Ashley,* 279.

[11] Reference to St. Vrain's first wife is based on probable date of conception of his
first son, Vincente. Birth recorded for May 10, 1827, in "Bent Family Bible." Historical Society of New Mexico Collections, Santa Fe.

[12] L. R. Hafen, "When Was Bent's Fort Built?" in *Colorado Magazine,* XXXI
(April 1954), 109; and Lavender, *Bent's Fort,* 65 and 375.

Santa Fe. Such a caravan did pull out of Franklin on June 1. Yet the not always reliable Henry Inman has declared that St. Vrain started westward with a party of forty-two men, driving twenty-six mule-drawn wagons from Ft. Osage during May 1826.[13] The caravan reached the New Mexican capital late in July.[14]

Later that year was the time of what has been called St. Vrain's Gila River expedition, but this is a misnomer, for St. Vrain was not its leader. It is true that on November 29, 1826, the governor of New Mexico, Antonio Narbona, issued passports to S. W. (W. S.?) Williams and Seran Sambrano (Ceran St. Vrain), with thirty-five followers, to travel to Sonora for purposes of private trade.[15] Similar passports were granted to other North Americans about the same time. Yet one document authorized the recipients to trap "the Gila and Colorado rivers for beaver," and since an estimated 100 American trappers headed for the Gila, it appears that all, including St. Vrain, intended to trap rather than trade. The trappers did not travel in one party, however, but in four separate groups. This fact alone suggests that St. Vrain was not the leader of the entire band.

Unfortunately, there are no details available as to the route, experiences or degree of success for the St. Vrain and Williams group. But it is known that by January 1827, St. Vrain had returned to Taos, where he joined a group of twenty-three trappers under the leadership of S. S. Pratte, which left the New Mexican settlements on a spring hunt.[16] Just where the band trapped is not recorded, although by the following June it is clear that St. Vrain was again back in Taos where he attended a wedding. One can hope that

[13] Henry Inman, *The Old Santa Fe Trail* (1897), 406-7.

[14] J. J. Hill, "Ewing Young in the Fur Trade of the Far Southwest, 1822-1834," reprint from the *Oregon Historical Quarterly,* XXIV, p. 1.

[15] T. M. Marshall, "St. Vrain's Expedition to the Gila in 1826," in *Southwestern Historical Quarterly,* XIX (Jan. 1916), 251 ff.

[16] Lavender, *Bent's Fort,* p. 376.

he had arrived there during the previous month, for on May 10, 1827, his first son, Vincent, was born.

St. Vrain's next trapping expedition lasted for nine months. The party was again headed by S. S. Pratte, and it included Milton Sublette and Tom Smith; St. Vrain served as clerk. The group set out hopefully from Taos in the fall of 1827 and traveled to the headwaters of the North Platte River in North Park, where it soon collected 300 beaver. While in the Park, Pratte was bitten by a dog that was infected with hydrophobia. A short and painful illness was followed by his death about October 1, 1827.[17] St. Vrain tried in every way possible to ease his leader's period of distress, and was terribly shaken when Pratte died.

After his burial the other members of the group, according to St. Vrain, confronted him with the question of what was to be done, or more particularly, who would pay them their wages. The men themselves, however, later claimed that they had unanimously requested St. Vrain to take command. In either case, Ceran accepted the role of leader and gave his companions his solemn promise that so far as he had or should have property or funds of the deceased under his control, the men would be paid their several demands. This promise was accepted as satisfactory to all concerned.

It was about this time St. Vrain undertook to caution the reckless Tom Smith not to expose himself so much to possible Indian attack.[18] But before the suggestion was completed, an Indian arrow pierced Smith's leg and necessitated its amputation. St. Vrain accorded Smith every attention and comfort. When the latter was able to be moved, the party left North Park and headed, according to Smith, southwestwardly for the Green River. There during No-

---

[17] Letter from C. St. Vrain to B. Pratte & Co., undated but received Sept. 28, 1828; and Deposition of Twelve Trappers, dated at Taos, Sept. 1, 1829. Bent and St. Vrain Papers, Mo. Hist. Soc.

[18] "Sketches from the Life of Pegleg Smith," 420-21.

vember, winter quarters were established. Shortly, a band consisting of forty lodges of Utes, friendly to Smith, encamped near them.

After surviving what St. Vrain described as "the most vigorous winter I have yet Experienced," the trappers began their spring hunt. Considerable success then caused a portion of the company, which had caught about a thousand beaver, to head eastward across the mountains for St. Louis by way of the Platte River. Yet after traveling on that course for four or five days, they "struck upon a large Indian trace which . . . [they] supposed to be the sign of a hostile party." Since the trappers were too short of ammunition to risk a fight, they decided to return to Taos, where they arrived safely by about May 23, 1828. There St. Vrain sold all that he could, to be able to pay off his men. A few months later he sent a report of his transactions, along with his available accounts, to Pratte and Co.[19] He had to confess that he could not then include "a Recappitulation of the Books, for these have been cep in such . . . [an irregular?] maner that I am at a loss in [a] grate meney accounts." He could only promise to send them later as nearly correct as possible. He added, with undoubted satisfaction, that there was a balance in his own favor of $522.26½, which he wished paid to his partner, Paul Baillio.

At the end of September, 1828, St. Vrain, Antoine Robidoux, David Waldo and Richard Campbell obtained passports from the governor of New Mexico for a trip to Chihuahua and Sonora.[20] If the evidence for David Waldo is any indication, the purpose of this expedition was trade, not trapping. Perhaps St. Vrain did embark on the venture, yet there is no certain record of just what his activities were

---

[19] Deposition of Twelve Trappers cited in fn. 17.

[20] "Mexican Passports, Aug. 14, 1828-Oct. 22, 1836. New Mexico." R.I. 108. Ritch Collection, Huntington Library.

during the winter of 1828-29. Then by the fall of 1829 he appeared to be in New Mexico.[21]

By the spring of 1830, St. Vrain had returned to Missouri. During April he signed a nine months' note in St. Louis in favor of Bernard Pratte and Co., for the sum of $2,570.63.[22] Probably the note covered the cost of goods that Ceran prepared to accompany to New Mexico. He may well have joined a caravan composed of 120 men and 60 wagons which left Franklin for Santa Fe on May 22, 1830.[23] In any case, he reached the New Mexican capital by August 4 and paid the full duty of sixty percent on the original cost of all the goods.[24] St. Vrain was the first to place his wares in the customs house, and promptly began retailing his merchandise. The market proved to be too slow to suit St. Vrain, so he decided to offer his goods at "hole sailes." He must have found a ready purchaser, or purchasers, because it was reported that he received $10,000 for the commodities that had cost him about $3,000.[25]

Instead of returning to Missouri, he signed notes in Santa Fe, for a total of $3,405.12, payable to B. Pratte and Co.[26] Then during the first week in September he went to Taos and purchased what furs were available – he confesses that he had arrived after the hunters had disposed of most of their catch.[27] A fortnight later he arranged with Andrew Carson and Savase Ruel to take charge of a wagon, eleven

21 F. X. DeLisle recalled in 1877 that in 1829 he went to New Mexico with St. Vrain and C. Bent. R.I. 2212. vol. 1, p. 79. Ritch Collection, Huntington Library.

22 Chouteau-Maffitt Collection, Mo. Hist. Soc. I am indebted to Dr. L. R. Hafen for lending me copies of this note and several other original sources cited herein.

23 Hafen, "When Was Bent's Fort Built?", 110.

24 Letter from C. St. Vrain to B. Pratte & Co., dated Taos, Sept. 14, 1830. Pierre Chouteau Collection, Mo. Hist. Soc.

25 Theodore Papin to P. M. Papin, Feb. 24, 1831. Mo. Hist. Soc.

26 Letter from C. St. Vrain to B. Pratte & Co., dated Taos, Sept. 14, 1830. P. Chouteau Collection. Also a sight-draft signed by C. St. Vrain to R. D. Shackleford at Santa Fe, August 31, 1830. Chouteau-Maffitt Collection, Mo. Hist. Soc.

27 C. St. Vrain to B. Pratte & Co., Sept. 14, 1830, cited in fn. 26.

mules, and 653 "Skeins of Bever," weighing 961 pounds, for shipment to Missouri, where they were to be credited to St. Vrain's account with Pratte and Co. A surplus wagon he lent to Charles Bent for returning to the States.

Later in the year, St. Vrain planned to head east, when Charles Bent proposed a cooperative arrangement for the two of them.[28] St. Vrain was to purchase half of Bent's goods and remain in New Mexico to sell them, along with Bent's half. Meanwhile, Bent would return to Missouri and purchase additional merchandise for the two of them. The offer appealed to Ceran, so he paid cash for his purchase from Bent, and the latter set out for the States. Bent carried with him $600 to be placed to St. Vrain's account with Pratte and Co., as well as a letter dated January 6, 1831, from St. Vrain explaining the foregoing developments.

It might seem that the cooperative effort of Bent and St. Vrain faced rather dismal prospects. St. Vrain himself had reported that money was very scarce in New Mexico, that goods sold at low prices, and that duties were high. Still he believed that prospects for trade were better in New Mexico than in Missouri. He probably planned to supplement the trade, as usual, by continuing to deal in furs.

While there are no statistics available for the value of Bent and St. Vrain's trade in 1831, the total worth of furs shipped from Santa Fe to Missouri that year was estimated at $50,000, which was nearly half the amount of the return estimated as coming directly from the Rocky Mountains to Missouri.[29] The $50,000 sum accrued to two unnamed companies fitting out in Santa Fe. Before the decade ran out, Bent and St. Vrain collected from $20,000 to $40,00 an-

---

[28] Letter from C. St. Vrain to B. Pratte & Co., dated at Taos, Jan. 6, 1831. Chouteau-Maffitt Collection.

[29] Letter from Wm. Gordon to Sec. of War Lewis Cass, Oct. 3, 1831. Quoted in A. H. Abel, ed., *Chardon's Journal at Ft. Clark, 1834-39* (1932), 347.

nually in their fur trade.[30] In short, the two men, through
the company which they formed at least by 1832, were to
build up what Hiram Chittenden termed "one of the most
important fur trading firms" of the West, ranking next to
the American Fur Company in the amount of business
transacted in the period about 1840.[31]

But to return to 1831. When St. Vrain had agreed to
remain in New Mexico as the merchant for his own and
Bent's goods, he committed himself to a new country. On
February 15, 1831, he became a naturalized Mexican citizen.[32] Actually, such a step meant a kind of dual citizenship, with benefits from both countries, though just how, if
at all, it affected St. Vrain's operations as a trader is not
clear. He did maintain a home in Taos and, by 1832, he and
his partner operated a store there on the south side of the
plaza. On the other hand, two years later he was appointed
U.S. Consul at Santa Fe, although he seems never to have
fulfilled the duties of his office.[33]

Meanwhile, the new company had erected a stockade fort,
called Ft. William, nine miles below the mouth of Fountain
Creek (near present Pueblo, Colorado), for trade with the
Cheyennes and Arapahoes.[34] A year later, that is in 1834,
the company erected the more famous Ft. William, also
called Bent's Fort, ten miles above the mouth of the Purgatoire River.[35]

For a dozen years after its founding, St. Vrain spent

---

[30] Letter from Alexander Barclay to George Barclay, dated at Ft. William, May
1, 1840. Barclay Papers. Colorado Archives and Records Service, Denver, Colo.
The Missouri Republican, June 12, 1840, reported that Bent & St. Vrain had obtained 15,000 buffalo skins during the past season.

[31] H. M. Chittenden, *American Fur Trade of the Far West* (1954 edit.), II, p.
543 fn.   [32] R.I. 113. Ritch Collection, Huntington Library.

[33] Lavender, *Bent's Fort,* 191.

[34] J. LeCompte, "Gantt's Fort and Bent's Picket Post," in *Colorado Magazine,*
XLI (Spring 1964), 115 ff.

[35] Letter from C. St. Vrain to Lt. Col. Eneas Mackey, dated at St. Louis, July 21,
1847. Quoted in N. Mumey, *Old Forts and Trading Posts* (1956), I, pp. 85-88.

considerable periods at Bent's Fort, trading with Arapahoes, Cheyennes, Comanches, Kiowas, and other Indians, supervising company activities, and welcoming both casual and important visitors, including members of the United States Army. From it, he occasionally traveled to the other forts the company established, namely Ft. St. Vrain (1837) on the South Platte River, and Bent's Fort on the Canadian (1842). He also, of course, accompanied company wagons to and from Missouri and still managed to spend some time in Taos and Santa Fe, with an occasional side trip to Washington.

Many of these activities were carried on jointly by St. Vrain and Bent. The two men complemented each other very well. Bent, a small man, was the more dynamic of the two and perhaps showed more initiative; St. Vrain, a large and portly man, with a Lincoln-like beard that caused the Indians to call him Black Beard, was more reserved, less in a hurry, and less volatile.[36] There is no record of a quarrel arising between the two men.

St. Vrain was on hand when Colonel Henry Dodge reached the Fort in 1835 while on a 1,600-mile swing up the Platte River and back by the Arkansas with a force of 120 troops.[37] Charles Bent was present, too, and one officer recorded that the proprietors greeted them "in a very friendly manner and invited them to dine at the Fort." The same officer observed that Bent and St. Vrain "appear to be much of gentlemen."

A year later, St. Vrain equipped R. L. (Uncle Dick) Wootton and a dozen other men with ten wagons loaded with goods for Indian trade and sent them northward into the Sioux country.[38] This party spent the winter north of

---

[36] G. B. Grinnell, *Bent's Old Fort and Its Builders* (1914), 7 fn.

[37] L. Pelzer, ed., "Captain Ford's Journal of an Expedition to the Rocky Mountains," in *New Mexico Historical Review*, XII (March 1926), 566.

[38] H. L. Conard, *Uncle Dick Wootton* (1950 edit.), 29, 42-43, 46-47.

Ft. Laramie and returned to Bent's Fort in the spring with robes and furs worth about $25,000.

Whether or not Wootton's trading expedition was the precipitating factor is uncertain, but in 1838, St. Vrain reached an agreement with Pierre Chouteau not to send men on the North Platte for trading with the Indians.[39] This step may have been taken as a friendly move, or as the result of rivalry – probably the former. The previous association of St. Vrain with the western agent for the American Fur Company (Pratte and Co.), and the continued close relationship of Bent, St. Vrain and Company with both the agent and the A.F.C., indicate harmonious, if not stronger, ties. For example, in May 1838, the Bent, St. Vrain firm purchased a total of $13,257.33 worth of goods and supplies from the A.F.C.[40]

In 1843, St. Vrain had also assumed charge of an experiment in shipping his firm's furs down the Arkansas River by boat.[41] Difficulties and delays developed en route, so that while the venture was described as "not altogether unsuccessful," it had to be abandoned west of Walnut Creek. St. Vrain then ordered five wagons from the fort and reloaded the peltries on them. This small caravan pushed on to Walnut Creek, which was flooded, and there it caught up with Charles Bent and his fourteen well-ladened wagons. Nearby, Captain P. St. G. Cooke and his troops, who were escorting westbound caravans, also waited for the flood waters to subside.[42] St. Vrain was able to inform Captain Cooke, "with apprehension and secrecy," that about 180 Texans under Colonel Jacob Snively were encamped near the Arkansas crossing, and they probably intended to attack

---

[39] Letter from F. Laboue to P. D. Papin, Dec. 15, 1838. Chouteau-Papin Collection, Mo. Hist. Soc.

[40] Ledger z, American Fur Co., under dates of May 11-18, 1838. Mo. Hist. Soc. Photostats in possession of author.

[41] W. E. Connelley, ed., "A Journal of the Santa Fe Trail," in *Miss. Valley Hist. Rev.*, XII (June 1925), 86.   [42] *Ibid.*, 90.

the Mexican portion (32 wagons) of the westbound caravan on Mexican soil. So Captain Cooke moved to the Snively camp and disarmed its men, for he believed it to be on United States soil.

After St. Vrain reached St. Louis and was prepared to return to New Mexico, during the latter part of August 1843, he was given a contract to establish a depot of provisions at Bent's Fort for Captain Cooke's troops, for they might have to winter nearby.[43] St. Vrain hurried to the captain's camp near the Arkansas crossing, found that the provisions would be needed, and so continued on to the Mexican settlements where he purchased and sent to the fort $6,500 worth of food. Meanwhile, Captain Cooke suddenly decided to return to Missouri, but St. Vrain was not informed of the decision. Subsequently, the military authorities refused to pay for the provisions, so early in the summer of 1844, St. Vrain went to Washington in connection with this and another company claim.[44] The second claim related to remuneration for a destructive Pawnee Indian attack on a small Bent, St. Vrain and Co. wagon train in 1837.[45] This claim Congress rejected, but finally in February 1848, Congress authorized payment for the 1843 supply of food.[46]

St. Vrain spent the winter of 1844-45 at Bent's Fort. During January 1845, he warned Bent in Taos of a large, suspicious looking party of whites camped near the Arkansas crossing.[47] A month later St. Vrain reported that he had learned from the Cheyennes that the party numbered 350.[48] He described them as "texians or rather robbers . . .

[43] *Sen. Rept. 115*, 29 Cong., 1 sess. (serial 473).

[44] *H. Rept. 194*, 28 Cong., 2 sess. (serial 468), 8.   [45] *Ibid.*, 1-8.

[46] *Sen. Misc. Doc. 67*, 30 Cong., 2 sess. (serial 534), 84.

[47] Letter from C. Bent to M. Alvarez, dated Rio Ariba, Jan. 24, 1845, in *New Mexican Historical Review*, xxx (July 1955), 252.

[48] Letter from C. St. Vrain to C. Bent, dated Ft. William, Feb. 11, 1845. Alvarez Papers. B. M. Read Collection, New Mexico State Archives and Records Center, Santa Fe.

[who would] remain there [at the crossing] for the express purpose of robbing whoever they chance to meet." St. Vrain therefore advised Bent that all parties who planned a trip to the East take the Platte River route.

At the end of June, St. Vrain and his partner Charles Bent, welcomed Colonel S. W. Kearny to the comforts of the fort.[49] He and some of his officers dined heartily and well there. Just a year later, the colonel returned to the fort with his Army of the West, as subsequent comment will develop.

During February and March of 1846, St. Vrain traded with the Comanches at the company's Canadian River fort; he was reported to be doing "very well and prospects good."[50] Less than two months later he had returned to Taos, and soon took part in the effort to develop one of the several Mexican land grants in which he and Charles Bent were interested.

The story of the grants that is pertinent here concerns first the Vigil and St. Vrain, or Las Animas, grant, originating in 1843, according to the official record.[51] It was one of the large Spanish and Mexican grants lying north and east of Taos that was based on documents of such questionable validity that it is difficult to be certain just what took place. But according to the official grant papers, on Decembre 8, 1843, Ceran St. Vrain and Cornelio Vigil, an alcalde of Taos, petitioned the governor of New Mexico for a large tract of land south of the Arkansas River and opposite Bent's Fort. Governor Manuel Armijo approved the petition and soon the claimants were placed in possession of an approximately four-million-acre tract. Some effort to develop or use this land, such as herding cattle on it, according

---

49 L. Pelzer, *Marches of the Dragoons in the Mississippi Valley* (1917), 137-9.

50 Letter from C. Bent to M. Alvarez, dated Taos, Mar. 6, 1846. *N.M.H.R.*, xxx (Oct. 1955), 52.   51 *H. Rept. 321,* 36 Cong., 1 sess., 269-78.

to later testimony, took place prior to the Mexican War. After the war, St. Vrain and his agents sold large portions of the land grant, far more in fact than Congress confirmed for it, namely 97,000 acres. The resulting conflict lies beyond the scope of this sketch, although the point should be added that Charles Bent had become a part owner of the grant in 1844.

The land grant which St. Vrain especially helped to develop in the spring of 1846 lay just south of the Las Animas grant, and was called the Beaubien and Miranda (later, the Maxwell) grant. During the latter part of May 1846, St. Vrain was delegated to select an appropriate site for a settlement on this grant, and he chose a place on the Cimarron River, across the mountains from Taos, which he called Montezuma.[52] Yet before there could be much of a follow-up on this beginning, the clouds of the Mexican War arose and Bent and St. Vrain hastily set out for Missouri.

The two partners left Taos on June 3, and after stopping at Bent's Fort, effected a rapid sixteen day crossing of the prairies, reaching Ft. Leavenworth on June 28.[53] They reported to Colonel Kearny on the leaders, the activities and the attitudes of New Mexican residents, and doubtless agreed on the army's use of Bent's Fort as a place of rendezvous for the invasion of New Mexico. Afterwards they boarded a boat for St. Louis. St. Vrain appears to have busied himself in the city for two months, while Bent returned earlier to New Mexico.

On August 24, St. Vrain began his return journey with a large supply of trade goods.[54] Accompanying him was the

---

[52] Letter from C. Bent to M. Alvarez, dated Taos, May 30, 1846. *N.M.H.R.*, XXXI (Apr. 1956), 163.

[53] *Missouri Republican,* July 3, 1846; and J. W. Cason, "The Bent Brothers on the Frontier," M.A. thesis, Univ. of New Mexico, 1939, p. 24.

[54] L. H. Garrard, *Wah-To-Yah and the Taos Trail,* R. P. Bieber, ed. (1938), 54 fn.

youthful and perceptive Lewis H. Garrard who later wrote
the following tribute:

> Mr. St. Vrain was a gentleman in the true sense of the term, his
> French descent imparting an exquisite, indefinable degree of polite-
> ness, . . [which] combined with the frankness of a mountain man,
> made him an amiable fellow traveller. His kindness and respect for
> me, I shall always gratefully remember.[55]

St. Vrain reached Bent's Fort before November 1, ahead of
his train, and later pushed on to Santa Fe, where Charles
Bent had been appointed first civil governor of New Mexico
on September 22. In the capital, St. Vrain divided his time
between managing the company store, furthering his rights
under the new government to his land grant, consulting or
advising with territorial officials, and enjoying social events
such as the splendid ball Governor Bent staged in the old
Governor's Palace on December 26.[56]

These activities were soon interrupted by the tragic circumstances of Governor Bent's death. Various aspects of
the United States occupation of the territory provoked an
attempted revolt of Mexicans and Pueblo Indians, which
broke out in Taos on January 17, 1847, and led to the
murder and scalping of Governor Bent, as well as several
other officials and citizens.[57] Shortly after the news of the
massacre reached Santa Fe, St. Vrain hurriedly organized
a company of sixty-eight mounted volunteers, composed of
Mexican and United States Mountain Men, traders and
residents of New Mexico, and joined Colonel Sterling Price
in a mid-winter march northward to suppress the spreading
revolt.[58] Captain St. Vrain and his troops played a notable
part in dispersing the rebel contingents, particularly in the

---

[55] *Ibid.*, 58.

[56] "Report of Lt. J. W. Abert of His Examination of New Mexico . . . 1846-
'47" *H. Ex. Doc. 41*, 30 Cong., 1 sess. (serial 517), 512-13.

[57] *St. Louis Republican*, Apr. 8, 1847.

[58] Inman, *Old Santa Fe Trail*, 124-132.

final struggle around the Taos Pueblo church. On one occasion, Captain St. Vrain dismounted to examine a powerfully built Indian who lay prone on the ground and whom the captain recognized.[59] This figure suddenly sprang to life and a deadly struggle ensued until the Indian was slain.

St. Vrain remained at Taos for a time and served as interpreter in the trials for some of the rebels who had been captured.[60] Meanwhile, he extended the hospitality of his home to Garrard, who was nearly overwhelmed at meeting the "dark-eyed, languidly handsome" Senora St. Vrain. It was during the post-revolt period that St. Vrain was unsuccessfully recommended for appointment as the new civil governor to succeed Charles Bent.[61]

In the summer following the Taos rebellion, St. Vrain returned to St. Louis. During July, he offered to sell Bent's Fort to the United States government for $15,000.[62] The offer was refused, although the military continued to use the fort for at least a year longer, and its owners supplied Major William Gilpin with some of his necessities during his 1847 expedition along the Santa Fe Trail to suppress Indian attacks.[63]

Meanwhile, Bent, St. Vrain and Co., was reorganized as St. Vrain and Bent, with William Bent as the junior partner. The new firm established a second store in Santa Fe, but almost immediately in 1847, St. Vrain sold out the entire stock there to Judge Joab Houghton and his partner J. W. Folger.[64] He then began to diversify his areas of busi-

---

[59] Conard, *"Uncle Dick" Wootton,* 183-4.

[60] Garrard, *Wah-to-Yah,* 234, 239.

[61] *St. Louis Reveille,* Apr. 12, 1847.   [62] See fn. 35 above.

[63] Letter from Wm. Bent to C. St. Vrain, dated Ft. William, Sept. 1, 1848, quoted in C. W. Hurd, "Bent's First Stockade, 1824-26," in *Denver Westerners Monthly Roundup,* Apr. 1960, p. 13; and O. L. Baskins, *History of the Arkansas Valley* (1881), 828.

[64] *Santa Fe Republican,* Nov. 20, 1847; and R.I. 1915, p. 5, Ritch Collection, Huntington Library.

ness enterprise, and probably by 1850 had dropped his association with William Bent.

The diversification included selling land within the boundaries of the Vigil and St. Vrain land grant, and speculating in land at what became Canon City, Colorado, and Denver City.[65] St. Vrain appears to have erected saw mills in the Rio Grande Valley, and, among other customers, supplied lumber to the Commissioners of Public Buildings in Santa Fe.[66] In 1855 he erected the first flour mill in Mora, New Mexico, and a decade later supplied the military forces of the territory with as much as $20,000 worth of grain and flour, along with beef, during a given month.[67] In 1853, he became interested in the railroad projects that were to affect New Mexico, and a decade later he was associated with the unsuccessful effort to secure official approval for the incorporation of the first national bank in New Mexico.[68]

Yet success did attend his entry into the publishing field, for not only did he join the organization which published the *Santa Fe Gazette,* but in 1858 he was designated the public printer of the territory.[69] At one time, it was reported that because of his great wealth and his desire for a new way of life he moved to New York, but he so missed the West that he returned to his home in Mora, where he had moved from Taos in 1855.[70]

The same year, St. Vrain was appointed lieutenant colonel of Mounted Volunteers and charged with recruiting troops to subdue marauding bands of Utes and Apaches.[71] He then served under Colonel F. F. Fauntleroy in fighting from the

---

[65] Mumey, "Black Beard," 12, 15.

[66] R.I. 588 and 591, Ritch Collection, Huntington Library.

[67] *Sen. Rept. 156,* 39 Cong., 2 sess. (serial 1279), 276-77.

[68] Mumey, "Black Beard," 10; and F. S. Fierman, "The Spiegelbergs of New Mexico . . .," in *Southwestern Studies,* I, (1964), 31-32.

[69] *Missouri Republican,* Jan. 29, 1858; and R.I. 1802, Ritch Collection, Huntington Library.   [70] A. D. Richardson, *Beyond the Mississippi* (1867), 255.

[71] R.I. 703, Ritch Collection, Huntington Library; and DeW. C. Peters, *Life and Adventures of Kit Carson* (1859), 480 ff.

headwaters of the Rio Grande to east of the Sangre de Cristo Mountains, and helped force the Indians to sue for peace in Santa Fe.

Several months after the opening of the Civil War, St. Vrain was commissioned colonel of the First New Mexican Cavalry, and promptly on August 16, 1861, he began to select his officers and recruit his men for the regiment.[72] These tasks proved to be too burdensome for him, however, so on September 30, 1861, he resigned his commission, and Lt. Colonel Christopher Carson, a scout in the 1855 expedition, took command.

St. Vrain's political activities in New Mexico readily developed from his abilities, his concerns, his prominence, and his association with men appointed to civil office by General Kearny in September 1846. By 1849 he was greatly concerned over the chaotic political situation, which was partly caused by disagreement and delay at the national level over the type of government New Mexico should have, and the slavery issue.[73] St. Vrain was chosen one of the three representatives from Taos County for the territorial convention which met in Santa Fe during the fall of 1849.[74] The convention confined itself to adopting a plan to obtain territorial status from Congress. About that time two parties or factions sprang up in New Mexico, and St. Vrain favored the territorial group, while Manuel Alvarez headed the state group. Despite this alignment, in 1850 St. Vrain was a candidate for lieutenant governor against Alvarez on a statehood ticket. Alvarez won by a vote of 4,586 to 3,465 and brought an end to St. Vrain's formal participation in politics, though not in public affairs.[75]

---

[72] R.I. 1059 and 2212 (vol. 2, p. 329), Ritch Collection, Huntington Library.

[73] A. H. Abel, ed., *Correspondence of James S. Calhoun* (1915), 41.

[74] H. H. Bancroft, *History of Arizona and New Mexico* (1889), 445 and fn.; and R. E. Twitchell, *Military Occupation of New Mexico, 1846-1851* (1909), 181.

[75] *Sen. Ex. Doc. 26*, 31 Cong., 2 sess. (serial 589), 16; and Bancroft, *History of Arizona and New Mexico*, 446-7.

From 1855 until his death at the age of sixty-eight, St. Vrain made Mora his home. He joined the Bent Lodge of the Masons in 1860, when it was founded in Mora. During his latter years he was married to the former Louisa Branch. This marriage was reported to have been the fourth of his career, and by each one he had had one child.[76] Three of these children were living at the time St. Vrain drew up his will in 1866.[77] His death at his home on October 28, 1870, was followed two days later by a funeral which more than 2,000 people attended, including officers and troops from Ft. Union.[78] He was buried by the Masons, with military honors, in the family plot near Mora, after a life full of accomplishments, service and honors.

[76] Letter from M. E. Jenkins, New Mexico State Records Center and Archives, to author, Jan. 31, 1964, citing records of Adjutant General.

[77] Reproduced in Mumey, "Black Beard," 14-15.

[78] *Rocky Mountain News,* Nov. 1, 1870. St. Vrain had been a member of the Masonic lodge in Santa Fe at least since 1855. A portrait of Ceran St. Vrain appears in this volume at page 18.

John Gantt

by HARVEY L. CARTER
Colorado College, Colorado Springs

The last of fifteen children, John Gantt was born at Queen Anne, on the eastern shore of Maryland, in 1790. His father, Edward S. Gantt, was a man of some distinction. He was born in Loudoun County, Virginia, on May 25, 1742, and spent some time in England, where he was ordained a deacon of the Anglican Church at Oxford, on January 25, 1770, by the Bishop of Oxford and ordained a priest by the Bishop of London on February 2, 1770. Returning to the colonies, he married Ann Stoughton Sloss, of Hagerstown, Maryland. He was a doctor of both medicine and divinity and a Fellow of the Royal Society. He served five terms as Chaplain of the United States Senate, and upon the completion of this appointment, removed from Georgetown, D.C., to Louisville, Kentucky, in 1808.[1]

Nothing is known of John Gantt's early years but, since he was appointed from Kentucky to the Army of the United States as a second lieutenant, it is a reasonable presumption that he must have accompanied his family when the migration was made to that state. His appointment as second lieutenant of a rifle company was made on May 24, 1817, and he was promoted first lieutenant April 5, 1818. Three years later, on June 1, 1821, he was transferred to the infantry, where he attained a captaincy on February 28, 1823.[2]

---

[1] The Francis W. Cragin Papers, in The Pioneer Museum, Colorado Springs, Colorado, Notebook IV, p. 2. Cragin's information was obtained in an interview with Mrs. Judith M. Gallup, a grand niece of John Gantt, at Pueblo, Colorado, on July 24, 1908. Alice B. Maloney in "John Gantt, Borderer," in the *California Historical Society Quarterly* (March 1937), XVI, p. 48, gives the dates 1738-1832 for the elder Gantt and 1810 as the date for his westward migration. Since Cragin's information was precise and definite, it may be assumed that it is correct.

[2] Francis B. Heitman, *Historical Register and Dictionary of the Army, 1789-1903* (Washington, 1903), I, p. 444.

Of his twelve years as an army officer, enough is known that it can be said that he was regarded as an able and efficient man and that he was also well liked by his company. Although doubtless much of the time was spent at Jefferson Barracks near St. Louis, some of it was spent on active service at frontier forts and in Indian campaigns, notably Colonel Leavenworth's Arikara campaign of 1823. We know that Capt. Gantt was officer of the day at Fort Recovery when, on May 13, 1824, two keelboats of the Missouri Fur Company arrived there from the Upper Missouri with a cargo of furs. Charles Bent and other traders reported to Gantt on this occasion, as recorded by James Kennerly.[3] He also participated in the expedition up the Missouri River to the mouth of the Yellowstone, made in the summer of 1825 by General Henry Atkinson and Major Benjamin O'Fallon, Indian agent. Treaties were made with twelve tribes for the better protection of fur traders operating on the Missouri. Captain Gantt is mentioned as riding ahead to the mouth of the Yellowstone, August 14 to 17, 1825, and again on the return he was detailed to remain with the repair crew of one of the boats, "The Rackoon," with orders to bring her on to Council Bluffs when repaired.[4]

Gantt's army service on the frontier gave him an opportunity to learn a good bit about the fur trade from contact and observation. His army career was suddenly terminated on May 12, 1829, as a result of his having been found guilty by court-martial, March 19, 1829, on two of four counts, involving the falsification of pay accounts. The court recommended clemency, which was refused by President Jackson, despite a petition signed by other officers of the Sixth Regi-

---

[3] Dale Morgan, *The West of William H. Ashley* (Denver, 1963), 253.

[4] *Ibid.*, 130, 136, quoted from Henry Atkinson's Journal, 1825. See also "Journal of the Atkinson-O'Fallon Expedition" in *North Dakota Historical Society Quarterly*, IV, p. 15, where it was reported, on May 31, 1825, that "a very large black bear was shot by one of Capt. Gantt's men last evening. . . ."

ment, on the ground that Captain Gantt had been tried and found guilty of a similar offence on March 26, 1828. The penalty of a year's suspension had been disallowed in the earlier case by General Winfield Scott. The court expressed its belief that Captain Gantt intended to redeem the accounts personally but had been slow in doing so.[5]

Some further light may be shed upon this affair by the fact that Lieutenant Colonel A. R. Woolley had been found guilty by court-martial shortly before Gantt's second trial, of "conduct unbecoming an officer and a gentleman towards Captain Gantt especially of procuring through a highly colored charge the court-martial of Captain Gantt" and also of punishing a private, Thomas Powell, by lashes.[6] This looks very much as if Woolley had brought the original charges against Gantt, that Gantt then got his revenge when Woolley was dismissed, but that new charges were then brought against Gantt, which produced his dismissal. However this may be, John Gantt now found himself out of the army and under the necessity of making a living for himself and wife, for he had married Virginia McClanahan in 1827, by whom he had one child who survived, N. Beale Gantt.[7] Nothing was more natural than that he should have turned to the fur trade, in which others had reaped fortunes in the past decade. Although dismissed from the army, he was still known as Captain Gantt and was so referred to for the rest of his life. Sometimes it was spelled Gant, or Gaunt, or Ghant, or even miscalled Grant, but it was always pref-

---

[5] *The Niles Register* (May 23, 1829), XXXVI, pp. 204-5.

[6] *Ibid.,* (July 11, 1829), XXXVI, pp. 325-6.

[7] Cragin Papers, Notebook IV, p. 2. N. Beale Gantt married Amanda Morgan, of Louisville, and resided there until his death in the 1890s. His widow is known to have been living in 1914 and to have had in her possession an oil portrait of John Gantt, done about 1829. Professor Cragin secured a photographic copy of this portrait but it has unfortunately disappeared from his collection. The portrait may possibly have been done by George Catlin. Efforts to locate it have, thus far, been unsuccessful.

aced by his military title. Perhaps it was not out of place, for in the fur trade he was the leader of nearly as many men as he might have commanded in the army.

During the year 1830 he matured his plans and formed a partnership with Jefferson Blackwell. A three-year license to trade for furs was issued to them on April 5, 1831. The license indicated several locations already exploited by Ashley and his successors as their intended destination but it is well known that the specification of locations was merely a form to be complied with. Also, it was taken for granted that the men would trap, as well as trade, for beaver.[8]

The route to the mountains followed by Gantt and Blackwell and their sixty or seventy men was from St. Louis, which they left on April 24, 1831, up the Missouri to Fort Osage, where they purchased food supplies, and continued along the Kansas and Republican rivers. They ran out of food on the latter and, finding no game, Gantt gave orders to kill two horses for eating. They went north to the Platte River, which they crossed by bull boats constructed for that purpose, and continued up the North Platte, where they at last found plenty of buffalo. On August 27, 1831, they reached the mouth of the Laramie River. Here they decided to divide into three companies and begin trapping. One group under A. K. Stevens was to ascend the Laramie, another under Washburn was to trap the Timber Fork, and Captain Gantt himself would lead a group up the Sweetwater; meanwhile, on September 3, Blackwell and two others returned to St. Louis for supplies.[9] Here, too, they encountered Thomas Fitzpatrick and a few men on their

---

[8] Abstract of Licenses in the Indian Affairs File of the National Archives, Washington, D.C. Places mentioned are "Camp Defiance on the waters of a river supposed to be the Bonaventura; Horse Prairie on Clark's R. of the Columbia; mouth of Lewis Fork of the Columbia. . ."

[9] *The Adventures of Zenas Leonard*, ed. by John C. Ewers (Norman, 1959), 3-8.

way from Santa Fe to join the rest of the Rocky Mountain Fur Company. Fitzpatrick was reticent about any information that might help this rival company to gather furs.[10]

The plan was for all three parties to return to the mouth of the Laramie River to spend the winter. The Stevens group, of which Zenas Leonard was a member, camped on the Laramie until January 1832, tried to go to Santa Fe and failed, and finally returned to the mouth of the Laramie about the end of April. Here they encountered Fitzpatrick with 115 men, who said that Gantt and Blackwell had become insolvent. The Stevens group then sold its furs to Fitzpatrick and joined him, going eventually to the rendezvous at Pierre's Hole in June 1832.[11]

At this rendezvous W. A. Ferris reported that he had learned from a party of trappers that they "saw Captain Ghantt at the head of fifty or sixty men, on Green River; he had procured horses from the Spaniards of New Mexico, and had made his hunt on the sources of the Arkansas, and tributaries of Green River, without molestation by the Indians."[12]

Another reference to this same activity is found in a letter from Captain B. L. E. Bonneville to Major General Alexander McComb, headed Crow Country, Wind River, July 29, 1833, which says, "Gantt came up in 1831 with about 50 men mostly afoot done little, then retired to the headwaters of the Arkansas where I understand he has opened a trade with the Comanche, the Arapahoes & Shians."[13]

In February 1833, Zenas Leonard and others camped at the mouth of the Laramie once more and found a letter in Captain Gantt's hardwriting which told what had occurred.

[10] LeRoy R. Hafen and W. J. Ghent, *Broken Hand: The Life of Thomas Fitzpatrick, Chief of the Mountain Men* (Denver, 1931), 93-4.

[11] *The Adventures of Zenas Leonard*, 9-29.

[12] W. A. Ferris, *Life in the Rocky Mountains*, ed. by Paul C. Phillips (Denver, 1940), 150-151.   [13] Maloney, *op. cit.*, 49.

Gantt and Washburn had returned as agreed upon but did not find Stevens and his men. Since their horses had been stolen by Indians, Gantt had gone to Santa Fe and purchased more. On his return, he had encountered Washburn and had made the hunt already alluded to by Ferris and by Bonneville. Meanwhile, Gantt had learned that the Stevens group had gone over to Fitzpatrick. He had received supplies from his partner Blackwell and they had left the mouth of the Laramie in September 1832 to go to the Arkansas River, where they had decided to establish a post for the purpose of trading with the Arapaho Indians.[14]

A letter of Gantt's headed San Fernando de Taos, February 20, 1832, and addressed to the Governor of New Mexico, Santiago Abreu, gives some further indication of his past operations and even more indication of his future plans.[15] He says that he left his camp at the junction of the Snake and Bear rivers on December 25, 1831, and came to Taos for the purpose of buying mules. He specifies that he has twenty-two trappers on the North Platte, eleven on the South Platte, twenty-five on the Snake, five with him in Taos, and that he will be joined by forty more from St. Louis on the Arkansas in July. All this is by way of leading up to the fact that he proposes to establish a trading post on the Arkansas River at its junction with the Purgatoire and that he wishes to cultivate friendly relations with the government in New Mexico. He speaks with assurance concerning the probable establishment of a fort by the Army of the United States on the Arkansas in the near future and indicates that the garrison of such a fort would cooperate

---

14 *The Adventures of Zenas Leonard*, 52-53.

15 This letter is ms. 1832 in the Ritch Collection of the Huntington Library, San Marino, California. It is translated and quoted in full in Janet Lecompte, "Gantt's Fort and Bent's Picket Post" in *The Colorado Magazine* (Spring, 1964), XLI, pp. 113-4. Mrs. Lecompte's authoritative and closely reasoned article settles the question of the location of the forts along the Arkansas and also proves that Gantt, rather than William Bent, was first to trade with the Arapaho and Cheyenne tribes.

with the New Mexico authorities in policing the Indians along the border and would also expect to draw its supplies from Taos. Thus, he cleverly holds out the advantages of trade to the governor, while at the same time hinting that he would have the backing of his own government's military power.

Gantt now returned to the mouth of the Laramie, only to learn that the twenty-two men he expected to find there, under Stevens, had gone over to Fitzpartick. He left the letter there for them at this time (early April of 1832) which Leonard found in February 1833, as has been related already. Gantt now returned to the Arkansas and met Blackwell, who brought needed supplies. He then returned to the mountains where he trapped until September, 1832. Either in South (Old) Park or North (New) Park, he was joined by Kit Carson and three companions who had heard from Alexander Sinclair on the Green River, that "Captain Gaunt, who was an old mountaineer, well known to most of the whites present" was trapping there.[16] Constructing a few log cabins enclosed by a stockade, Gantt left his men on the Arkansas in September and went to Taos for two months. On his return they wintered in the new quarters, presumably at the mouth of the Purgatoire. They spent a comfortable winter, except for the fact that the Crow Indians stole their horses which Carson and others succeeded in recovering.[17]

In the spring, having cached three hundred pounds of beaver skins, they set out for the Laramie once more. On the South Platte, two men deserted and Gantt sent Carson and a companion after them. As had been suspected, these men had stolen the cache but Carson was unable to overtake them and he and his companion spent a month forted up at Gantt's

[16] Blanche Grant, ed., *Kit Carson's Own Story* (Taos, 1926), 21, says New Park. DeWitt C. Peters, *Kit Carson's Life and Adventures* (Hartford, 1874), 59, says South Park. It seems impossible to determine which is correct. Peters, p. 60, says they later trapped in North (New) Park.   [17] Grant, *op. cit.*, 22-25.

Post until Blackwell arrived with fresh supplies. Shortly after this, four of Gantt's trappers came with the news that Gantt was in the Bayou Salade (South Park) and all six trappers went there to join him. However, they did so poorly that Carson and two others detached themselves and took up free trapping with some little success.[18]

Gantt's thoughts now turned to the possibilities of trade with the Indians at some fixed point on the Arkansas, which he had already begun in a small way. He had met with many losses and misfortunes in his trapping ventures and it was clear that beaver were becoming scarce and that there were too many competitive companies scouring the mountain streams.

Contemporary evidence indicates that Gantt began trade with both the Arapaho and Cheyenne tribes in the winter of 1832. Rufus Sage, writing in 1843, said, "About the year 1832, Capt. Grant succeeded in effecting a treaty with the Arapahos. ." One of the items discussed was the possible return of Friday, the Arapaho boy, found by Fitzpatrick a year earlier.[19]

Writing in 1837, the Rev. Moses Merrill, a missionary among the Oto Indians, recorded that "the Shiennes, a tribe of Indians on the Platte River, were wholly averse to drinking whisky but five years ago – now (through the influence of a trader, Captain Gant, who by sweetening the whisky induced them to drink the intoxicating draught) they are a tribe of drunkards."[20]

Then Ferris, a contemporary trapper, also mentions "Capt. Ghant, whose firmness and liberality they (the Arapahos) have reason to remember long, has established

18 *Ibid.*, 27.

19 Rufus B. Sage, *Letters and Scenes in the Rocky Mountains,* ed. by LeRoy R. and Ann W. Hafen in *The Far West and the Rockies Series* (Glendale, 1956), V, p. 303.

20 "Diary of Rev. Moses Merrill" in *Transactions and Reports of the Nebraska State Historical Society* (1892), IV, p. 181.

a post among them on the Arkansas, four days march from Taos. . ."[21]

Liberal Gantt may have been, but the 180 gallons of whiskey which he was authorized to have for trading purposes when he first went to the mountains, was to last for three years and, unless the supply was replenished in much greater quantity, it was not enough to make the Cheyennes into a tribe of topers.[22] Nevertheless, it is clear that Gantt was the first to trade with these two important tribes, although it is not clear which of Gantt's trading posts Ferris had in mind.

For Gantt built a second fort and trading post on the Arkansas in 1834, which he named Ft. Cass.[23] It was located on the north bank of the river, but near to it, about six miles below the mouth of the Fontaine Qui Bouille. It was built of adobe which was made by Guadalupe Avila and Dominguez Madrild, who were sent from Taos for that purpose by Jim Wilkes, a friend of Gantt's in that place. Construction was begun in May 1834, only three miles above a log trading post of William Bent's, known as Ft. William, which had probably been there less than a year.[24]

During that summer, William Bent and his men made an unprovoked attack on some Shoshone Indians encamped near Ft. Cass. Gantt and several of his men witnessed this fight, in which three Shoshones were killed and scalped, thirty-seven horses and all the camping equipment belong-

[21] Ferris, *op. cit.*, 312.

[22] Indian Affairs File, 1831, in the National Archives, Washington, D.C. Gantt and Blackwell were issued a permit for 180 gallons of whiskey for three years on April 10, 1831. By contrast, the American Fur Company's permits were for 2,666 gallons for a year and a half.

[23] See Lecompte, *op. cit.*, XLI, pp. 117-125. The location of this fort, and that of William Bent's Ft. William, is fully discussed and definitely established in this important article.

[24] F. W. Cragin Papers, Notebook II, pp. 35, 68-69, and Notebook X, p. 38. The location of Fort Cass was near present Baxter, Colorado, and that of Ft. William just east of present Devine, Colorado. Cragin's informant was Tom Autobees, son of Charlie Autobees, and nephew of Guadalupe Avila.

ing to eight lodges taken.[25] The importance of this episode has not been generally appreciated. It was the turning point in Bent's career and a fatal crisis for Gantt. By 1835 Bent was established in his adobe castle, to be known as Bent's Old Fort, and Gantt was out of the fur trade forever. The question may well be raised as to why Bent succeeded where Gantt failed.

It has generally been believed that Gantt and Blackwell became insolvent, but it is certain they were not insolvent when Tom Fitzpatrick started the rumor that they were, in 1832, because Blackwell brought supplies to the mountains and Gantt continued to trap and trade for two years after that. It is not even certain that they were insolvent in 1834, when they went out of business. William Bent had the backing of an established Santa Fe trading company but Gantt had the advantage of good will among the Cheyenne and Arapaho tribes. This good will was destroyed at one stroke, and gained for Bent Brothers and St. Vrain, when William Bent attacked the Shoshone interlopers in the shadow of Gantt's own fort and before his very eyes, on July 29, 1834. Bent by this act established himself as a stronger power than Gantt, in the eyes of the Indians of the region. As his trade fell off in the months that followed, this must have become so evident to Gantt that he saw it was hopeless to continue the competition with Bent. The fur trade was a cut throat business and Fitzpatrick by his crafty lie and Bent by his attack on Gantt's customers had both helped to ruin Gantt, who was too much of a gentleman for such a lawless business. But it was Bent who delivered the decisive blow.[26]

---

[25] Gantt may possibly have been the writer of the unsigned letter reporting this incident to the Indian agent, Major Cummings, at Ft. Leavenworth. This letter is reproduced in full in Lecompte, *op. cit.*, XLI, p. 121.

[26] David Lavender, *Bent's Fort* (Garden City, 1954), 151-2, considers this affair to be "the blackest mark on William Bent's record." It is a black mark from any

George Bird Grinnell tells us that among the Cheyennes, Gantt was known as "Bald Head," and Blackwell as "The Crane," because he was tall and thin. But "Little White Man," as the Indians called William Bent, had supplanted them in the trade, which they were the first to conceive and attempt.[27]

In the summer of 1835, Colonel Henry Dodge led a regiment of Dragoons to the front range of the Rocky Mountains for the purpose of conferring with the Indian chiefs of the high plains and establishing better relations with them. He left Ft. Leavenworth in May, and traveled up the South Platte with John Gantt, ex-army officer and ex-fur trader, as his guide. Gantt also did a good bit of the hunting, made a bull boat for crossing rivers, and had the task of finding and bringing in the chiefs for conferences.[28] The Dragoons passed from the South Platte to the Arkansas and, on August 1, 1835, were at an "old trading establishment formerly occupied by Capt. Gant," as reported by Hugh Evans who kept a diary of the expedition. Lemuel Ford, another diary-keeping member of the group, made a map

moral viewpoint and the same can be said of Fitzpatrick's lie about Gantt and Blackwell's financial position. But Fitzpatrick obtained twenty-two men and 120 beaver belonging to John Gantt; and Bent drove Gantt out of business at the cost of the lives of only three Snake Indians. The pragmatist will approve what the moralist will condemn. Gantt fought fairly; his rivals were less scrupulous and more successful.

[27] See George Bird Grinnell "Bent's Old Fort and its Builders," in *Kansas Historical Society Collections* (1919-22), XV, p. 18. But George Bent, William Bent's half-breed son, writing to Professor Cragin from Colony, Oklahoma, on September 23, 1905, said that Gantt was called "Tall Crane" and that Blackwell was called "Bald Head." He also said that "Tall Crane" had a child among the Cheyennes. In the absence of any known likeness of either Gantt or Blackwell, it is difficult to decide which name belonged to which partner or which one fathered the child.

[28] "Report on the Expedition of Dragoons under Colonel Henry Dodge," in *American State Papers, Military Affairs,* VI, pp. 130-146. See also Fred S. Perrine, editor, "Hugh Evans Journal of Colonel Henry Dodge's Expedition to the Rocky Mountains in 1835," in *Mississippi Valley Historical Review* (September 1927), XIV, pp. 192-214.

which shows the locations of both Fort Cass and Fort William, as already designated.[29]

Four years later, Sidney Smith, on the way to Oregon with T. J. Farnham, recorded in his journal, under date of July 15, 1839, "encampt on the fontinkaboya [Fontaine Qui Bouille] passed two forts that have been abandoned."[30] Gantt returned to Missouri after having guided Colonel Dodge for over 1600 miles.

The next that is heard of Gantt is that, along with William Stoner, he agreed to mine and sell coal from a mine in Missouri owned by William L. Sublette, another well known Mountain Man. How long this arrangement lasted and with what success it was pursued, is not known.[31]

While with the Dragoons, Gantt had made the acquaintance of Lancaster P. Lupton, an officer who was soon to follow Gantt's example and engage in the fur trade. Doubtless he was influenced by what he learned from Gantt. Also accompanying the Dragoons was George Catlin, the famous painter of Indians. A testimonial signed by Gantt and dated November 27, 1837, New York City, was used by Catlin in connection with his exhibit there.[32] Gantt's father had died in Louisville, on September 24, 1837, at the age of ninety-five. This event may have taken him there and he may have continued to New York and also to Washington, for we know that he served as Indian agent for the Pottawatomies at Council Bluffs during 1838 and 1839, and he may have procured the appointment on his trip to the East.[33]

From 1839 to 1843 nothing is known of Gantt's move-

29 Louis Pelzer, editor, "Captain Ford's Journal of an Expedition to the Rocky Mountains" in *Mississippi Valley Historical Review* (March 1926), XII, pp. 550-579. The map is reproduced in LeCompte, *op. cit.*, XLI, pp. 122-123.

30 LeRoy R. and Ann W. Hafen, editors, *To the Rockies and Oregon, 1839-1842* in *The Far West and the Rockies Series* (Glendale, 1955), III, p. 72.

31 Sublette Papers, Missouri Historical Society, St. Louis, Mo.

32 Maloney, *op. cit.*, XVI, p. 53.

33 *House Document 103*, 25 Cong., 3 Sess. (Serial No. 346), p. 9.

ments but, in the latter year, he contracted to guide as far as Fort Hall 875 emigrants bound for Oregon, at a price of one dollar per person. This "Great Emigration" left its rendezvous, twelve miles west of Independence, Missouri, on May 22, 1843. They reached Independence Rock on July 26 and Fort Hall a month later. Gantt performed his duties well and is uniformly mentioned with approval in the various journals of the emigrants. James Nesmith refers to him as "our respected pilot" and Jesse Applegate later wrote: "The pilot (a borderer) who has spent his life on the verge of civilization and has been chosen to the post of leader from his knowledge of the savage and his experience in travel through the roadless wastes stands ready, in the midst of his pioneers and aids to lead the way. . ."[34]

Having fulfilled his contract, Gantt left Fort Hall on August 27, 1843, with a party, led by Joseph B. Chiles and Joseph Reddeford Walker, headed for California. This party divided, Walker taking the wagons over Walker Pass, while Chiles, with a few men on horseback went by a new route along the Feather River and eventually reached Sutter's Fort. Gantt accompanied the latter group.[35]

In 1844 and 1845, Gantt played an important part in California public affairs. He was elected captain of a company of one hundred mounted riflemen. This company was formed by Sutter, who expected to command it himself, for the purpose of aiding Governor Micheltorena against discontented groups who were in arms against him. However, Gantt's company of Americans found that there were many Americans aiding the rebels when they met them at Cahuenga Pass on February 21, 1845, and they refused to engage in battle with them. The result was the defeat and exile of

---

[34] See Jesse Applegate, "A Day with the Cow Column," in *Oregon Historical Society Quarterly,* I, p. 373; Peter H. Burnett, "Recollections and Opinions of an Old Pioneer" in *ibid.,* v, pp. 67-8; Maloney, *op. cit.,* 53-6.

[35] See W. J. Ghent, *The Road to Oregon* (New York, 1934), 72-77.

Governor Micheltorena by General Alvarado, with Gantt and his command taking no part. The outcome was not satisfactory to Sutter and John Bidwell but was highly so to Gantt's friend, Dr. John Marsh. Pio Pico was chosen governor and Gantt and Marsh contracted with him to recover horses from thieving Indians, although it is thought that they were never active in carrying out their contract.[36]

Two letters of Gantt's to John Marsh, in the spring and fall of 1845, are of interest. In the first, headed New Helvecia, March 11, he speaks of having had a rupture with John Bidwell over the Cahuenga Pass affair. He indicates that Sutter owes him money but that he will not take worn out horses in payment. He plans instead to go on a trapping expedition to the mountains and then to go south. In the second, headed Feather River, October 21, 1845, he says that he has just returned from a beaver hunt on the Trinity River, where the whole party was sick and did not put a trap in the water. He says further that he has been ague and fever proof for thirty years and that he has become almost mosquito proof.[37]

Nevertheless, it appears that Gantt took no part in the events of the Mexican War in California in 1846 because he was in very bad health at that time. Edwin Bryant found him very ill at Dr. Marsh's ranch in September, 1846. He wrote, "Capt. Gant, formerly of the U.S. Army, in very bad health, is residing here. He has crossed the Rocky Mountains eight times and, in various trapping excursions, has explored every river between the settlements of the United States and the Pacific Ocean."[38]

---

[36] Maloney, *op. cit.*, XVI, pp. 56-58; H. H. Bancroft, *History of California,* IV, pp. 516, 543.

[37] Alice B. Maloney, "Three Letters of John Gantt," in *California Historical Society Quarterly,* XX, pp. 148-150.

[38] Edwin Bryant, *What I Saw In California* (London, 1849), 247. Bryant was a newspaper man. The exaggeration, concerning the area trapped over, is probably his rather than Gantt's.

It seems probable that this was the beginning of the heart trouble which caused his death. He recovered sufficiently to go to the Napa Valley, where he formed a partnership known as Gantt and Hannah and projected the building of a saw mill. This was in 1847 and 1848. A letter of his to Dr. Marsh, headed Napa Valley, August 22, 1847, urges Marsh to get married and promises to introduce him to some ladies, if he will pay him a visit. It also contains some humorous references to the efforts being made by old Mountain Men Moses Carson and George Yount to find wives for themselves.[39]

John Bidwell recalled that Gantt attempted to do some gold panning near Bidwell's Bar in the fall of 1848 or the spring of 1849. If so, he soon gave it up and returned to the Napa Valley where, at the ranch of George Yount, he died on February 14, 1849. He was buried in the Yountsville cemetery.

John Gantt was one of the few men who made friends with the eccentric Harvard graduate, Dr. John Marsh. Apparently, Marsh recognized Gantt as a gentleman and an equal and they got along well.[40] Though Gantt was dishonorably discharged from the army, it seems clear that he was, by training and by nature, an honorable man and that he was unsuccessful in the fur trade, at least partly, because his competitors were less honorable and more unscrupulous than he was. His greatest claim to fame must be that he was the first to perceive the opportunity for a trading post on the Arkansas River, a project which was carried out successfully by his rival, William Bent.

---

[39] Maloney, *op. cit.,* XX, pp. 150-151.   [40] Maloney, *op. cit.,* XVI, pp. 58-59.

Charles Bent

by HAROLD H. DUNHAM
University of Denver

Charles Bent, fur trapper and trader, Santa Fe trader, part owner of Bent's Fort on the Arkansas, and governor of New Mexico, was born November 11, 1799, at Charleston, (West) Virginia.[1] His father was Silas Bent, a native of Rutland, Massachusetts, who had been sent west as a young man in 1788 to select a home site for his parents at the Ohio Company's new village of Marietta.[2] A short time later, Silas moved to Wheeling to study law, and afterwards he went to Charleston to become a storekeeper. There he married Martha Kerr, of a Virginia family, and their first child was Charles. Silas subsequently received an appointment as deputy surveyor, then judge in a Common Pleas Court in Washington County, Ohio.

When Charles was six years old, his father was appointed deputy surveyor for Louisiana Territory, so the family embarked for St. Louis, arriving there during the middle of September, 1806, a few days before Lewis and Clark returned from their epic trip to the Pacific Ocean. Silas promptly assumed his duties as surveyor and found them somewhat arduous, first because of the extent of territory for which he was responsible, and second because of complica-

---

[1] A. H. Bent, *The Bent Family in America* (1900), 121. The most extensive coverage of the life of Charles Bent may be found in D. Lavender, *Bent's Fort* (Garden City, N.Y., 1954). See also H. H. Dunham, "Governor Charles Bent: Pioneer and Martyr," in N. Mumey (ed.), *The Westerners Brand Book, 1951* (Denver, 1952), 219-67; P. A. F. Walter, "The First Civil Governor under the Stars and Stripes," *New Mexico Historical Review*, VIII (Apr., 1933), 98-127; and I. W. Cason, "The Bent Brothers on the Frontier," M.A. thesis, MS., University of New Mexico, Albuquerque, 1939. See Charles Bent's portrait, page 13 herein.

[2] Bent, *Bent Family*, 58.

tions resulting from the existence of Spanish and French land grants in the area.[3] There is a certain relevance in these factors for the life of Charles, in that he became classified as a surveyor in New Mexico, and that he was instrumental in the promotion of some extraordinary land grants in New Mexico during the early 1840s.

After serving less than a year as Louisiana surveyor, Silas again transferred to the judicial field and filled successively positions of increasing responsibility, the most important of which was that of Justice of the Supreme Court of Missouri Territory, 1813-1821.[4] He lived an honorable life with his large family (Charles had a total of ten brothers and sisters), in a fine residence in Carondelet, then a suburb of St. Louis. He became associated professionally and as a friend with the region's leading citizens, including fur merchants such as Bernard Pratte and Auguste Chouteau. These latter persons may well have been significant in the subsequent lives of his sons, four of whom took part in the fur trade.

Charles Bent grew to manhood under comfortable family circumstances and in the environment of a city that was emerging from its more primitive and provincial characteristics. As St. Louis grew to become America's western fur capital it lost some of its French cultural orientation. Doubtless Charles was aware of these changes and opportunities, but as a matter of fact, not much is known about his youth, including his education, either along the Ohio River or in Missouri.[5] Sometime during his teens he did attend school at Jefferson College in Canonsburg, Pennsylvania. His brother John studied at the same institution, although neither boy received a diploma. Reports or indications of later times demonstrate that while Charles possessed

---

[3] Lavender, *op. cit.*, 20-21.

[4] Bent, *Bent Family*, 59. A picture of the Silas Bent home is contained in C. W. Hurd, *Bent's Stockade* (1960), 18.

[5] Lavender, *op. cit.*, 25-6.

an erratic method of spelling, he probably picked up some beneficial training in mathematics and medicine. Assertions that he attended or graduated from West Point are not substantiated by the official records of the Academy.[6] Nevertheless, in maturity, he displayed a keen, vigorous, clear, and logical mind.

In view of his later classification as a surveyor,[7] it is possible to speculate that Charles engaged in surveying work as a young man, but whether he did or not, it is certain that he entered the fur trade. One author declares that he enlisted with Gen. William Ashley's first group of trappers and went up the Missouri in 1822, although for some undisclosed reason he returned to St. Louis within less than a year.[8] The family historian places Charles with the American Fur Co., by 1823,[9] but later research has shown that at that time he was identified with the Missouri Fur Co. Within two years it is recorded that he had become a partner in that firm, and within two more years he joined the partners in an expedition to the Colorado River of the West. Despite the lack of adequate information and in the face of some conflicting records, it seems likely that for the period of the early 1820s Charles had served the Missouri Fur Company in St. Louis and had been able to participate in its activities on the Big Muddy, so that first a brief review of the company's history for the period is in order; then Bent's known connections with it can be described more fully.

Upon the death in 1820 of its founder and mainstay, Manuel Lisa, the Missouri Fur Co. had been taken over by Joshua Pilcher.[10] He began to re-expand its area of operations in the western fur trade revival that commenced about

---

[6] *Ibid.*   [7] *Ibid.*, 164, 393.   [8] Hurd, *op. cit.*, 20.

[9] Bent, *Bent Family*, 121. See also *Dictionary of American Biography*, II, p. 205.

[10] H. M. Chittenden, *A History of the American Fur Trade* (2 vols., 1954 edition), I, p. 150; and P. C. Phillips, *The Fur Trade* (2 vols., 1961), II, p. 391.

that time. In 1821, Pilcher pushed beyond the old head-quarters at Council Bluffs and built Ft. Recovery at the mouth of the White River in Sioux country. He sent Robert Jones and Michael Immel to the mouth of the Yellowstone to trade with the Crows. A year later, the company erected Ft. Vanderburgh in Mandan territory.[11] Government li-censes issued to Indian traders that year, 1822, show that both in April and September, Pilcher's company declared the valuation of its capital goods at $50,000.[12] It is said to have employed 300 men along 1,000 miles of the Missouri River, from Council Bluffs to the Yellowstone.[13] Mean-while, competition along the river steadily increased, enter-ing a new phase when in 1822 the American Fur Company created its Western Division and began its efforts to dom-inate the trade.

David Lavender asserts that by 1822 Charles Bent had become "firmly established in the lower echelons" of the Pilcher outfit.[14] Yet it is not known whether he served the company at Ft. Recovery, at Ft. Vanderburgh, with Immel and Jones, at Council Bluffs, or elsewhere. And for the next, or fateful year of 1823, when the Blackfeet Indians de-spoiled Jones and Immel and attacked Andrew Henry,[15] the Aricaras repulsed William Ashley, and Colonel Henry Leavenworth's expedition encountered mockery from the Aricaras,[16] there is no unequivocal word of the role played by Bent. It does seem fairly certain that after these events had occurred, he spent the following winter at Ft. Recovery in the Sioux country.

In the spring of 1824, Charles Bent, identified by a con-

---

[11] P. C. Phillips, "William Henry Vanderburgh: Fur Trader," in *Mississippi Val-ley Historical Review*, XXX, (Dec., 1943), 381-2.

[12] *Ho. Exec. doc. 7*, 18 Cong., 1 sess. (ser. 93).

[13] Chittenden, *op. cit.*, I, p. 150.   [14] Lavender, *op. cit.*, 31.

[15] H. C. Dale (ed.), *The Ashley-Smith Explorations and the Discovery of a Central Route to the Pacific, 1822-29* (Glendale, Calif., 1941), 65.

[16] Dale Morgan, *Jedediah Smith* (Indianapolis, 1953), chaps. 2 and 3.

temporary as employed by the Missouri Fur Company, accompanied one of the Papins down the River with two fur-loaded keelboats.[17] On May 4 the men put their boats ashore at Ft. Atkinson, the Army post located at Council Bluffs. There Bent donated ten buffalo tongues to James Kennerly, the post sutler. Such a courtesy suggests previous acquaintanceship with the staff at the post. Undoubtedly Bent resumed his river voyage and landed at St. Louis to unload his furs. Perhaps he subsequently returned upstream with a shipment of fresh supplies and barter goods.

In any case, by 1825 Bent became one of the partners in the reorganized Missouri Fur Company. The losses which it suffered in 1823 seem to have crippled it greatly. Pilcher's license for October 27, 1824, showed that the total capital to be employed was listed at only $3,175, a mere fraction of the amount for the previous year.[18] Dale Morgan has found that the company became bankrupt by 1825,[19] and yet it was at that time that Pilcher was able to effect another company reorganization. In the new concern, Bent stepped up to full partnership, with Lucien Fontenelle, William Vanderburgh, Andrew Drips and Pilcher. On July 4, 1825, the partners obtained a license from Superintendent William Clark "to trade at the mouth of the Kanzas River, Bellevue Trading establishment, eight miles below Fort Atkinson, Pania Villages; at the mouth of L'eau Qui Cours [Niobrara River], Fort Lookout [Ft. Kiowa]; mouth of the Cheyenne River, Ricara and Mandan Villages; and mouth of the Yellowstone River." [20] The amount of capital involved was $7,712.82.

Where Charles Bent operated that year, as well as the next, when the company license showed little change in the

---

[17] E. B. Wesley (ed.), "Diary of James Kennerly, 1823-1826," in *Missouri Historical Society Collections*, VI, p. 69.

[18] *Ho. doc. 54,* 18 Cong., 2 sess. (ser. 115).

[19] Morgan, *Jedediah Smith,* 298.

[20] *Ho. doc. 118,* 19 Cong., 1 sess. (ser. 136).

amount of capital employed and areas of trade, is a matter of guesswork, at present. William Waldo's later comment on Bent's experience prior to 1829 that he "had spent some years in the Rocky Mountains," offers only general information for locating Charles during the period.[21] However, it was during 1826 that he was officially recommended for the post of sub-agent to the Ioway Indians,[22] and in 1827 his appointment was approved. This position might have at least proved interesting, but Bent could not take it, and within a few months of his appointment, another man was assigned to the work.[23]

Later in the year Bent accompanied his partners on a trading and trapping expedition to the Colorado, or Green River, as previously mentioned. Pilcher has described how he arranged for "more extensive operations," in 1827 than his outfit had attempted for some time.[24] He organized a party of forty-five men, including all his partners and probably William Bent, Charles' nineteen-year-old brother. Stocked with ample merchandise for trade, the expedition headed west from Council Bluffs in September, struck the Platte River, and continued up its north branch. When they reached the mountains, the Crow Indians stole all but a few of their horses, so it became necessary to "make a depot [cache] of merchandise and property . . . by burying it in the ground." Thereafter the expedition resumed its journey, on foot, through deep snow across South Pass.

---

[21] Wm. Waldo, "Recollections of a Septuagenarian," in Missouri Historical Society, *Glimpses of the Past,* v, (April-June, 1938), 72. Waldo also testifies that Charles Bent and David Waldo were partners in trading and trapping at a very early period. *Ibid.,* 62-3.

[22] LeRoy R. Hafen, "When Was Bent's Fort Built?" in *Colorado Magazine,* xxxi, (Apr. 1954), 111.

[23] Letter from Wm. Clark at St. Louis, April 27, 1827, to M. L. Clark (his son). MS. Missouri Historical Society, St. Louis. Photostat in the possession of the author. See also Lavender, *op. cit.,* 46.

[24] Chittenden, I, pp. 155-6; Morgan, *Jedediah Smith,* 298-9; and *Sen. doc. 39, 21* Cong., 2 sess. (ser. 203), 7-8.

The rest of the winter of 1827-28 was spent in camp on the Green, or what Pilcher called the Colorado, River. When spring returned, most of the party either hunted or trapped, while one of the partners obtained horses from the Snake Indians and returned to the depot on the Platte. To his dismay he found "a considerable part of the merchandise destroyed, the water having penetrated the place where it was buried." The goods which were still usable were carried back to Bear Lake, "then a rendezvous for hunters and traders." There at the rendezvous of 1828, Pilcher, Bent, and the other partners traded for what additional furs their diminished supply of goods would permit, and ended up with a total of less than twenty packs of beaver. This was a discouragingly small return for forty-five men, in view of their labors, losses, and expenses; so the company was dissolved.

After the break-up of the partnership, Bent, Vanderburgh, Fontenelle and a majority of the party embarked during July on the return trip to Council Bluffs via South Pass and the Platte River.[25] Enroute, the expedition suffered an attack by the Crows and lost two men.[26] When the survivors finally reached the old company headquarters, they learned that the American Fur Company had achieved a virtual monopoly of the Missouri River fur trade during their absence. The former partners appear to have accepted the situation for what it was and approached the American Fur Company official, J. P. Cabanné, at a nearby post, requesting the necessary financial backing to return to the mountains.[27] Only Bent seemed to have had certain reservations about undertaking a new expedition, though on what grounds is not stated.

[25] Morgan, *Jedediah Smith*, 299; Lavender, *op. cit.*, 82.
[26] *Ibid.*
[27] Letter from J. P. Cabanne at "Pres du Bluffs" Oct. 14, 1828, to P. Chouteau, Jr. MS. Missouri Historical Society, St. Louis. Photostat in the possession of the author.

Cabanné debated their request for, as he wrote Pierre Chouteau, Jr., he recognized that by enlisting these experienced traders under the company banner there would be less competition in the year ahead. Yet he decided not to back them because they could contribute so little in the way of supplies and equipment. Bent's financial status seems to be indicated by the fact that he was forced to borrow money from Cabanné in order to return to St. Louis that fall, 1828.

The following winter marked a turning point in Charles Bent's career. His interest became drawn to the Santa Fe trade. Whether this resulted from a meeting with Ceran St. Vrain, his future partner, operating out of Santa Fe during the time of the 1827-28 Pilcher expedition to Green River, as Lavender surmises,[28] or from persuasion of his long-time friend, David Waldo, who had recently returned to St. Louis from a trip over the Santa Fe Trail, or from some other cause or causes, is difficult to determine. But whatever the reason, by the spring of 1829 Charles was determined to join a Santa Fe caravan with Waldo. During the latter part of May of that year he brought his goods to Round Grove, the rendezvous center for traders, forty miles west of Westport.[29] Here he found a party of seventy-eight, possessing thirty-eight wagons loaded with trade goods.

At the suggestion of David Waldo, Bent was chosen captain of the caravan, and so became responsible for conducting the outfit over the 775 miles of prairie and mountain trail to the New Mexican capital.[30] Charles' brother William became a member of the expedition, as he had done with some of those of the fur company on the Missouri River. Captain Bent's party became marked by two firsts: one was the protection afforded by four companies of U.S. infantry under the command of Major Bennett Riley; the

---

[28] Lavender, *op. cit.*, 79.　　　　　　　　[29] Waldo, "Recollections," 72-3.
[30] O. E Young, *First Military Escort on the Santa Fe Trail, 1829* (Glendale, Calif., 1952), 75.

second was Bent's testing of oxen on the western part of the Trail, after Major Riley had brought them as far as the Arkansas River.[31]

On June 12, 1829, Bent started the expedition with its escort out of Round Grove, and by July 9 it had reached the international boundary at the Santa Fe crossing of the Arkansas. Here the military escort was to wait while the traders took their goods into Mexican territory and returned; Bent promised to be back at the river early in October. Bent also borrowed a yoke of oxen from Major Riley, and the subsequent trip proved that they were able to get through to Santa Fe better than the mules.

After fording the Arkansas River, the caravan set out on the Cimarron branch of the Santa Fe Trail. It had progressed only nine miles beyond the crossing when a large band of Indians, perhaps 500 Kiowas, violently attacked it.[32] At one point during the assault Captain Bent is said to have charged alone at a group of fifty Indians that were pursuing a trader, and he dispersed them by his audacity. Meanwhile, he dispatched messengers requesting assistance from Major Riley. Ignoring the international boundary, the latter came to the rescue of the caravan, and then accompanied it for a few days toward the Cimarron, before returning to his vigil on the Arkansas.

The traders continued westward under Bent's leadership with some apprehension because of a report from Mexicans of large numbers of marauding Indians.[33] The Mexicans joined the traders for safety's sake, and later a protecting force of nearly one hundred men under the leadership of Ewing Young escorted the combined group into Taos. The members of the caravan then pushed on to Santa Fe, where they were well received, and judging by the value of their

---

[31] *Ibid.*, 86; *American State Papers, Military Affairs*, IV, p. 277.
[32] Young, *op. cit.*, 89-91.   [33] *Ibid.*, 140-1.

return cargo they enjoyed a profitable sale of their merchandise.

The return journey to the states was begun under the protection of a Mexican military force, and in company with a party of wealthy Spaniards who were being expelled from Mexico. According to William Waldo, Charles Bent again was the captain of the non-military part of the expedition, and he rendered significant aid to the New Mexican military force on whom the Indians attempted a trick.[34] The caravan's cargo consisted of furs, specie, and mules to the value of $240,000 (amounting to one hundred percent profit on the goods that had been brought out).[35] The caravan reached Major Riley on the Arkansas in October, just as he had started to return to the States because he believed it was not coming through.[36]

One confusing factor about Bent's captaincy arises from a document showing that early in October he was assigned a guide in Santa Fe to accompany him on a trading trip to Chihuahua and Sonora.[37] There is a similar conflict of evidence for his activities in 1831. Nevertheless, it is helpful to learn from his 1831 passport that he stood five-feet seven-inches tall, possessed a high forehead, common nose, mouth and chin, and gray eyes and black hair.[38] In later years the Indians were to call him gray-haired whiteman.

In the second year of his life as a Santa Fe trader, that is in 1830, Bent established a business agreement with another trader-mountain man, who was the courteous, capable, ex-

---

[34] Waldo, "Recollections," 75.

[35] *Ibid.,* 59.   [36] Young, *op. cit.,* 139.

[37] Charles Bent – Declaration of Goods and Petition for a Guide, Oct. 8, 1829. Folder 2330. R. E. Twitchell Collection, New Mexico State Archives and Records Center, Santa Fe. It is possible that this applied to a trading venture of his brother William and Robert Isaacs west of Santa Fe in 1830. See an account of the trip in an abstract from Isaac's Journal in the *Missouri Intelligencer* of Columbia, Oct. 6, 1832.

[38] L. H. Garrard, *Wah-To-Yah and the Taos Trail,* R. P. Bieber, ed. (Glendale, Calif., 1938), 179.

perienced Ceran St. Vrain. The latter had gone to Santa Fe as early as 1824, and had established business contacts with Bernard Pratte and Co., fur merchants of St. Louis.[39] Bent and St. Vrain may have known each other in St. Louis, they may have discovered their common business interests while accompanying the 1830 spring caravan to Santa Fe, or possibly they met during the winter of 1827-28 on Green River, as mentioned earlier. It is assumed that Bent traveled with the 1830 caravan, one which consisted of 140 men, seventy wagons, and $120,000 worth of trade goods.[40] But whatever the origin of their agreement, Bent seems to have undertaken the return trip to the States in September, after St. Vrain lent him a wagon.

Returning to Santa Fe again, it is certain that before the year 1830 had closed, the two traders reached an understanding whereby St. Vrain purchased half of Bent's goods for cash and agreed to remain in New Mexico to sell them, while Bent crossed the plains to St. Louis in order to obtain additional merchandise for both.[41] Thus commenced a business association which endured until Bent's death in 1847. Known first as Bent and St. Vrain, it later was called Bent, St. Vrain and Co., and it became the largest and strongest merchandising and fur trading firm in the Southwest.[42] Important as were the contributions of both St. Vrain and Charles' brother William, it appears that Charles Bent played the dominant role in the firm's operations.

As indicated above, just how or when Bent traveled back to Missouri early in 1831 is not clear. He may have gone directly there from Santa Fe, for he carried St. Vrain's letter of January 6 to B. Pratte and Co., telling about the arrange-

---

[39] Hafen, "When Was Bent's Fort Built?", 108.

[40] *Ibid.,* 112; Lavender, *op. cit.,* 123.

[41] Letter from Ceran St. Vrain at Santa Fe, Jan. 6, 1831, to B. Pratte & Co. MS. Missouri Historical Society, St. Louis. Photostat in the possession of the author.

[42] Waldo, "Recollections," 62, fn.

ments for trade the two men had made. On the other hand, since Bent had obtained a passport for Mexican provinces to the south of New Mexico, he may have gone southward and then either returned through New Mexico or headed for the east coast of Mexico and taken a boat to New Orleans and thence up-river to St. Louis.[43] Whichever route he followed, he was loading goods in the latter city by May, and Josiah Gregg has indicated that he preceded Bent in his summer crossing to Santa Fe.[44]

Granted that Gregg's report is accurate, Bent must have made a hurried journey back to St. Louis, for he obtained a passport there in July,[45] and early in August was preparing to head westward along the Trail again.[46] At Independence in September, the party of seventy-five men, with ten wagons, purchased some oxen, repaired their wagons and added to their stores before pressing on to Council Grove. One member of the party was Albert Pike, the later famous author, lawyer, and soldier.[47] He has related how Captain Bent's train made a much slower than expected crossing of the prairie and then was caught in a blizzard in the mountains east of Taos, so that not until the middle of November did all the travelers reach the haven of that town.

According to Hiram Chittenden, in both 1832 and 1833 Charles Bent captained the principal westbound caravans over the Santa Fe Trail.[48] He seems also to have brought in to the States the major returning train in 1832, one which carried with it $100,000 in specie and $90,000 worth of other property. The outgoing caravan of 1833 consisted of 184

---

[43] Lavender, op. cit., 127.

[44] Josiah Gregg, Commerce of the Prairies, M. L. Moorhead, ed. (Norman, Okla., 1954), 51.

[45] Garrard, op. cit., 179.

[46] A. E. Jones, "Albert Pike as a Tenderfoot," in New Mexico Historical Review, XXXI, (Apr. 1956), 141.

[47] M. G. Fulton and P. Horgan (eds.), New Mexico's Own Chronicle (Dallas, 1937), 103-4.

[48] Chittenden, American Fur Trade, II, p. 510.

men, 103 vehicles and cargo worth $100,000. One report credits Bent with the ownership of goods valued at $40,000 in this expedition.[49] It was escorted by a force of U.S. Mounted Rangers, the first military convoy since 1829. A special feature of the caravan was that its members fell into a dispute about the election of a captain at Council Grove, and decided to push on to Diamond Spring without agreement; at the Spring, however, Bent was finally selected.[50]

Obviously by 1833 Bent was recognized as one of the leading Santa Fe traders. Moreover, he and St. Vrain had established a store in Taos, at least by that year, and later they were to add another in Santa Fe. Charles' frequent crossings of the prairie seem to reflect an increase of trade, and he was to continue to average one round-trip a year until the time of his death. In this connection, a new phase and increase of the business is associated with the year 1833, for, as will be described shortly, it was marked by the construction of Bent's Fort on the Arkansas River. This meant that Bent, St. Vrain and Co. would trade with several Indian tribes at or near the Fort, send out trappers and traders to deal with Indians, later erect two additional forts (one on the South Platte and one on the Canadian River), enjoy the increased business of supplying the necessary trade goods, and haul wagon-loads of furs to Missouri markets annually. So after 1833, Charles Bent's trail travel was apt to proceed by way of Bent's Fort.

Charles was the leader in the company's efforts to plan for and to erect Bent's Fort, or Fort William, as it was also called, because William Bent supervised much of the construction and the management of the establishment.[51] There has been considerable controversy over the dates for the

---

[49] Hafen, "When Was Bent's Fort Built?", 114.

[50] O. E Young, "The U.S. Mounted Ranger Battalion, 1832-33," in *Mississippi Valley Historical Review*, XLI (Dec. 1954), 463.

[51] Lavender, *op. cit.*, 132, 136.

building and completion of the fort, though more recently the year 1833 has been accepted as the time when it was finished for the opening of Indian trade.[52] It became one of the leading three or four fur trading posts in the West, and certainly it was the most outstanding one in the Southwest. Its ground plan showed measurements of approximately 180 feet by 137 feet; its adobe walls were three feet thick and fourteen feet high, with two watchtowers eighteen feet high.[53] Attached to the main courtyard with its shops, living quarters, and other facilities, was a large enclosed courtyard for the protection of animals. The fort served as a business emporium, a haven for travelers, a rendezvous for the military, a home base for trappers, and a center for Indian trade and conferences. At its peak, the fort might place anywhere from 100 to 150 men on its payroll.

Rather curiously, Bent and St. Vrain did not obtain a license to trade with the Indians until December 13, 1834.[54] Furthermore, the license was issued by Indian Superintendent William Clark to Charles Bent, rather than to the company or partnership. It was, nevertheless, to be valid for two years, and it showed that the total amount of capital to be employed was $3,877.28, and the number of employees, twenty-nine. As to places and tribes for trading purposes, the license stipulated:

> at Fort William, on the north side of the Arkansas, about 40 [80] miles east of the Rocky Mountains, about 20 miles north [90 miles northeast] of the Spanish Peaks, and about five miles below [above] one of the principal forks of the Arkansas, near the foot of the Rocky Mountains, about ten miles below the Black Hills [Black Forest?]; and at a post near the mouth of the Bear river, on the waters of the Grand River, or the Colorado of the West; with the Arapohoes, Cheyennes, Kiawas, Snakes, Sioux and Aricharees.[55]

---

[52] *Ibid.*, 386; and Hafen, "When Was Bent's Fort Built?", 119.

[53] N. Mumey, *Old Forts and Trading Posts: Bent's Old Fort and New Forts* (Denver, 1956), 23-4.

[54] *Sen. doc. 69*, 23 Cong., 2 sess. (ser. 268), 3. Lavender has given the license the date of 1833, which I believe is in error.

Licenses issued at later dates show certain changes as to location of trade and Indians with whom to trade. For instance, in 1838 the names of the Snake and Arickaree Indians no longer appear, nor does the Grand River;[56] the names of the Comanches were included.

Charles Bent's trips to or by way of Bent's Fort might find him present when military groups made periodic visits there. Some well-known military visitors were Colonel Henry Dodge, Colonel John C. Fremont, and Colonel Stephen W. Kearny. Bent was present in 1835, for instance, when Colonel Dodge stopped in after nearly completing a sixteen hundred mile sortie out of Ft. Leavenworth to conciliate plains Indians.[57] Early in August he and his officers were accorded a hospitable invitation by both Charles Bent and Ceran St. Vrain to dine at the Fort.[58] The Colonel believed and reported that Fort William was favorably located for establishing an Indian agency to deal with the upper bands of the Kiowas and Comanches, as well as the Cheyennes, Arapahoes, Gros Ventres, and Blackfeet that frequented the vicinity.[59] To one of the other officers, Captain Lemuel Ford, Bent and St. Vrain appeared to be conducting a lively fur trading business with the Indians.[60] He observed the loading of fifteen wagons, or packs, principally of buffalo robes, for transporting to Independence. He seemed to be impressed by the fact that the proprietors purchased each robe for about twenty-five cents worth of

[55] Because Col. Henry Dodge visited Bent's Fort during October, 1835, about ten months after the 1834 trading license was issued to Charles Bent, and because Dodge reported that the Fort was located about 130 miles from the Rocky Mountains, I have assumed that the license referred to that fort, rather than to any other Bent's Fort. See: *American State Papers, Military Affairs*, VI, p. 145.

[56] Mumey, *Old Forts*, inset, opposite p. 12.

[57] *American State Papers, Military Affairs*, VI, pp. 130ff.

[58] L. Pelzer (ed.), "Captain Ford's Journal," in *Mississippi Valley Historical Review*, XII, (Mar. 1956), 566.

[59] *American State Papers, Military Affairs*, VI, pp. 140-2.

[60] Pelzer, "Captain Ford's Journal," 566-67.

goods, and later sold it in St. Louis for five or six dollars. A further indication of alluring profits for the company is evident in the report that a gallon of brandy which cost two dollars in New York was sold for twenty-five dollars at the Fort.

Since Charles Bent frequently captained the annual fur-ladened caravans sent to Missouri from the Fort, a few of his experiences on the Trail are relevant. For instance, in the late spring of 1839 his caravan consisted of thirty men and ten wagons loaded with peltries.[61] On the Trail about the middle of June, the train had halted for the evening when a party of hunters came up from T. J. Farnham's Oregon-bound party. Bent and his associate, probably Antonie Leroux, treated the hunters kindly, served them an evening meal, and offered to share the shelter of their tent for the night. It is just possible that Captain Bent hoped these hunters would subsequently keep a sharp lookout for thirty mules and seven horses that had run away from his train a few days before, and if he did, his hospitality was rewarded, for the strays were found and driven back to the Fort. The 1839 caravan drove with it two hundred sheep for marketing in Missouri. News of Bent's cargo preceded him to St. Louis. On June 1, J. F. A. Sanford, writing from that city, informed Pierre Chouteau, Jr., that the Bent and St. Vrain train was expected to bring in about six hundred packs of robes and ten packs of beaver by the end of the month.[62]

Again in 1840 Bent captained the company shipment of furs from the Fort to St. Louis. The *Missouri Republican* for June 12, 1840, reported that the firm had enjoyed remarkable success during the previous season, for it had obtained fifteen thousand buffalo skins. Again the following

[61] LeRoy R. and A. Hafen (eds.), *To The Rockies and Oregon, 1839-1842* (Glendale, Calif., 1955), 36, 99.

[62] Letter from J. F. A. Sanford at St. Louis June 1, 1839, to Pierre Chouteau, Jr. MS. Missouri Historical Society, St. Louis, Mo.

year Bent supervised the firm's eastbound caravan. He reported from Bent's Fort that the company had made a fine trade during the winter, that eighteen company wagons loaded with "peletrys" had started for the States.[63]

During the journey of the 1842 caravan, Bent was able to arrange for special trading relations with the Comanches and Kiowas. As early as the spring of 1841, while he was in Taos, Bent learned from the Fort that thirty-one Comanches had come to make peace with the company.[64] Apparently this move was preliminary to what was described as "a kind of peace or truce" that Bent himself made with both the Comanches and Kiowas during the summer of 1842.[65] It occurred on the Trail when he met a combined band of those two Indian tribes and drew up the "truce." Consequently, that fall Bent established a trading post on the Canadian River, within the present Panhandle of Texas, and began a more systematic trade with what Captain Phillip St. George Cooke estimated were approximately six thousand Comanches and twelve hundred Kiowas. From them, one or the other partners of the firm obtained buffalo robes in trade each year, at least through 1846.[66]

One other of Charles Bent's eastward trips might be noted because of two distinctive features associated with it, namely, cattle and boating. The summer fur caravan from Ft. Bent in 1843, consisted of fourteen well-laden wagons drawn by ox and mule teams.[67] Additional hides were being trans-

---

[63] Letter from Charles Bent at Ft. William, Apr. 30, 1841, to M. Alvarez. *New Mexico Historical Review*, xxx (Apr. 1955), 159.

[64] Letter, same to same, Mar. 15, 1841. *Ibid.*, 155. Six years earlier, that is in 1835, Col. Henry Dodge reported that on August 8, Mr. Bent (Charles or William?) had arrived at Bent's Fort after a visit to the Comanches on the Red (Canadian) River, where he had been treated with great kindness. *American State Papers, Military Affairs*, VI, p. 145.

[65] W. E. Connelley (ed.), "A Journal of the Santa Fe Trail," in *Mississippi Valley Historical Review*, XII, (June 1925), 239.

[66] Letter from Charles Bent at Taos, N.M., Mar. 6, 1846, to M. Alvarez. *Ibid.*, xxx, (Oct. 1955), 352.

[67] Connelley (ed.), "Journal of the Santa Fe Trail," 85.

ported on hoof, for Bent was taking a drove of cattle raised near the Fort to his farm in Missouri. This trip was held up about ten days near Walnut Creek, largely because his chief partner, Ceran St. Vrain, was coming up with five more wagonloads of peltries.[68] St. Vrain's delay had been caused by what Captain Cooke described as a not altogether successful experiment in conveying furs by boat down the Arkansas. The wagons had had to be called up to take over from the boats.

Of course, not all of Bent's time was spent at the Fort or on the Santa Fe Trail. By 1832 he had established his residence in Taos, seventy miles north of Santa Fe.[69] Probably in 1835, Bent married Maria Ignacia Jamarilla, a beautiful widow who was related to several prominent families in Taos. The couple's life together appears to have been most congenial, and to them were born three children: Alfred, Teresina, and Estefina. Domestic felicity and local business enterprise were accompanied by a certain political prominence amidst the factionalism of Taos.[70] Charles not only held minor political positions, but established friendship with such prominent men as Cornelius Vigil and Charles Beaubien. Yet he developed a strong antipathy to the politically powerful Martinez family, headed by Padre Antonio Martinez, the most outstanding religious leader of the region.[71] The antipathy between Bent and the Padre was mutual, and the latter denounced certain practices of Anglo traders like Bent and St. Vrain, and sought to thwart Bent's activities in connection with land grants.

---

[68] *Ibid.*, 86. Again in June, 1844, Charles Bent's train was held up at Walnut Creek, but on that occasion by flood waters. However, his brother William, who had crossed the Creek earlier after a trip from Chihuahua, reached St. Louis ahead of the flood. "Letters and Notes From and About Bent's Fort, 1844-45," in *Colorado Magazine*, XI, (Nov. 1934), 223-4.

[69] Dunham, "Governor Charles Bent," 231-2.

[70] *Cf.* Election List of Taos, N.M., March, 1842. Item 6750, New Mexico State Records and Archives Center, Santa Fe.

[71] Dunham, "Governor Charles Bent," 237-8.

Bent's contacts naturally extended to leaders at the capital, Santa Fe. Besides American traders with stores there, particularly the U.S. Consul, Manuel Alvarez, Bent became well acquainted with New Mexican traders and political leaders.[72] He developed a special standing with Governor Manuel Armijo, who held the chief political post throughout most of the period 1837-1846. Bent's connections enabled him to secure an occasional reduction in tariffs on merchandise his friends brought into New Mexico and to promote the acquisition of title to large sections of public land in this northern Mexican province.[73] All of which is not to say that Bent avoided antagonisms and even periodic assaults, from the governor down to the lowliest citizen, that were directed toward Anglo traders. Moreover, the government could and did adopt discriminatory practices toward that group. To his credit, Charles Bent stood in the van of those who protested such treatment, and persisted in demands for justice where too frequent official shortcomings occurred in regard to his fellow countryman.[74]

Another way in which Bent sought to help Santa Fe traders and fur traders, including his own firm, was to support the movement seeking to allow drawbacks to traders.[75] Drawbacks meant that traders who imported their goods from abroad and paid the standard U.S. tariff rates, and then transported their merchandise to New Mexico and paid the Mexican tariff, should be permitted a refund on their United States duties. This movement was finally successful shortly before the Mexican War.

Another benefit for traders along the Santa Fe Trail could have come from the establishment of U.S. Army forts in appropriate locations. In 1842, Bent responded to a

---

[72] The available letters from Charles Bent to Manuel Alvarez have been published in the *New Mexico Historical Review*, XXIX (1954), no. 3 et seq.

[73] Dunham, "Governor Charles Bent," 247-9.

[74] *Ibid.*, 250-3.

[75] *Ibid.*, 254.

request from Senator L. F. Linn of Missouri for advice on such a fort, one that would offer protection to Oregon immigrants as well as Santa Fe traders, by holding in awe Indian tribes living between the two routes indicated.[76] Bent's suggestion was that the junction of Fountain Creek with the Arkansas River was the most likely spot, near the trading post called Fort Pueblo that had recently been established. A further step by the government that might have benefited Bent's firm much more than traders in general related to the Cheyenne and Arapaho Indian tribes. The issue had developed earlier, that is, after 1835, when Colonel Dodge promised those two tribes that official tokens or medals would be presented to their principal chiefs. Some kind of delay occurred so that by 1838 the medals had not been delivered, and as a consequence Bent then urged that these tokens of friendship be supplied.[77] Indian Superintendent William Clark favorably endorsed Bent's proposal, but the available records do not indicate the outcome.

The latter portion of Charles Bent's all-too-brief life is highlighted by two features arising partly from the so-called forces of Manifest Destiny and their relation to the onset of the Mexican War. The first feature is associated with the promotion of land settlement in New Mexico and grew out of the opportunities for obtaining extra large land grants during the 1840s from New Mexico's authoritarian governor, Armijo. Bent was reputedly instrumental in securing for various claimants the Beaubien and Miranda (or Maxwell) Grant – 1,714,000 acres; the Sangre de Cristo Grant – 1,000,000 acres; the Vigil and St. Vrain (or Las Animas) Grant – claimed amount, 4,000,000 acres; and the Nolan Grant – claimed amount, 500,000 acres.[78] They formed a

---

[76] Letter from Charles Bent at Taos, Sept. 19, 1842, to M. Alvarez. *New Mexico Historical Review,* xxx, (Apr. 1955), 161-3.

[77] Letter from Wm. Clark at St. Louis, Apr. 30, 1838, to C. A. Harris, Com. of Indian Affairs, Wash., D.C. Photostat copy in the Missouri Historical Society, St. Louis.

compact unit athwart the trails running to and from the upper Arkansas River and Taos and Santa Fe. While Bent's name does not appear in the original title papers to these grants, the records show that he soon obtained possession of a portion of three of them from the original grantees. Two of the grants, the Beaubien and Miranda and the Vigil and St. Vrain, developed stock ranches and settlement projects at Bent's instigation between 1844 and 1847. On his last trip to the States, in early June, 1846, Bent accompanied a group of settlers from Taos to the company's Poñil ranch or farm on the Beaubien and Miranda grant, some miles south of Raton Pass.[79] Perhaps Bent and his associates had become aware of the value of such foreign-made grants to claimants when the United States acquired the territory from another country, because of their knowledge of the value of French and Spanish grants along the Mississippi, especially in Missouri after 1803.

The other prominent feature in Bent's later life was political, for in September, 1846, he was appointed the first U.S. civil governor of New Mexico.[80] Two years before, he had become concerned over the election of James K. Polk as President of the United States, apparently because it threatened war with Mexico. Subsequently, Bent had established friendly relations with Colonel Stephen W. Kearny, at least by the time of the latter's 1845 visit to Fort Bent. In the late spring of 1846, with American preparations for war in progress, particularly those for raising Kearny's army that was to invade New Mexico, Bent and his partner Ceran St. Vrain hurried from Santa Fe to Ft. Leavenworth, conferred with Col. Kearny, and assured him of the possibility of an easy and perhaps peaceful conquest of the department. Ostensibly, too, arrangements were completed at

---

[78] Dunham, "Governor Charles Bent," 249-50.

[79] Letter from Charles Bent at Taos, June 1, 1846, to M. Alvarez. *New Mexico Historical Review*, XXXI, (Apr. 1956), 164.

[80] Dunham, "Governor Charles Bent," 257-61.

that time for assembling Kearny's Army of the West at Bent's Fort.

When that army entered Santa Fe on August 18, 1846, without having fired a shot, Bent had not yet returned from St. Louis. Nevertheless, he reached the New Mexican capital a few days later, and within a month was appointed governor.[81] Other high ranking territorial officials were selected from American or Mexican residents of the territory, and several of them were connected with the large land grants mentioned above. The new governor promptly undertook to fulfill the burdensome and exacting duties of his office, and seemed to succeed except in gauging the degree of social unrest resulting from General Kearny's conquest. During December, 1846, it is true, Governor Bent was able to forestall an incipient revolt because he was secretly advised of it in time. Believing that he had scotched any further efforts of the kind, he sought a vacation in his home at Taos.

Unfortunately the forces of discontent had persisted, and they burst out in connection with a disagreement over the treatment of local prisoners so that there resulted the Taos Revolt of January 19, 1847.[82] Governor Bent was brutally slain in his own house, and other officials and citizens also lost their lives. The revolt was suppressed by troops under Colonel Sterling Price, assisted by a body of volunteers commanded by Ceran St. Vrain. The Governor's death cut short a life of great accomplishment and great promise. Among the many tributes that have been paid him by his contemporaries, that of William M. Boggs seems particularly fitting: Bent "was a noble man and was a great business man."[83]

[81] *Ibid.*, 262-5.

[82] R. E. Twitchell, *Military Occupation of New Mexico, 1846-1851* (Denver, 1909), 125-32.

[83] L. R. Hafen (ed.), "The Wm. M. Boggs Manuscript about Bent's Fort," in *Colorado Magazine,* VII, (Mar. 1930), 57.

Dick Wootton

by HARVEY L. CARTER
Colorado College, Colorado Springs

Richens Lacy Wootton was born on May 6, 1816, in Mecklenburg County, Virginia, the son of David C. Wootton, who moved to fertile Christian County, Kentucky, in 1823. When he was eighteen he left his father's tobacco farm and joined an uncle on a cotton plantation in Mississippi. In the spring of 1836, he took a trip to Independence, Missouri, where he yielded to the lure of the Rocky Mountains and hired to a Bent Brothers and St. Vrain wagon train.[1] Thus was begun a long and eventful career in the West.

Twenty years old, of an open and frank countenance, well muscled, and above the average in height and weight, Dick Wootton could handle a gun and a team and take care of himself. The small train of seven wagons overtook a train of fifty-seven, and he soon learned the essential military precision of a large wagon train. Before the small train was dropped off at Bent's Old Fort on the Arkansas, within sight of the Rockies, he had shot his first buffalo and participated in a brush with the Comanches. He was then sent, with thirteen men and ten wagon loads of goods, to trade among the Sioux. After a profitable trade, somewhere north of Fort Laramie, he returned to Bent's Fort in the early months of 1837 and, except for a quick trip to Taos with

---

[1] Howard Louis Conard, *Uncle Dick Wootton* (Chicago, 1890), 28-29. *The Denver Republican,* Aug. 23, 1893, in an obituary article states that the Woottons were a Scottish family in origin. Conard's work is essentially Wootton's autobiography, since it was written from interviews during which he told his life story. It has been cited in preference to Henry Inman, *The Old Santa Fe Trail* (New York, 1898) and Glenn D. Bradley, *Winning the Southwest* (Chicago, 1912), both of which contain chapters on Wootton which are almost wholly based on Conard.

Ceran St. Vrain, spent the rest of the winter at the fort.[2] In the summer of 1837, he went down the Arkansas to the Pawnee Fork to meet a wagon train and, with eight men, killed thirteen of sixteen Pawnees.[3]

Deciding now to strike out for himself, he got up a party of seventeen free trappers, upon his return to Bent's Fort, and headed into the Colorado Rockies. On Grand River they had a fight with a band of Snake Indians, killing twenty of them. The trapping was good and he sold his peltry in Westport for over $4,000. With great optimism, he wrote to his mother that he would soon be rich and would be home in a year or two![4]

In the fall of 1838, he set out upon one of the most extended trips of which there is any record in the annals of the fur trade. Nineteen free trappers, accompanied by six or seven Shawnee and Arapaho Indians, left Bent's Fort in September, 1838. It was nearly two years before they returned. Their route lay up the Arkansas to its source; thence northward over the mountains and up the Green; thence over the Wind River range to the Big Horn; down that stream to the Yellowstone and westward along its course; thence over the continental divide to the Salmon and the Snake and on to the Columbia. At Fort Vancouver, they sold their furs to the Hudson's Bay Company and passed across Oregon and into California by an unspecified route, except that they struck the Pacific Ocean near San Luis Obispo and continued on to Los Angeles. Then heading east, they trapped the Gila and the Colorado, catching plenty of beaver but of inferior quality; thence into Utah and back to Bent's Fort by an undetailed route. The party had traversed the great western circuit which Jedediah

---

[2] *Ibid.*, 41-44. Wootton's story that he shot a mule, thinking it was a skulking Indian, on his first trip west was the stock story told on all greenhorns and need not be credited as true. It may also be doubted whether Wootton was in charge of his first trading venture as he claims to have been.

[3] *Ibid.*, 46-51.   [4] *Ibid.*, 54-62.

Smith had covered twelve years earlier, but in a counter-clockwise direction.

Five of the trappers were killed on this circuit, three by the Bannocks on Green River and two by the Pah-Utes. La Bonte, a noted character among the early trappers, was cut off by the Pah-Utes when he lagged behind the main party. His bones were found and buried by his companions but most of the flesh had been taken off and eaten by his slayers. Le Duc was shot by a poisoned arrow and died after twenty-four hours of agony. The Snake Indians also beat in the skull of August Claymore (Clermont), but he recovered, surprisingly, and lived for many years. Another French-man, Charlefoux, was chased by Nez Perces and fell into a fissure, breaking both legs. He was rescued and carried in a litter for two months, but the notched stick, whereby he kept track of the days for the party, was lost.[5] For most of the trappers this trip was a last fling; for some it was their swan song; for young Dick Wootton it was his first great adventure. Henceforth, he could regard himself as a seasoned Mountain Man.

During the final stage of this trip, Wootton had sent furs to Taos by some Mexican slave traders who had been encountered. So, in the fall of 1840, he went from Bent's Fort to Taos to collect his money. On his return trip, he rescued an Arapaho woman who had escaped from her Ute captors but who was nearly naked and perishing from cold. Her kinsmen gave him two ponies as a reward and the Arapahoes

[5] *Ibid.,* 65-82. *The Denver Republican,* Aug. 23, 1893, refers to Wootton's having trapped on the Yellowstone and his having visited Fort Vancouver. It does not refer to the further excursion into the Southwest. There seems to be no positive evidence upon which it may be questioned, although it seems strange that no other reference to so extensive a trip by so large a party seems to exist. Wootton's account to Conard is a sketchy one, fifty years after the event, but the newspaper reference indicates that he had talked of it before and that it had become a matter of commonly accepted knowledge. Conard attributes the death of the three unnamed men to the "Monarch" Indians but he obviously misunderstood Wootton or did not hear him clearly. The Bannocks lived in the area west of Green River which is the locality of the incident in question.

were always his friends thereafter. Their name for him was
Cut Hand, because he had lost two fingers off his left hand
in an accident during childhood. On one occasion, some
years later, he was pursued by a band of nineteen Pawnees,
who came upon him after his horse had given out and he
had walked over twenty miles. They chased him for six
miles until he reached an Arapaho village near where
Greeley, Colorado, now stands. Wootton had killed one
Pawnee but was too exhausted to mount and go with his
Arapaho friends, who killed and scalped all but one of his
pursuers.[6]

Falling prices had dealt the fur trade a heavy blow by
1840, so, for the next two or three years, Wootton made his
living by contracting to supply buffalo meat to Bent's Fort.
This, he felt, was combining business with pleasure, for he
considered buffalo hunting to be the finest of sports. Around
this time, he built a corral where the city of Pueblo, Colorado, is now located, and used forty cows to raise buffalo
calves for him. He claimed that, when they were three years
old, he broke several to work as oxen and drove them to
Kansas City, where he sold them for shipment to zoos in
the East.[7]

In 1842, he is said to have run a weekly express for a time
between Bent's Fort and Fort St. Vrain, with an occasional
trip from Bent's Fort to Taos, sometimes carrying as much
as $60,000 in silver on pack mules. In the winter of 1843,
he got a license to trade with the Utes. With only a Delaware Indian as a helper, he made a successful trade with
an Indian village on the Canadian River in the Texas Panhandle region, but his profits were lost when Comanches
killed and robbed a man named Tharp, by whom he had

---

[6] *Ibid.,* 91-95; 315.

[7] *Ibid.,* 88-89. This tame buffalo story has a most improbable sound. However,
other similar claims have been made. It is likely that all such accounts are basically
true but exaggerated as to detail.

sent his robes and skins to Kansas City. Next, he traded with Yellow Wolf's Cheyenne band in northern Colorado; then, after supplying meat again for Bent's Fort, he traded with the Utes in New Mexico. He paid ten to twelve dollars for mules and a little less for ponies, in trade goods. This trade was always rather dangerous. On one occasion, a Shawnee Indian employed by Wootton killed a Ute, and Wootton and his party of eight men had to hold off a large number of Utes who sought revenge.[8] At another time, Jim Walters [Waters] was wounded while in company with Wootton and Old Bill Williams, but they were able to bring him safely in to Bent's Fort.[9]

In the fall of 1846, Wootton was in and out of Taos a good bit, but he was not there when the famous Taos uprising occurred in January, 1847. He was at the old Pueblo on the Arkansas when John Albert brought the news of the massacre. Wootton and four others set out at once for Taos and kept watch on it from the mountains to the east until Captain Burgwin, with two companies, and St. Vrain, with sixty volunteers, appeared on February 3, 1847. They joined this force during the night and engaged in the fight next day which ended the rebellion. Wootton said that St. Vrain, seeing a supposedly dead Taos Indian, dismounted, when the Indian wrestled with him until Wootton intervened on St. Vrain's behalf with an ax. His estimate of the losses in the battle, on both sides, is probably too high.[10]

Immediately after this, Wootton received a letter from Colonel Doniphan requesting his services as a scout. By hard riding, he overtook Doniphan's column south of El

---

[8] *Ibid.,* 98-108. Wootton's dates are frequently in error. Here he may have confused the order of his trading with the Cheyennes and the Utes, as Bill Tharp was killed in 1847.

[9] LeRoy R. Hafen, "Colorado Mountain Men," in *Colorado Magazine,* xxx, p. 26; Conard, 147-48.

[10] LeRoy R. Hafen, "Mountain Men – John D. Albert," in *Colorado Magazine,* x, pp. 60-61; Conard, 178-84.

Paso and was present at the battle of Sacramento on February 28, but was sent back to Albuquerque by Doniphan with dispatches telling of his success. He reached there in nine days and this ended his service in the Mexican War.[11]

In March, 1848, and for four months thereafter Wootton and Antoine Leroux acted as guides for Colonel Newby and Major Runnels against the Navajos.[12] In common with other Mountain Men, Wootton felt that army officers paid little heed to experienced advice. This impression was strengthened in October, 1849, when word was received in Taos of the capture of a Mrs. White and her child by Jicarilla Apaches in eastern New Mexico, where the Santa Fe stagecoach had been ambushed. Soldiers, under Colonel Greer, set out to attempt a rescue, accompanied by Kit Carson, Antoine Leroux, Tom Tobin, and Dick Wootton. These scouts located the Indian encampment undetected, but the rescue could only have been effected by a sudden onset, which was rendered impossible by Colonel Greer, who decided to parley before fighting. The Indians had time to kill their captives and Wootton and the other scouts were thoroughly disgusted.[13] In this period, also, Wootton and others set out from Taos to rescue Lucien Maxwell and a party who were beleaguered by Utes and met them, in bad condition, about thirty miles from Taos.[14]

In 1848 Wootton was married to Dolores, daughter of Manuel Le Fevre, a French-Canadian, of Taos.[15] The

[11] *The Denver Republican,* Aug. 23, 1893, says he "worked as scout for Colonel Doniphan's army down in Old Mexico." Also Conard, 189-97.

[12] Conard, 218-32.

[13] *Ibid.,* 205-14. Henry Inman, *The Old Santa Fe Trail,* 161, gives January, 1847, as the date for the White tragedy. Neither Wootton nor Carson could possibly have been along with Greer at that time. Jacob Piatt Dunn, *Massacres of the Mountains,* 374, gives the correct date.   [14] Conard, 214-17.

[15] *Ibid.,* 235, 320. Lewis H. Garrard, *Wah-to-Yah and the Taos Trail* (original edition, 1850) in Ralph P. Bieber and LeRoy R. Hafen, *Southwest Historical Series* (Glendale, 1938), VI, pp. 246-47, refers to Señorita LeFevre, the daughter of Manuel LeFevre. This was about a year before her marriage to Wootton. Garrard was much taken by her appearance and is highly complimentary in his remarks.

English traveler, George F. Ruxton, who had become acquainted with Wootton in 1847, endowed him with a bride from Sonora in his book, *Life in the Far West,* but this is a work of semi-fiction.[16] By reason of his being newly married, Wootton escaped the worst of the California gold fever, contenting himself with unsuccessful searches for lost Spanish mines in the Sandia Mountains.[17] He made his home at Taos until 1854 but spent a part of his time at the old Pueblo on the Arkansas. He is said to have turned back from Fremont's ill-fated expedition of 1849 when he saw the unusual amount of snow on the Sangre de Cristo Mountains, and he seems to have been in Taos when the demoralized survivors of the winter disaster straggled in.[18]

Faced with the necessity of providing for a family, Wootton extended and diversified his business operations.[19] In the winter of 1849-50, he conducted a trade with the Comanches at Adobe Walls, one of the few trading ventures to this hostile tribe, and got twelve old-fashioned Pennsylvania (Conestoga) wagons full of robes and skins.[20]

Then came two long trips. In 1851, he went to St. Louis

[16] George F. Ruxton, *Life in the Far West* (New York, 1849), 178-79, 186, 193, 199. Ruxton calls his character "Young Ned Wootton" in the first two citations, and "Young Dick Wootton" in the other two. Wootton was thirty-one, but he was five years older than Ruxton, who also adds six inches to Wootton's stature. Joseph Wootton, a younger brother of Dick, was in the West with him only in 1857-59, and so could not have been the original of Ruxton's "Ned" Wootton. Dick Wootton's eldest daughter told F. W. Cragin that there was no truth in Ruxton's story of how her father got a wife by abduction. See below, note 19, for Cragin Papers.

[17] Conard, 236-38.

[18] *Ibid.,* 197-200. The statement that Wootton turned back was made by Thomas E. Breckenridge, "The Story of a Famous Expedition," in *Cosmopolitan,* XXI, p. 400. Conard says nothing of this and it is obvious from what he does say that Wootton had no first-hand knowledge of this expedition.

[19] The Francis Whittemore Cragin Papers, "Interview with Eliza Ann Walker (née Wootton), widow of William R. Walker, December 4, 1907," in Notebook XI, p. 5. There were five children by Wootton's first marriage, of whom those reaching maturity were Eliza Ann, born February 1, 1850; Richens Lacy, Jr., born March 26, 1851; Frances Dolores, born April 14, 1853. – Cragin Papers, Pioneer Museum, Colorado Springs.

[20] Conard, 241-44.

to buy goods. He won a bet with Colonel Greer as to who would arrive first, covering the distance between Taos and Westport in a little over seven days on horseback and continuing by river steamer to St. Louis. On his return to Westport, he learned of a cholera epidemic and set off at once for the mountains, leaving his goods to come later.[21] In 1852, he bought nine thousand sheep around Watrous, New Mexico, and drove them to California, thus preceding the famous drives of Carson and Maxwell by one year. He employed fourteen Mexicans and eight Americans and used mules instead of horses. Starting on June 24, 1852, he arrived in Sacramento 107 days later on October 9, with a loss of only a hundred sheep. When the Ute chief, Uncotash, disputed his passage in western Colorado, Wootton grappled with him and forced his consent at knife point. In Salt Lake City, he met Ben Holladay and Brigham Young and, in Sacramento he witnessed the famous fire and flood. Taking a steamer from San Francisco to Los Angeles, he bought some mules and traveled home via Yuma and Tucson to avoid the Apaches, arriving back in Taos on January 8, 1853, after thirty-three days on the road. He brought with him $14,000 in gold and more than twice that amount in drafts on a St. Louis bank.[22]

---

[21] *Ibid.*, 245-46. It seems most probable that the well-known picture of Wootton in trapper's costume (Conard, 64), was made while he was on this trip. This portrait is reproduced herein at page 19.

[22] *Ibid.*, 249-62. Wootton's claim that Brigham Young served him some very good wine may, perhaps, be open to question. See also the letter written by Wootton, dated at Don Fernandez de Taos, New Mexico, October 22, 1853, and published in the *Missouri Democrat*, November 28, 1853. This letter is reproduced in LeRoy R. and Ann W. Hafen, *The Far West and the Rockies Series* (Glendale, 1957), VII, pp. 269-72. Wootton recommends the route to California which he had recently traveled, via Robidoux (Mosca) Pass, Cochetopa Pass, and the Old Ute Trail, and takes occasion to advertise the settlement at the mouth of the Huerfano, which he was then in the process of establishing. Wootton was the active partner in the sheep venture. He and Charles Williams furnished $3,143.23 and Jesse B. Turley furnished $6,132.12 of the capital. The agreement of the partnership, formed June 26, 1852, and dissolved Feb. 9, 1853, is in the Scrapbook of Jesse B. Turley, in the possession of the Missouri Historical Society.

During these years he also kept cattle at the junction of the Huerfano and Arkansas rivers. In July, 1854, he moved his family to this location, where he and his partner, Joseph B. Doyle, built houses about one hundred yards apart. They also built a blacksmith shop and operated a mill and an irrigation ditch.[23] At Christmas time, the Utes wiped out the old Pueblo settlement, but they did not attack the Wootton-Doyle ranch.[24] Doyle now moved to Fort Barclay, New Mexico, but Wootton stayed on, raising some corn and wheat and trading one sound ox for two sore-footed ones when California-bound emigrants came by.[25] However, Doyle persuaded him to engage in the freighting business. Just as the Woottons prepared to move to Fort Barclay, Dolores Wootton died, May 6, 1855. Her husband took the children to their grandfather, Manuel Le Fevre, in Taos[26] and joined Doyle in freighting goods between Kansas City and Albuquerque, via Fort Barclay, near which the army established Fort Union.

While in this business, Wootton became acquainted with A. S. Johnston, H. H. Sibley, and E. R. S. Canby, among other army officers. Wagons going east were only half loaded, but those coming west carried from six to ten thousand pounds each. The freighters received eight dollars per hundred pounds. The train had thirty-six wagons, each pulled by five span of oxen. On one occasion, Wootton raced William Bent to Fort Union, winning by a day and a half. He played cards with Bent while his men moved their train ahead of Bent's at night. In 1857-58, Wootton made his longest freighting trip, covering the 1225 miles between Fort Atkinson, Kansas, and Salt Lake City in ninety-seven days. Doyle was along on this trip and, after they started

---

[23] Cragin Papers, Notebook II, p. 61.

[24] Conard, 282-307.   [25] Cragin Papers, Notebook II, p. 61.

[26] Conard, 320; Cragin Papers, Notebook II, p. 32; XI, p. 5. Dolores Wootton died in childbirth. The infant also died. Interview of Wootton by a reporter for the *Chicago Inter-Ocean*, reprinted in *The Denver Republican*, March 18, 1888, p. 21.

Bent's Fort, as depicted by Lieutenant J. W. Abert, 1845. Courtesy of Western History Collections, University of Oklahoma.

back, Wootton sold out to him and went on horseback to Taos to visit his children.[27]

Returning to Bent's Old Fort (abandoned by Bent), he married Mrs. Mary Ann Manning, a widow from Pike County, Missouri, who was with an emigrant train. They were married there by contract and later by a priest at Mora, New Mexico.[28] Leaving his wife at Fort Barclay, Wootton decided to make a last trading trip among the Cheyennes and Arapahoes, after which he would take his family "back to the States." [29]

However, he reached the Arapaho village on the Platte to find that gold seekers had established the infant settlements of Denver and Auraria. This was in December 1858, and the settlers persuaded him to remain and set up a trading post by giving him a quarter-section of land. For the next three years, he ran a saloon and a hotel, as well as a general trading and loan business. The hotel failed because he would never turn a man away hungry, whether he had money or not.[30] In the loft of one of Wootton's cabins, W. N. Byers brought out the first issue of his newspaper on April 23, 1859.[31] His brother Joseph returned to Kentucky in this year, taking with him Dick Wootton, Jr., who returned to his father in 1865.[32] His wife joined him in Denver, but

---

[27] Conard, 323-63.

[28] Cragin Papers, Notebook XI, p. 5. Conard makes no mention of Wootton's second and third marriages. W. J. Ghent in his sketch of Wootton in the *Dictionary of American Biography*, XX, pp. 525-26, mentions only his first and last wives and only three children. There were three sons by his second marriage. Those surviving were: Joseph, born at Barclay's Fort, December, 1858; and William, born at Denver in 1861. Mrs. Wootton died at William's birth.

[29] Conard, 371-72.

[30] *Ibid.*, 372-84; see also LeRoy R. and Ann W. Hafen, *The Far West and the Rockies Series,* XIII, p. 200.

[31] Wilbur Fisk Stone, *History of Colorado,* I, p. 782. Henry Villard, *The Past and Present of the Pikes Peak Regions* (original edition, 1860) gives a description of Wootton's place of business. It will be found in Hafen's edition (Princeton, 1932), 14.

[32] Cragin Papers, "Interview with Maria Paulina Wootton (née Lujan), Dec. 4, 1907, in Notebook XI, p. 3.

died in 1861. It may have been partly for this reason that Wootton sold out in 1862 and built a house at Pueblo and another dwelling eight or nine miles above, on the east side of Fountain Creek, where he farmed till his crops were destroyed by a great flood in May 1864.[33]

Meanwhile, he had married a Miss Fanny Brown in 1863, at Doyle's ranch on the Huerfano, and his older children lived with them. However, his wife died a year and twelve days after the marriage, leaving an infant daughter.[34] After giving up the farm, he kept a store at Pueblo for a time, but all his real estate in this area was confiscated by Colorado Territory because of his pronounced secessionist sympathies during the Civil War.[35] Wootton said his opinions were only natural to one of his Southern antecedents. On one occasion, in 1863, he found it prudent to get out of Denver rather suddenly, having expressed his opinions in a manner that Denver citizens objected to.[36]

In 1865 he decided to engage in a venture that he had been considering for some time – to build a toll road over Raton Pass, on the Colorado-New Mexico line. He secured legal authorization for this project from the Colorado and the New Mexico territorial legislatures and, with George C. McBride as his partner, built twenty-seven miles of road, including many bridges, at considerable expense.[37] They operated it for the next thirteen years. At first, Wootton lived in a tent, then he built a three-room cabin and, in 1869, a comfortable and commodious home, with a veranda

---

[33] Conard, 403-04. Another reason for his leaving Denver was his opinion "that it would never amount to much."

[34] Cragin Papers, Notebook XI, p. 5. This daughter, named Frances Virginia, married a man named Fitzgerald.

[35] After Wootton lost his property he was overseer on Doyle's ranch until Doyle's death in 1864. Doyle's widow was engaged to marry Wootton but she died the night before he arrived for the wedding. He suspected she had been poisoned to keep him from getting control of Doyle's property. *Ibid.,* Notebook IX, p. 38.

[36] Conard, 395-400. It was at this time that the amusing incident of Fagan's ghost, apparently one of Wootton's favorite yarns, occurred.

[37] *Ibid.,* 417-30.

across the front in the best ante-bellum Southern architectural tradition.[38]

Wootton said that the toll road was a financial success. Wagons were charged $1.50; lesser vehicles, $1.00; horsemen and pack animals, 25¢. Herded livestock on foot passed at 5¢ a head. Indians had to be allowed free passage. Wootton simply tossed the coins into a whiskey keg and, when the keg was full, took it to the bank in Trinidad. However, McBride kept books for a period in 1869-1870, when Wootton was absent. The later years were probably more profitable, but these books show that, for a fifteen month period, the gross receipts averaged over $600 a month.[39]

In 1878, the Atchison, Topeka, and Santa Fe Railroad built over Raton Pass and Uncle Dick "got out of the way of the locomotive." The railroad company allowed him a credit of $50 a month, as compensation for having put him out of business. After his death, this was continued to his fourth wife, Maria Paulina Lujan, whom he had married on June 17, 1871.[40] They continued to live in their mountain home until it burned on March 3, 1890.[41] For some years after the toll gate closed, Wootton enjoyed hunting and engaging in shooting contests with visiting Utes.[42] Then he became nearly blind, but about 1886 an operation partially restored his sight. It was after this that he told his life story to Howard Louis Conard, of Chicago. Wootton died Au-

---

[38] Cragin Papers, Notebook XI, p. 5. For a picture of the large house at Simpson's Rest, see Conard, 465.

[39] Bess McKinnon, "The Toll Road over Raton Pass," in *New Mexico Historical Review*, II, pp. 83-89.

[40] Cragin Papers, Notebook XI, p. 3; Glenn D. Bradley, *Winning the Southwest* (Chicago, 1912), 101-02. Maria Paulina Wootton was sixteen at the time of her marriage; Wootton was nearly forty years older. She died at the age of eighty, in Albuquerque, in 1935. They had ten children, six of whom survived childhood. Five were living in 1935: Ida (Baca), Fidelis Wootton, and John, Frank, and Jesse Wootton. See obituary article in the *Rocky Mountain News* (Denver) March 3, 1935.

[41] *Ibid.* After the house at Simpson's Rest burned, Wootton lived in Trinidad, Colorado. [42] Conard, 427-30.

gust 22, 1893, having been bedfast for the last three months of his life.[43]

His familiar title of "Uncle Dick" probably dates from 1858. Though only forty-two when he came to Denver, the newcomers there thought of him as a relic of a bygone age, and he was indeed an old settler, having been in the area for twenty-two years. He was always an active man, of great physical endurance. His temper was somewhat unpredictable. He killed a Mexican teamster who asked him a second time for a hickory shirt when he was reading and did not want to be bothered.[44] He also shot Luke Murray (Moran) in the right arm. Murray was considered harmless and people said Wootton "ought not to have done it" although he considered that Murray was set on killing him.[45] He also had to be restrained from shooting up some troublesome Comanches in Denver.[46] No doubt he mellowed in the last years of his life, for Conard calls him "a genial warmhearted old man" and speaks of his "honesty, simplicity, and candor," his "modest manly manner," and his "tears at his own recollections."[47]

He never softened much toward the Indians. The Comanches he considered the meanest of all, but as merely the worst of a bad lot.[48] He thought the Crows and Cheyennes

---

[43] *The Denver Republican,* Aug. 23, 1893. On the basis of this article, *The Dictionary of American Biography* gives the date of Wootton's death as Aug. 21, 1893. However, his widow said it was August 22. Cragin Papers, Notebook XI, p. 3. Rufus Rockwell Wilson, *Out of the West* (New York, 1936), 29, makes the curious and unwarranted statement that Wootton died in 1908, at the age of ninety-two. Wootton went to Chicago in 1888, where a Dr. Olin removed a cataract from his eye. Details are in an interview given by Wootton to a reporter for the *Chicago Inter-Ocean,* reprinted in *The Denver Republican,* March 18, 1888, p. 21. Where dates given by Wootton in this article conflict with those given in Conard, the latter has been followed.

[44] Cragin Papers, Notebook III, p. 74. This was in 1858; Wootton had been drinking.

[45] Cragin Papers, Notebook VIII, p. 75. Conard, 317-19, gives Wootton's extenuation of his action.

[46] Conard, 383.   [47] *Ibid.,* 469-72.   [48] *Ibid.,* 41.

to be the best fighters and conceded that the Maricopas and Pimas were handsome and intelligent.[49] He was almost the only Mountain Man who defended Chivington's action at Sand Creek in 1864.[50] He was also fond of pointing out that far more Indians were killed by other Indians than were killed by white men.[51] Wootton has been called "second only to Carson as an Indian fighter."[52] Like Carson, he seems to have had a level head in an emergency and a strong element of caution, which was occasionally supplanted by swift, daring action. He passed through so many skirmishes unharmed that he began to feel confident that it was not his destiny to be killed by Indians.

Wootton's business qualities were well developed and, although he never made a fortune, he was never in want and none of his varied enterprises ever failed completely. Better than most of the Mountain Men, he kept abreast of the changing times. He held office as a county commissioner and lived to see his eldest son a respected member of the state legislature of Colorado.[53]

The fact that he reminisced for Conard has provided a detailed record of his life that is unusually complete. His memory was remarkably reliable, and there are only a few instances in which his reputation for veracity can be questioned.[54] The year that marked his death was the same in

[49] *Ibid.*, 121; 275-76.   [50] *Ibid.*, 409-11.   [51] *Ibid.*, 118-21.

[52] Henry Inman, *The Old Santa Fe Trail* (New York, 1898), 341.

[53] *The Denver Republican,* August 23, 1893. Conard's book is dedicated to Richens Lacy Wootton, Jr., who apparently helped to finance its publication.

[54] Wootton's statement (Conard, 289) that he put Tom Tobin on the trail of the Espinosa bandits is dubious. Conard (149-153) provides an instance of Wootton's having appropriated the story of Thomas Fitzpatrick's escape from the Indians, which was said to have caused his hair to turn white. Wootton tells it of an army officer named Fitzgerald but the fact that he says he was afterward a noted Indian agent is sufficient to identify him as Fitzpatrick, whose adventure occurred before Wootton came west. It was undoubtedly one of the tales he heard in his early days and Conard was thirsting to hear hair-raising adventures. On the whole, Wootton must be accounted a reliable raconteur, except as noted occasionally in these footnotes.

which Frederick Jackson Turner called attention to the disappearance of the American frontier. Uncle Dick would have agreed that the frontier was gone. In fact, he would have placed its passing a few years earlier, perhaps in 1876 when he made his last buffalo hunt in the Texas Panhandle or, perhaps in 1878, when the iron horse came chugging over Raton Pass. The Denver paper, in taking note of his passing said, "He has trapped beaver where Denver now stands; he owned a buffalo farm on the site of Pueblo, and he fought wild animals and Indians where other prosperous communities now are. The pioneer of Colorado pioneers, (he) has been a maker of history." [55]

---

[55] *Denver Republican,* August 23, 1893.